ALSO BY KAREN ABBOTT

Sin in the Second City

American Rose

American Rose

A NATION LAID BARE:
THE LIFE AND TIMES OF
GYPSY ROSE LEE

KAREN ABBOTT

RANDOM HOUSE
NEW YORK

Copyright © 2010 by Karen Abbott

Published in the United States by Random House, an imprint of The Random House Publishing Group, a division of Random House, Inc., New York.

RANDOM HOUSE and colophon are registered trademarks of Random House, Inc.

Grateful acknowledgment is made to Alfred Publishing Co., Inc., and Imagem Music for permission to reprint "Zip" from *Pal Joey*, words by Lorenz Hart and music by Richard Rodgers, copyright © 1951, 1962 (copyrights renewed) Chappell & Co., Inc. All rights reserved. Reprinted by permission of Alfred Publishing Co., Inc., and Imagem Music.

Library of Congress Cataloging-in-Publication Data
Abbott, Karen.
American rose : a nation laid bare : the life and times of Gypsy Rose Lee / by Karen Abbott.
    p. cm.
ISBN 978-1-4000-6691-9
1. Lee, Gypsy Rose, 1911–1970. 2. Stripteasers—United States—Biography.
3. Authors, American—20th century—Biography. I. Title.
PN2287.L29A63 2011
792.702'8092—dc22
[B]

Printed in the United States of America on acid-free paper

www.atrandom.com

9 8 7 6 5 4 3 2 1

First Edition

Book design by Caroline Cunningham

FRONTISPIECE: Rose Louise Hovick posing as "Hard-boiled Rose."

For my grandmother,

Anne Margaret Scarborough,

another indomitable lady of the Depression

Genius is not a gift, but the way a person invents in desperate circumstances.

—Jean-Paul Sartre

May your bare ass always be shining.

—Eleanor Roosevelt to Gypsy Rose Lee, 1959

Contents

Author's Note

My interest in Gypsy Rose Lee stemmed not from the movie or play based on (part of) her life but from television—reality television in particular—a medium and genre that didn't even exist when a girl named Rose Louise first talk-sang lyrics on a stage. In our current cultural norm, where the route to fast (if fleeting) fame is to package and peddle moments once considered in the private domain, there is something compelling about a woman who achieved lasting, worldwide renown without letting a single person truly know her. The "most private public figure of her time," as one friend eulogized Gypsy, sold everything—sex, comedy, illusion—but she never once sold herself. She didn't have to; she commanded every eye in the room precisely because she offered so little to see.

Trying to discover Gypsy the person, as opposed to Gypsy the persona, became the sort of detective story she herself could have written. Her memoir contains nuggets of truth—the rotating collection of pets, the struggles during the Depression, the family's wary views of men—but these were tempered throughout by invention and fantasy, whatever Gypsy decided would best benefit the character she'd so meticulously created. It was fitting that *Gypsy* the musical—a production Frank Rich of *The New York Times* called "Broadway's own brassy, unlikely answer to 'King Lear' "—was and is billed as a "fable": Gypsy had always preferred stories that favored ambiguity over clarity, humor over revelation.

I spent many hours thoroughly engrossed in Gypsy's archives at the New York Public Library for the Performing Arts, and after a while even the most prosaic bits of information (or lack thereof) became suspect: Were the New Year's goals listed in her diary ("Speak well of all or not at all," "I will try to live each day as tho I'm meeting god that night," "To be right too soon is to be in the wrong") written honestly in the moment, or with an eye toward posterity? Wasn't it odd that she spent a month detailing her mother's hospice care, yet recorded her death in four succinct words? ("Mother died at 6:30.") Wasn't it odder still that she was similarly terse in noting the death of Michael Todd, the one great love of her life? ("Mike was killed in a plane [crash] at 4:30.") And how could an iconic sex symbol write a memoir without once mentioning her own sex life?

So I read and reread and fact-checked everything I could, tasks that helped me clarify supporting characters and timelines but did little to unravel the layers of Gypsy's mystique. To that end, I was incredibly fortunate to connect with the two persons who knew Gypsy best: her only son and her only sister. The relationship a woman has with her child vastly differs, of course, from the one she has with a sibling, and the intensely personal anecdotes and insights Erik Preminger and June Havoc were kind enough to share went a long way toward revealing parts of Gypsy I would otherwise never have seen. From Erik, I gathered that his mother was an array of complexities and contradictions: a "madly self-assured" woman who hid her nerves and insecurities; an avid student of Freud who disdained introspection; a "fairly sad person" and "wounded soul" despite a desperate need to "keep her heart close"; an authority figure capable of inspiring awe and exasperation and loyalty and fury and love, often within the very same moment.

June's memories are darker and more melancholy, which I attributed partly to the fact that she'd expected to die relatively young, just like her mother and sister before her. It is hard to fathom that the brave, brilliant girl she knew as Louise has been gone, now, for forty years—nearly half of June's remarkably long and wonderfully rich life. I first met June in March 2008, exactly two years before she passed away, hoping she would guide me through Gypsy's mythology, peeling away the punch lines and fanciful digressions to reveal a core of truth.

When I arrived at June's Connecticut farm I found her lying in bed, her hair done up in pert white pigtails, a snack of Oreos and milk arranged on a side table. Her eyes were a bold shade of blue and painfully sensitive to light; she couldn't go more than a few moments without moaning and clenching them shut. She was ninety-four years old, give or take (her mother, the infamous "Madam Rose," was a prolific forger of birth certificates), and the legs that once danced on stages across the country were now motionless, two nearly imperceptible bumps tucked beneath crisp white sheets. She painted a deceptively frail picture, I learned soon enough; this wisp of a woman had retained her survivor's grit, her cannonball voice, her savvy instinct to question any stranger prying so deeply into the past. A part of me believed, all physical evidence to the contrary, that, if so inclined, she could leap up and strangle me with quick and graceful hands.

But she was welcoming and funny (lamenting a life steeped in "rumorsville"), and genuinely appreciative of my gift—a video of her four-year-old self performing in a 1918 silent film. She gave canned answers to certain queries—answers I'd heard or read elsewhere that nevertheless seemed illuminating when delivered face-to-face, by that deep and resonant voice. If her sister had shown any talent at all, she, June, would never have been born. Her vaudeville audience was like a "big, warm bath," and the closest thing she had to family. Her mother was by turns tender and pathetic and terrifying, broken in a way that no one, in that time or place, had any idea how to fix. The musical Gypsy distorted her childhood so thoroughly it was as if "I didn't own me anymore." The tone of her fan mail changed overnight, from sentiments of "loving affection" to "what a little brat you must have been." June realized her sister was "screwing me out in public," and that, in the end, there was no stopping either Gypsy or Gypsy; the play was both her sister's monument and her best chance for monumental revisionism.

It took another visit for June, just as private as Gypsy, to share bits of memories she'd never written about or pressed into a scrapbook, memories that defined her life even as they long lay dormant and unspoken. Money was Gypsy's "god," and she would do anything to anybody, in-

cluding June, to make more of it—and not just with regard to the musical. Gypsy did in fact do things, not only to June but to herself—
"terrible" and "awful" and "shocking" things, things beneath her sister's
formidable intellect and keen wit, things that made June believe, to that
day, that love (even love fraught with competition and jealousy) never
existed between them at all.

I asked and listened, for as much time as June gave me. I asked until
her patience wore thin and her eyes watered with the effort to stay
open.

"I hope I didn't upset you today," I whispered, bending down to her
ear. "That's not my intention."

"I know," June said. Those startling eyes found their focus, settling on
mine. "I know you're on a story . . . and I'm sorry I couldn't be more
open about some things. Some things are just . . . I'm still ashamed for
her. I'm still ashamed. I wish they hadn't happened."

"Would Gypsy wish the same?" I asked.

"She had no shame."

A pause, and I said, feebly, "You were a good sister to her."

One of those quick and graceful hands emerged from the sheet. She
coiled long, blade-thin fingers around my wrist.

"I was no sister," June said. "I was a knot in her life. I was nothing."

She retracted her hand, gave her eyes permission to close. I kissed
her cheek and crept out the bedroom door. I was grateful she let me
inside—even on the periphery, even briefly—and I suspected she was
saving her own questions for the day she reunited with the sister she did
profess to love, the one she still called Louise.

What follows is my story of the legendary Gypsy Rose Lee and the
people lucky enough to have known her, in any capacity. These pages
relate tales of deception and betrayal, triumph and tragedy, ambition
and failure and murder—much of it sensational, and all of it as true as
I could tell it. Anything that appears in quotation marks, dialogue or
otherwise, comes from a book, archival collection, article, journal, government report, or interview. When I occasionally slip inside Gypsy's
head, I do so using the most careful consideration of my research, and
with the tantalizing, agonizing knowledge that there is certainly more

to the story. Gypsy Rose Lee, herself a master storyteller, knew better than to give everything away.

Karen Abbott
New York City
May 2010

American Rose

The "City of Light" was the world's largest diorama, containing four thousand buildings that stretched three stories high and filled an entire city block. During two seasons of the 1939–1940 World's Fair, the exhibit drew more than 11,400,000 visitors eager to observe the cycle of the city ("the great stone skyscrapers," E. L. Doctorow wrote of the experience, "the cars and buses in the streets, the subways and elevated trains, all of the working metropolis, all of it sparkling with life") compressed into twelve-minute intervals—a meticulous and spectacular illusion, just like Gypsy Rose Lee herself.

Chapter One

Everybody thinks it's all so easy. Sure. Mother says I'm
the most beautiful naked ass—well, I'm not. I'm the
smartest.

—GYPSY ROSE LEE

New York World's Fair, 1940

In late spring, across a stretch of former wasteland in Flushing Meadows, Queens, a quarter-million people pay 50 cents each to forget and to dream. In the last decade they lost jobs and homes and now they face bleaker losses in the years to come: fathers and sons and husbands, a fragile faith that the worst has passed, the hope that America will never again be called to save the world. They come by boat and train and trolley and bus, hitchhike across four states in as many days, engagement rings tucked deep inside pockets along with every dollar they own. Not one inch of the fair's 1,216 acres betrays its inglorious past as a dump, Gatsby's valley of ashes come to life, where towering heaps of debris meandered in an ironic skyline. Instead, beyond the gates, a "World of Tomorrow" beckons, offering flamboyant distractions and bewitching sleight of hand, a glimpse of fantasy without the promise that it will ever come to pass.

They have never seen anything like the Trylon, its gaunt steel ribs stretching seven hundred feet high, carrying bodies skyward on the largest escalator in the world. They chase salty scoops of Romanian caviar with swigs of aged Italian Barolo. On one soft spring day they admire Joe DiMaggio as he accepts the Golden Laurel of Sport Award. At the Aquacade exhibition they watch comely "aquabelles" perform intricate, synchronized routines, the water kept extra cold so as to stimulate goose flesh and nipples. They hear Mayor Fiorello La Guardia boom with optimistic predictions: "We will be dedicating a fair to the hope of the people of the world. The contrast must be striking to everyone. While other countries are in the twilight of an unhappy age, we are approaching the dawn of a new day." The Westinghouse Time Capsule, to remain sealed until A.D. 6939, contains fragments of their lives: microfilm of *Gone with the Wind*, a kewpie doll, samples of asbestos, a dollar in change. At night, when fireworks begin, they fall silent watching the colors crisscross overhead, hot tails branding the sky, imprinting a patchwork of lovely scars.

They wait in lines for hours to glimpse a reality that seems both distant and distinctly possible. Revolving chairs equipped with individual loudspeakers transport them through General Motors' Futurama exhibit, a vast model of America in 1960, where radio-controlled cars never veer off course on fourteen-lane highways and "undesirable slum areas" are wiped out. They witness a robot named Elektro issue commands to his mechanical dog, Sparko. They marvel at an array of new inventions: the fax machine, nylon stockings, a 12-foot-long electric shaver. One thousand of them watch the fair's opening ceremonies on NBC's experimental station, W2XBS. "Sooner than you realize it," advertisements for the telecast predict, "television will play a vital part in the life of the average American."

But this World of Tomorrow can't obscure the dangers of the world of today, despite the fair committee's efforts. The new official slogan, "Peace and Freedom," is absurdly incongruous with the hourly war bulletins that blare over the public address system. Visitors who brave the foreign section find only a melancholy museum of things past. The Netherlands building is dark and vacant, the Danish exhibit downsized into smaller quarters. Poland, Norway, and Finland still have a presence, but fly their flags at half-mast and display grim galleries that show photographs of demolished historical buildings and list names of the distinguished dead. The Soviet Pavilion is razed and replaced by a space called the "American Common," complete with "I Am an American Day." Fairgoers line up at the Belgium Pavilion when that nation falls to Germany, as if waiting to pay their respects at a wake. They wish this slim wedge of time between troubles past and future could pause indefinitely, but understand that New York is capable of everything but standing still.

On May 20, thousands of them—a crowd larger than the turnout for President Franklin Delano Roosevelt and Wendell Willkie combined—find temporary solace at the Hall of Music, where they wait to see Gypsy Rose Lee in her World's Fair debut. A forty-foot-tall billboard flaunting her image looms above the entrance, those skyscraper legs and swerving hips a respite from the hard lines and stark angles of this futuristic fantasy. She wears an expression both impish and imperious, a baited half smile that summons them closer yet suggests they'll never arrive.

Inside her dressing room, Gypsy reclines on a chaise longue and holds a glass of brandy in shaking hands. The smoky-sweet scent of knockwurst drifts over from her hot plate, but her appetite is gone. She can hear them, the dull thrum of their expectations, the drumbeat chants of her name. Gypsy Rose Lee, voted the most popular woman in America, outpolling even Eleanor Roosevelt. Gypsy Rose Lee, who boasts that her own billboard is "larger than Stalin's." Gypsy Rose Lee, the only woman in the world, according to *Life* magazine, "with a public body and a private mind, both equally exciting." Gypsy Rose Lee, whose best talent—whose *only* talent—is becoming whatever America needs at any given time. Gypsy Rose Lee, who, at the moment, is as mysterious to herself as she is to the gathering strangers outside.

She sips her brandy, lights a Murad cigarette. The voices beyond these four tight walls grow louder still, but can't overtake her thoughts. At age twenty-nine, she stands, precisely and precariously, on her own personal midway, cluttered with roaring secrets from her past and muted fears for her future, an equal number of years ahead in her life as behind. A half-dozen scrapbooks are fat with clippings from vaudeville and burlesque, her first marriage and Hollywood career, her political activism and opening nights; a half-dozen more, blank and empty, wait for her to fill the pages. Not a day passes without her retelling, if just to her own ears, the densely woven and tightly knotted story of her own legend, and not a day passes when she doesn't wonder how its final line will read.

She senses that the next chapter might begin with Michael Todd, the man who said he'd give his right ball to hire her, who granted her the Stalin-sized billboard and a second chance with New York. Earlier that afternoon, he banged on her dressing room door, and she took her time letting him in.

"What's the matter in there?" he asked, pushing his way inside. "Can't you read?" He pointed his cigar toward a sign on the notice board: NO COOKING BACKSTAGE.

"Of course I can read. It saves money," Gypsy said in that inimitable voice. She's worked for years on that voice, scrubbing the Seattle out of it, ironing it smooth, tolling her words like bells: "rare" became *rar-er-a*. It is both charming and affected and, when either raised a decibel or compressed to a whisper, positively terrifying. It makes babies cry and one of her dogs urinate in fear.

"On your salary," Mike responded, "I can't afford to have you stinking up the theater."

Gypsy invited him to try her knockwurst, and he sat down across from her. She smiled at his singular philosophy about money and success: "I've been broke but I've never been poor," he told her. "Being poor is a state of mind. Being broke is only a temporary situation." She noted his graceful, fluid movements, strangely at odds with his features: rectangular, filet-thick hands dead-ending into tubular fingers, a head that sat atop a brick of a neck. He nearly licked the plate, and afterward ripped down the sign.

A cheapskate, Gypsy thinks, but not a hypocrite. Just like her, on both counts. She suspects they'll work well together now and in the future, since they both understand that ambition comes first and money matters most.

She sets her brandy down on her vanity, making room amid a *Roget's Thesaurus,* millipede-sized pairs of false eyelashes, an ashtray, a typewriter. Whenever she's not performing she plans to work on her novel, a murder mystery set in an old burlesque theater; the book counts as one bold step into her blank and waiting future. She's told favored members of the press about her literary ambitions, confessing that she's lousy at punctuation due to her limited schooling and sharing her theories about storytelling. "I don't like poison darts emerging from the middle of the Belgian Congo," she says, "and I think there is no sense having people killed before the reader is acquainted with them."

She doesn't mention that she has a few authentic, true-life murders in her past, or that the person responsible has recently resurfaced, sending a terse, cryptic note that concludes: "I hope you are well and very happy."

Which, coming from Mother, signals another gauntlet thrown.

The four syllables of her name thrash inside her ears. It's time, now, and she makes her body comply. One last review in the full-length mirror, a slow turn that captures every angle and inch. She knows the crowd outside doesn't care who she plans to be. They want the Gypsy Rose Lee they already know, the one whose act has remained unchanged for nearly ten years; they delight in the absence of surprise. They'll look for her trademark outfit: the Victorian hoop skirt, the Gibson Girl coif, the plume hat slouching over one winking eye, the size 10½ brocade heels, the bow that makes an exotic gift of her long, pale neck. They'll wait for the slow roll of stocking over knee, strain to glimpse a patch of shoulder. They'll beg for more and will be secretly pleased when she refuses. She knows that what she hides is as much of a reward as what she deigns to reveal.

The curtain yields and admits her to the other side. She senses the spotlight darting and chasing, feels it pin her into place. Voices circle one last time and collapse into silence, waiting.

"Have you the faintest idea of the private life of a stripteaser?" she begins, caught between her personal, unwritten World of Tomorrow, and deeper and deeper yesterdays.

Rose Thompson Hovick, "a beautiful little ornament that was damaged."

Chapter Two

Do unto others before they do you.

—ROSE THOMPSON HOVICK

Seattle, Washington, 1910s

No matter what Rose Hovick tried—hurling herself down flights of stairs, jabbing herself in the stomach, refusing food for days, sitting in scalding water—the baby, her second, would not go still inside her. A preternaturally stubborn little thing, which she should have taken as a sign. She wanted a boy, even though men did not last long in her house. Her first child, Ellen June, was a chubby brunette, twelve pounds at birth, tearing her mother on her way out. The house had no running water, and the attending midwife washed the baby clean with snow. A caul had covered her face, which meant she had a gift for seeing the future as clearly as the past. But she was clumsy, too, and by age three already diluting Rose's dreams.

Ellen June's new sibling arrived early and when it was most inconvenient for Rose, during a trip to Vancouver, but the baby was instantly forgiven—even for being a girl. This second daughter had a sprig of bright yellow hair and blue eyes with dark circles etched beneath them, as if she were already weary, and her head seemed tiny enough to fit into a teacup. She could spin perfect circles on her toes before she could

WASHINGTON STATE BOARD OF HEALTH
BUREAU OF VITAL STATISTICS
CERTIFICATE OF BIRTH

STATE OF WASHINGTON
DEPARTMENT OF HEALTH

Record No. **193**
File No. **1388**
Registered No.

PLACE OF BIRTH

County of   KING
City of   SEATTLE
or
Town of   (No. 4314 Frontenac Str.   St.   Ward)
{ If child is not yet named, make supplemental report, as directed.

FULL NAME OF CHILD   Ellen June Infant Hovick

Sex of Child   Female   Twin, Triplet or other?   and { Number in order of birth   Legitimate?   Yes   Date of Birth   Jan.8,   1911
                                                                                          (Month)   (Day)   (Year)

FATHER
Full Name   Jack O. Hovick
Residence   SEATTLE
Color   White   Age at last Birthday   25 (Years)
Birthplace (State or Country)   Minn.
Occupation   Adv. Solicitor
Number of child of this mother   1

MOTHER
Full Maiden Name   Rose Thompson
Residence   SEATTLE
Color   White   Age at last Birthday   19 (Years)
Birthplace (State or Country)   N.D.
Occupation   Housewife
Number of children, this mother, now living   1

CERTIFICATE OF ATTENDING PHYSICIAN OR MIDWIFE.

I hereby certify that I attended the birth of this child, and that it occurred on   Jan.8,   1911   at   M.

(Signature)   F.G.Gardner,

*When there was no attending physician or midwife, then the father, householder, etc., should make this return.

Give name added from a supplemental

report

(Physician or Midwife)

Address   SEATTLE
Filed   Jan.14,   19 11   J. E. Crichton
Registrar.   Registrar.

QOH 01-003 (5/99)

Rose Louise Hovick's birth certificate, amended to read "Ellen June."

talk, and Rose decided that since the girl had refused to be destroyed, she might consent to being created.

Rose would give the baby everything—even things not rightfully hers to give—including her older daughter's name, the first and favorite name. From then on the original Ellen June was called Rose Louise, Louise for short—a consolation prize of a name, half borrowed from her mother. It was the first of many times she would become someone else.

$\mathcal{I}$n the beginning the family lived in a bungalow on West Frontenac Street in Seattle, built of crooked wooden slats and a sloping shingled roof, squat as a bulldog, four rooms that felt like one, the kind of dank, dreary home that looked inviting only in a rainstorm. A porch jutted from the front, supported by columns where Rose could string wet laundry, had she been that kind of housewife. The place had a single grace note: the tiny square of Puget Sound visible from one window.

No matter where Louise or Ellen June (nicknamed "June") hid, their mother's voice could find them. "Her low tones were musical," June said, but "her fury was like the booming of a cannon." Rose had married John "Jack" Hovick in 1910 at age eighteen, one month pregnant with Louise, and by 1913, when her dainty baby June was born, she had already left and returned to her husband half a dozen times. She vowed to memorize his offenses, real or imagined, so that when the day came she could recite her lines in just one take.

Rose got her chance in the summer of 1914, when she placed her hand on a Bible in a King County courtroom, a box of tissues by her side. Your Honor, she began, her husband, Jack Hovick, forced her and their daughters to live in an apartment on Seattle's Rainier Beach that was "damp and full of knot holes"—unacceptable, especially for a woman suffering from the grippe and weak lungs. Their next apartment was no better, what with its "bad reputation" and tenants of questionable character. She and her husband separated, reconciled, separated again. Rose so feared for her and her daughters' safety that she had applied for a restraining order against Jack, and nailed shut the door and every window. He had threatened to steal Louise and June, never to bring them back. "If I could only get the kids," he'd said, "it is all I would want."

She wept for a moment at the horror of the memory. The courtroom quieted, waiting for her to compose herself.

Once, Rose continued, Jack broke through the glass, trashed all the furniture, and stole the bedrails, leaving her to sleep on the floor. He also "struck and choked" his wife and once beat Louise "almost insensible, slapped and kicked her and put her in a dark closet on account of some trivial matter."

Her husband made $100 a month as an advertising agent for *The Seattle Sun* yet refused, during all of their married life, to buy Rose even one hat or a dress suit or "any underwear to speak of." He never gave her money to spend on herself or for "any purpose whatever"—including private dance lessons for Louise and June, although she omitted this last grievance from her public testimony. Rose would use the girls not to escape a life she'd never wanted, but instead to access one that had always stood just out of her reach.

No longer, though. That life crept closer the day she took her daughters to a group lesson at Professor Douglas's Dancing School in downtown Seattle. Four lines of girls bobbed up and down to sounds from the professor's piano, thumpy renditions of "Baby Shoes" and "A Broken Doll," and not a talented one in the lot. Especially not Louise, always a half beat behind, swatting at the air rather than stroking it. Rose stood on the sidelines, making elegant butterfly swoops with her arm and pointing her toe, hoping Louise would follow her lead. June stood nearby, grasping the ballet barre, watching as if hypnotized. She toddled toward the line of dancing girls and they parted, making room. "I cannot recall the compulsion that led me out onto the floor," June said, "but I can close my eyes and still thrill to the memory of being there."

Rose understood compulsion and recognized its worth. Compulsion, along with indomitable women, had propelled her family through generations of misery, failure, and boredom; it was by far their finest trait. She shared with her daughters a favorite bit of family lore. Their great-great-grandmother emigrated from Norway and set out for the West Coast in a covered wagon. She made it as far as the Sierra Nevada mountains when her party was stranded by a blizzard. Most of the party died, frozen or starved or devoured by wolves. Rescue workers whisked Grandma to the nearest settlement and undressed her, discovering what appeared to be horsemeat strapped around her body, hidden from the other survivors. She alone appeared plump and healthy. On closer inspection, the rescue team discovered that it wasn't horsemeat after all but rather the flesh of her less fortunate companions. It was a fairy tale, Hovick style, in which drama trumped veracity and the women always won.

On that afternoon in Professor Douglas's studio, Rose's eyes shifted from Louise to June. She watched June lift up until her tiny feet were perpendicular to the tile floor, and then her baby's body let itself fall, legs parting into a split, seamless as opening scissors.

Professor Douglas pulled at his beard. "In a few years," he said, "bring her back to me."

"What's the matter with her now?" Rose asked.

"Mrs. Hovick, here you have a natural ballerina. But let me implore you to heed my warning. Do not buy her a pair of toe shoes until she is at least seven years old. You will ruin her."

But Rose wouldn't—couldn't—wait, she told Jack that night. June was double-jointed; any child who could stand on her toes and do splits *had* to be. It was a gift, couldn't he see that?

"We simply haven't the money for private lessons," Jack said. "I have faith in the future, but right now I am forced to be frugal."

"Frugal!" Rose yelled. "You're Norwegian, that's what you are. I should have listened to my mother. She tried to save me from throwing my life away." The marriage was over, Rose declared. She would leave and take the girls with her.

Jack Hovick told a different story. Instead of dance lessons he bought his daughters a kitten, and watched them pet the soft length of its belly as he left the next morning for work. When he came home, he found the pet's body, the sweet little face severed from the torso and cotton fluff of its tail. A bloodied hatchet stood propped in a corner, mute testimony to what his wife had done, and what she might be inclined to do.

He fled that evening and never returned.

*R*ose was finished with Jack Hovick, but not yet with men. Seattle had stretched from a sleepy frontier town into a bustling city, home to upward of a quarter-million people. Would-be millionaires from around the world passed through on their way north to the Klondike fields, hoping to find gold. Rose knew her strengths. Men noticed her bonnet of shiny brown curls and her striking eyes—nearly violet, with feathers for lashes. She had a compact, curvy figure and a flash-beam smile she used at her discretion. She was a proper lady, uneducated but ruthlessly shrewd, by turns vulnerable and witty and savage. In her own words she was a "jungle mother," and knew to evaluate the worth of a thing or a person before bothering to stake her claim.

She decided that Judson Brennerman, a traveling salesman from Indiana, would be her next husband. Surely someone in his profession would understand how rare her baby was, and agree that June needed an act, and an audience, as soon as possible.

Rose and Judson were married at the First Unitarian Church in May 1916, on the same day newspapers reported that Seattle had surpassed Reno, Nevada, as the divorce capital of the United States, averaging twenty-five splits a week. Rose told the girls to call her new husband "Daddy Bub." The following September, Daddy Bub bolstered the statistics by filing for divorce from Rose. He alleged that she was "cruel in many ways," causing him to "suffer personal indignities ever since his marriage, rendering life burdensome." The judge ordered Brennerman to pay Rose $200 in cash immediately, and $500 more over the course of the year.

"Men," she told her daughters, "will take everything they can get and give as little as possible in return. . . . God cursed them by adding an ornament here." Rose pointed to between her legs. "Every time they so much as think of a woman, it grows. . . . Why girls, when I married Daddy Bub he promised me faithfully that he would educate my two little baby girls, I would run his house, and we would just be good friends. The very night we were married, he tried to enter my room. He had no intention of just being friends! That's why Daddy Bub is no longer with us."

Rose ended this lesson by telling the girls exactly where they'd come from: she'd found June tucked inside the petals of a lovely red rose, and Louise had been plucked from a cabbage leaf.

Rose took the settlement money and paid for more dance lessons, even for Louise. The girls had never brushed their teeth or seen the inside of a classroom, but they were ready for their first dance recital at Professor Douglas's school. The professor, at Rose's repeated insistence, let June wear toe shoes and kept any thoughts about her potential ruin to himself. June was no bigger than the dolls she longed for in toy store windows, spinning circles in slow-motion perfection, a music-box dancer come to life. Louise jerked her arms and wobbled on her kicks, self-conscious until she realized that not one eye was on her.

$\mathcal{R}$ose took the girls to stay with her family at 323 Fourth Avenue, in West Seattle. Her father, Charles Thompson, owned the house, but the women he lived with ran it. His wife—Rose's mother—was Anna, but Louise and June called their grandmother "Big Lady." She had a glorious pelt of thick dark hair and was tall enough to look down, literally and figuratively, on her husband. She had never wanted to marry him, especially not at age fifteen, and wanted her four children even less. Rose's only brother, Hurd, accommodated Big Lady by drowning when he was nine.

A search party discovered Hurd's naked body trapped beneath a sunken log in the middle of Lake Union. The neighbors whispered about the strange circumstances: everyone knew the boy had been petrified of water, and why were his clothes folded neatly by the bank? But the mystery was buried along with Hurd, and the Thompson women took some solace in the fact that the boy was spared from becoming a man.

Rose's older sister, Mina, died of a drug overdose when she was just twenty. Afterward the younger sister, Belle, clung to Rose, absorbing her philosophy, noting the patterns of her behavior. Big Lady's mother, Dottie, rounded out the crew. She, too, shared the family penchant for marrying young, wedding Big Lady's father at age fourteen and then simply losing track of him. Big Lady, Rose, Louise, and June knew nothing of their father, grandfather, and great-grandfather. "Of course, he was only a man," June said, "so it didn't much matter."

Big Lady often fled her dull, untidy life in Seattle and ventured out to San Francisco or Juneau or Tonopah, lugging a trunk of hand-sewn corsets and garters dotted with beads and jewels. Undergarments were her specialty. On the backs she embroidered hearts and across the fronts naughty angels who cracked jokes in bright, cursive lettering. In Goldstream, Nevada, the prostitutes were among her best customers. But she catered to all kinds, even embroidering an altar cloth for the nuns of Sacred Heart Convent.

Once, after Rose, Louise, and June moved in, Big Lady took an extended trip. Rose asked her to knit an afghan throw rug while she was on the road. Months passed, and Rose wondered when it would be finished. "Dozens of tiny squares don't knit themselves together, dear," Big Lady told her. Rose accepted this, and kept sending her mother money for yarn.

Meanwhile, Rose described the project to a few neighbors in West Seattle, who told her that they, too, were waiting for this same afghan. They'd also sent money for yarn. Next time they spoke, Rose accused her mother of running a scam.

"Now, Rose," she explained, "I keep track of every penny sent by each person, so when I finish knitting I'll add up the score. You see, darling, the one who has paid the most gets the prize. It's a sort of auction, only it's private and it goes on during, not after, I make the afghan."

Impressed, Rose told the story to her daughters. "There's nothing ordinary about your Big Lady, girls," she said, and only hoped she could pass on such valuable lessons.

———

During Rose's childhood, Charlie Thompson quietly tolerated both Big Lady's long absences and her brief appearances. His hair was bone white by the age of twenty-seven, and he held the same job his entire life, working as a cashier for the Great Northern Railway. He escaped only as far as his own backyard garden. There, at least, nothing talked back or disobeyed or seethed with disappointment.

Rose didn't care to pass her time at Seattle's Alki Beach with neighborhood girls, stringing "Indian necklaces" made of wild rose seed pods. Instead she longed to be on the stage, and Charlie Thompson indulged her, but only for one summer. He had no choice, really; each night the child cornered him with tales of vaudeville routines past and present, and she wasn't alone in her fascination. "Vaudeville was America in motley," wrote one historian, "the national relaxation . . . we flocked vicariously to don the false face, let down our back hair, and forget."

Variety, as the entertainment was originally called, had its roots in

Europe, where itinerant performers trouped from town to town and village to village. Later in the century, "vaudeville" became the more popular term, derived from vau-de-Vire, the valley of the Vire River in Normandy, where locals gathered on mild nights to show off whatever odd or remarkable talent they happened to possess. Similarly, it had always been American tradition to enliven a play with entr'acte performances by singers, dancers, magicians, and acrobats. George Washington, in black satin court dress, always preceded by an usher carrying lighted wax candles in silver candlesticks, used to stroll down the aisle of the old John Street Theatre in lower Manhattan. From the decorated presidential box Washington reportedly saw *The School for Scandal* no fewer than three times, but not because he enjoyed the play. "His Excellency," confessed one colleague, "seemed greatly charmed with Mlle. Placide, the lively tight-rope dancer from Paris, who appeared in most gracious diversions between the acts."

Vaudeville became a community enterprise, cheap entertainment for new immigrants, offering something for everyone: skits, jugglers, singers, minstrel acts, and "coon shouters" (the most famous of whom was a Jewish woman named Sophie Tucker, who donned blackface and sang "Nobody Loves a Fat Girl, but Oh How a Fat Girl Can Love"), gymnastics, animal and human tricks, comedy sketches, choreographed brawls, innovative dancing (in one popular number, a woman spun and leapt and pirouetted among two dozen eggs, never breaking a one), and bluntly ribald humor. A perennially popular skit, "The Haymakers," began with a group of harvesters, boys and girls, working on a farm. Eyebrows waggled, bawdy quips were exchanged, and each boy lined up to visit the same girl behind the haystack, shocked expressions and disheveled appearances betraying their indiscretion.

Dime museums, such as P. T. Barnum's famous place on Broadway, staged 10-cent shows in divided buildings—one for freak exhibitions, the other for variety acts—showcasing fat ladies, bearded women, pickled embryos in jars, Bertha Mills and her nineteen-inch feet, Laloo and the parasitic, headless twin sprouting from his stomach, Down syndrome children passed off as "Aztecs," and a few entertainers who would go on to achieve legitimate success, including comedians Weber and Fields and magician Harry Houdini.

For years Houdini was the highest-paid vaudeville star in the country, and crowds flocked to see him, hoping to learn his secrets. One renowned songwriter, Gerald Marks, recalled following Houdini from show to show. Every time the magician appeared wrapped in heavy chains and prepared to submerge himself, upside down, into a tank of water, he warned the crowd, "This is a very dangerous thing I'm about to do, and I don't know if I'm going to come out alive. I always kiss my wife good-bye." With that, Bess Houdini rose solemnly from her seat in the front row, approached the stage, and embraced her husband. One night the songwriter discovered the secret: Bess, too, was an illusionist, distracting everyone with her sweet, stoic smile and then slipping a key beneath Houdini's tongue.

In New York City a producer named Tony Pastor introduced "refined" vaudeville, shows to which respectable men could take their wives, sisters, or sweethearts without fear of encountering harlots or drunken revelers. Pastor favored sweet, wholesome performers such as the minstrel duo who first sang the tune "While Strolling Through the Park One Day." The idea spread, and managers across the country advertised theaters with "no wine room" and exhorted the new commandments of vaudeville: Keep it clean, keep it neat, keep it dainty. No hells, no damns, no mention of any deities. Ladies will wear silk tights to the hip. And if you have to stoop to dirt to get a laugh, you're in the wrong theater.

In 1904, the summer she was twelve, Rose joined a group of child vaudevillians, practicing the mandolin and dance routines, but when the days shortened again Charlie Thompson told her enough was enough. He enrolled her in a Catholic boarding school for girls in Seattle, where, according to Big Lady, she could "learn manners and obedience from the sisters." Big Lady herself claimed to read the Bible regularly and warned of God's growing wrath. "God wouldn't like the way men have turned everything around," she said, "to make things easier."

Rose came to believe that God witnessed her every act and heard her every thought, and that He cleared a path especially for her. She didn't need outside channels or people to get His attention. To underscore her point, she used her Bible to make a paper doll family. When the silence of the halls grew unbearable, Rose told the nuns she had to go home to visit her sick father. Instead she joined any roving vaudeville troupe that happened to pass through. After a few weeks the nuns caught on, dispatched a search party, and found her, invariably, in the front row of a chorus, singing out louder than anyone.

A dozen years, two divorces, and two children later, Rose begged her father to assist his granddaughters' burgeoning careers. Charlie Thompson acquiesced when she asked for two favors: a recital at the Knights of Pythias lodge hall, where he would play piano, and money for costumes. Rose still had a flare of hope for Louise—the girl had done one thing right, scoring first prize in a "Healthy Baby" contest when she was a year old—and decided to dress her in a sensible ensemble: striped skirt and black sweater, feathered hat, and white stockings tucked into thick-heeled Mary Janes. June got a pink tarlatan ballet dress and toe shoes and a butterfly pin that nested inside her blond curls, which Rose touched up with a dab of peroxide. Every night she knelt before her baby and massaged cold cream onto June's knees, and every afternoon she took June to the best vaudeville houses in Seattle. Watching from the wings of the Orpheum or the Admiral or Pantages, Rose ordered her daughter to memorize all of the best songs and steps, and she did, within hours. "We always," June said, "stole our stuff."

The Hovick girls' debut followed the induction of new Knights of Pythias officers, and once the men took their seats Louise found herself in the center of the room. Her brown hair was bobbed at midear, Dutch boy style, and the hat's tight string gave her an extra chin. She was wide and round and curveless—her grandpa called her "Plug"— and both her front teeth sloped to a point, like sharpened pencils. Every month Charlie stashed some money away, saving up for the dentist.

She sang a tough tomboy number—"I'm a hard-boiled rose, everybody knows"—and executed a series of poses too disjointed to be called a dance. Knee bent, heel lifted, hands on hips, swivel and repeat from the other side, scowling all the while. A stage direction on the sheet music instructed, "Pull skirt up," and at the appropriate place in the song Louise did, sliding a gloved hand up one pudgy thigh.

Rose kept silent as Louise performed, waiting in the wings for June's turn. "Baby June" was her new name, her official name, though by now she was two and a half years old. Charlie Thompson struck a chord and his granddaughter spun out, splitting in the air and raising herself up. "The rose step," Rose called out, hands clasped as if in prayer. Her voice carried to every corner in the room. "Smile, dear, smile. That's right. Now, arabesque, arabesque." Baby June was more graceful than either Leland sister and prettier than Anna Pavlova, the famous Russian ballerina.

Charlie Thompson could play the piano by ear but kept his eyes fixed on the sheet music, never once glancing up at June. "Fank you," she said, falling into bow after bow, her forehead flush against her knees, compact as a folding chair. "Fank all of you." Inside her tiny toe shoes the Baby's feet were bleeding. Rose had just enough money for a brand-new pair, filched from her father's account. Louise's teeth could wait; the girl didn't need a proper smile to sing about being a rose, hard-boiled or otherwise.

Chapter Three

A Minsky never says die, or if he does, he says it softly.

—*THE NEW YORK TIMES*

New York City, Late Spring 1912

"Billy Minsky!" a voice called from behind, and the man who owned that name turned. It was late, and the street lamp cast a dim semicircle of light on the corner of 14th Street and Second Avenue. He couldn't see who was wielding the gun, just its long silver finger of a barrel, pointing and accusatory.

He should have known this was coming. Wasn't it just a few weeks ago that four gangsters pulled up to the Metropole Café in a Packard touring car and shot Beansie Rosenthal dead? Beansie had been Billy's source, telling him all about a crooked police lieutenant and his graft and gambling and prostitution rackets. Billy knew it was risky to write about the scandal for the *New York World,* but he had always been one to take chances. He embodied the times, preferring swift action to careful planning, no matter the consequences. "This is a get-things-done-quick age," *Life* editorialized that year. "A ready-to-put-on-and-wear age. A just-add-hot-water-and-serve age. A new-speed-record-every-day age. A take-it-or-leave-it-I'm-busy age." He penned article after article about the lieutenant and his henchmen, thugs with names like Billiard Ball

Rivington Street on the Lower East Side, circa 1912.

Jack and Gyp the Blood. His exposé had sent several of them to jail earlier in the year, and now one of them was out here, waiting for him by
the stoop of his family home.

Beneath the ceaseless clamor of the Lower East Side, the most
crowded neighborhood in the world, Billy Minsky heard the cock of the
gun. The silver finger quaked and lowered, pointed directly at his forehead. Billy dropped to the pavement.

If Billy were a spiritual man—as his father, the son of a rabbi, wished—
he might have taken that moment to reflect on how he'd made it this
long, this far. He spent all of his twenty-three years operating at only
one speed and in one direction, furious and forward, convinced that a
collision could only improve the ride. As a child he played in the alleyways of the Lower East Side, outrunning his brothers and outwitting
his friends. He learned the nuances and advantages of pitting people,
and even entire blocks, against one another: Rivington Street hated
Allen, Allen scoffed at Delancey, Delancey considered Forsyth a band of
savages, and they all looked down on Uptown—except for Billy.

A chronic fugitive, he skipped school, fled to the Houston Street station (always dodging the attendant), and took the El to 42nd Street,
watching the neighborhoods shift, the East Side's murky scrim yielding
to Broadway's gaudy brilliance. He took frequent trips to the grand old
mansions along Fifth Avenue. Not his style, he decided, though he certainly appreciated the money required to live there. When the time
came for his bar mitzvah, he addressed his beaming relatives with elo-
quence beyond his years.

"As I enter a new phase of my life," he said, "the New World I live in
enters a new phase too, its twentieth century. . . . I will take from the
new century what is good, and just, and right. . . . I will give to the new
century what is mine to give, my gifts from the past, the gift from my
parents, from all my people since the days of Abraham. I will take and I
will give."

He meant the last words literally, having cribbed his entire speech
from a book he'd found in the public library titled *Anthology of Orations
for All Occasions,* and then given to it his singular flair for showmanship.
His mother wept, convinced that her unruly boy—"such a trouble," she

called him—had finally come around, and his father, though he'd be loath to admit it, knew all too well which parent was responsible for Billy's dramatic gifts. A few years later, the boy dropped out of high school. It didn't matter, he insisted, since he'd earned something more useful than a GED—a GE, his "gutter education."

He had already grown into his adult height of barely five feet four, a short, squat doorstop of a man, and gave the impression of being too big for himself. He approached work with the same relentless energy he'd applied to everything else, tending to the jumble of schemes in his head careening along like overloaded freight cars, threatening to veer off track, always one more charging around the bend. A Wall Street firm hired him as a messenger boy, the New York Stock Exchange let him answer telephones, and Joseph Pulitzer's *New York World* decided he'd make a fine journalist.

He did. He was the only reporter who talked his way into the office of J. P. Morgan, Sr., hoping to get the financier's opinion on President Theodore Roosevelt's decision to remove "In God We Trust" from American currency. For hours Billy sat in a leather chair in Morgan's office, waiting. He filched a cigar from a humidor on the desk, lit up, puffed away, and waited some more. The smoke from the Havana clogged the air, and Billy's empty stomach began to churn. *I'm going to be sick*, he thought, and couldn't find a trash can. Indeed, the only available receptacle was Mr. Morgan's silk hat. Fleeing from the office, clutching the cigar with one hand and his mouth with the other, Billy recounted the story often and with great verve to anyone who would listen. A week later, J. P. Morgan issued a statement declaring his thoughts on the matter: he liked God and he liked money, and saw no reason to separate the two. Billy counted it as a win.

He also crashed Gladys Vanderbilt's wedding to Count László Széchenyi of Hungary. While the choir from St. Patrick's Cathedral serenaded the couple, Billy slipped into the Vanderbilts' Fifth Avenue mansion wearing his old messenger-boy uniform. After the reception, twenty of his colleagues hoisted him up on their shoulders and carried him to the Plaza Hotel, eager to hear tales of what went on behind the event's barred doors. Impressed, his editor made him a society reporter, and every night from then on the high school dropout wore a crisply pressed tuxedo no matter where he went or whom he talked to, including underworld characters such as Beansie Rosenthal and shadowless, armed thugs who followed him home.

———————————

$\mathcal{B}$illy was lucky, really, that the neighborhood itself hadn't already killed him. The city that would one day make Gypsy Rose Lee was filled with people who wouldn't make it to tomorrow. At the turn of the century, Jews fled pogroms in Russia only to find that life in New York's Lower East Side was scarcely safer. Two thousand people to an acre, fifteen people squeezing into tenement apartments measuring just 325 square feet, all connected by a dingy web of laundry lines. Dead-eyed women stood half naked in streets, babies suckling openly at breasts. Children were warned never to enter the Orchard Street lairs of the Gypsy women, with their billowing skirts and gold flashing from ankle to teeth; no fortune in this neighborhood was worth hearing, anyway. Hit men abided by a strict pay scale: $10 for the administering of a sound beating, including discoloration of eyes and, perhaps, the loosening of teeth; $50 for breaking the subject's nose or blinding him; $100 for preparing him for delivery to a hospital; and $500 for murdering him outright.

Billy's father had faced certain death himself when, in 1883, he was conscripted into the army of Russian Tsar Alexander III. Panicked, he made inquiries and connections among his fellow Jews and finally found a man who was willing to sell his identity card. A private meeting, a discreet exchange, and, just like that, Louis Salzberg became Louis Minsky.

Louis fled Russia and settled in New York's Lower East Side with his wife, Esther, and young son Avrum ("Abraham" in his new country). He worked as a peddler and saved enough money to buy a building on Grand Street. A natural marketing savant, he sewed a string of bedsheets to use as a screen, projecting images of his dry goods interspersed with old Jewish proverbs and neighborhood gossip, complete with English subtitles. He offered free matzohs during Passover and a soda fountain for customers, who arrived parched and weary after riding cramped Manhattan El cars or the Brooklyn ferry. Soon Minsky's Department Store was luring customers from long-established emporiums such as Arnold Constable, Lord & Taylor, and Milgrim's. He told his sons a story that would shape the way they came to view the nature of business in general, and of thievery in particular.

One night their father was walking home with a friend. The two men passed the home of one of the Minsky cousins, a floor manager at the store. "How can you stand it?" the friend asked, shaking his head. "Look in those windows—the velvet drapes, the crystal chandelier. How can a man live like that if he isn't stealing you blind?"

"It's like this," Louis Minsky answered. "*If* I fire him, I'll have to hire a new man. This *schmendrick* has stolen so much already that he doesn't need any more. But if I hire a new man, he'll have to start robbing me from scratch. I'll lose twice as much!"

The Minsky patriarch continued to study the Talmud in his spare time, but the old country was loosening its grip. He filled his closet with hand-tailored suits, fastened a diamond stickpin to his lapel, and carried a silver-topped cane. Tammany Hall, the unabashedly corrupt political machine that had ruled New York since the end of the Revolutionary War, took notice of Louis and asked him to run for alderman of the Sixth Ward—what better way to secure the Jewish vote than to make a hero of one of their own? "The politicians used to come fishing on the East Side," one resident recalled, "because they had a raw crowd— a crowd that was not polished yet. They could make them into a frenzy. They would talk about capitalism, and socialism, and sweatshops. The problems were always there, and Tammany Hall was always on your tongue."

Louis Minsky knew that the Tammany politicians, who put a price tag on every city position from janitor to judge and collected millions of dollars in graft, were largely responsible for the horrific conditions in the Lower East Side. But if elected, he could ensure that his fellow Jews and neighbors—the future songwriters George and Ira Gershwin and actor Eddie Cantor among them—received their share of the ten thousand pounds of turkey, six thousand pairs of shoes, and eight hundred tons of coal Tammany doled out annually to supporters. He won handily, and supporters dubbed him the "Mayor of Grand Street."

The new alderman began his tenure confident he could mend a broken system from within. Never once did Louis suspect his own constituents of contributing to the disrepair, until one of them, a poor tailor from his hometown back in Russia, duped the alderman into supporting his wife after he'd allegedly abandoned her and their five children. The tailor and his wife, a witting accomplice, lived off the alderman's own dime until neighborhood gossips ratted them out.

Alderman Minsky was hurt—"I would spend $10,000, if I had it, rather than pay that alimony," he said—but the incident marked his transformation into a true Tammany man, with all the cunning and treachery that title implied. A few years later, Louis declined to run for reelection but kept his connections, and then devised a scam of his own. A friend hired him to solicit accounts for the Grand Street branch of the Federal Bank, promising a kickback on all new deposits. In March 1904, another poor tailor from the neighborhood wandered into the bank.

"Hello," Louis greeted him. "Do you know who I am?"

"No."

"Why, I am the ex-Alderman, and I supposed everybody on the East Side knew me. I am the boss of this bank . . . and my bank is the safest in the world. You ought to put your money in it."

The tailor deposited his entire savings of $555, and Louis found dozens more just like him. The kickbacks having been duly handed over, the bank failed within weeks, and Louis was arrested on a charge of grand larceny. The ex-alderman swiftly put his marketing savvy to work, announcing that he himself had made a deposit in the bank just a half hour before it went under. Furthermore, he would pay 50 cents on the dollar to all customers who had accounts of $100 or less.

"I will have stories in all the papers about my philanthropy to the poor people," Louis confided to his lawyer. "And I will have pictures of myself, and everybody will think I am a very fine man."

A fellow Tammany man posted bail, the press let the story drop, and the scandal fizzled, especially in the Minsky household. To his sons and two daughters Louis Minsky was always above reproach, fully within his right to dispense advice and pass judgment on their respective paths in life. In the coming years, his eldest son, Abraham, endured the brunt of parental scrutiny. The boy clearly understood what money could buy, that much was clear, but he showed neither interest in nor aptitude for making it.

———

*A*be was a rotund mama's boy, moody and mercurial. Nothing—not his sartorial elegance, not his Tammany pedigree, not his growing bank account—made Louis Minsky feel as American as having a child with a sense of entitlement, this strange belief that one could be idle and still prosper. Abe had inherited his father's penchant for fine things but none of his work ethic. And Esther, doting mother that she was, developed a cyclical pawning system to ensure he didn't have to. She gave her favorite child watches, rings, and silver hairbrushes, which he promptly hocked in favor of suits, cologne, and dinner dates at Rector's and Delmonico's, a different woman on his arm each time. He married one of them in 1907, a union as short-lived as one of his cherished Havana cigars and not nearly as pleasurable—owing mainly to his scheme to defraud his father-in-law of $150,000, which earned him a $500 fine and five months in prison.

The incident mortified Louis and Esther Minsky, and they were relieved when their eldest son found a business venture that actually inspired him to work. An abandoned Protestant church in the neighborhood, Abe announced, would make the perfect venue for a nickel theater. The country was newly obsessed with motion pictures, with more than 45 million Americans attending shows every week—nearly every second person in the United States. "It amounts practically to a revolution," *Billboard* opined, "and yet those who are conversant with the inside workings of the business maintain that it is still in its infancy." For a nickel or dime, customers could watch films that were sweet or silly or lewd, all ingeniously produced: a series of photographs, each with a slight variation, was reflected on a screen in such rapid succession that the images appeared to move, one action flowing seamlessly into the next.

Abe bought the old church, called it the Houston Street Hippodrome, and opened for business, positioning the screen where an altar used to be. Customers didn't complain about sitting on the hard pews; they could wedge salamis, frankfurters, and tongues from nearby S. Erschowsky & Sons Deli into the racks that had once held hymnals. In the dark, no one could see the New Testament murals that still decorated the walls: a stoic Joseph with staff in hand, Jesus falling for the third time. Nor did the masses mind the pricey 5-cent admission for such racy pictures as *The Butler and the Upstairs Maid*. Between films Abe projected slides in Yiddish and English warning people against spitting, noisemaking, pickpockets, and the rude practice of reading titles aloud.

The Hippodrome prospered for three years without Louis Minsky once passing through its doors. When he inquired about business, his son had a careful answer. "You know those slides you used to show when you ran for alderman?" Abe asked. "Well, now I show slides, too, and for holidays I hire actors to act out lessons from the Talmud."

When Louis finally discovered the true nature of Abe's films, he ordered his son to shut the place down. No member of *his* family would make a living showcasing smut. Abe balked, but they reached a compromise. Louis had his eye on another project: the National Theatre on Houston Street and Second Avenue, a perfect venue for Jewish plays; the area was, in fact, becoming known as the "Yiddish Broadway." Abe could show movies on the sixth-floor rooftop, as long as they depicted great dramas—*Uncle Tom's Cabin, Ben Hur, Queen Elizabeth*—and not the randy rompings of butlers and maids. Father and son shook hands.

The long silver finger fired, and the gunshot was the loudest sound Billy Minsky ever heard. He lay facedown on his stoop, his immaculate tux now stained with dust and grime, and it occurred to him that if he heard the shot, he must still be alive. Then he heard something else that confirmed it: the sound of running—furious, swift wing-flapping strides that grew fainter, then barely perceptible, then silent. He raised his head an inch, dared to peek through parted fingers. Second Avenue was as peaceful as he'd ever seen it.

First thing next morning, Billy made yet another rash decision, one that would shape not only his life but the life of a toddler living on the opposite side of the country, a failure as soon as she could walk. He sat down with his father.

"Listen, Pop," he said. "You know that deal you've been talking to Abe about, showing movies on the National Theatre roof? Well, I think I'm interested in it after all. I think I've just about had it with the newspaper business."

Chapter Four

He was just a taker. She was a taker in her way too.
They were taking each other, and they loved each
other for that.

—JUNE HAVOC

New York City, Fall 1940

For five months, the entire length of their World's Fair show, Gypsy devises ways to be near Mike Todd. She finds herself in the unfamiliar process of falling in love, or at least the facade of it; nothing in her past has taught her the difference. They stroll past the Lagoon of Nations, find privacy in the cloistered corner near the Temple of Religion. They pose for pictures in the photo booth: she behind a cutout of a pregnant woman with voluminous breasts, legs akimbo, scratching at her thigh; he behind a baby clad only in a diaper, one fat fist tucked inside the woman's shirt and a cigar clamped between his teeth. Besides her mother, he is the only person capable of amusing and angering her at the same time.

"I am not a stripper," Gypsy tells him one day between shows. "A stripper is a woman who puts on a sex spectacle. My act is straight comedy."

"I don't care what you call it," Mike says, waving a cigar, "as long as you zip."

Michael Todd.

It's a familiar misconception, and she checks her temper when she corrects him.

"I never use a zipper," she explains. "A zipper is cheap and vulgar. And suppose one got stuck? I use ordinary straight pins. I used to toss 'em into the bell of a brass tuba in the band. They would go ping every time I hit the target." She pauses, adds a punch line; she wants to amuse him too. "But it was too expensive, the guy wanted union wages."

After the closing ceremonies they watch workers dismantle the World of Tomorrow, artifact by artifact, returning the future to dust. Mike announces he's heading back to Chicago, his hometown, to discover what he'll become next. Gypsy wants to keep seeing him, but also let him miss her. After all, she has a murder mystery to write, her own image to update.

She's been in relationships before, with a comic, a socialite, a salesman, and a gangster, but stayed on guard in all of them, as modest with her emotions as she is onstage—in these later years, at least. But Mike is, to Gypsy's frustration, exactly her type. "I like my men on the monster side," she confides to a friend, not entirely in jest. "A snarling mouth, an evil eye, broken nose—if he should happen to have thick ears, good! And I like a little muscle, hair on the chest, none on the head. A nervous tic excites me and if with all these things he wore green suits—BANK NIGHT!"

Certainly part of the attraction is that they come from the same place. He, too, remembers the Great Depression's long plain brown days, the light pockets and empty stomachs, the desperate things one did to fill them. As a kid he daydreamed about money. When he was nine his tonsils were removed, and he convinced his classmates to pay two cents each to peer down his throat. He hawked newspapers, shined shoes, played the cornet in a boys' band, worked as a roustabout at a carnival where he rigged the games of chance, and became an expert craps player before the age of twelve. As a teenager during Prohibition, he partnered with his neighborhood pharmacist to sell illegal alcohol. Michael Todd is his own creation just as Gypsy Rose Lee is hers; he'd said to hell with "Avrom Goldbogen" a long time ago. He understands why she never stops moving, her fear that the past will come galloping forward and override the present.

The past is already too close, panting against her neck, lurking inside her mailbox.

"Dear Louise," Mother wrote recently from Tucson, while on the road with her female lover.

> Well I waited for you to write to me. . . . and as I told you I only had ten dollars left. We sold our radio for six dollars got a second hand tire and drove as far as we could. . . . Now for God's sakes get me some money here as soon as you can. . . . I had to sleep in the car and I have had darn little to eat in the last three days. No matter how you feel about me or my plans right now I must have help and at once. I would not ask you unless it was absolutely necessary. Love, Mother.

Gypsy doesn't quite trust Mike's endearments—Mother taught her well in the ways of both money and men—but the sound of them still lands soft in her ears, looks lovely typed across the page. "I thought you would like to know that your mind is more beautiful than your body," reads one missive from Chicago. "Will see you Wednesday. Be good— but only till Wednesday." It is the last thing she needs right now, to get involved with a married man who already has one girlfriend on the side, especially since she's still technically married herself. Matters of the heart are not immune to her pragmatic judgment, and she revels in the irony that most defines her: the great sex symbol is, at her core, asexual. She has to be; one can't discover the comedy in sex unless observing it from a wide, safe distance. It is smarter to make a living from sex than to incorporate it into her life, but she makes careful exceptions: sex for protection, sex for position, sex for power—sex for any purpose that will further her creation while leaving the girl inside it alone.

Business with Mike is pragmatic, but not so a romance. She knows she should listen to her instincts and not his sweet, sly promises. Besides, no matter what his letters say, she can't shake the sense that he is never more absent than when he is by her side.

Chapter Five

However paradoxical this may seem, a child is at the mother's disposal. The mother can feel herself the center of attention, for her child's eyes follow her everywhere. A child cannot run away from her as her own mother once did. A child can be brought up so that it becomes what she wants it to be.

—ALICE MILLER, *THE DRAMA OF THE GIFTED CHILD*

Hollywood, California, 1916

Here they were again, Rose and June, two states away from home, where the Baby's star could begin its rightful ascent. After her debut at Grandpa Thompson's Knights of Pythias Lodge, she performed for the Elks and Masons and Shriners and every fraternal organization around Seattle, tumbling across hard linoleum, split-leaping from wall to wall, collecting calluses along the knuckles of her toes. Each time, Rose talked Charlie Thompson into playing the piano and convincing his lodge brothers to attend, although he remained skeptical about the whole enterprise. For these local bookings Louise trouped, too, occasionally scoring bit parts independent of June's developing vaudeville act. In a stage production of *Blue Bird* she played a frog, while June was a good fairy and Rose a witch. Usually, though, Louise shuffled along in

Baby June in her toe shoes, age three.

her too-tight striped skirt and labored through "Hard-boiled Rose," the points of her teeth spiking her bottom lip as she talk-sang.

Small concerts and benefits clogged their calendar, and at one of the latter Rose gripped June's forearm and pulled her to the front entrance. "Come quickly, darling," she said. "She's standing in the wings waiting to go on. She watched you." She crunched June's curls, tugged at her dress. "Stop breathing so hard . . . when I speak to her, be sure you stand directly in front of her. Then look up and smile."

June was just over three years old, and when she lifted her head she stared directly into stiff pink layers of tutu. The edges tickled the tip of her nose.

Anna Pavlova.

"Madame, if you please," Rose said in a reverent voice, straight from her convent days. "I would like your opinion. . . . Would you say my baby was a natural dancer?"

June peered into the ruffles, her teeth dry from her unbroken smile. She couldn't see Madame Pavlova, but heard her stilted reply.

"One cannot tell such a things. She is not even yet borned. Her feets have not formed enough to hold her." She spun and glided away, her toe shoes rasping across the floor. June released her mouth from the smile.

"Foreigners," Rose muttered. "I could hardly understand a word she said."

Nevertheless, she quickly forgot the ballerina's slight. When they left for Hollywood, Rose announced her daughter's new billing: "Baby June, the Pocket-sized Pavlova."

———

They had been down to Hollywood before for minor vaudeville shows and benefit concerts; the write-ups had made every trip worthwhile. "Baby June Hovick, whose three years weigh lightly on her dainty shoulders," wrote the *Los Angeles Times*, "has danced on her toes since she learned to walk, and is altogether the most adorable little creature in captivity." Most satisfying, the press bought into Rose's marketing scheme: "Baby June delighted the large crowd last night, a baby Pavlova," the *Seattle Times* reported. "Her little legs and feet speak poetry." Los Angeles society women elected June the queen of their annual carnival, where the "little tot" led a parade of Tommy Tuckers, Cinderellas, Aladdins, and Little Bo Peeps and performed "a toe dance as dainty as Pavlova ever dreamed of." Rose saved every clipping, underlining the most flattering phrases with red pencil, beginning a scrapbook she would keep for the rest of her life. The Baby's toe shoes didn't last nearly so long. Blood gathered in the tips, hardly wider than thimbles, spreading across the satin like a blooming rose. At night, Rose dabbed salve on June's cuts and calluses and taped the tips of her cracked nails. There was always a new pair of shoes waiting to be broken in.

Sometimes the entire tribe came along: Great-grandma Dottie, Big Lady, Aunt Belle, Rose, June, Louise, and the family dogs. During one occasion they all crammed into a boardinghouse room when it became clear Dottie was nearing death. She was tiny but innately resilient, like all their female kin, and Rose sent June and Louise out to play. When they returned, they saw their mother, Aunt Belle, and Big Lady locked in a hug, weeping. Not because their great-grandmother had finally passed, although she had, but because Rose found the missing diamond from one of her engagement rings under Dottie's body.

"Hush, children," Rose said, placing a finger over each daughter's mouth. "I had given up hope of ever seeing it again . . . wouldn't Granny be pleased if she knew that by dying she had saved me from accusing anyone of stealing my diamond?" The girls found themselves trapped in a grid of arms, Mother and Big Lady and Aunt Belle all squeezing tight, and for one moment the family felt incredibly, indestructibly, close.

———

*L*ater, the sisters would remember things differently, as sisters do, old grudges and misunderstandings refracting each memory, bending them in opposite directions. June looked at her big sister and saw "the most beautiful child alive," with eggshell smooth skin and a shiny brown cap of hair, instead of an overweight, ungraceful tomboy. She, not Louise, was awkward, with wiry, bruise-mottled legs and a "Norwegian beak" of a nose, her talent more slapstick than refined. In her view, Louise didn't lack ability so much as interest. "She was haughty," June said, "and not sure she wanted to be there because she didn't *have* to be there."

To Louise, June was born for the sole purpose of gracing a stage, as if those oddly tired eyes and miraculous little feet had been specially ordered by Dionysus; even the barrel curlers their mother wound in her hair every night couldn't diminish the effect. "Only actresses," Louise thought, not without jealousy, "could be so pretty." But she resented the Baby's talent most of all. Of course Louise *tried* to make her steps light and quick and her voice carry without cracking, but her body refused to obey her brain. "I wanted desperately to sing and dance as well as June," she insisted, "but she learned everything so fast. . . . I couldn't help looking at myself and I hated the person I saw."

The one thing the sisters came to agree on, after years of being entrapped by her words and mauled by her will, was their mother, a woman whose every thought and action defied her last, who raised her daughters as if they were two grizzled generals preparing for war—with men, with her, with each other. From year to year, month to month, even moment to moment, neither Louise nor June nor Rose knew the true status of their relationship: the tornado of slights (real or imagined), remorse (genuine or feigned), and resentment (always authentic, always deep) scythed too fiercely through their paths.

Rose was forthright in her dishonesty. "Never lie, never steal," she'd advise, "it does no good in the long run," but she did both every day they spent on the road. A self-professed prude, she invoked God often and disdained makeup (for herself; the Lord understood the girls needed rouge onstage), nail polish, and silk stockings, yet ventured this opinion about marriage: "If you don't succeed the first time, try, try again, only don't try to squeeze oil out of a rock." Her petite hands, with their fragile, baby-bird bones, were capable, literally, of murder. She was by turns tender and pathetic and terrifying, broken in a way that no one, in that time or place, had any idea how to fix. "Mother was," June thought, "a beautiful little ornament that was damaged." Her broken edges cut her daughters in ways both emotional and physical, and only sharpened with age.

Louise recalled many injuries from these days, long before Rose's un-yielding focus turned from June to her, long before the Minsky brothers stepped in and rearranged her world, long before she trained her mind to ignore messages from her body. At first Rose tried desperately to fit her into the act. "I know that Louise is destined to be a great, great something or other," she insisted to Big Lady and Belle. "My children are rare." She bought Louise a saxophone she couldn't play and spoiled her with presents, such as a Helena Rubenstein makeup box, to make her forget how jealous she was of June. But Louise knew she was a lia-bility most of the time; her mother made that clear when she called her "excess baggage" and sighed in her direction, asking, "What *is* the mat-ter with you, Louise? Is it that you don't want to do the dance? Is that it? What *do* you want?"

What Rose wanted, at least part of the time, was for Louise to go away, although she worried about strange influences warping her elder daughter. "When she's away from us," Rose fretted, "she's in a nest of civilians. Oh God, please don't let it rub off on her." But on several oc-casions she made it happen, allowing the girls' father, Daddy Jack Ho-vick, a rare visit (despite her fury at his remarrying), or taking her to live with Aunt Hilma, Daddy Jack's sister in Seattle. Aunt Hilma was married to an advertising executive for the *Seattle Times,* and they owned a grand white house on Queen Anne Hill.

Their daughter, Helen, died at age seventeen. Aunt Hilma and her hus-band went out one evening and came home to find Helen in a pool of her own blood—a freak menstrual hemorrhage, the doctors concluded—and they were overjoyed at the idea of taking Louise in. Rose enrolled Louise in the local public school and told her she could stay in Helen's room. She and June would send for her just as soon as they landed ei-ther a string of movie deals or a long-term circuit contract, and they would all troupe together, across the country, hoping, ultimately, to perform at the Palace Theatre in New York City, the heart of vaudeville in the heart of everything.

Forty years later, when Gypsy Rose Lee told the story of little Louise, her old self, the identity she traded in with the hope of trading up, she said that living in Seattle with wealthy relatives sounded just fine. She explored her cousin's things while a neighborhood girl, Helen's best friend, provided narration. This silver mirror and matching comb came from "Tiffany's in New York," and here was a "real pearl necklace," to which a new gem was added on each birthday.

"Mother says you're the luckiest little girl in the whole world," Helen's friend said. "Everybody doesn't get a chance to be adopted into such a nice family."

At that, Louise felt the comb slip from her fingers, and informed the girl that she wasn't going to be *adopted*. She was merely staying for a visit, "until Mother gets back on her feet."

"Oh no," Helen's friend insisted. "I heard my mother and father talking about it after dinner. They said the papers are all drawn up and all your mother has to do is sign them."

In the doorway stood Mother and Aunt Hilma. Rose blew her nose, poked a tissue at her eyes.

"Louise, dear," she said, "you're old enough now to know how hard life has been for me these past few months, what a fight I've had just to keep our heads above water. It might be years before June is where she belongs in the theater. Years of hard work and struggle . . ."

"But if I'm adopted I won't be yours anymore," Louise said. Her mother must not understand what "adoption" truly means, she thought. That was the only explanation. "I'll work harder in the act, Mother. I'll practice every day, honest I will. I'll do anything but, please, don't let me be adopted."

After a moment Rose sighed, crumpled the tissue in her palm, and ordered her daughter to get her coat. Outside, Louise turned her face upward, willing her mother to look down.

"I'll make up for it some way," Louise promised. "You'll see."

———

By now, Rose figured June had been to Los Angeles enough times and scored enough film cameos to merit another moniker: "The Holly-wood Baby." The Hollywood Baby was a natural, perfect at taking direction, with a face that could reflect anything you wished to see. On one visit, for instance, June was in competition for a part along with five hundred other "beribboned, beflowered, overbleached, overcurled moppets." Rose noticed the director looking their way. "Smile, baby," Rose instructed, and pinched June's cheeks until she whimpered.

The director, Hal Roach of "Our Gang" fame, approached and asked June if she knew any rhymes. June launched into a song:

> *Nobody knows me number*
> *Nobody knows me name.*
> *Nobody knows where I gets me clothes*
> *But I gets them all the same.*

"She'll do," he said. "Stop slapping her face for color. She's right as she is. She plays the part of a hungry, beat-up waif."

Rose was furious but accepted the job on the Baby's behalf. June would do it because June did it all; clearly, her younger daughter had inherited her work ethic and drive. Hal Roach loved the Baby, booking her for film after film, many of them silent, so all June had to do was let those sad eyes work for her. Before each take, Rose bent down and leveled her face with her daughter's.

"Darling," she said, "your dog has just been run over. It was killed." June's four-year-old brain tried to process her mother's tone and expression, to dig at the truth of her words. "NeeNee is dead," Rose continued. "Run over—dead." She shoved June, gently, toward the set. For four straight takes, all from different angles, the Baby cried fat, perfect tears, and her mother's applause beat a wondrous rhythm inside her head.

A glittering, shiny world opened up and made room for them. The film star Mary Pickford planned a party, a high-profile fete that Rose anticipated for weeks. That afternoon June developed chicken pox, and the doctor advised Rose to let her rest. Instead she sat on the bed and made up her daughter's face: mascara, dollops of rouge, lipstick, thick greasepaint to hide the splotches and bumps. "You're my trouper," she murmured, leaning in to kiss June's cheek. "Nobody could ever guess now by looking at you that your temperature is 103." And off to the party they went.

Baby June *en pointe*.

The Baby didn't always have to cry, or look sad and neglected, to score parts. Harold Lloyd, second only to Charlie Chaplin as a silent-film leading man, heard about June and wanted to work with her. His movie *On the Jump* was standard comedic fare for the time—choppy, disjointed scenes that each vied independently for a laugh. A midget balances books on his head, a man whacks passersby on their behinds with his cello, people chase each other around for no apparent reason, someone pulls a dog out of a purse. In one scene, Harold Lloyd hoists a box and stumbles under its weight. He lowers it to the ground, runs off to the side, and then lifts two tall tiers of china. From the corner of his eye, he sees the box's lid fly off, and a cumulus cloud of yellow hair rises over the edge. The girl it belongs to is improbably tiny, no higher than his knee, and it's as if an unseen hand lifts her slowly to her toes. She unfurls her arms and begins to dance. The camera pans back to Lloyd, who is so enchanted he drops his china. He makes no move to sweep up the pieces. She knows he's watching her, and for his benefit she leaps around the box, weightless, a leaf being kicked by the wind. She wears a calm expression—regal, almost—as if Rose had told a different sort of story before this take, one that promised everything would be okay, now and always, for all of them.

Chapter Six

America is the only country that went from barbarism
to decadence without civilization in between.

—OSCAR WILDE

Paris, France, Summer 1916

Abe Minsky was in a hurry. He had paid $100 for a first-class ticket on
the SS *Lafayette* and sailed 3,142 miles, docking in Bordeaux, France. He
traveled another 362 miles to Paris by train, drumming his fingers
against the window, watching the lolling countryside slip past him,
ideas somersaulting in his brain. He had decisions to make and he knew,
better than anyone, that New York could not be persuaded to wait.

The First World War was raging in Europe and inching closer to U.S.
shores, despite President Woodrow Wilson's campaign promises to the
contrary. On Sunday mornings Manhattan's faithful sat rapt in pews, listening to unsettling sermons and adamant predictions. "The second
coming of Christ," warned a minister at Fifth Avenue Presbyterian, "is
not only certain, but signs of the time point to an early coming. Might
it not be well if His coming were to be now and bring about the end of
the great war?"

Every incident was spliced, examined, threaded with conspiracy. An
early-morning explosion on Black Tom Island, in New York Bay off Jersey City, killed seven men and destroyed $40 million worth of property

Blondinette d' Alaza
des Folies Bergères

Performer at the Folies Bergère, 1916.

within a twenty-five-mile radius. Shells and shrapnel intended for Allied ships continued to burst for three hours, breaking windows along Wall Street, shattering plate glass all the way to Times Square. German saboteurs were to blame, everyone believed, since the country's agents were infiltrating New York's neighborhoods, depositing millions of dollars in its banks. Even the city's socialites prepared for potential disruption, hosting a rash of "war weddings" and "war engagements."

Abe was not interested in developments on the western front or, for that matter, on the Upper East Side. He only wanted to visit France before it fell to Germany, especially the grand burgundy-and-gold music hall, now almost fifty years old, tucked away at 32 rue Richer in the foothills of Montmartre.

He knew the history of the Folies Bergère well. Here Charlie Chaplin made his vaudeville debut at age fourteen, and the crafty Anna Pavlova surrounded herself with inferior dancers so she appeared even greater than she really was. Elephants, seals, and rats shared the stage with jugglers, acrobats, clowns, cyclists, and an Indian "rubber man." A performer called "The Kangaroo Boxer" challenged his marsupial rival for three two-minute rounds; the animal, using gloved paws, always won (owing, in part, to the performer's reluctance to permanently maim his livelihood). Before the turn of the century the Impressionist genius Édouard Manet sat here for hours studying the barmaids, and a thick-lipped, bearded cripple named Henri de Toulouse-Lautrec drank his signature Tremblement de Terre ("Earthquake") cocktail—equal parts absinthe and cognac—while forging an unlikely kinship with the ladies who ruled the back promenade.

These ladies were tradition, one of the Folies Bergère's oldest, as much a part of the scenery as the striped crimson ceiling and sham indoor garden. Folies Bergère management distributed cards only to the best dressed and best behaved, passes that were valid for two weeks. On the appointed day the general manager hosted a parade to decide which prostitutes deserved a renewed card. Pretty boys offering paid companionship circulated as well, although gentlemen for hire were excluded from the pass system.

Abe had been to the Moulin Rouge, too, before a fire closed the famed hall down a few years earlier. The Folies Bergère was older and, in his opinion, just as grand. There it stood, at the end of a long line of literary cafés, next door to a mattress shop named Les Colonnes d'Hercule. With its golden speared bars winding around the top floor, the place looked to Abe like an eighteen-karat jail.

The theater's door swung open, and he waded through a forest of gilt and plush. Patrons laid claim to every square foot of the hall, hundreds of them laughing, blowing spires of smoke, singing lyrics he couldn't understand: *"Allons, enfants de la Patrie, Le jour de gloire est arrivé; Contre nous de la tyrannie, L'étendard sanglant est levé."* Soldiers in brocaded képi hats and hobnailed boots sipped bourbon at Toulouse-Lautrec's green bar, flirting with women in the more subdued costumes of wartime: dresses in dour grays raised to a practical midcalf length, hats adorned with a single feather, a dab of Vaseline on the eyelids instead of charcoal liner. Professional linguists strolled about the theater wearing caps marked INTERPRETER, facilitating some conversations and eavesdropping on others. Promenade ladies fanned themselves, and the ripe scent of their underarms mingled with the weak perfume of dying flowers pinned along their necklines.

No matter what happened on the western front, Paris would *not* have its pleasures curtailed. "To deprive Paris of a chance of smiling, even in war time," said one theater owner, "is like depriving it of air to breathe." As a New Yorker, Abe appreciated a city that knew its priorities, especially when those priorities included black leotards, red garter belts, and the tease of nearly bare flesh. He sank into an armchair seat, impatient for the curtain to rise. This was not pleasure but research; Paris shows were the best ones in the world from which to steal.

———

*A*fter Billy's close call with the gunman, Abe accepted his little brother's offer to join his movie theater business—on one condition: he, Abe, was boss, and would have final approval on all decisions. Abe was going to build an empire, make the Minsky name famous across the country, and Billy was lucky just to be standing with him now, at the beginning.

Billy looked at his brother for a long, silent moment. He agreed and left it at that.

Privately the brothers marveled that anyone made it to their National Winter Garden at all. Access to the seats was maddeningly difficult, requiring patrons to ride a rickety, temperamental elevator, squeeze through a narrow lobby, and then shimmy around the theater's back wall by way of the fire escape landing. A swarm of shrewd thieves infiltrated the crowd, picking pockets while their victims focused on reaching their seats alive. Customers didn't care much about the quality of the films or music; they were willing to risk robbery or injury for the rooftop atmosphere alone.

Rooftop gardens were the height of fashion. On summer nights wealthy New Yorkers flocked to the roof of Madison Square Garden, where braids of colored lights connected a forest of palm trees and Chinese lanterns swung low from rafters. The Minskys' rooftop wasn't quite so glamorous, but it offered a rare luxury for tenement dwellers. For once they could look down on the city rather than being trapped in the thick of it, high above the screams of slum boys playing slugball and hit-the-crack, the first-floor parlors crowded with old men hunched over hands of pinochle, the rotten scent of the street vendors' overripe peaches.

Despite the rooftop ambiance, the brothers soon realized that a local, family-based operation couldn't compete with new movie chains, like the nearby Loew's Delancey Street Theatre. Nor could they book any major vaudeville acts, since the big-time palaces outbid them. They knew they had to transform their operation, one way or another, into a house that could draw the stars. Maybe films and vaudeville weren't the way to go, Billy suggested. The Minskys were, after all, men who took risks and who appreciated the risqué—men more suited to burlesque.

What began in ancient Greece as an art form that mocked social conventions, spoofed politics and current affairs, and titillated audiences with suggestive dialogue became, ultimately, a bold celebration of the female form. Just after the Civil War, a play called *The Black Crook*—considered the original Broadway musical—debuted, marking the first time in the history of the American stage that women appeared naked not as an integral part of the plot but for the brazen appeal of nudity itself. Burlesque evolved further, drawing from circuses and dime museum freaks, dance-hall honky-tonk and minstrel shows, behind-the-barn tent and cooch dancers, and by the turn of the twentieth century it had fully distinguished itself, for better or worse, from vaudeville. While middle-class men took their wives to see Tony Pastor's sweet dancers and clean comics, working-class men flocked alone to watch the gyrations of ample blondes and "screaming farces" with titles like *Did You Ever Send Your Wife to Jersey?* "Variety became vaudeville and aligned itself with talent," as one historian put it. "Burlesque became itself and aligned itself with dirt."

Abe and Billy vowed to reinvent the National Winter Garden as the best burlesque house in New York, dubious though that distinction may have been. Their Lower East Side comrades would appreciate burlesque—what man in his right mind would choose *Ben Hur* over *Bend Her,* complete with scantily clad chorus girls as Roman charioteers? They learned that the business of burlesque revolved around "wheels," organizations that supplied shows to theaters across the country: the Columbia Wheel, the Mutual Wheel, and the American Wheel. A typical year for the American Wheel took seventy-three shows on tour to eighty-one theaters from New York to Omaha, playing to about 700,000 people. The wheels supplied a different road show every week, including costumes, scenery, jokes, and music, and the theater owner simply had to open the doors, sell tickets, and sweep up.

Nothing to it, the Minskys thought, so in late spring of 1916, Abe and Billy booked a show from the American Wheel. The night before the grand opening, a tawdry procession slinked down Houston Street, blackface comics in clown shoes, zaftig derrières peeking from leotards (belonging to shiksas, naturally, since Jewish girls did not engage in such scandalous behavior), and cardboard cutouts of tenement buildings almost as tall as the originals. Perfect, all of it, except the brothers realized too late that there was no way to transport the enormous stage sets up to the sixth floor in their tiny elevator. Plan B involved piano movers, who tried to haul the sets up via the roof, only to smash the windows of the adjacent building.

Undeterred, Billy—with Abe's consent—canceled the show and posted fliers proclaiming that the National Winter Garden would reopen in the fall with a live burlesque show—stock burlesque, which meant autonomous burlesque, unencumbered by any rules or any wheel. They should regroup, Billy said, and take the summer to strategize. He recruited their little brother Herbert and ordered him to study classic comedy, the works of Cratinus and Menander and Aristophanes. Billy ventured up and down the East Coast, scouting out every burlesque show he could find, noting what flopped and what deserved to be stolen. And Abe set off at once for Paris, where he now sat in an overstuffed armchair watching the curtain lift, just like wrapping falling away from the gift he wanted most.

The girls were magnificent, red lace hugging thighs, peacock tail feathers rising from bottoms. Their heads reared back like thoroughbreds'. Legs kicked in flawless unison, high at first, knees almost meeting noses, and then level with hips, a line so straight and perfect you could have set a table across the shins. His fellow New Yorker Irving Berlin was sadly mistaken, singing "Why do they rave about beautiful France . . . we can enjoy all their joys here at home," because Abe saw one idea, one *brilliant* idea, that he'd never spotted at home— not along Broadway, not in any music halls, not even in the old, short-lived, New York–style Folies Bergère, where a woman dressed as the Statue of Liberty mounted a pedestal to flirt with the audience. The Parisian Folies Bergère had a *runway*, of all things, and when the music neared its crescendo those glorious legs stepped closer and closer still, a bracelet of spotlights following each stride. The men hollered and stretched their arms, every curve of ankle and spike of heel just out of reach. It was a revelation: Abe had traveled 3,504 miles to see the best girls in Paris, but now they were coming to him.

Gypsy Rose Lee, working on her novel backstage.

Chapter Seven

You have made your stake, you would kill anyone who
tried to steal from you; you ache to accumulate more
and more.

—GEORGE DAVIS TO GYPSY ROSE LEE

Brooklyn, New York, Fall 1940

After the World's Fair, after Michael Todd leaves for Chicago, she moves in with some of the most important writers and artists of the time: Carson McCullers, W. H. Auden, Benjamin Britten, Peter Pears, Chester Kallman, and George Davis, the openly gay fiction editor of *Harper's Bazaar* and an old friend—the only one who knew her before she became Gypsy Rose Lee. After all, she is a writer now, too, although her work on *The G-String Murders* proves sporadic and frustrating. "If I have night lunch with a smarty pants like Saroyan," Gypsy confesses to a friend, "I want to spit on the whole damned manuscript."

This sleepover literary salon was George's idea, something positive to counter the increasingly grim news from Europe, and the house at 7 Middagh Street is like no other on the block. Its facade resembles a playing card, with intricate moldings etched in the shape of diamonds and clubs, and it operates strictly by anarchic rule. Cocktail hour commences at 4 P.M., dinners (prepared by Eva, Gypsy's personal cook) often stretch into breakfast, and party guests include everyone from the soldiers in port to Columbia University professors to *Vogue* editors to Salvador Dalí. After feasting on Eva's roast beef and gravy, boiled potatoes, and chocolate cake, they migrate to the parlor and take turns entertaining. Auden pops Benzedrine tablets and does wicked imitations, George's observations about his friends cut with scalpel precision, and no one tells a story like Gypsy Rose Lee, who, one visitor notes, pervades the house "like a whirlwind of laughter and sex."

Holding a brandy in one hand and a cigarette in the other, Gypsy recounts her days in vaudeville, embellishing as she pleases (could they believe she played the back end of a cow?), about Mother's schemes and attitudes toward men, about raids at Minsky's and her striptease mentor, Tessie the Tassel Twirler, who proffered some sage advice: "Leave them hungry for more—you don't just dump the whole roast on the platter." Carson McCullers sits at Gypsy's feet and stares up at her, enthralled. She loves this witty, exotic creature, whose legs seem to stretch longer than Carson's whole body, whose spontaneity and warmth are the perfect antidote to the distant coolness of Annemarie Clarac-Schwarzenbach, a Swiss writer and painter who has broken her heart. Carson hears rumors that Gypsy entertains women as well as men, and it is certainly true that the stripteaser cultivates homosexual fans. She wants to spend every minute with Gypsy but keep things light and fun, and luckily, Gypsy won't have it any other way.

Nearly every night, Gypsy invites Carson to her third-floor suite, greeting her at the door in a sheer nightgown—worn, on cold nights, over baggy long underwear that sags at the knees. A fin-shaped clip holds her hair from her face, still smudged with makeup she never bothered to remove. All of which is to say, without words, that Gypsy views stripping as work, not fun, and portrays herself as a sex symbol only when paid to do so. Carson flops on Gypsy's bed, keeps her whiskey bottle within reach, and confides all of her troubles. She is under immense pressure to match the critical and commercial success of her debut novel, *The Heart Is a Lonely Hunter,* and to redeem herself after the disappointing reception of her second, *Reflections in a Golden Eye.* Work is going so slowly on *The Bride and Her Brother,* her tale of a twelve-year-old misfit, Frankie, who feels like an "unjoined person." How Carson misses writing for the simple joy of it, without worrying about readers or a career. Her estranged husband will probably soon show up in Brooklyn again to pick another fight. And she can't help it: she misses Annemarie terribly. Gypsy listens and soothes and fetches her friend homemade strudel she's made with apples from the backyard garden. If their visit lasts past midnight, Gypsy lets Carson sleep in her bed.

On Thanksgiving night, after another raucous party, Gypsy hears a caravan of fire engines whine down Middagh Street. She jumps out of her chair and beckons to Carson, and together they chase after the commotion, hand in hand. "We ran for several blocks," Carson recalled. "It was exhilarating to be out in the chilly air after the close heat of the parlor." They're almost at the scene when Gypsy feels a hard yank on her arm. She turns to Carson, who looks half crazy, the pupils of her wide doe eyes shrunk to pinpoints under the streetlights. "Frankie is in love with her brother and his bride," Carson says, breathless, "and wants to become a member of the wedding!"

With that, her slump is over. She knows exactly how to write *The Bride and Her Brother*, the book that would become *The Member of the Wedding*.

Gypsy, meanwhile, is finally making progress on her own novel, with George's guidance. She rambles about her days in burlesque as he sits at her typewriter and serves as stenographer, taking down every word. Then he helps arrange her stories, like puzzle pieces, into a rough sketch. She names the burlesque impresario "H. I. Moss" and molds him after Billy Minsky—stout, with hound-dog jowls and a fondness for speaking of himself in the third person. The surname, "Moss," is an ironic tribute to one of the Minsky brothers' foes, a New York City license commissioner.

"H. I. Moss didn't care much whether I wanted to be a strip teaser or not," Gypsy writes. "He thought of himself as a star builder."

Once Gypsy feels comfortable facing the blank page alone, she rises at six every morning, wraps herself in a housecoat, and types with the pads of her fingers so as not to break her three-inch nails. George knocks on the door in the afternoon to offer his critique, navigating the snowdrifts of crumpled paper layered across the floor. As he scribbles in the margins, she resumes her natural state of restlessness, making calls, scanning her datebook, filing her nails. If she's feeling bloated or lethargic, she summons her masseuse from Manhattan to "get my ass pounded" while George questions her dialogue or plot twists. And occasionally—more than she cares to admit—she finds herself thinking about Michael Todd.

The letters keep coming. "I read you are too smart to be happy," he teases. "I don't think you are so smart, so you can get happy with me—try it sometime." He has another grand idea, one guaranteed to be even more lucrative than their show at the World's Fair. He plans to open a club in Chicago—a glittering spectacle, catering not to the elite "Chez Paree crowd" but to families and "your average working-class Joe," with a dance floor suspended above a sixty-foot stage, champagne cocktails for 25 cents, and a Ben Hur chariot race. He'll call it the Theatre Café, and the advertisements will read: ALL THIS AND GYPSY ROSE LEE TOO. The best part of all—they'll be together again.

He implores her to think about it, and she promises she will. Maybe, she thinks, she could prove her theory wrong. Maybe she doesn't have to be foolish in order to indulge this strange bright flash in her heart.

Chapter Eight

Our true intent is all for your delight.

—WILLIAM SHAKESPEARE,

A MIDSUMMER NIGHT'S DREAM

Seattle, Washington, and on the Vaudeville Circuit, 1917–1920

Rose sat behind the piano this time instead of her father, graceful fingers arched and poised, engagement rings stacked to her knuckle. She had scored at least one more marriage proposal since her two divorces; her daughters couldn't keep track. They just knew what Rose meant when she "removed" a man from their lives, as if he were a dirty dish or a wart. Once in a while the numerous removals came in handy, as when they got stranded in Bend, Oregon, in 1918, without any money or bookings. Rose surveyed the town to find the biggest lodge hall, then reached into her bag and fished out the proper insignia pin for her lapel. A swipe of powder across her face, a wad of tissues clutched in her fist, Louise and June squeezed close on either side, and she was ready to call on the head man of the lodge.

"They are little show kiddies," she said, the tears threatening to fall. "I thought we were supposed to play your lovely little town, but it seems I got my engagements mixed up again. I'm not much of a businesswoman and I—we were really due in Prineville but I bought the

Baby June and Rose Louise, "the Doll Girl."

wrong tickets. I used our last cent in the world to get to the wrong town."

She lay the back of her hand against her forehead, wilted a bit to the right. The mogul jumped from his desk. She'd be fine, Rose assured him, so long as she and her babies got something to eat and just enough money to get home to Seattle. She fingered the lodge pin and the mogul noticed her rings, just as she knew he would.

"What about your husband?" he asked.

"He deserted us a year ago," Rose said, sotto voce, and lowered her eyes.

"A lodge brother! To think a lodge brother would do a thing like this! Let his wife and two babies go out into the world alone!"

Within minutes, the mogul had an event booked at a hall and a guaranteed audience of lodge brothers. The hall manager even agreed to split the proceeds fifty-fifty and pay for all publicity and "exploitation," as Rose called it. Seventy-eight dollars and ninety cents, quite a take for one night. She called it their little "nest egg" and said they mustn't tell Grandpa Thompson.

He still didn't approve of their trouping or of the "harum-scarum" Hollywood excursions, running up and down the West Coast without proper food or rest, just asking to catch that influenza pandemic now circling the globe. The carnage was unfathomable. A cough gave way to a pain that settled behind the eyes and tunneled through the ears. Your heart rate soared, your body caught fire inside, your own lungs fought to drown you. People died walking on the way to work. Four women played a late-night game of bridge and three of them passed by morning. Volunteers drove horse-drawn carts through neighborhoods and called for people to bring out their dead. Bodies couldn't be buried fast enough. Children skipped rope in alleyways, singing, "I had a little bird, its name was Enza, I opened the window, and in-flu-enza."

Theaters across the country shut down for weeks at a time. Hollywood carried on, but Rose had finally given up on her silver screen dreams. After June's early successes, her progress came to an abrupt and puzzling halt. She wept on cue for Cecil B. DeMille, yet another child, who couldn't cry at all, got the part. It happened again with a Mary Pickford film, *Daddy Long Legs*. Rose blamed the failures on her refusal to visit the casting couch. "June would be in pictures today," she told anyone who would listen, "if I would have stooped to what those other mothers stooped to." Back in Seattle, she told Grandpa Thompson that June was never in the movies at all, aside from being an extra in a crowd. It was proof, Grandpa said, that Rose hadn't forgotten her upbringing.

She decided, finally, that vaudeville was the Baby's surest path, and so here she sat behind the piano inside Seattle's grandest theater, waiting for both her girls to take the stage.

The Palomar loomed over the corner of Third and University, bulbs spelling PANTAGES in bright lemon letters along the facade. Before Alexander Pantages built his vaudeville empire, he worked as a waiter, a bartender, and a pimp. He owned fifteen theaters throughout the northwestern United States and Canada and had a controlling interest in twenty-eight others. He rivaled the team of Timothy Sullivan and John Considine for dominance in the region's vaudeville market, and the three of them resorted to all manner of nastiness and trickery, trying to outbid each other for acts, making threats they weren't afraid to carry out.

Each man shanghaied performers, literally dragging them off railway trains. Pantages offered fourteen weeks of playing time, even though he could guarantee thirty-two, and he made certain the tours always ended on the West Coast. Stranded, the performers had little choice but to sign on for another eighteen weeks—at a 25 percent cut in salary. "Take it or leave it," Pantages told them. He also vowed to burn the musical instruments of any performer who defected to Considine, a tactic that never failed.

Pantages wasn't exactly the "big time," in the parlance of vaudevillians, but his circuit was a requisite stop along the way. His lineups were idiosyncratic and occasionally disturbing: Alice Teddy, a 236-pound roller-skating bear; an ex-convict who had spent sixteen years in solitary confinement; Guglielmo Marconi and his "electrical act"; Fatty Arbuckle, on an ill-advised comeback tour after three trials for the murder of starlet Virginia Rappe. But the building was grand and stately, more like a castle than a theater, with Corinthian columns upholding the balcony seats and a soaring dome ceiling carved like lace. One of Pantages's booking agents now sat in a velvet front-row seat, listening to the pushy lady at the piano instruct her two daughters to sing out, sing out, even louder now.

"You'll hear from us, one way or the other," he said. "Next act, please."

———

*E*ach afternoon, Rose stared out the window of her father's home, watching for the mail carrier. When Big Lady wasn't traveling she huddled next to Belle on the couch, trading complaints and criticisms as the neighbors did recipes, stitching garters for Nevada's sporting girls. Charlie Thompson reported for work at the Great Northern Railroad and weeded his garden, where the fall air had dimmed all the blooms to brown. Louise watched June arabesque and rose-step through the streets. "She was so ruffley, fluffley," according to one neighborhood child, who always mistook Louise for a boy.

Two weeks after the Pantages audition the mail truck lumbered up to Charlie Thompson's house, carrying a letter for Rose. She slammed the door behind her and held the envelope aloft, letting bills and catalogs flutter to her feet.

"It's here, papa, it's here! Girls, the letter is here!" Rose closed her eyes. "Oh, please, please God, make it good news."

She ravaged the envelope and read its contents, lips moving wordlessly. God still listened to her every thought.

———

*A*gainst his better judgment, and after a calculated chorus of weeping by Rose, June, and Louise, Grandpa Thompson fronted the money for a wardrobe trunk, publicity photographs, winter coats, and new costumes. With the addition of a boy named Kenny, whom Rose rechristened "Master Laddie Kenneth," the "King of the Ballad Songsters," Baby June and Louise became "Baby June and Her Pals." Rose couldn't decide what role Louise would fit best, so her older daughter was billed, alternately, as "Honey Louise," "The Doll Girl," and just plain "Rose

Louise," a "clever Juvenile character actress." Pantages offered $100 per week, about $5,000 in today's dollars, for twenty-five consecutive weeks. But the act wouldn't get top billing, and they'd be stuck, invariably, with the dressing room on the very top floor.

They trouped by car since it was cheaper than by train, cramming into Charlie Thompson's early-model Tin Lizzy alongside props, costumes, Rose's two dogs, and NeeNee, June's dog from her Hollywood days, still alive and well despite her mother's frequent insistence to the contrary. Rose strung a sign across the passenger side door with the words TO-NIGHT! TO-NIGHT! VAUDEVILLE emblazoned boldly. On to Tacoma, Portland, Vancouver, Spokane, San Francisco, Salt Lake City, Winnipeg, and Victoria, where Rose, Louise, and June slept in one bed, the mutts sprawled across their feet. Master Laddie Kenneth merited a mattress on the floor. Rose cooked breakfast and lunch over a Sterno stove or gave the kids coffee and rolls. Dinner was at the closest Chinese restaurant. They must order yaka mein noodle soup, she insisted,

Master Laddie Kenneth, Louise, Baby June, and NeeNee.

the cheapest dish on the menu. She set down saucers of coffee for the dogs.

During every free moment they practiced the act. Rose reminded them to sing out and speak out—they were performing in theaters that seated three thousand people, remember, without microphones or amplification of any kind, and they had to train themselves to be heard.

Louise and Master Laddie Kenneth appeared onstage first, dressed in what Rose considered the fashion of "rich children"—a tailored velvet suit for him and a short dress for her, long shiny necklace skimming the hemline. Tapping a drumbeat rhythm on slates, they sang:

> *I think and think and think and think*
> *Till my brain is numb*
> *Put down six and carry two*
> *Oh, I guess I'm just that dumb!*

June skidded into sight on her rear end, shoved out by stagehands. Barefoot and in grubby coveralls, she held up a thick piece of rope.

"What a vulgar child!" Louise said. She loved any line that made her feel superior to June.

"C'mon, help me, will you?" June begged. "C'mon, take an end of this rope."

An exaggerated count of three, a swift tug, and the other end of the rope rose into view, revealing a small dog. Rose believed that even the animals had to earn their keep, and NeeNee's cameo got a big laugh.

"Don't talk to her, sonny," Louise said to Kenny. "She's just an adopted child."

"Oh, yes?" June lisped. Her mother insisted that she blur all of her consonants so she still sounded like a baby. "Well, just remember this. When my ma got me, she picked what she wanted. But when your ma got you, she had to take what she got."

Another big laugh.

The girls then met backstage for June's costume change. When the Baby reemerged she waited, expectantly, for the spotlight to follow her. She wore a short tight skirt held together with a safety pin. A straw hat sprouting a plume sat askew atop her curls. The end of the feather pierced June's scalp, sharp enough to draw blood. She sauntered across the stage gangster style, hands on swinging hips, a seven-year-old version of Texas Guinan, one of her vaudeville idols.

"'ullo, Gov'nor!" June shouted. Master Laddie Kenneth, dressed like a miniature hoodlum, stepped out to join her. The music swelled, all mournful violin and menacing bass. He clutched her, lowering her into a deep dip. She sprang forward, taking the lead. Back and forth they went, an underworld brawl masquerading as dance, bumping knees and elbows and shins. June would awaken black and blue and scabbed all over but prepared to do it again—hours of practice, matinees, evening performances. "I got hurt a lot but it wasn't important. I just had to cover that bruise and get out there again," she said. "It was safe. The affection of the audience was like a big, warm blanket."

From behind the curtain, Louise watched her sister, halfway wishing it were hers—the broken body, the salve of applause, the endless bows—and all the way pretending not to care.

———

They returned to the circuit the following year and Rose hired six little boys, scouting them out at dance schools and amateur contests. After renaming the act "Dainty June and Company," she updated her advertising posters and invested in some velvet curtains that looked almost new. She filed away every success and indignity from the first season, determined to repeat what had worked and fix what hadn't, and remembered, specifically, some advice from the Glencoe Sisters: get an agent. "Ten percent, right off the top," one sister said. "But you just got to have an agent. And if you're smart, you'll slip him a little extra, as an incentive, you know."

Rose didn't know, but she learned. A mother had to be wary. Unscrupulous agents targeted desperate performers. "What are you getting?" the sham agent typically asked. "Two hundred dollars? I'll get you three hundred for twenty percent." The performer readily agreed, and the agent, in concert with a theater's booker, put the act through for $500. Then he paid the performer $300 and split the difference with the booker. On the whole bookers weren't any better, changing schedules on a whim and ordering jumps, at a moment's notice, from New York to Philadelphia or Baltimore to Washington, with the performers absorbing all travel costs. Any complaints, and another act would gladly take the job.

Rose believed that Dainty June and Company deserved William Morris, the top agent in vaudeville, a German immigrant and former advertising solicitor based in New York City. But in the meantime she kept her options open, and during a booking in Detroit one presented itself.

Louise and June were playing in the hotel lobby, as they often did, running around and sitting on the laps of strange men. "It's a wonder," June later mused, "why I wasn't taken off and raped." A group crowded at the cigar counter, playing poker dice, calling out, "A horse on you!"— a signal to the loser to pay for drinks. One of them hoisted June up on the counter so she could get a better look. She loved it there, being higher up than her big sister, clicking her heels against the thick wood, breathing in the scents of tobacco and pomade, giggling when someone dropped coins in her palm and said, "You keep the change, honey." These men seemed so much nicer than the ones her mother met occasionally on the road, fleeting and temporary "uncles" who slid next to June in bed and slipped her hand inside their trousers. Now, in the lobby, June noted a man striding toward her with purpose and concern. He wore a proper suit and a gold watch chain that grabbed and held the light. He leaned in close enough for June to smell the soap on his face, and said, "What are you doing here? What do you think you're doing?" June felt small and oddly displaced; a moment she later identified as her first pangs of shame—of her background, of her upbringing, of her business.

Just then Rose started down the lobby stairs, taking her time, lifting her skirt so the hem kissed her knee. June watched her mother, and the man followed her gaze. "I'll never forget the expression on his face," June said. "He fell in love with her at first sight."

He introduced himself as Murray Gordon Edelston. He was tall, with an elegant gait and dark hair everywhere, even in penny-sized tufts along his knuckles. Certainly he was wealthy, Rose thought—look at that silk tie, those imported shoes, the leather briefcase covered in stickers from around the globe; so what if the gold initials stamped on the

June, Gordon, Louise, and NeeNee.

side weren't his? He looked like a broker, maybe, or a banker, but he told Rose he sold soda pop for a small company there in the Motor City.

It took Rose just one afternoon to talk him into becoming a vaudeville manager. He was a businessman. He could switch from selling soft drinks to entertainment; the same techniques and confidence applied. He could get them to the big time—the Orpheum Circuit, the Palace Theatre on Broadway. He was smart and talented and could make them more money than she'd ever dreamed possible. And if he left his wife and child behind, a child nearly the same age as June, Rose promised she and her girls would replace them, become his brand-new family.

Rose suggested they all go out for ice cream. Louise sat across from her mother and this strange man. By now she knew all of Rose's tricks and signals—the lowered eyes, the flushed cheeks, the fanciful, patchwork story of their past. "I lost their father when the baby was two and a half," she said. "June could dance on her toes almost before she could walk, so naturally when I was faced with having to earn a living, I thought of show business." June, too, seemed to take to Murray Gordon right away, since he promised to buy her a doll. "I'm Baby June," she said, by way of introduction, "and I'm going on four and a half." In truth, she was nearing seven. But four and a half years was the age currently sanctioned by Rose, and June recited her lines just as well offstage.

But Louise hated him on sight, and said so aloud. "I hate him," she told June. The girls had been forbidden to say that word, and she was pleasantly surprised by the sound of it. She hated him even more the following evening, when he climbed aboard the Chicago-bound train with the entire act, squeezing close as he could to her mother. Louise watched Rose during the ride—the way she laughed, throwing her head back, the curve of her hand, like a delicate vise, around his shoulder—until her eyes insisted on turning away. Every time her mother behaved like this she ended up marrying the man, and Louise was tired of it. Tired of men appearing, tired of them being removed, and, most of all, tired of vying for her mother's attention. June was competition enough.

June Havoc (with Van Johnson) in *Pal Joey*.

Chapter Nine

If you cry, June, I'll beat the hell out of you.

—GYPSY ROSE LEE

Philadelphia, Pennsylvania, December 1940

Their dynamic as sisters now feels familiar and rehearsed, roles given to them rather than established by them, an act without the payoff of applause. June is idealistic and Gypsy pragmatic, Gypsy untalented and June unbright. Gypsy makes life fun and June infuses it with drama; June is generous and Gypsy tight. June is an actress but Gypsy is a presence. They understand each other implicitly but neither seek nor offer approval, and they never, June said, "talked about the things that would make us fight." June defers to her big sister and listens to her stories, even the ones that make her blush rather than smile, the kind Gypsy tells once they've receded far enough into her past.

To Gypsy's surprise, the Baby is back onstage again, stopping the show, just as God—or at least Mother—had always intended. The show is *Pal Joey,* a Rodgers and Hart musical with a nightclub setting, starring an unknown dancer named Gene Kelly. June plays a chorus girl, Gladys Bump, and had so impressed producer George Abbott with her "original juke box voice" that her two numbers grew to five. *Pal Joey* would debut on Broadway on Christmas Day but the initial date is in Philadelphia, and the play promises to be a much greater success than *Forbidden Melody*, June's initial "comeback" vehicle of a few years prior. Gypsy drives from Brooklyn to see her sister at the Forrest Theater. For the first time in years every eye is on June; it's like vaudeville all over again.

But even on June's big night, Gypsy shares the spotlight. In one scene the actress Jean Casto appears, playing a jaded newspaper reporter, clad in a dowdy sweater, clunky oxford shoes, and thick glasses. In a song called "Zip," she mocks a certain burlesque queen's most famous routine, making reference to stripteaser colleagues Margie Hart and Sally Rand, miming undoing a zipper during each refrain:

> *I interviewed Leslie Howard*
> *I interviewed Noël Coward*
> *I interviewed the great Stravinsky*
> *But my greatest achievement*
> *Is the interview I had*
> *With the star who worked for Minsky*
> *I met her at the Yankee Clipper*
> *And she didn't unzip one zipper*
> *I said, "Miss Lee you are such an artist.*
> *Tell me why you never miss.*
> *What do you think while you work?"*
> *and she said, "While I work*
> *My thoughts go something like this."*
>
> *Zip! Walter Lippmann wasn't brilliant today*
> *Zip! Will Saroyan ever write a great play? . . .*
> *Zip! I'm an intellectual*
> *I don't like a deep contralto*
> *Or a man whose voice is alto*
> *Zip! I'm a heterosexual.*
> *Zip! It took intellect to master my art*
> *Zip! Who the hell is Margie Hart? . . .*
> *Zip! My intelligence is guiding my hand*
> *Zip! Who the hell is Sally Rand?*

Gypsy refuses to be upstaged—not by someone spoofing her routine, not by her sister, not by anyone. She begins sobbing at June's first
entrance, wailing with such force that songwriter Richard Rodgers
leaves his seat at the rear of the theater, walks discreetly down the aisle,
and escorts her back to sit with him. She continues crying through the
homage to her act, through the final scene, through the curtain call and
standing ovation. It is by far one of her most convincing performances—
if only 20th Century–Fox could see her now—and she knows June will
understand. Sooner or later, her sister always does.

Photographers catch each frame of her movement, her rush to em-
brace June when she slips backstage. She presses her sister's face into
her ermine coat and fits her mouth tight against June's ear. "You always
stopped the show, June," she whispers. "You used to have to go out in
front of the damn newsreel to take a bow, remember?" A throng of reporters fringes out around them. Gypsy sniffs, pulls away, and says, "I
stop the show, too."

June pulls back and stares at her, notices the haughty lift of her chin,
that sleek white ribbon of neck. She realizes that Gypsy Rose Lee the
creation is slowly killing the only sister she has. "It wasn't hilarious and
funny at all, when you got back to the dressing room," June said. "She
put on this wonderful, sophisticated, glamorous, I-know-more-than-
you-do attitude with such conviction, she convinced the world. But she
would come home and cry because she'd been on an interview and all
they wanted her to do was take off her gloves, slowly. They wanted to
leer. It made her sick, and nobody ever knew that."

How Gypsy envies June's freedom, that elusive trick of hiding inside
your own skin. A month earlier, she'd asked June her opinion of her
own Broadway performance, when she briefly replaced Ethel Merman
in *Du Barry Was a Lady*.

"I . . . I didn't think you were ready," June had said. "You couldn't
sing."

Silence, and then Gypsy replied, "Well, you see, June, if you are
Gypsy Rose Lee, you don't have to act, you don't have to sing. All you
have to do is keep up your strength so you can carry your money to the
bank."

In this moment, on the night that was meant to be hers, June wants badly to say something to her sister—something specific and ugly, something heavy with the weight of their history: "Men yelling 'Take it off, come back and take it off' is not stopping the show." The words push against her closed lips, but she never lets them out. They don't need to be spoken in order for Gypsy to hear them.

Within the week, Gypsy breaks the news to George Davis: she will be leaving the house on Middagh Street and heading to Chicago to star at the Theatre Café. Michael Todd, not to mention her adoring public, is waiting. Gypsy Rose Lee is a brand before branding exists, and she knows instinctively the danger in growing predictable or stale. She'll give the people what they love best, all the things that hurt her most.

Chapter Ten

New York City, 1917–1920

As soon as Abe Minsky returned from his field trip to Paris, he summoned Billy for a conference at the National Winter Garden, eager to share the details of his potential European import.

"Ya know," he said, "if we could only get lights somehow, there's quite a stunt they pulled at the Folies Bergère. They paraded girls on a runway—"

That got Billy's attention. "Runway? What kind of runway?"

"There was a raised platform coming down from stage right into the theater," Abe explained, pointing with his cigar. "The audience went crazy when they paraded down in spotlights. If we could manage a few spots—"

"Spots, hell!" Billy interrupted. "If it's in the house, we'll use the house lights. They may not be glamorous, but they'll be able to see the girls. For the moment we can do without the glamour, or at least until we have some more money for spots."

The following Sunday, when the National Winter Garden was closed, the Minskys brought in a team of carpenters and watched the

From left: Morton, Billy, and Herbert Minsky.

runway come to life. They planned to advertise it as the first such contraption in American theater history—who cared if it were true?—and it was a beauty, a long gleaming strip that ran from the orchestra pit up the center of the house to a point just under the rim of the balcony. The crew had to dismantle forty-eight orchestra seats, a painful but necessary concession, and the brothers added one more decorative touch to their theater, this time with homegrown rather than Gallic flair: American flags pasted flush along the edges of the exterior windows and jutting at jaunty angles on either side of the doorway.

Sacrifice and patriotism had become New York's latest trends with the United States' formal entry into World War I. For the first time the city had more motor vehicles than horses, and the streets were crowded with Studebaker sedans, red, white, and blue ribbons streaming from bumpers. One couldn't window-shop without encountering artist J. Montgomery Flagg's finger-pointing, craggy-faced portrait of Uncle Sam beseeching young men to join the army. A group of New York society matrons calling themselves "The First Fifty" announced that they would diminish waste and extravagance by "pruning their lunches to two courses, and dinners to three." (Of course, one editorial writer pointed out, women of that milieu tended to eat lightly, anyway.) The Anti-Saloon League of New York argued that responsible citizens should support an immediate halt in distilling and brewing to conserve fuel and grain for the troops, developing slogans such as "Booze or coal?" and "Save 11,000,000 loaves a day."

City Hall bowed to the pressure, passing an ordinance forbidding hotels, restaurants, saloons, cabarets, and roof gardens to sell liquor after 1 A.M., and imposing new taxes on everything from cigars to telegrams to tickets for Broadway shows. Despite the added expense, the theater industry, as in Paris, managed to thrive. The blocks from 38th to 50th Streets offered fifty-five amusement houses, all but five of them devoted to theater, and all but thirty-four of them belonging to the three Shubert brothers, sons of poor Jewish immigrants. Lee Shubert, whose formal education had ended at age ten, was an odd-looking man—"a fascinating cross," Gypsy Rose Lee noted, "between a wooden Indian and a hooded cobra." He was reportedly illiterate but a genius with numbers. Although he knew nothing about directing or the creative process, he

Minsky "Rosebuds" on the runway at the National Winter Garden.

worked to cultivate an image as a businessman with highbrow taste, and Billy Minsky considered him the greatest showman in the country. "The people must be amused," Lee Shubert said. "The war, even with its ticket tax, will have no appreciable effect upon theatrical entertainments, provided, of course, they are what the people want."

Downtown, in a decidedly more modest family empire—so far, at least—the Minsky brothers prepared to debut their new attraction. When the show opened on Monday, Minsky's six showgirls, all of them over thirty, christened the runway with a sad parade. The harsh yellow house lights were unkind to their skin, showcasing every clump of foundation and wayward smear of rouge. Even worse, the footlights seemed to cut the girls in half, illuminating the bottoms but not the tops of their legs, and shining beams directly on their chins—or, in some cases, double chins. Still, they walked *through* the audience, so close the men could smell their perfume and hear them lose their breath as they strutted and twirled. Close enough for the men to look directly up their legs—bloated legs encased in garish pink tights, but legs nonetheless.

The National Winter Garden was sold out all that week. Billy, still troubled by the footlights' distortion of the girls, asked little brother Herbert to study the psychology of color. Blue was remote and cool; green, soothing; yellow cheerful. Red or magenta signified drama, romance, mystery, and sex—the proper colors for Minsky's. With Billy's and Abe's permission, Herbert spent $2,000 on power cables for stage lighting and tried a rich magenta, which seemed to flatter every skin tone and evoked, subtly, the feeling of an old-time brothel.

Billy and Abe kept their focus on business matters while Herbert took over "culture," commissioning an artist to transform the concrete walls into a mural celebrating *Othello:* Iago and Roderigo frozen in banter; a drunken Cassio; Desdemona, lovely even in death. He himself fashioned whimsical backdrops in the style of Aubrey Beardsley. Deep crimson paint created borders between each scene, and lush, multicolored silk drapes swept down from the ceiling. The hard wooden seats stayed—let the uptown joints waste money on velvet—but Herbert added one last touch: "The play's the thing" etched along the proscenium, with proper credit to "Will" Shakespeare.

Even with these upgrades, the Minsky brothers well knew they weren't Florenz Ziegfeld, the impresario behind the famous *Ziegfeld Follies,* and this was precisely their intention. The Minskys understood the National Winter Garden audience, the ethos of the working man. Fantasies had to have a tangible, realistic shell. The sort of girls the Minskys advertised—"plenty of short girls, tall girls, fat girls"—sounded, above all, attainable. A man paid 50 cents to see a Minsky show, more than double the cost of a ticket at a lesser burlesque house, but this was the closest he might ever get to the *Follies.* The rest of Manhattan was full of reminders of what a workingman could never have, but the Lower East Side stood level with his gaze, spoke his language, deigned to shake his hand.

Ziegfeld, on the other hand, traded in fantasy. In 1907, he produced a Parisian-style "revue" on the roof garden of the Jardin de Paris near 44th Street, and the *Ziegfeld Follies* was born.

"No name in the history of American entertainment ever had such a magic connotation," wrote the comedian Eddie Cantor. "When an Arabian wizard said, 'Open sesame!' you expected diamond fountains and platinum flowers to sprout out of a rock. When a Hindu fakir said 'Abracadabra!' you knew he'd change into a flying horse or a singing tree. But when somebody said, 'The Ziegfeld *Follies*!' you expected the Seven Wonders of the World to stand at attention and say, 'Yessir!'"

Ziegfeld sought tall, pin-thin ladies with absurdly long legs who were more decorous than dirty and who could stretch the limits of New York law, which permitted a nude woman onstage as long as she stood still. He aimed to transform the American chorus girl into an abstract objet d'art, a remote, glittering ornament too delicate to touch. After the *Follies* found a permanent home at the New Amsterdam Theatre, Ziegfeld produced a cabaret number called "Midnight Frolics" that evoked Marcel Duchamp's *Nude Descending a Staircase*, with girls parading across the stage in flawless unison, all lithe limbs and blade-edged bones, a Cubist tableau in motion. "One type is missing," Ziegfeld wrote, explaining his criteria, "because the public has eliminated it. Time was when big women were admired onstage. They were so tall and broad that skirts were imperative. One sees them on the boards no more."

In addition to "glorifying the American girl," Ziegfeld offered the best comedic talent in the business: Eddie Cantor, Will Rogers, W. C. Fields, and the gawky Fanny Brice, whose clever parody of *Follies* girls made her the most famous of them all.

———

By mocking Ziegfeld and satirizing his skits, the Minskys offered burlesque in the original, truest sense of the word. That distinction allowed the brothers to skim the edges of class and elegance without being limited by them. Billy planted signs on Second Avenue that read WHAT THE FOLIES BERGERE IS TO PARIS, MINSKY'S IS TO NEW YORK and THE POOR MAN'S ZIEGFELD FOLLIES and hired a first-rate soubrette named Mae Dix, an "energetic Amazon" known for flashing her "censorless ginger."

One summer night, toward the end of the season, a thick heat skulked through the auditorium. Men huddled in large packs, heaving toward the stage, shirts polka-dotted with sweat stains. The place smelled of greasepaint and talc and cheap cigars. Spirals of smoke unraveled upward, fogging the air, blurring the Shakespeare quotes on the walls. Mae Dix sauntered across the stage and down Abe's runway, wearing a short black dress with white collar and cuffs, French maid style. The collar and cuffs were detachable, so they could be washed daily, although Mae tried to make them last for at least two shows.

At the end of her number, after a final twirl and shake, she pulled at her collar, holding it away from the thick makeup on her neck, but she was not yet behind the curtain. A man in the audience hinged his fingers on his lips and whistled, begging her to stay onstage and do it again—take off something else, the cuffs this time. Mae obliged, fell into a bow, and thought the show was over.

But there was a stampede of clapping now, furious and unrelenting, and Mae slowly, tentatively, undid her bodice, one button at a time. She stepped back behind the curtain, where Nick Elliott, the house manager, stood glaring at her.

Ten-dollar fine, he said. She knew perfectly well that showing more than what the script called for was a punishable offense.

He threw on the house lights, pushed the curtain aside, and took center stage.

"The Minsky brothers," he yelled above the frenzy, "run a decent theater. There won't be any more of that, and if you don't like it, you're free to leave."

Billy Minsky panicked at the words. He rushed to Nick, clamped a hand around his shoulder, and yanked him back behind the curtain.

"If people want it," Billy said, "we'll give it to them. When a court finds that I've broken some law, I'll stop. Until then, we'll sell tickets." The way Billy saw it, men had seen Mae's routine countless times at private stag shows. He hadn't invented the strip, but he'd bring it out from the back room.

Give Mae back her ten dollars, Billy ordered. Moreover, she'd score a ten-dollar raise as long as she repeated her "accident" every single night.

$\mathcal{A}$ few weeks later, a man named John Sumner, the secretary of the New York Society for the Suppression of Vice, requested that police pay a visit to the National Winter Garden. Sumner never expected to become the city's premier vice quester, having lost his virginity to a prostitute at the old Haymarket "resort" in Chelsea, but he strove to match the efforts of his predecessor, Anthony Comstock (who reportedly "died of joy" after procuring the conviction of birth control advocate Margaret Sanger).

A horse-drawn paddy wagon pulled up to Second Avenue and Houston Street, and the officers handcuffed the first Minsky brother they spotted, who happened to be Herbert. They took him for a ride downtown to chat with Inspector McCaullaugh at the precinct station.

The Minskys knew the law wasn't on their side. Two years prior, in 1915, the courts had decreed that movies and theater were popular entertainment, not art, and therefore unprotected by the First Amendment. Burlesque, not surprisingly, fell into this category. For two hours the inspector railed at Herbert and for two hours Herbert took it, eyes downcast, threading and unthreading his fingers as if they might produce a singing cat or length of rope, some vaudeville trick on the fly.

"I have never before or since," he confessed to his brothers, "felt quite so mean and worthless."

When the inspector ran out of condemnations, Herbert stood and grimly shook his hand. "Have your men drop in anytime," he said. "They'll never see anything off color at Minsky's."

The following afternoon, Herbert installed red, white, and blue lights in the center of the footlight trough and wired them to the ticket booth, where he was stationed every night. If he saw a cop in uniform or suspected one had infiltrated the audience in disguise, he threw on the red light. At once the act downgraded into a tamer version of itself—a "Boston," they called it, named for that city's especially vigilant enforcers of decency. Bodices remained buttoned, hips swayed to a halt, and the officer would leave disappointed, not having seen anything remotely objectionable.

Never let it be said that the Minskys weren't men of their word.

Chapter Eleven

Michael Todd was the toughest, lowest kind of man,
that close to being a gangster. And Gypsy was mad
about him. *Really* mad about him.

—JUNE HAVOC

Chicago, Illinois, 1941

After arriving in Chicago, Gypsy does what Michael Todd will not, filing for divorce from a spouse she doesn't love. Just as her mother did nearly thirty years earlier, Gypsy claims her husband, Arnold "Bob" Mizzy, treated her "cruelly" by using "obscene and abusive language" and knocking her down twice. She requests that the decree apply to her two wedding ceremonies, one in a water taxi off the Santa Ana coast and another at Long Beach, both sanctioned by 20th Century–Fox and attended by the press.

Reporters follow Gypsy to Chicago, covering her divorce (GYPSY ROSE LEE "STRIPS" HUBBY, headlines blare) and the grand opening of Mike's Theatre Café on the city's North Side. Teenage waitresses wear gingham skirts and serve Jell-O and milk along with highballs. Children swing back and forth on the railing while their parents watch Gypsy work the stage, using every one of her old tricks. She pays a woman in the audience to scream as she pulls off her last pin. A beat later, a busboy drops a tray of dishes. While the audience roars, Gypsy pretends to faint. "I never try to stir up the animal in 'em," she confides to Chicago's press corps. "Did you ever hold a piece of candy or a toy in front of a baby—just out of his reach? Notice how he laughs? That's your strip audience."

She keeps her word to George Davis and pounds on the typewriter between performances, rereading while she soaks off her body paint in the tub, a process that often takes hours. His connections help her land a contract with Simon & Schuster. "I'll do my specialty in Macy's to sell a book," she writes to her publicist. "If you would prefer something a little more dignified, make it a Wannamaker's window." She's eager to finish now. George is a great friend but a stubborn, temperamental critic, and his letters often have less to do with *The G-String Murders* than with his own floundering literary career, the daily chaos at Middagh Street, pointed comments about her decision to leave ("I'm delighted to hear that Todd wants you to stay on and make more money"), and, most maddening, his insights into her future.

"I think it very funny," George writes, "that you were once arrested for playing in a sketch called 'Illusion.' By rights you should have been given a life sentence: you've been playing it constantly. . . . Over and over I catch myself staring the mask of youth off you, the way dirty boys stare the dress off their teacher, and what I see scares the bejesus out of me. Not for myself, but for you." More foreboding than his words is the fact that she had thought them first herself, the looping, silent sound track in her mind since becoming Gypsy Rose Lee.

She and Mike spend nearly every hour of every day together operating the Theatre Café, and if he leaves Chicago he sends letters: "Darling, I reread your pink letter at least 10 times. . . . I feel exactly like you do and wish I could say it as good as you do—somehow I can't make with gags & funny words."

His wife, Bertha, has her suspicions, and Mike still insists on discretion, mostly for the benefit of his son. If Bertha discovers their affair, she will keep him from seeing Michael Todd, Jr. One night, when Gypsy is expecting Mike for dinner, she hears a knock at her door. To her surprise she finds Junior, dressed in a suit, comb lines visible across his hair.

"My father was unavoidably detained," he says. "He has asked me to take you to dinner."

The kid is eleven years old.

He orders Gypsy's favorite dish and brand of champagne, discusses his burgeoning business philosophy. At the end of the meal, he drops his hand over the check.

"Dad is paying for dinner, Miss Lee," he says, "but your split of champagne, that's on me."

Gypsy thinks, not for the first time, that Mike would be a good father to her own child, should she ever decide to have one.

With the Theatre Café making $55,000 per week, Mike takes an extended business trip to New York, seeking a show to produce on Broadway. In his absence, Gypsy notices one of the managers making some curious changes. A pinup-pretty girl now stands behind a green felt box and encourages patrons to play a dice game. He also raises drink prices, imposes a minimum, and fires half of the waitresses.

Mike is furious upon his return and demands that everything revert to the way it had been. The manager explains that certain business "connections" demanded the changes, connections who could not be reasoned with. The next day, two henchmen for the Chicago Mafia stop by to underscore that point. Mike withdraws his name from the Café, sells it to the Mob for one dollar, and flees the city.

Gypsy leaves with him and takes the act on the road, traveling across the country, three shows a day, six days a week. In August, as the tour nears its end, Bertha Todd bursts into her dressing room in Syracuse, weepy and wild-eyed. She aims a shaking finger at Gypsy.

End your affair with Mike, she demands. Immediately.

There is no affair, Gypsy says, her tone calm and cool.

She has her superstitions, developed during childhood and deepening as she ages. Eat twelve grapes on the twelve strokes of midnight every New Year's Eve. Never lay your hat on your bed. Don't whistle in the dressing room. No hint of the color green backstage. And truth is malleable, something to be bent or stretched or made to disappear, but direct lies always find the path back to the one who tells them.

Dainty June, at the height of her career.

Chapter Twelve

Forty-five weeks of two shows a day, seven days a week, in states that permitted Sunday shows. And if you made good you stayed on the wheel, show after show, until you were too old and shaky to play any part at all.

—SOPHIE TUCKER

On the Vaudeville Circuit, 1920–1924

By now Louise was nine and June seven, but Rose Hovick didn't need the calendar to tell time. She had a private clock, set precisely to her needs and preferences, years tacked on and stripped away within mere moments. Birth certificates were forged and forged again: locations chosen at whim; dates substituted or invented entirely, always younger for train travel and older for evading child welfare. Had she not wished so desperately for her girls to be seen, they might not have existed at all.

Murray Gordon—"Gordon" to Rose, "Uncle Gordon" to June, and still a nonentity to Louise—applied a veneer of order over the chaos, slowing time just enough to establish rules and routines. He would sleep separately and alone; the girls never once caught him trying to enter their mother's room. "We never saw or heard a thing about them being intimate," June said. "It was strictly hidden." And no salary for the boys in the act, an edict Rose found brilliant. "The experience they'll get," he told their parents, "is worth more than money." He discovered the boys in hotel courtyards and small-town alleyways during stops on the circuit, and their parents, for the most part, were happy to be rid of them.

One singer, from Shamokin, Pennsylvania, had never owned a pair of underwear or socks. He sang in clear, pitch-perfect Italian, but was so deformed he couldn't straighten his legs. Gordon positioned him close to the wings, in near darkness, with a pin spot illuminating only his face. The sight of the audience terrified him, and at the high notes he sometimes wet his pants.

Another boy slept in one room with twelve siblings and had a father who spent more time in jail than at home. Rose named this second boy Sonny Sinclair. Within a week Gordon had taken him to see three doctors, the last of whom determined that Sonny, ten years old, had syphilis.

"The disease is incurable," Rose told Louise and June, "and there is only one way you can get it—by letting some man enter your room. Most important of all, nearly all men have it."

Except, she hastened to add, for Gordon.

Gordon also put an end to games of hide-and-seek in between rehearsals and performances. No more wasting their energy or wandering into situations they were too young to understand, such as the time June spied on a fellow vaudeville star, a man with a lioness. The animal was the most regal creature June had ever seen, and she crept backstage at every opportunity to watch them practice their act. One day she noticed the man touching his animal, petting her again and again between her hind legs. She made a strange, unfamiliar sound, somewhere between a purr and a roar, and June ran and told her mother that the lioness was hurt. The following afternoon, Rose hid backstage with June so they could watch together. "He fondled her and fondled her," June remembered, "and finally he entered her." She felt her mother stiffen, heard her sharp intake of breath, but Rose said nothing about this man trespassing into a room where he didn't belong.

Gordon tried to break Rose of her bad habits as well, insisting that she stop chewing the animals' food before feeding it to them. Impossible, Rose countered. How else could her darling pup Mumshay eat, since all of her teeth were gone? Gordon sighed and gave up, but Rose must start taking better care of Louise and June. Their usual breakfast of rolls and coffee was forbidden—"It's a wonder their stomachs aren't ruined," Gordon scolded—although Rose still sneaked them each a mug if he stepped out. Their teeth, however, were practically beyond repair. "The toothbrush," June said, "was something we had never considered." While trouping in Milwaukee, Gordon made appointments with a dentist. "Why, they are only little kids, Rose," Big Lady protested from Seattle when she heard the news. "That man has them brushing the enamel off their teeth twice a day just like they were sick or something."

For once a man prevailed against the Hovick clan. June nearly had to be knocked out in order to have eleven cavities filled. Louise had just as many cavities, two fanglike incisors pushing through her top gums, and a severe case of trench mouth. The doctor removed and replaced the offending incisors and instructed Rose to swab her mouth with iodine every day. But the problem persisted, and Louise grew more self-conscious, memorizing the angle of each wayward tooth, noticing a slight lisp that sounded, to her ears, as forceful as a crashing wave. In photos from that era she smiles with her mouth closed, lips gripped and upturned tightly, as if holding hostage a secret not ready to be told.

━━━━━━

𝓛ouise and June met vaudeville's characters and learned its rules. They recorded everything, taking mental snapshots and filing them away. Certain memories resonated only later. The kindly stagehands who acted like uncles hung pictures of Klan rallies and lynchings backstage. One of them hoisted June on his lap and presented her with a gold pendant etched with the letters "KKK"—an image that "chilled" her, though she didn't yet understand why. The sisters noticed that the colored and foreign vaudevillians disappeared after the shows, heading to their own "special" bars and restaurants and hotels. They heard the

Dainty June and Co., top billing on the vaudeville circuit.

colored artists talk about a separate vaudeville circuit, as well, an organization known formally as the Theater Owners Booking Association and informally as "Tough on Black Asses."

They encountered the strangest hotel mates along each of their
stops: the man who sold leeches as a cure for black eyes; a brash, redheaded hooker and her pimp; a man who carried tiny dead babies in
glass bottles. "Look at the umbilical cord hanging on this one," he
boasted. They met a performer named Gentle Julia, who one day made
a bold proclamation neither girl ever forgot: she was pregnant and saw
no reason to tell anyone who the father was, not even the father himself. They learned that proud and true vaudevillians turned to déclassé
burlesque only if bookings on the circuit were scarce. And it came to
them, piece by broken piece, that they would never be normal, every-
day people, and that they had lost their childhoods while they were still
children.

The act had steady offers now, just as Gordon had promised, including a booking in Buffalo for $750 per week, about $32,000 today. Rose
clutched the contract to her chest and wept. It was unclear whether she
was moved by the astonishing sum of money, or the shock that a man
had finally kept his word to her. From now on, Gordon said, they would
ride to the theaters in taxicabs instead of streetcars. And instead of just
one hotel room, they would rent a suite. Still, Rose haggled over prices,
once arguing with a hotel manager for an hour when the bill was $7
more than expected. "It's not the principle of the thing," she explained.
"It's the money."

Rose vowed to follow each rule of the contract (no profane language, no intoxication, no impromptu lines or jests interpolated into
the dialogue) and began packing the props and costumes and animals,
an ever-growing and ever-shifting menagerie that included, at one time
or another, Mumshay, her favorite dog, June's beloved NeeNee, Bootsie
the poodle, guinea pigs, rabbits, chameleons, white mice, rats, turtles, a
poisonous horned toad, a goose, a lamb, and Louise's monkey, Gigolo,
who kept constant vigil on her shoulder, turning heads wherever she
went.

The guinea pigs and rats slept in dressing room drawers or in the
girls' pockets, leaving them wet and filled with droppings—"licorice

buttons," Rose called them. When a pet died on the circuit, Louise and June insisted on great pomp and ceremony, and tiny makeshift graves were scattered across the country. Mumshay was one of the more spectacular casualties, squashed in the crevice of a folding bed in Syracuse, and June's elderly guinea pig, Samba, perished after a nightlong three-some with a magician's lady pigs. (June cried for hours, and Rose pressed cold towels onto her eyes to reduce the swelling before her performance.) The animals, more than anything else, gave Louise, June, and the boys a sense that every budget hotel and cramped train car was home, even if windows never offered the same view twice.

Most of their fellow vaudevillians loved Louise and June and the boys, but there were exceptions. Some of the other kiddie acts grew suspicious when, seemingly out of nowhere, things began to go wrong: props were destroyed, wigs and wardrobes disappeared, the sheet music got lost. Rose expressed sympathy and joined in the search, and occasionally found the missing item—always too late. "They shouldn't have left the things lying around so carelessly," she'd scold. One performer known as "The Darling Devina—Female Adonis" warned others not to breathe too deeply when passing by their room and called Louise and June "imitation children." Another played on the same bill with them several times and insisted that Dainty June was a midget, since no actual child could dance that well. Rose took a particular dislike to her, and conferred with her daughters over coffee.

"She needs a lesson," she said. "A good scare, that's what she needs."

"She's mean," Louise said. "I don't think you ought to tackle someone so mean."

Mother smiled, and she spoke her next words in a blunt whisper. "Tackle? Oh, no . . . I'll write a letter she won't forget. I'll say, 'Someone is following you, and within two weeks your body will be found floating in the river.' "

———

Louise was the only child who'd spent any time, no matter how brief, in a formal classroom, but Rose believed the circuit taught everything they—and she—needed to know. Consistency was the key to success in vaudeville, polishing an act until it became the prettiest, shiniest version of itself. Consider how many times Chaz Chase, the "Eater of Strange Things," consumed lit matches in order to make the trick appear effortless, or the practice schedule of Hadji Ali, the master regurgitator, famous for swallowing a gallon of water followed by a pint of kerosene. After his assistant set up a small metal castle a few feet away, Hadji Ali spat the kerosene in a six-foot stream and set the structure ablaze. He then opened his throat and, with the aim and velocity of a fire hose, purged the water and killed every flame.

These sorts of acts dominated the circuit, vaudevillians possessed of talents invented rather than innate. The man who guzzled hot molten lava and belched up coins, the man who swallowed a goldfish and a baby shark and asked the audience which should reappear first, the man who lit gunpowder on his tongue, the man who discovered that his sneeze made audiences laugh and worked it into his routine, honing, over the course of a year, the mechanics of twitching his nostrils and cranking his jaw, the exaggerated intake of breath and sputtering of lips. A performer called "The Human Fish" ate a banana, played a trombone, and read a newspaper while submerged in a tank of water. Another had a "cat piano," an act featuring live cats in wire cages that meowed Gregorio Allegri's *Miserere* when their tails were pulled (in reality the performer yanked on artificial tails and did all the meowing himself). Alonzo the Miracle Man lit and smoked a cigarette, brushed his teeth and combed his hair, and buttoned his shirt—miracles since he had been born without arms. Louise and June were particularly fond of Lady Alice, an old dowager who wore elegant beaded gowns and performed with rats. The runt settled on the crown of her head, a miniature kazoo clenched between teeth like grains of rice. He breathed a tuneless harmony while the rest of the litter began a slow parade across Lady Alice's outstretched arms, marching from the tip of one middle finger to the other. The girls never understood how Lady Alice controlled the rodents—their own animals weren't quite so obedient—until one day she revealed her secret: a trail of Cream of Wheat slathered on her neck and shoulders.

Vaudevillians called these signature bits "insurance," gimmicks they kept tucked away in their repertoire, always close at hand if a new routine failed. (Fred Astaire once learned this lesson the hard way, when he was replaced by a dog act.) Child performers were considered the surest bet of all; "kids," June said, "were an automatic gimmick." Her mother sifted through identities for the Baby and added layers to her history, each more impressive and fantastic than the last. Once again Rose renamed the act, settling on "Dainty June and Her Newsboy Songsters." They were playing the big time now, the Orpheum Circuit. It meant something when Martin Beck, the Orpheum's manager, believed in an act; he had discovered Houdini and booked the phenomenal Sarah Bernhardt at the New York Palace for $7,000 per week. No more lodge halls or the indignity of decay, the frayed traditions of worn plush and peeling sequins, the old piano just barely in tune.

June was now the "sophisticated little miss" of the Orpheum Circuit, dubbed "Pavlova's Own" by the famous diva herself, at least according to Rose; an "infant prodigy"; both "the greatest of all juvenile screen notables" and star of "the greatest juvenile musical comedy on the American stage." One columnist—aided, perhaps, by suggestions from Rose—could barely contain his exuberance. "I have seen and talked with the Eighth Wonder of the World! She is a tiny creature, weighing about 75 pounds when all dolled up." Three nuns went blind sewing her $1,000 dress, which blinked with the brilliance of a million rhinestones. When she wasn't dazzling audiences with her preternatural talent, Dainty June dabbled in politics, advocating on behalf of a proposed bill that would raise wages for postal workers. Carrying the bill to every stop on the Orpheum Circuit, she vowed to collect enough signatures to present the petition to Speaker of the House Frederick Gillett. Dainty June and Her Newsboy Songsters would soon set sail on the SS *Olympic* and tour abroad in England, France, Belgium, South Africa, and Australia. When the time came, Rose would know exactly how to doctor the passport applications.

She encouraged Gordon to contribute to June's persona, as well. "She is the most tender-hearted child you ever saw," he said. "It distresses her to see anything suffer." Sometimes June spoke for herself. "I love everybody," she announced, and the papers assumed she meant her mother most of all, who "taught her virtually everything she knows." Dainty June, in fact, had become such a hot commodity that she needed a patent: "DAINTY JUNE (Hovick), The Darling of Vaudeville, Reg. U.S. Patent Office." Even the pronouncement of the patent became part of June's official persona.

It was the surest advertising paradigm, which Gordon knew by trade and Rose by instinct: discover what could make you famous, and then proclaim that it already has. In Rose's opinion, her own image was just as crucial to the act, and with that in mind she began inserting herself into the newspaper stories, telling reporters she once taught acting to the members of "Our Gang." She bought a beaver fur coat and insisted there was no other in the country like it. She had designed it herself, se-

Advertisement for
Dainty June and Her
Newsboy Songsters.

lecting the skins and taking just a few at a time to the furrier. As a further guarantee that the furrier wouldn't switch skins, each one had Rose's name written on it, in indelible pencil.

"You know I wouldn't pay that much money for a coat," she reasoned, "unless it was to put up a front." A stack of new diamond baubles adorned one finger, complements to her engagement rings. The rings could be pawned if they ever ran out of money, and besides, she said, "they do impress the managers." No objections, no arguments—Gordon wouldn't want her asthma to act up, now, would he? She also took to carrying money in a grouch bag, a gray suede pouch worn around her waist that bulged oddly under her dress, although she often insisted that there wasn't much hidden inside.

The most crucial change, however, was to her name; the public would know her, from now on, as "Madame Rose." Still not satisfied, she tagged on a suffix: "The Developer of Children."

———

*D*ainty June and Her Newsboy Songsters traveled for months at a time, performing at theaters across the country, Chicago to Minneapolis, Pittsburgh to Detroit, Indiana to Salt Lake City, three cities a week, two shows per day, more on weekends. Louise and June split the burden of packing a cretonne bedspread, a trunk cover, a coffeepot, and a lampshade for every trip. As soon as they checked into their hotel, Louise said, "We started fixing our room to make it look homey." Every Christmas, Louise lugged a half-dead, needle-deprived tree aboard the train that dwindled to skeletal by the time they retrimmed it for her January 9 birthday. Musty green curtains enclosed the sleeping cars, each one a dank, gloomy cave. June slept alone in the lower bunk, her neck smeared with Vicks VapoRub and sheathed in a stocking, while Louise shared the upper with two of the younger boys. Sometimes she cried at night, uncertain of her age but certain enough to know she should no longer be bunking with the opposite sex. With her heavy rubber boots, tweed cap (which doubled as a bed for her guinea pig), and bluntly cut dark hair, Louise couldn't blame the porter for thinking she was one of them.

"I just can't stand it any longer," she confided to her guinea pig, wiping her tears on his fur. "Not if I never sleep again. I can't. I can't."

She mostly kept to herself during layoffs and lulls, reading and rereading Gordon's birthday gift, a book titled *Dreams: What They Mean*. She studied the various interpretations and incorporated her own occult visions. "You can charge a nickel a dream," Gordon said, but Rose shushed him. "Don't go putting ideas into her head," she muttered. "People will think she's a Gypsy."

Louise also devoured every book supplied by their tutor, Olive Thompson: *Painted Veils*, *The Rubaiyat of Omar Khayyam*, Honoré de Balzac's *Droll Stories*. Miss Thompson, no relation to the family, had joined the troupe at the reluctant behest of Rose. She hated to spend the money, but frequent inquiries from the police and child welfare agencies didn't leave much choice. The Society for the Prevention of Cruelty to Children, called the "Gerry Society" after its founder, Elbridge Gerry, was especially zealous in monitoring child performers under the age of sixteen. "These child slaves of the stage," Gerry wrote, "[are] subjected to a bondage more terrible and oppressive than the children of Israel ever endured at the hands of Pharaoh or the descendents of Ham have ever experienced in the way of African slavery."

Officers kept slinking backstage and cornering the girls, asking them all sorts of ridiculous questions: Who was the vice president under Woodrow Wilson? Under Warren G. Harding? Who killed Cain? Louise and June could no sooner answer such inquiries than they could recall, without hesitation, all the years in which they might have been born. Most of the time the officers nodded grimly, scratched some notes on a pad, and warned that they'd be back, but in January 1923, on a bitter Saturday afternoon in Rochester, New York, they kept their word.

Dainty June and Her Newsboy Songsters were in the middle of the matinee finale, a military number featuring a gun drill, when a whistle pierced the orchestra's cheery tune. No questions this time, just two officers marching down the aisle, motioning for everyone to exit the stage. They wrapped Louise and June in coats and herded all eight members of the company into the back of a police van. Through the windows, Louise watched her mother in the taxi behind them, weeping on Gordon's shoulder.

"They won't make me talk," Sonny whispered, squeezed between the girls. "My father talked once, and the gang busted two of his ribs and almost poked his eye out."

The other children at the station were all cases of neglect or abuse and June noticed she stood out even among them, with her prop badges of honor and face painted like a watercolor. What a relief, she thought, that the officers did nothing more than lock them in a stuffy room that smelled of bleach. But Louise hoped they would fingerprint or interrogate or at least throw them in a cell—something exciting to make for a good story. She hushed the others and listened to Rose plead with the officers. Would they please let the children go? They had another show scheduled for that night, and the contract . . . fine. Well, would they at least let her contact her father in Seattle? He could straighten out this whole mess right away.

The officers consented, and Rose sent a Western Union wire to Charlie Thompson:

```
GO IMMEDIATELY TO MASTER OF YOUR MASONIC LODGE TELL HIM
TO WIRE HORACE OLIVER MASONIC TEMPLE ROCHESTER NY THAT
HE KNOWS YOU AND ME TO BE OF GOOD CHARACTER AND PROPER
GUARDIANS FOR LOUISE AND JUNE DO THIS IMMEDIATELY BE-
CAUSE LABOR AUTHORITIES HOLDING CHILDREN FOR INVESTIGA-
TION
```

Twenty-six hundred miles away, Grandpa Thompson read his daughter's plea. He sighed and did as Rose asked. The lodge master hurried with a response:

```
SEATTLE WASH
HORACE OLIVER
CARE MASONIC TEMPLE ROCHESTER, N.Y.


HAVE KNOWN CHAS J THOMSON AND DAUGHTER FOR PAST 5 YEARS
THEY ARE OF EXCEPTIONALLY GOOD CHARACTER AND WORTHY
GUARDIAN OF TWO CHILDREN NOW PLAYING ORPHEUM CIRCUIT
NAMELY JUNE AND LOUISE YOUR EFFORTS IN THEIR BEHALF
```

WILL BE GREATLY APPRECIATED SAMUEL A. COX WORSHIPFUL
MASTER IONIC LOGE NO. 90

The judge, an active and honorable Shriner, dismissed the case with the stipulation that Rose hire a tutor immediately.

A graduate of the Minnesota State Normal School, Miss Thompson was formally certified to possess the "character, skill, and experience required by law." The girls liked their tutor immediately, but Rose thought her too pretty. To dowdy her up a bit, she suggested that Miss Thompson wear horn-rimmed glasses, flat, sensible shoes instead of black patent pumps, and a black dress with white piqué collar and cuffs—proper attire for a governess. Newspapers were intrigued by this insight into troupers' lives, the strange logistics of a migratory classroom. Rose arranged real school desks in the dressing room, hid the makeup mirror behind a large blackboard, and stole a prop globe from another act on the bill. Gordon encouraged the press to come see for themselves how stars were educated on the Orpheum Circuit, a vaudeville act in its own right.

Math and spelling made June nervous. Between acts, the stagehands taught her the alphabet and how to sound out words phonetically. They listened as she read vaudeville advertisements aloud and corrected her pronunciation. Slowly she was learning, although she much preferred the "See for Yourself" field trips Miss Thompson organized in each city, tours through carpet plants and steel mills and salt mines. But Louise, for all her trouble memorizing dance steps, remembered everything her teacher said. She tried on new words as if they were her mother's gleaming rings, recoiling at June's "hideously" thin arms and proclaiming her sister "gauche." June couldn't tell if she should be flattered or offended, but she envied Louise's brilliant, facile mind, the way it left nothing unexamined or unclaimed.

By now Rose's grouch bag held at least $25,000 and swung pendulously between her legs. She did not believe in banks. Once, June watched while her mother fanned piles of bills across the floor, counting them one by one.

"It's a trillion dollars, I bet," June whispered to Louise that night.

They had made a pretend tent, pulling the bedspread taut over the foot posts. "Even more than a trillion, maybe. So I don't see why I can't have a doll that goes 'Mama' wiff a buggy to match. I could even have a live pony if I wanted it, and a stove wiff a real oven—"

"I want a boat," Louise interrupted. "A boat that's big enough for me to sit in with a sail and oars."

"What is the meaning of this?" Rose said, standing in the doorway that connected their two rooms. She threw on the light and whisked up the bedspread, ruining the tent. "We're taking an early train tomorrow, and here you are talking all night. What are you talking about?"

Louise kept quiet. This was June's game, and she was obligated to explain herself.

"We were saying what we'd do wiff the money in the belt," June said.

A pause. Rose stepped closer and calibrated her words.

"Who told you about any money?" she asked.

"Nobody," June replied, quick and adamant. "I seen—I mean I saw it."

Rose sat down on the foot of the bed. The windows were open, and the wind gusted her flannel nightgown around her hips. Her cheek bore deep creases from her pillow.

"Remember the story about the poor little match girl?" she asked.

Louise and June nodded, waiting.

"Well," their mother said, "her mother was a very foolish woman. She gave all her money to a bad wolf and the wolf left her alone with her little girl to starve. Remember how hungry she was? And how cold? And how they found her dead one morning, all frozen?"

June began to sob. "Please don't tell any more," she whimpered. "It's too sad."

Rose patted June's foot. "Mother doesn't want that to happen to *her* babies," she said. "That's why she hides the money away so no one can find it. That money belongs to the three of us. You mustn't tell a soul that we have it."

June studied her mother. "Not even Uncle Gordon?" she asked.

Rose yanked the bedspread up tight, pulling the top around her daughters' necks. She kissed them both, and the room went dark again.

"Not even Uncle Gordon," she said, closing the door gently.

It was quiet until June rustled and turned. Louise felt her sister's breath soft against her cheek.

"That wasn't the story about the poor little match girl at all," June said. "There was no wolf in that story."

Neither girl questioned Rose about the grouch bag again.

$\mathcal{E}$ach afternoon during break, Louise and June took one dollar apiece from Rose, a sum expected to stretch for all three meals. They strolled to the local Woolworth's, by now used to stares from the civilians. Look at the little blonde dressed cap-à-pie in dirty white rabbit fur, the pumpkin-sized muff encasing her hands, the missing buttons, the tattered hems, how precious and peculiar she was, all at once. And the taller one, with knickers tucked into boots and—could that be?—a *monkey* perched on her (or was it his?) shoulder. It was easy for June to distract the clerk with her blond curls and eager little face and talk of how she loved "Woolworff's," while Louise skulked up and down the aisles, grabbing here and there, nothing she wanted or needed. A tin spectacles case, a compass, a jar of pomade, a can opener, a tea strainer. Then they switched places and, once safe outside, compared their booty to see who won. After one such trip a pair of flat, sensible shoes appeared next to their pile, and they looked up to see Miss Thompson glaring down.

"Where did you children get those?" she asked. Clamping a hand on each girl's shoulder, she turned them around, guided them back into Woolworth's, and made them confess. "I'm sowwy and I'll never steal again," June said. Louise repeated that line, her voice sounding hollow and far away.

An hour later, back in the dressing room, the story came tumbling out. June began to cry and Rose joined in, a raspy gasp chasing each sob. Louise cried into the dip of her mother's neck and they all rocked back and forth. "We were together," Louise said. "We were warm and safe from outsiders who didn't understand us."

Without warning Rose unclasped Louise's grip and pushed June aside. She took a step toward Miss Thompson. Her face took on an expression of terrifying calm, those violet, coin slot eyes, that fault line of a mouth.

"How dare you?" she said. Even the pauses between words carried a threat. "How dare you subject that little bundle of nerves to such a strain?"

June sniffed from the corner. Miss Thompson knew better than to defend herself.

"Get out! You're fired!"

The door shut behind her. The next time a reporter visited their dressing room, his camera captured the children bent over desks and Rose standing before the blackboard, posing as Miss Thompson, complete with proper governess uniform and horn-rimmed glasses.

Louise conducted her own private lessons, updating her reading list, carving out private niches of time to scavenge for unfamiliar phrases and exotic words. She replaced *Sarah Crewe, Tanglewood Tales,* and *A Child's Garden of Verses* with Boccaccio's *Decameron, Indian Love Lyrics,* and *Das Kapital,* always carrying one or another under her arm. June regarded her with unabashed awe and the boys mocked her playfully. Look at this bookish, haughty version of plain old Louise, the clumsy girl who couldn't even carry a tune—"The Duchess," they now called her. She taught herself to sew, too, a gift passed on from Big Lady, and made costumes for the entire company during long train rides from town to town. They all read tea leaves, a popular pastime for troupers, but Louise insisted she had a true gift for seeing the future; the veil over her face at birth, which Grandma Dottie had pressed between the pages of her Bible, had marked her as special.

"I'm going to marry a king or somebody," she boasted to June. "In any case, I'll be rich." As reinforcement, she doodled just one word, "Money," in her careful child's cursive script, until the page was filled edge to edge with her intent.

———

*B*y now, Dainty June and Her Newsboy Songsters were so successful other acts spied on them, memorizing Sonny's solos, imitating June's steps. There was even a rumor that the Pantages Circuit was developing a new young starlet named "Baby June" to follow Dainty June's act across the country, a ploy Rose grudgingly admired. Gordon occasion-

Dainty June

(HOVICK)

"The Darling of Vaudeville"
(Reg. U.S. Patent Office)

and Her Newsboy Songsters

OPENING: Dainty June and

Her Newsboy Songsters

"Dear Mary" Dainty June

"Just a Step" George Trailord

"Duet" Dainty June and Danny Montgomery

NOTE: The Rhinestone Dress worn by Dainty June

contains 24,000 imported stones and cost $1000.

"Ballad" Joseph Dare, "the boy Caruso"

"Nobody's Darlin'" Dainty June

"The Dumbells" Danny Montgomery and George Trailord

"Sole Mio," sung in Italian, Joseph Dare

"Two Little Wops" Dainty June and Sonny Sinclair

Fast Eccentric Dancing: George Trailord

"Hello! Mag!" Rose Louise, Danny Montgomery

and Dainty June

FINALE: Dainty June and Her Newsboy Songsters

ally altered the roster of boys; they succumbed to the grueling schedule or demands of their families back home, but new talent waited in every city. Dainty June played after intermission, a coveted position on the bill, much preferable to opening or closing (called "playing to the haircuts," since the audience typically began exiting the theater). One of their programs featured a cover image of June clad in angel wings, so high on her toes that her feet arch perfectly, improbably, like crescent moons.

Not one false note in any of their performances, according to the critics. George's dancing was phenomenal—not surprisingly, since he performed before the royal court in Italy, according to Rose. The skit done in blackface by two boys named Nixon and Sans was "hilarious." Another boy's solo was made more "interesting" by the fact that his cracking, pubescent voice slid between tenor and bass. Louise displayed a flair for comedy and character acting, especially during her "excellent" Scandinavian singing impersonation and "Frances, the Bowery Tough" number. They loved everything about Dainty June, especially her rendition of the melody "Won't You Be My Husband?," during which the star, "still in her babyhood," crossed the footlights to find an elderly gentleman with a gleaming bald head. Reaching into "parts unknown," she produced a massive powder puff and caressed the man all over, performing as if for him alone.

No one seemed quite sure of June's age—the guesses ranged from eleven to fourteen to sixteen—and despite the "wealth of chuckles" and "world of laughter," there was something disturbing, something off, about the whole spectacle.

"Dainty June and Company," one critic noted, "are not very childish, with their uncomfortable sophistication. The more meager is the period of childhood, the hastier, relatively, does withering old age creep on."

It would not be long before Dainty June had her first nervous breakdown.

Outside the insular world of vaudeville, the 1920s were updating everything America knew about itself. Sigmund Freud introduced the idea that all people are born bisexual. Franklin Delano Roosevelt, as assistant secretary of the navy, got enmeshed in a scandal when young sailors went undercover to collect evidence against homosexuals in Newport, Rhode Island. President Warren G. Harding met with his mistress, a pretty young blonde named Nan Britton, in clandestine corners of the White House. There was, she said, "a small closet [where] we repaired many times, and in the darkness of a space no more than five feet square the President of the United States and his adoring sweetheart made love." America had finally completed her noble task overseas and now anticipated a promising future.

But the future had ominous undertones. The deaths of more than 15 million people, 130,000 of them Americans, ushered in an era of violent change—the great turning point of modern history. A postwar malaise gripped the country. People felt untethered. Their traditions were uprooted, their belief systems unmoored. Two Chicago boys named Nathan Leopold and Richard Loeb murdered a neighborhood boy "just for the thrill of it." On a cloudless September day, a brown wagon draped in canvas and pulled by an old bay horse stopped at 23 Wall Street, the headquarters of J. P. Morgan in lower Manhattan. The driver crept away, and as the clock on Trinity Church struck 12:01 P.M., a blast rattled the entire district. Shards of iron shot through the air, shattering pedestrians' skulls. Windowpanes blasted out as far as ten blocks away and clerks in sixth-floor offices suffered severe burns. The property damage neared $3 million, 39 people died, and 130 were injured. It was the deadliest attack on U.S. soil to date, and the perpetrators would never be discovered. In this new world of random bombings and genocide and poison gas and machine guns that fired six hundred rounds per minute, it wasn't difficult to believe that young men could kill each other over a truckload of booze.

Drastic change was encroaching on vaudeville, too, and even the best insurance bits were no guarantee against the growing new threat. Since KDKA in Pittsburgh broadcast the 1920 presidential election returns, radio, though still an inchoate and primitive medium—one would be lucky to tune in and hear a harmonica played by whomever, wherever—seemed poised to revolutionize every aspect of daily life. It could cure disease, solve crimes, soothe the lingering tensions with Europe. And to say nothing of the entertainment possibilities! Mme. Luisa Tetrazzini, standing in her apartment in Manhattan's Hotel McAlpin, gave an opera concert for hundreds on board naval ships cruising the Atlantic Ocean. The Park Avenue Baptist Church, where John D. Rockefeller, Jr., worshiped every Sunday, had an evening service broadcast by station WJZ. An engineer in Ossining, New York, hosted a "wireless vaudeville" performance from the comfort of his own home. Music and comedy soared invisibly across prairies and lakes to reach audiences in Connecticut, Illinois, Arkansas, Ohio, and Colorado. A family could enjoy a night out without paying a single dime for admission.

"Those earphones will never take the place of vaudeville," Rose insisted, but she consented to tweak the act. A cow would join them, she announced. Yes, a cow. It had appeared to her in a dream and told her exactly what to do. Gordon understood that such omens were not to be ridiculed, and immediately ordered the cow to be made. It had a papier-mâché head with nostrils the size of rabbit holes, a brown-and-white body made of felt, trousers for legs, and leather spat hooves. One boy occupied the head, two crouched inside its torso, and one controlled the hind legs. Louise, contrary to the myth she would one day create, never played any part of the cow's body. In June's opinion, "she couldn't dance that well."

"I've got a cow and her name is Sue," June sang, while the cow pranced and dipped alongside her, "and she'll do most anything I ask her to." The cow became an Orpheum headliner in its own right. "Bring the kiddies," the advertisements exhorted, "to see Dainty June and the Funny Dancing Cow."

The cow helped, but Rose still relied on her own version of insurance: stealing from other performers' acts (although she was now more selective about who was worthy of the effort). When she learned they would be on a bill with the great Fanny Brice, on break from the *Ziegfeld Follies,* during an upcoming stop in San Francisco, she reminded the girls to watch every single show, and closely.

Fanny Brice was a star not easily copied, a true original with a honed philosophy about her craft, and she would have scoffed at Rose's plan to spy on her act. "Every successful artist, no matter what his medium," Fanny wrote, "has his own individual methods of getting his result, and anyone who attempts to borrow another's method becomes a mere impersonator. . . . You never can tell what an audience is going to do. That is what makes the search for the feel of the audience such a fascinating and lucrative pastime."

But Rose forgot her spying scheme when the manager of the Orpheum in San Francisco approached her. Did Madame Rose have anyone in her act who could do a scene with Fanny Brice? The role called for a teenage girl, able to speak five lines, and he needed her right away.

She decided that Louise, now thirteen, would do the part. Not a natural like June, but she handled herself reasonably well onstage and knew how to deliver a joke. Besides, June was still a baby and could never convincingly play a teenager, not even when she became one.

Louise could scarcely believe her luck. All those nights spent ducking in the shadows of the stage, resenting June's talent and her own irrelevance. All those rehearsals where it became clear she was interchangeable, her characters not truly her own. All that time wasted hating the act simply because it could carry on, indefinitely, without her. And now, finally, performing was an opportunity rather than an obligation, a chance to prove she was an intrinsic part of their future, that Mother had been wise not to leave her behind.

𝒜 dozen years later, when Gypsy Rose Lee considered Fanny Brice her mentor and best friend, she would recall nearly everything about the day they first met, the day she had her first solo without June or the Newsboy Songsters. Fanny looked different than she'd expected, clothed in a plain black dress, no bustle or fur or feathers, not even a glint of jewelry. She invited Louise to sit in her dressing room so they could discuss the scene: Louise is the drunken flapper, a know-it-all kid named Mary Rose, and she struggles while a cop tries to arrest her. Fanny talks him out of it, then steps in and delivers a lecture about her gutter ways. Louise listened to every word Fanny said, each one amplified in the intimate space of the dressing room, and told her she was sure she could do it, even though she wasn't sure at all.

She tried on her costume, a bejeweled orange chiffon dress with a floaty skirt of feathers. "I can't wear this in front of an audience," Louise whispered. "It isn't modest." Fanny shook her head, and noticed that the girl looked scared to death. "Look, kid," she said. "You can't be too modest in this business." Louise slipped into a pair of gold brocade heels that pinched her growing feet—so badly she had to retrieve the clunky oxfords from her newsboy costume, and hope the feathers would hide them.

She felt June watching her and heard her sister's question—"Does Mother know you're wearing a dress like that?"—accompanied by a wise little smile; for once, the Baby played the big sister. With each moment an internal shutter clicked, imprinting everything: the numbness in her legs; the grace of the conductor's hands, waving like "pink wax birds" over the black expanse of audience; the remote, untamed sound of her voice as it recited each line. What Louise remembered most of all was how the spotlight felt hotter, somehow, when it had only her to shine on.

Chapter Thirteen

If only you knew how difficult it is to strip one's heart
clean, and to tell you boys how proud I am of you for
the fine service you are giving to your country and to
the strengthening of the arsenal of Democracy.

—GYPSY ROSE LEE, IN AN OPEN
LETTER TO SERVICEMEN

New York City, 1942

A few weeks after the attack on Pearl Harbor, while 2,500 Japanese residents are being rounded up and shipped to Ellis Island, Gypsy receives a phone call from Michael Todd.

While walking along 42nd Street, he tells her, he was struck by an idea. He wants to revive burlesque, transform the tired old bump and grind into a flashy, expensive Broadway musical—a brilliant marriage of Minsky and Ziegfeld on a grand and opulent scale; Americans crave nothing in times of hardship so much as the distractions of beauty and noise. He'll call the production *Star and Garter* and stage it at the Music Box Theatre. Mayor La Guardia won't dare interfere with one of Broadway's most prestigious venues.

Gypsy is intrigued. She'll be the lead in her own Broadway show as

Souvenir program from *Star and Garter*, 1942.

well as a producer, roles she never played before. Even better, she'll get to work with Mike again.

They stay up nights perfecting skits and sharpening jokes, but as the June 24 premiere date approaches, he is still $25,000 short. He knocks on Gypsy's dressing room door to tell her *Star and Garter* is finished before it even starts.

"You have to open," she protests. "I bought two gallons of body paint. Two gallons, Mike. That's enough for years!"

"One of my backers, Herb Freezer, wants his G's back. And I'm tapped out."

"I'll buy Freezer's interest," she says, casually.

"I said G's, not G-strings."

"I heard you."

"Twenty-five big ones, Gypsy. You can't dig up that kind of scratch in twenty-four hours."

She bends her lips into a smile. "One hour."

It is that easy and it isn't. Gypsy has the money, but it's stashed in banks throughout Manhattan. Right on schedule she meets Mike and his lawyer, Bill Fitelson, with $25,000 in hand.

"How much percentage do I get?" she asks.

Mike's lawyer seems incapable of speaking in words, just fractions and numbers. Gypsy might have forced her way through Proust's oeuvre, but she still uses her fingers to count. She sighs, exasperated.

"Can't you just give me a pie?" she says.

"A pie?" Fitelson asks, confused.

But Mike understands right away. "For chrissakes!" he yells. "The dame wants a pie, give her a goddamn pie." He draws the pie himself, slicing up each investors' share, shading in her cut until she is satisfied.

Star and Garter premieres to mixed reviews, but the show is sold out far in advance. "It was wartime," Gypsy said, "and it was the first girlie show that had been done on Broadway in a long time—beautiful girls, scanty costumes, low comics. . . . It was beautiful, lush, extravagant, and wonderful. I remember one matinee, one of the ladies was leaving— my dressing room faced the street—and there were some friends waiting for her when she came out. She said, 'Mabel, I have just seen without a doubt the dirtiest, filthiest show I've ever seen in all my life. Don't miss it.' "

She has yet to regret her investment in Mike, personally or professionally. The time has come, she decides, to go all in, to push her last coin across the counter.

I've never been close enough to anyone to share an honest feeling, she tells him, let alone an intense one, and now I'm sharing both with you. Get a divorce, and marry me.

Once it leaves her hands there is no taking it back, even when he says he could never divorce Bertha—not because he loves her, of course, but because he loves his son. She asks again in different ways with different words but receives the same answer. No one misses their raucous fights behind the curtain of the Music Box Theatre after each closing. Pleas morph into demands, anger into desperation. After two months, in August, she decides to withdraw her offer and bluff. Fine, Gypsy tells Mike. If he won't marry her, she'll find someone who will.

She doesn't have to find William Alexander Kirkland, a perfectly nice, blandly handsome, closeted bisexual actor, known as Alexander in business and Bill in private. He is already there, calling her his "princess," courting her in his patient, sensible way. At a party for her *Star and Garter* costar Bobby Clark, she decides to hurry things along. Climbing atop a crate, she calls for everyone's attention and makes her announcement: she and Bill Kirkland are getting married.

Gypsy looks directly at Mike as she speaks. Around her the room fills with movement and noise, whistles and applause and men rushing to shake Bill's hand. Mike remains the only still thing, pinning her with unblinking eyes, until he rises without a word and leaves her alone with the crowd.

Chapter Fourteen

We'll get drunker and drunker, and drift about nightclubs so drunk we won't know where we are. We'll go
to bed late tomorrow morning and wake up and begin
it all over again.

—HARLEM RENAISSANCE WRITER
CARL VAN VECHTEN

New York City, 1920–1924

As midnight approached on January 16, 1920, Billy Minsky prepared to meet the new needs of his patrons and his city, stocking his office at the National Winter Garden with ice buckets, crystal tumblers, bottles of the finest whiskey, scotch, bourbon, and cognac, fruit juices to make Orange Blossoms and Old-Fashioneds and Sidecars, sugar cubes and maraschino cherries and lemon peels for garnish. Outside his windows New York was in the throes of a citywide wake, up and down every avenue, across every street. Black-bordered invitations had been dispensed weeks before, announcing "Last rites and ceremonies attending the departure of our spirited friend, John Barleycorn." The death was premeditated and met with sadness and gaiety, mockery and contempt, and few predicted the resurrection soon to come.

The ice-slicked streets did little to deter the "mourning parties,"

A grand finale at the National Winter Garden, "slumming" destination for up-towners.

which began at dinnertime and multiplied as the hours advanced. Guests paid their respects at the Waldorf-Astoria, hip flasks peeking from waistbands, champagne glasses kissing in farewell toasts. Park Avenue women in sleek ermine coats and cloche hats gripped bottles of wine with one hand and wiped real tears with the other. Uptown at Healy's, patrons tossed empty glasses into a silk-lined casket, and eight waiters at Maxim's, clad entirely in black, carried a coffin to the center of the dance floor. Reporters on deadline tapped out eulogies for John Barleycorn and imagined his final words. "I've had more friends in private and more foes in public," quoted the *Daily News*, "than any other man in America."

Past and future purveyors of vice marked the night with anticipation, a sense of déjà vu, or no feeling at all. The "Lester sisters"—two former madams exiled from Chicago—spent a quiet evening in their Upper West Side brownstone, sipping champagne and marveling at the lunacy of the reformers. A Brooklyn boy named Alphonse Capone, considered a minor player in the old Five Points Gang (or what remained of it), had been discharged from the army the previous year. The dawn of Prohibition fell, coincidentally, on his twenty-first birthday, but all of its possibilities had not yet occurred to him. One of his Five Points cohorts, twenty-three-year-old Charles Luciano—soon to earn the nickname "Lucky"—had served time as a teenager for trafficking cocaine and heroin and knew precisely how to take advantage of the new law. "I never was a crumb," he said, meaning a common workingman, "and if I have to be a crumb I'd rather be dead."

Arnold Rothstein, pawnbroker to the underworld and future inspiration for *The Great Gatsby*'s Meyer Wolfsheim, was deep into a card game on the night Prohibition struck. He was no stranger to grand schemes, having fixed the World Series of 1919, and would soon join bootlegging forces with a Lower East Side gangster named Irving Wexler. Better known as Waxey Gordon, Wexler stood poised to become one of the country's premier rum runners. On at least one occasion he would use his resulting fortune for an ostensibly benevolent purpose: ordering a New York City dentist to fix Gypsy Rose Lee's teeth.

All across the city, speakeasies sprouted in unexpected places: tucked behind receptionists' desks in office buildings; amid the rubble and machinery of construction sites; in the cellars of fashionable hat shops and the back rooms of pricey town houses; across from police stations; and even at the top of the Chrysler Building. Revelers bet one another who could find the oddest location for their next libation. In one apocryphal story, a young man spent hours drinking at a speakeasy that felt "vaguely familiar." Slowly, it came to him that he was standing in his childhood home, in the very room that had once been his nursery. Two federal agents named Izzy Einstein and Moe Smith, donning disguises that ranged from fishermen to firefighters, football coaches to bums, sophisticated operagoers to matronly Italian women, made bartenders faint when their true identities were revealed.

The Minskys welcomed every new speakeasy that graced their neighborhood. Dozens lined East First, East Fourth, Rivington, Chrystie, and Stanton Streets, the Bowery, and Second Avenue. The best in the neighborhood, and perhaps all of New York, was Manny Wolf's at Forsyth and Grand, just a few hundred yards away from the National Winter Garden's door. Moneyed uptowners arrived in their Cadillac limousines, afflicted with, as one reformer noted, "an itch to try new things." Drinking now required cunning, an urbane wit, the code to a secret and thrilling language. "Give me a ginger ale," they said, and waited for the bartender's wink and knowing reply: "Imported or domestic?" The correct answer, imported, earned the customer a regulation pre-Prohibition highball.

Occasionally, Billy noticed, these uptown visitors wandered over to the National Winter Garden, sufficiently sober to make it up to the sixth floor but tipsy enough to enjoy the show. They sat among the factory workers and longshoremen and blacksmiths, all of them grimacing at the comics (WAITER: Would the lady like some tongue? WOMAN: Sir, I'll have you understand that I never eat anything that comes out of an animal's mouth. WAITER: Then how about a couple of eggs?) and ogling the girls. It was fine by Billy if those uptowners thought they were "slumming" at his theater, if they made jokes about needing a passport to venture so far south on the island. Instead of being insulted he invited such guests to his office for a postshow nightcap and frank, enlightening conversation about what they most wanted to see onstage. A hefty wallet and a string of numerals after his name didn't prevent a man from enjoying the more vulgar sketches. Often such patrons laughed hardest when a comic shook a bottle of seltzer and squirted the contents into a girl's waiting buttocks, or when she perched herself on a toilet seat and burbled lines about going to Flushing and buying stock in Consolidated Gas.

"Burlesque, like Broadway, is changing in its ever-vacillating clientele," *Billboard* observed. "This is especially applicable to Minsky's National Winter Garden, for no more do we see the ever-yawning smokers of hop and dreadful degenerates, [but] out-of-town slumming parties and would-be sporty boys and girls who demand an indecent thrill."

At the same time, Billy wanted the interlopers to know that the National Winter Garden was superior to the rest of the neighborhood's stock burlesque houses, that the brothers were familiar enough with the so-called legitimate producers to parody them properly. To that end, he took out pointed half-page ads in the *New York Clipper:*

WANTED

for

MUSICAL STOCK BURLESQUE

PRINCIPALS OF CLASS AND QUALITY

Comedians, Straight Man, Characters Man, Dancing Juvenile,

Prima Donna, Soubrettes, Ingénue, Leading Woman

ONLY THE VERY BEST WILL BE CONSIDERED

SALARY NO OBJECT. WRITE YOUR OWN TICKET

IF YOU CAN DELIVER.

THERE IS NOTHING TOO GOOD FOR

THE MINSKY BROTHERS

Billy also sought the services of Anne Toebe, widely acknowledged as the burlesque industry's first stripper, and Carrie Finnell, the first teaser (despite Mae Dix's fortuitous wardrobe mishap back in 1917 as she exited the Minsky runway). The monikers were self-defining. A teaser sashayed, strutted, winked. She exited the stage each time she showed skin, even if just a square of collarbone or the dip of her waist, and returned until adorned only in her girdle and brassiere and G-string, offering, if the men begged sufficiently, a flash of breast at the end.

A stripper was more focused in her approach, unhooking clasps and hooks with connect-the-dots predictability until clad in her "union suit," a one-piece garment designed to look like bare flesh. The chubby, redheaded Toebe engaged in "rough" flirtation with the audience, imprinting scarlet kisses on the pates of bald jewelry salesmen. One of her most popular songs went, in part:

> *My face ain't much to look at*
> *I gotta shape like a frog*
> *But I can make the boys in the gallery*
> *Sit up and yell "Hot Dog!"*

Carrie Finnell, years after her heyday at the National Winter Garden.

Finnell, by contrast, performed in baby blue silk and rabbit fur boots, and was known as "the girl with the $100,000 legs" after her manager, in a well-publicized move, had them insured. The teaser, Billy figured, would do much to dispel the unfortunate nickname the Minsky runway had earned since its inception: "Varicose Alley."

Last but far from least, Billy brought back Mae Dix, who was by now one of the biggest draws in burlesque, demanding $175 per week and top billing. Wearing nothing over her union suit but a handkerchief, the point falling strategically between her legs, Dix announced the following week's attractions and invited the audience to share suggestions. "I'll do anything at all for you," she said, adding with a wink, "within reason." She had a supporting cast of chorus girls who specialized in cooch dancing, a tradition derived from Little Egypt's slinky undulations during the 1893 Chicago World's Fair, and one that had come to burlesque to stay.

Sex, Billy predicted, would soon be the predominant component of burlesque, edging out the corny comics and suggestive repartee and animal-bladder bashings, and he would do everything in his power to hasten that change along.

——————

$\mathcal{B}$illy celebrated success with his customary zealous focus. He zipped a brand-new Stutz Bearcat sports car through the Lower East Side's narrow streets and bought a vacation house in Seagate, a private, exclusive community on Coney Island. He sent his wife, Mary, and their young son to live there permanently; she wouldn't like the theater, he insisted. Too vulgar for her refined tastes, and she should take her exclusion as a compliment. In truth, he and Abe—by now remarried—spent most of their downtime competing for the affections of various Minsky "Rosebuds."

The brothers also continued to spy on the big uptown productions. One night, Billy ventured to a Shubert theater on Broadway and settled, as inconspicuously as possible, into a back row. Critics had raved about *Cinderella on Broadway,* calling it "a lavish and bounteous extravaganza." At the close of the first act, a great silver slipper transformed into a staircase, down which paraded an impressive cast of beauties.

Billy was watching closely, noting which set designs and physiques would work downtown, when he felt a finger drill into the back of his neck. He turned and found himself staring at the bedraggled brows of Lee Shubert, obsidian eyes glaring beneath them.

"Look out, Minsky," he said. "Don't let me catch you using any of this stuff in your show at the National Winter Garden."

Billy smiled. "Too late," he said.

It was time, the brothers decided, to bring the Minsky name to Broadway. The press greeted the news with enthusiasm and praise. "They are far seeing youths," the *Times* wrote of the Minskys, "and have old heads on young shoulders." The new venture would be housed in the Park Theatre at Columbus Circle. Billy envisioned an entirely new type of show, a superior sort of burlesque—"Burlesques," he called it, emphasis on the final *s*, a brand that would become as recognizable as the *Follies*. Calling it the Park Music Hall instead of the Park Theatre would evoke a more elegant age, the height of Old New York. The company consisted of an English pony ballet (in which sixteen girls danced on the backs of live ponies), fifteen leading actors (called "principals"), and forty chorus girls, who must weigh less than 170 pounds—the first time Billy imposed such a restriction, never having forgotten the mean-spirited review that described the Rosebuds as "hulking." No unsightly veins, either; Broadway wouldn't tolerate a Varicose Alley.

A jazz orchestra of twenty began rigorous rehearsals, and a Hawaiian octet set up in the foyer to play during intermissions. The Minskys would keep the same company but change the show every week. Two dollars and twenty cents per ticket was several times the cost of their shows downtown, but a bargain compared to the overpriced and overrated *Follies* at $6.60. Forget the New Amsterdam or the Winter Garden, the Park Music Hall would be the new Victoria, Oscar Hammerstein's opulent, grand old theater that set a standard back in 1899. "The Victoria," the *New York American* wrote that year, "at a bird's eye view, looks like a big twinkling pearl, all white and gold with the opals of electricity studding it in profusion. . . . Gorgeous carpets, splendid lounges and all the ultra-elegance the metropolis loves were to be seen everywhere." Better to forget the Victoria's ultimate disgrace at the hands of Hammerstein's son Willie, who took over operations in 1904 and turned it into a freakshow venue, booking acts like "Sober Sue—You Can't Make Her Laugh." Willie posted a $1,000 reward and several of the best comics of the day tried their best, but all failed. When the engagement ended, it was discovered that it was physically impossible for Sober Sue to laugh since her facial muscles were paralyzed.

The Park Music Hall would require much time and effort, but the Minskys couldn't neglect their flagship burlesque theater. Billy suggested that Herbert stay downtown and make sure the National Winter Garden kept attracting ethnics and uptowners alike. To keep an eye on audience rowdies and drunks, Abe hired Albert and Walter, two retired Pinkerton detectives with barrel-sized arms and convincing costumes—gold-plated badges and stiff-brimmed police caps filched from the Minskys' props department. Patrolling the rooftop, they smacked billy clubs against beefy palms and tossed out "sleepers," bums inclined to loiter until the next day's matinee. They also kept an eye on the oddball who engaged in loud, intense conversations with his penis during the show.

Billy devoted his energy to the Park Music Hall and offered the youngest Minsky brother a proposition: how would Morton like to work the Park's outdoor box office, where patrons could buy premium seats closest to the girls? It was time for Morton to stop hanging around aimlessly and bothering the soubrettes (his crush on Ethel De Veaux, for instance, was cute but wearisome; he was always offering to escort her to the subway and staring, entranced, as she cracked her wad of Juicy Fruit gum). With some tutoring and hard work, Morton could be an asset to the growing Minsky franchise. Morton immediately dropped out of New York University, and begged Billy to teach him everything he knew.

No one, unfortunately, mistook the new Minsky theater for the old Hammerstein Victoria. "The long-awaited uncorking of the Park Music Hall," wrote the New York Clipper, "was attended by a loud pop! it is true, but the ensuing flow of its contents proved it to have no new flavor."

The list of complaints was long as a chorus line. The main dancer seemed "unacquainted with the art of makeup." A leading lady wore a hideous outfit while singing "Pretty Clothes," and the number wasn't meant to be ironic. Vaudevillian Bob Nelson's dancing was more St. Vitus than tap. The almost-nude dancing by a single girl seemed exploitative and gratuitous, as though the producers "felt the need to give the boys in the balconies a little spice for their money." For once, even Billy didn't know what to give them or how to put it on.

"People," Morton said, "were staying away in droves."

The Park Music Hall closed after just twenty-three weeks. Billy returned to the National Winter Garden hazy and unfocused, wondering how his pitch-perfect instinct had failed so miserably. Maybe the very idea was flawed: why would uptowners want a downtown version of glamour when they already had the original, legitimate thing? Maybe the Park Music Hall had offered slumming prices with none of the fun and ambiance of actual slumming. Maybe they would forever be stuck providing toilet humor and fat girls and inflated animal bladders over the head. Maybe some things in New York City were too good for the Minsky brothers, after all.

Chapter Fifteen

By the time you swear you're his,

Shivering and sighing,

And he vows his passion is

Infinite, undying—

Lady, make a note of this:

One of you is lying.

—DOROTHY PARKER

Gypsy's Country Home, Highland Mills, New York, August 1942

Gypsy Rose Lee wears black for this wedding, her second, knowing she'll be in mourning if the ending isn't a happy one. The ending she hopes for has nothing to do with the gathering downstairs, absurd as a burlesque skit: the famous stripteaser Georgia Sothern as maid of honor; Carl Van Doren as best man; Lee Wright, her editor at Simon & Schuster (and rumored lover), as a bridesmaid; *Life* magazine as the official photographer; the impressive assemblage of guests, including Carson McCullers (who still recalls, longingly, their time together on Middagh Street), Peggy Guggenheim, Janet Flanner, Christopher Isherwood, Clare Boothe Luce, George Jean Nathan, and Max Ernst; one of her trained Chihuahuas as the entertainment; a chimpanzee as ring bearer; and the minister, who is dozing on the couch. It has nothing,

Gypsy Rose Lee, preparing for her wedding to Bill Kirkland.

even, to do with the groom, Bill Kirkland, who truly seems to believe he loves her.

It has everything to do with the ultimatum she gave another man, Michael Todd, and the clock's willful march toward her midnight deadline. It has to do with the view outside her bedroom window—no sign of headlights boring through the darkness, no wisp of smoke from his omnipresent cigar, no demand from that booming voice to stop this charade, for God's sake, he has come to call her bluff.

And how ironic that this wedding has forced a tepid reconciliation with her mother when her first resulted, eventually, in their bitterest estrangement. Rose is downstairs now, in the country estate that she used to call home, laughing with the very people she once derided as "night club bad company, reefers, fags" who brought "unpleasant" things into their lives. It is Gypsy's turn to deal with Rose, Big Lady, and Aunt Belle; June has made that clear. "Dear Bride Gypsy Rose Lee," her sister writes,

> I shall now explain to you why you will have to wear the whole
> crowd of vultures—I have worked three weeks out of seven
> months. . . . I sent Rosebud fifty bucks a week until I simply
> couldn't . . . you are the moneyballs in the family. . . . Please write
> me and tell that man you're living with that I personally don't think
> he has a chance—all the smart money is on a Hovick.

In some ways it's a shame Gypsy has her genes and temperament and timing, that Bill, through no fault of his own, fails to be her match. The press calls him Hollywood's most desirable bachelor, describes him as "young, good-looking, successful, and well-endowed." He seems earnest, smart, considerate, classy. "I don't think a woman should hold her love back," he says, "and use it as a means with which to bargain for what she wants of life. I think that is cheapening love. Marriage ought to be on a finer, higher plane than that of barter and trade."

A secret, tucked-away part of her heart recognizes how ugly this is, letting a man believe he's a groom at his own wedding when he is merely leverage, a chip to be turned in if only she wins this hand. From the moment he met Gypsy he adored her, for the same reasons she is adored by both New York's literati and its longshoremen. She is a strutting, bawdy, erudite conundrum, belonging to everyone but known by none. She has to admit that Bill, for all that he isn't and for all he'd never be to her, understands her better than most.

A year from this night, after they decide never to consummate their marriage but before it is officially over, he writes a letter that she presses into her scrapbook:

Dearest Gypola,

I've been thinking a lot about us. I am proud that we are not very different, you and I—at least fundamentally. You are a lot more scared of failure than I am—a little more anxious for success— I think it all comes from that childhood which would have been so devastating to any person not made of platinum and moral courage like you. Even with all your character it has made you a bit of a lone wolf and strangely enough my weird upbringing has made me one too. So you see I know that even when we are baying most ferociously and looking our fiercest, we are just a couple of lonely and rather frightened "near-dogs." I know at the present clip we'll achieve a really sinister old age—solitary. I also know that we can change all that—but I honestly don't know that we are going to. There are a lot of things that may keep us from finding the answer together. . . .

Deep down you have the husband-pattern of the women of your family—the marriage pattern. I dislike it intensely. It savors of the Life of the Bee, and I will never willingly be a drone. . . . I sometimes wonder whether [here Bill crossed out "I" and replaced it with "we"] have the force to break through this life-dream to a really workable marriage for us. . . . I wish it could be because I love you with a strange deepness—considering that we are both such strong minded jerks. Darling, it would be the easiest thing in the world to stop thinking and tumble through emotions with you, but I am afraid of that little bit of bad in you that would transform me into grandpa (Big Lady's) and then send you away from me to sell corsets in the Yukon. You wouldn't love me that way, and that you love me is of the greatest importance to me . . . well, black angel, that's enough.

Her mother's laughter, quick and light as beating wings, climbs the stairs and invades her room. Rose fools even Bill, who says she can "charm the birds out of the trees," who finds it endlessly amusing when she dances with one of the apes from *Star and Garter*. She cheers Bill on when he feeds the animal an entire bottle of beer, and cheers the animal on when it then relieves itself down the front of Bill's lapel. She is in her element, the matriarch of this grand and sardonic charade, and the thought of watching Mother lord over the proceedings gives Gypsy another reason to stall.

With a crimson fingernail, the black angel bride adjusts the twig of grapes entwined in her hair. For once the grapes' promise of good fortune has failed her. It is half past midnight and she will not tell a direct lie this time, not even to herself. Mike isn't coming. He might never come again. Time to turn her back to the window, to the driveway that remains silent and unlit. Never in her life has she moved so slowly as she does descending those steps.

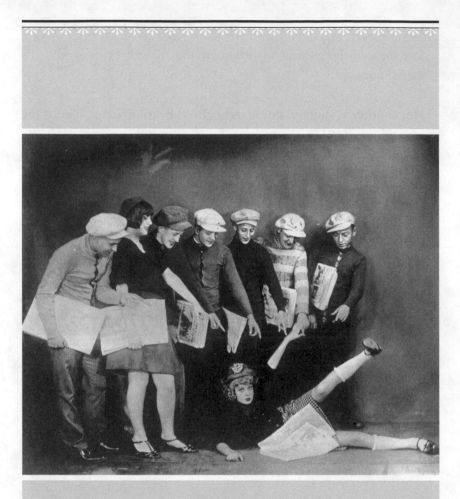

Dainty June and Her Newsboy Songsters (including Louise), near the end of the act.

Chapter Sixteen

Their sincerity was greater than their artistry—their

eagerness to please was beyond their capacity to

please—but they gave their hearts and their lives and it

was not their fault that that was not enough.

—ALFRED LUNT, VAUDEVILLE STAR

On the Vaudeville Circuit, 1925–1928

Louise had watched her sister work through measles and chicken pox and ruined feet, so she was as surprised as anyone when, one morning in Chicago, June literally could not lift her head. Her blue eyes appeared dull and unseeing, her cheeks were leached of color, her limbs as thin as the blinds darkening her room. "I wanted to die," June said, "just for the vacation." Nothing Rose tried worked: threats, scolding, praise, promises of extra yaka mein at dinner. Sensibly, she refrained from mentioning what might have caused, or at least contributed to, June's condition—a recent conversation with a theater manager in New York, who said that June had true talent. With singing, dancing, and acting lessons, she could be a triple threat, a bona fide star, and he was so sure of her potential he'd foot the bill himself, so long as Rose promised not to interfere. "Mind your own business," Rose told him. "There's no man in the world going to take my baby from me. . . . What school on earth can teach her anything she doesn't already know?"

Louise stood at June's bedside until the hotel doctor arrived and declared that the twelve-year-old had suffered a breakdown. For two straight weeks she must lie in bed in perfect quiet with no outside visitors—not Louise, not the boys, not Uncle Gordon, not even Mother. Rose nodded at the doctor's instructions, clasping his hand and thanking him for taking such good care of her baby, and when he left she sat by June's head and stroked her daughter's hair.

Now there, Rose said. The Baby had never let anything stop her before, and she wouldn't now, would she? Not when she knew how Mother and Louise and the boys and Big Lady and Aunt Belle and Grandpa depended on her?

June stared at her, quiet and rigidly still. She willed her mouth to pry itself open, then had no energy left to give it words.

"Go and do it," Rose said, "and we'll talk about it later."

It occurred to Louise that her sister was losing herself, in quick but agonizing stages. First the death of Samba, her cherished guinea pig. Then closing her contract on the Orpheum Circuit, with no guarantee she'd ever make it back, and losing the only chance she might ever have to study acting. And now this, her body turning on her just when she—and Mother—needed it most.

Louise grew more conscious of her own problems, as well. She was fourteen now and 165 pounds, not yet tall enough for the weight to settle evenly around her frame. No bust or waist to speak of, just thighs and a bottom that appeared larger every time she looked. She studied her legs, pinched at the loose skin. Fanny Brice had told her it was nothing personal, but she was taking Louise's scene out of the show and wouldn't need her again. "Don't feel bad about it," Fanny said. "It was too much to ask of a kid your age, with no experience." Louise thanked her for the opportunity, returned that gorgeous orange Creamsicle of a dress, and pulled on her old long underwear with the baggy knees.

Louise, around age fourteen.

Now, with this body, she feared she would never again have the stage all to herself.

She blamed this development entirely on their vaudeville act; her body changed because nothing else had. June was no longer a baby or even dainty, and Louise was no longer a demure Doll Girl or a tomboy Bowery Tough. Turnover was so fast that they now rehearsed in the wings, and the Newsboy Songsters who remained barely fit into their costumes. Yet, night after night, they performed the same old routines. They dressed up like rough Tenderloin kids and "shook the bones," cavorted with Susie the Dancing Cow, and encircled June during the big finale, all of them pointing down at her as if depending on their star to do something.

Louise knew her sister sensed the expectation. June drew all of her strength and "nutrition," as she called it, from the boys in the act and her audience, and she was too much of a pro to let either of them down.

True, the crowds had thinned a bit. Lately the applause merely crackled instead of thundered, and even the most prestigious theaters had clusters of empty seats. Panic seized managers and booking agents across the country. No fewer than 540 broadcasting stations now provided Americans with entertainment inside their homes, playing the scores of the same shows currently in production throughout the country. "There is no more important question before the theatre than the radio," declared the president of the American Society of Composers, Authors, and Publishers during an emergency meeting in New York. "I want to warn all present against the peril of ridiculing or underestimating its effect on the theatre." Vaudeville impresario E. F. Albee went so far as to forbid his acts from appearing on radio, or from even mentioning radio onstage unless the remarks were scathing.

Advances in the film industry were no less troubling. The ten-minute short "flickers" that had once rounded out a vaudeville bill were now the main attraction, and, one by one, old-time vaudeville houses succumbed to the enemy. In 1921, a quarter of the theaters that had played both films and vaudeville dropped the vaudeville shows, and by 1925 only a hundred "straight," no-flicker theaters remained. Dozens of talented vaudevillians followed Charlie Chaplin's lead and made forays into film: W. C. Fields, Buster Keaton, Will Rogers, Harry Houdini, Rudolph Valentino.

The "film peril," as theater managers called it, delivered another blow to vaudeville with Warner Bros.' introduction of Vitaphone, a device that synced sound recording with films. The following year, in 1927, the studio released *The Jazz Singer*, the first feature-length "talkie," starring erstwhile vaudevillian Al Jolson. Though only five hundred theaters nationwide were wired for sound, it was the best-selling film of the year, and other major singers and comedians signed on for talkies.

Members of the American Federation of Musicians amassed a $1.5 million "defense fund" to prevent the installation of Vitaphone in more than a thousand additional theaters. Their concern, shared by other artists' agencies, was as cultural as it was mercenary. If this modern technology were implemented nationwide, wouldn't the American theater and musical traditions stagnate and die? A change in public taste was one thing, they argued; purposeful, absolute lack of choice was quite another.

Still, for now, the century-old art form of vaudeville—"that big boisterous American wench," as one critic put it—limped along. People continued to pay 50 cents to see vaudeville acts of every provenance and scope, including Jean Boydell, the "Unique Pepologist," Nancy Decker, "The Joy Girl of Syncopation," and, of course, Dainty June and Her Newsboy Songsters, a "festival of splendor, fun, music, and dance." June was a trouper in every sense of the word, and Louise sensed that she would make a move at the last possible moment, only when she had to—when her performance ceased to please herself or, consequently, her audience, and when Mother was looking the other way.

Rose, too, noticed a change in June after her breakdown. She was at a loss to explain this newly defiant, sulking child who no longer appreciated her gift or the mother who so tirelessly developed it. Louise was old enough to distinguish fear from anger, and terror was Rose's latest and most severe affliction. It weighted her gait like the grouch bag once did, marched with glum purpose behind her eyes. Mother behaved the only way she knew how when she felt threatened: she stomped and yelled and made a horrific scene. One snide word or seething silence and she would raise her hand to June, striking that face, that cherubic, aging face that could no longer rely on its own practiced expressions. Whether she meant to or not, Louise watched her mother carefully, and learned.

"Malcontent!" Rose yelled at June one night. "After all I've gone through for you!" She began to cry, her slight shoulders shaking. "Ungrateful, selfish—oh, God. You were put on earth to make my life a misery."

Louise rushed to Rose, took her in her arms. She held a handkerchief to her mother's nose. They switched roles often now, a seamless transition both ways.

"June, it's bad enough everything's so rotten," Mother continued, weeping. "Why must you be a . . . a . . . Bolshevik!" She broke free from Louise's grip and moved forward, cornering her younger daughter. "Undermining the army, challenging the rules!"

June thrust back her shoulders, lifted her chin. Louise saw the words rise inside her sister. A vicious, furtive part of her—the part that once made her bite June's favorite stagehand, the part that yearned to be closest to Mother—hoped to God June said them.

She did.

"Yes!" June screamed. "Yes I am!"

That was it. Mother was turned wholly inside out; no sweet traces or soft instincts remained. She raised her fist like a scepter and lowered it like a gavel, connecting with June's mouth. Louise watched her sister spin—graceful even under the circumstances—careening and landing facedown on the carpet. She spat into cupped hands, and her fingers were slick with blood. Crimson bubbles swelled and popped at her lips.

It was the worst blow yet.

Louise braced herself as Mother took another step, but she kept her hand by her side. "Look at yourself," Rose said, dicing her words. "You're going to look just fine on that stage, just fine. See what you made me do!"

A streak of blood carved a marionette line down June's chin. She grabbed the blanket from her cot and crept to the bathroom.

"You'll see," Rose yelled at the back of her head. "God will punish you. He's started already. You're a failure—a failure. After I've spent my whole life on you, too. I can't book you anywhere anymore."

Louise curdled with guilt, as if her own mouth had said those hateful words, as if her own hand had split June's lip. She stroked her mother's hair and waited until she fell asleep before following her sister. June lay curled up in the tub, her head resting on the drain. When June looked up, Louise pressed a finger against her lips and locked the door behind her.

"Shhh," she said. "Mother's asleep. She is exhausted, June. These fights are getting worse and she can't stand it."

She was referring, also, to Mother and Gordon. Louise still didn't trust him, but she marveled at his patience and restraint. When Mother stole from other acts and from hotels, Gordon said nothing. When Mother piled their laundry for him to wash, he hunched over the bathtub and scrubbed each garment without complaint. Their fights were frequent but one-sided. "The kids aren't babies any longer," he said recently. "June can't get by with what she used to get by with—"

Mother lunged at him and rapped at his chest with her fists.

"Shut up!" she said. "She'll always be a baby. She'll never grow up. Never, do you hear me?" He stood there and took it, using his forearms as a shield while her nails tore at his skin. Sometimes he disappeared after these episodes, just long enough for Mother and June to miss him. Louise wondered what they would do if one day he didn't come back.

"What fights?" June said, bringing her back to the moment. "She just slugs me. It's always one slug and out. That's no fight."

Louise considered her next words, weighing what they might give and what they might take, and the fact that she couldn't empathize with June without betraying Mother.

"I know how you feel," she said, finally. "About the act, I mean."

"You do?" June said. Her mouth widened, cracking the line of drying blood. "But you don't have to do the act—you never have."

Louise sighed. As if she needed to be reminded she wasn't necessary.

"That's right," she said. "All that sweating, practicing every minute. I've watched you enjoying your broken toes and scratches. Dancing so hard you black out in the wings. No, you do the act because you enjoy all that. I never have and what happens? You don't enjoy the act any more than I do now. Do you? So, we sit here in the same bathroom with the same problem."

The sisters regarded each other for a long, silent moment. This was the first confidence they had ever shared.

————

*L*ouise consulted her tea leaves. Peering into the cup, letting all other objects around her recede, a vision appeared that she couldn't unsee. A steel beam, like a willful, deliberate streak of lightning, shot from the back of a truck and aimed straight at someone she knew, a former Newsboy Songster traveling in the next car. It pierced him, sheering his tendons and veins, severing his head from his neck. Three days later, through the vaudeville circuit grapevine, she learned the boy had been in a fatal accident, so similar to her premonition it was as if she'd cho-reographed the death herself.

She never read tea leaves again.

Instead, Rose adopted the superstition. Her tea leaves signaled omi-nous days for the stops in Wichita and Kansas City, but the grouch bag was light and they needed to work. Their bookings were miserable—one theater manager threatened to cancel the act on the ground that they no longer resembled their press photos—but there was, as Louise later put it, "one bright spot"; the blankets on the hotel beds were the nicest she'd ever seen, soft, pure white wool. Rose decided that Louise should make coats out of them. Their trunk was too full, so Rose wrapped them around her body and wore her beaver coat on top. No one in the hotel lobby suspected a thing when they left.

In Omaha, their next stop, Louise made coats for everyone, including her monkey, Gigolo. His had a shawl collar, dolman sleeves, and a tam-o'-shanter to match. On closing night, she put Gigolo to bed in his new outfit. She found him in the morning, lifeless and limp, a mess of gor-geous wool coiled tight around his neck. He died because of her, she re-alized, and began to cry quietly, so no one could hear. Louise promised God she would never again take anything that didn't belong to her, even if she felt she deserved it.

Mother soothed Louise, promising to get her a new monkey, but her fights with Gordon escalated. They had been laid off for four weeks and had trouble getting booked anywhere, despite Gordon's connections in Detroit.

"Everything going out, nothing coming in," he said. "We're damned near broke."

"And whose fault is that?" Mother retorted. "The act is as good as it ever was. It's your fault we're not back on the Orpheum Circuit, where we belong. A fine man you are, blaming your failure on a baby—a child."

June found solace with the boys in the act, shooting craps and play-ing tag, and Louise buried herself in her books. No one knew about her secret hiding place next to the Dixieland Hotel. She spent hours prowl-ing the aisles of the Seven Arts Book Store, where batik scarves looped brightly across the walls and exotic-looking young men talked in low, sure voices about F. Scott Fitzgerald and James Joyce and Carl Van

Vechten. She eavesdropped, memorizing fragments of their conversations: "His very lack of pretension is pretentious . . . having asthma doesn't make a hack writer another Proust." The manager was young, too, and he didn't seem to mind that Louise had browsed for a week without buying anything. She learned that his name was George Davis.

"Have you read Shakespeare's sonnets?" he asked her one day, handing her a cloth-covered book.

"I don't care much about reading plays," she said, making her voice low and deliberate, unfurling each word. "Being in the theater myself I—"

"These are poems," George said evenly.

Louise didn't like poems but she liked George Davis. He had kind eyes and an encouraging smile, and he spoke to her as if they were equals. She bought the book with her lunch money and ran back to the Dixieland Hotel, heading straight for the alcove of desks behind the elevators. She yearned to speak in an important voice about characters and themes, to laugh at jokes understood only by the exceptional few, to become someone who inspired second glances and curious whispers. She wanted to write—but what? About herself, maybe—not who she was now but who she'd become: the rich husband, the money money money, the life she would seize for herself when the moment was right and ripe.

On a piece of hotel stationery, she wrote:

PAGE ONE

Scene One

I enter.

———

That night, hours into the hollering, Gordon pulled on his overcoat. "You've told me to get out for the last time, Rose," he said. Louise had never heard his voice so angry or certain. "I'm leaving, and so help me God, I'm not coming back." He left behind only a photograph of Rose in a leather frame, set on the bureau. Mother secluded herself in her room with her curtains drawn, weeping and wheezing, and the air grew thick with the scent of her asthma powder. Three of the boys slept on the floor so Louise and June could share their bed; no one wanted to disturb Rose. They brought her food that went uneaten. Ten days later, her eyes still swollen and her hair unwashed, she summoned all of them and announced they were going to New York. She put a down payment on a secondhand Studebaker after realizing that train travel consumed much of their profit, and ticket fares, unlike cars, had to be paid for in cash, all at once. "I'm going to start all over again," Louise heard Rose whisper to herself. "Alone with my two babies against the world."

They settled, along with their menagerie, costumes, and props, in the Langwell Hotel on 44th Street and Sixth Avenue. Rose sent the native New Yorkers in the act to stay with their parents so she could save space and money on the hotel room. The two remaining boys slept on a daybed in the sitting room, and Rose, Louise, and June shared the bedroom. It wasn't clear how much longer the current crop of boys would last, anyway. Meals could no longer be counted on. June was so thin she was nearly translucent, and Louise was hopeful that she might finally lose some weight. Mother gave them pep talks. "We'll just have to tighten our belts, girls," she said. "It's only temporary, until we get going." Neither Louise nor June asked what happened to all of the money that once weighted Mother's grouch bag, and they never learned the truth. They had repaid Grandpa Thompson's numerous loans, bought him a Model T Ford sedan, fixed the roof of the Seattle home, supplemented Big Lady's and Belle's meager savings, bought the dogs an entire wardrobe of wool sweaters and red leather shoes with lace-up legs, and spent untold thousands on costumes and transporting their elaborate collection of props. But still, they should have had plenty left over. "That's interesting," June said eighty years later. "I don't know. We had lean times—very lean times."

By eleven in the morning, Rose had the girls up and dressed and ready to make the rounds. Louise noticed a marked difference in the way the booking agents treated Mother, and she felt humiliated for all three of them. Gordon had sat on the edges of their desks, slapped backs, and handed out cigars. If they made a lowball offer, he laughed and walked out the door. With Mother, they continued to bark on the phone while sifting through scrapbooks and piles of faded clippings, and barely glanced at the old, lucrative Orpheum contracts she "accidentally" dropped on the desk. When they made a lowball offer, she shoved the papers back into her briefcase and spoke in a huff. "Why, that's an insult," she said. "Two hundred and twenty-five dollars for eight people! You know our salary and you know how our little act goes over. You've been booking us long enough to—"

"Take it or leave it," was the typical response. "Plenty of acts around will grab it if you don't."

And so they took all of them, at theaters with moldy curtains and rank lobbies and marquees dotted with dead bulbs: one day at the Victoria Theatre in Lansford, Pennsylvania, for $116.67; two days at Central Park Theatre in Chicago for $175; four days in Los Angeles for just $70 total. One of the boys, finally fed up with Rose's antics and the dwindling crowds, decided to quit. "It is understood and agreed upon," Rose scribbled on the back of the contract, "that Henry Elias is remaining here in Los Angeles with his own free will, transportation has been offered him by Rose E. Hovick to New York City. This he has refused." Louise and June stared out at the audience, the seats more empty than full. It gaped back at them, a wide black mouth with so many missing teeth.

Hoping to inject some new energy into the act, Rose scoured the streets for talent, telling each boy she'd get him onto the Orpheum Circuit—they wouldn't believe the paychecks, the acclaim, the adoration of the audience. "The experience will be so valuable," Rose promised, "and of course the prestige of appearing with Dainty June. You realize, of course, that my baby has headlined all over the country?" A seventeen-year-old boy named Bobby Reed signed on. He "danced like a bubble" and played the saxophone, and he seemed to be auditioning for June alone. Suddenly, Louise noticed, June wasn't running around outside like a savage in between rehearsals. She and Bobby practiced separately in the wings or climbed to the organ loft when they thought no one was watching.

Louise still played "The Duchess," holding herself apart and above, but she found herself drawn to another seventeen-year-old, Stanley Glass. June considered him a "snoot," but clearly she didn't understand

Louise, "Bobby Reed," and June.

the difference between self-confidence and conceit. True, he was a bit boastful, and did "show-offy" things like changing all of his money into ones and folding a ten over the thick wad of bills—habits Louise told him were "cheap-looking." But he was ambitious and clever and performed his solo beneath a lobster scope, a metal disk that fitted over a spotlight and was rotated via an electric motor. The contraption spliced the light and seemed to slow it down so it looked as if he were dancing underwater—a sure showstopper, and he wasn't afraid to say so.

"I like being with you," he told Louise one night, while they were sitting together in the stage alley at a theater in Trenton. "You aren't like most of the girls I know, giggling all the time and always talking about themselves. I like serious girls."

The moon bloomed full and bright, and she leaned against the wall so her face dipped into shadow. She was shy, suddenly, and acutely aware of her double chin.

"I have a very serious nature," she said in her most sophisticated voice, the one she'd been practicing since meeting George Davis. "Maybe that's because I read a lot. Do you like to read?"

She'd lost him. He was tap dancing now, listening only to the staccato symphony of his shoes.

"Thus by day my limbs, by night my mind," she recited, "for thee, and for myself no quiet find—that's from Shakespeare's sonnets. Have you ever read them?"

He spun a circle and stopped short, his lithe body outlined against the moon.

"This sure is a dumpy theater, isn't it?" he said. "I never would have joined this crumby act if your mother hadn't told me we were going on the Orpheum Circuit."

"Oh, we'll be going back. It's just that vaudeville is in a slump right now. Mother says that's because of the talking pictures."

He had big plans, he told her: his own professional act, called Stanley Glass and Company. He'd find a partner, a pretty, dainty girl who could sing and dance. They'd practice right outside the Palace Theatre in New York and catch the eye of the most important agents in town. Would Louise mind humming "Me and My Shadow" so he could show her a few steps? She complied, and he launched into a figure eight and over-the-top, fell into his knee drops, sprang back up, and executed nip-ups and after-beats. He became a blur and she tried to capture each frame of his movement, the right angle of his muscled arms, the perfect arc of his kicks. She felt him land beside her, heaving, soaked through his shirt with sweat. His hand covered hers, and he searched the shadow for her face. "Quickly, like the fluttering of the moth around the electric bulb over the stage door sign, he kissed me," Louise remembered. "My mouth burned from the light touch of his lips." For just a moment she relinquished control. As if on cue Rose appeared, her body silhouetted inside the stage door. Louise broke free and scuttled back in the theatre, catching Rose's look as she passed, and all those years of her mother's advice rose like cream in her mind.

She decided she both agreed and disagreed with her mother. A boy couldn't get you pregnant just from a kiss; how silly and naïve that sounded, now that she was older. But Mother was right about the power they held as women, about the one currency that never lost its value. She would give it away whenever and to whomever she saw fit, but always—and only—for something in return.

———————

They continued on their tenuous, makeshift circuit, each theater shabbier than the last, one-night stands in Buffalo, Sedalia, North Platte, Toledo, Trenton, and Appleton, Wisconsin. At the Folies Bergère on Atlantic City's boardwalk they were fifth on the bill, below both the Three Ormonde Sisters (tagline: "A Wee Drop of Scotch of the 'Grab Bag Show' "), and Evelyn Nesbit, the former Manhattan ingenue—now, at age forty-three, eight years older than Rose. Even Bingo, Bank Night, and Dish Night had higher billing. They had long layoffs in between when the grouch bag got even lighter, the boys angrier, and June more distant and cagey. Rose, perhaps wishing for a self-fulfilling prophecy, decided to change the act's name for a gig in Albuquerque, New Mexico: "Dainty June and the Happy Gang Revue" performed at the Kimo Theater.

Rose feigned a positive attitude, insisting that God was watching over their little act, that He wouldn't "knock vaudeville out from under us." But Louise knew her mother better than anyone; she alone could follow the seismic shift of her moods, the weather-vane spin of her thoughts. Improbable as it seemed, she was now nearly Mother's age when she'd escaped from the convent so long ago, when Rose first learned the importance of timing: when to latch onto someone and when to let go; when to beg and when to threaten; when to yield and when to take charge; when there was no choice left but to disappear. Louise might not sing or dance as well as June but she had inherited Mother's gifts of timing and tenacity, the ability to walk into a picture just as the shutter clicked and smile until the flash went dim. Rose was falling and Louise would rise to meet her halfway, accept a permanent exchange of innocence for control. It was a matter of both necessity and choice. She wanted to become her mother's equal, her other, willing half, as much as she had to.

Louise tried on her new role slowly, an inch at a time, since this was one costume she could never take off. When they were out in public, she looped her arm through Rose's and whooped and hollered so loudly that June slunk away, mortified, to the other side of the street. Mother loved the attention, and Louise would deliver it to her. When the two girls ran into Gordon by chance in New York City, June jumped into his arms while Louise regarded him, warily, from a distance. "Mother will be so glad to see you," June said, breathing into his neck, forgetting, for the moment, that she was now fifteen years old. "She thinks you're dead." Gordon set her down and stepped away. "I never want to see her again," he said. "Never, do you hear me?" June hid her face in her hands and wept, but Louise was thinking of Mother. She decided that Rose should never know the truth. And if any man ever professed his love for her, she would recognize the words as lies.

When Mother finally lost it, when she did the worst thing she'd ever done in her life—so far, at least—Louise willed herself to understand. These were desperate times, their entire world creeping away from them, and Louise had to wonder how she would have reacted in the same situation, if she were the oldest, the mother, the one ostensibly in charge. An unnamed hotel manager in an unnamed city affronted Rose in an unspecified way. He insulted her daughters, or threatened eviction because their room was overrun with boys, or looked at Rose in a way that dredged up every sore moment with Daddy Jack and Daddy Bub and Murray Gordon and the rest she never cared to name. Louise had to ask herself: if she were Mother under these circumstances, would she have stood by passively and withstood yet another indignity? Or would she have allowed her best instincts to meld with her worst, thinking of her daughters, broken and diminished, while she closed her eyes tightly and pushed that manager out the window?

The why didn't matter after the fact, only that the police accepted Rose's alibi of self-defense, and that the murder was never spoken of again. Louise honored this pact even later, when Rose knew all of her secrets and threatened to remember them out loud.

*A*nd Louise was there for Rose when the end finally came. On December 28, 1928, after performing at the Jayhawk Theatre in Topeka, Kansas, Louise heard her mother scream, a fierce, high-pitched keening that sounded vaguely inhuman. A note rested on the windowsill, and Louise saw her sister's childish scrawl:

> We were married two weeks ago in North Platte so you can't have it
> annulled. Please don't try to find me. I can't go on doing the same
> act all my life. I'd rather die. Bobby loves me . . .

Louise let Mother weep into her shoulder and cry for the baby she had once tried to destroy. "She's only a baby," Rose said, over and over. "She's thirteen, Louise. Thirteen years old! She can't leave me like this." Louise didn't remind her mother of June's true age or stop her when she reached for her coat. It wouldn't be Rose without a dramatic denouement, and Louise would be waiting when she returned.

Two detectives arrived, their flashlights sweeping golden streaks across each corner, beneath the gnarled branches of leafless trees. "She can't have gone far," Rose told them, her voice trailing down the street. "She isn't very bright and won't know what to do." Louise pictured her sister hiding in some slim wedge of space, willing herself to be smaller than she was.

Mother never stopped talking. "He's been in trouble before," she said. "He's just a tramp traveling around with burlesque companies. That's all he's ever known before—burlesque! My poor baby. Oh, my poor baby! Thank God there are men like you in the world to help a poor widow."

The officers escorted her to the police station, told her to sit tight. Before long, they returned with Bobby and presented him to Rose. June was nowhere to be found.

"Marriage isn't the electric chair," one officer reasoned. "I would like to see you and Bobby shake hands and be friends."

Bobby took a step toward Rose and extended his hand. She reached inside her coat and pulled out a small automatic pistol. Ten inches from his chest she fired once, twice. The gun jumped in her hand but no bullet discharged. She hadn't unhinged the safety lock. The detective ripped the gun away and locked her inside barrel arms, but she would not be confined. She wrestled free and tackled Bobby, kicking his shins, pounding his head, scratching at his eyes. The entire night staff approached cautiously, as if closing in on a rabid, feral animal, and then it was over. Rose lay flat on her back, the rhythm of her screams ceding gradually, like a tree swing slowing to a stop after a child jumps off.

When Rose returned, Louise was waiting. She took her mother back into her arms and held her upright. "You're all I have now, Louise," Rose whispered, breathing hot against her neck. "Promise me you'll never leave me. Promise me that, dear." She gripped Louise's arms and pulled back far enough to look at her directly. "Say you'll never leave me! Promise me!"

Louise stared back. They were even, now, shoulder to shoulder, eye to eye.

"No, Mother," she said. "I can't promise that." Rose fell into her arms again, but Louise was already gone—thinking of orange chiffon and ostrich feathers, the sweet refrain of "Me and My Shadow," the spotlight's halo encircling her every spin and stride. She thought of June, lost but *free,* and in that moment wanted only to be one step ahead of her.

Gypsy with Mike Todd and George S. Kaufman.

Chapter Seventeen

All I ever wanted was to have one husband and one
house and one garden and a lot of children.

—ACTRESS JOAN BLONDELL

Highland Mills and New York City, 1942–1943

The slow descent down those steps finally ends, and in the roomful of spectators she becomes Gypsy Rose Lee again. At the makeshift altar, she jokes about feeling like "an Aztec virgin being prepared for sacrifice" and cries as the service concludes. "My Gawd," Georgia Sothern says, patting her back, "what a performance!"

Gypsy doesn't smile when she cuts the cake with a knife the length of a machete, and smiles hugely, falsely, when she and her new husband, Bill Kirkland, pose for a photograph with their mothers that will soon appear in *Life* magazine. Gypsy wrenches away from Rose, as if her mother's skin is painful to the touch, and Rose leans in, resting her chin on Gypsy's shoulder, closing a hand around her daughter's neck.

After removing the grapes from her hair, Gypsy dresses in flannel, slathers herself with Vicks VapoRub, and picks up a book, ignoring the champagne and flowers Bill sets by the bed. Ten months later gossip columnist Walter Winchell is the first to break the news. The demise of their relationship makes him so disillusioned, Bill Kirkland claims, that he will "stay a bachelor forever." Rose, as always, offers her own unsolicited opinion. "Sorry you are having trouble with Bill," she writes. "It must be your fault."

Mike Todd is still married to Bertha and seems intent on remaining so, but he never stops teasing Gypsy with his letters: "I miss you," he writes, "so don't marry any actors." The situation brings to mind her mother's easy gift for uprooting men, the same way Grandpa Thompson used to weed his garden. Rose's ruthless instinct lives inside Gypsy, to both her occasional frustration and frequent relief, but with Mike its edges are softened, its sting mild. She has no idea how to unweave him from her life, or even if she wants to.

They are together again, on his terms, and he is producing her play, *The Naked Genius,* titled after the way she signs off letters to her editor. It strikes Gypsy that the saga behind *The Naked Genius* is more compelling than the play itself, what with its plot that manages to be at once semiautobiographical and contrived—yet another instance of her mining her past to ensure she'll never relive it. A stripper named Gypsy hires a ghostwriter to pen her memoirs, a surprise critical and commercial hit, and she becomes the unlikely toast of New York's literati. She falls in love with her slick, unavailable press agent and, to spite him, decides to marry her wealthy book publisher, who promises to save her from a lowly life in burlesque.

By now Gypsy is a literary force, a self-fulfilling prophecy she finds both thrilling and ludicrous. Here she is, the author of two novels, *The G-String Murders* and *Mother Finds a Body* (the latter also based on true events), several *New Yorker* articles, and now a Broadway-bound play, her only academic degree a "Doctor of Strip Teasing" issued by the Minsky brothers. After the successful adaptation of *The G-String Murders* into the movie *Lady of Burlesque,* Hollywood has kept a close eye on her literary efforts. Pulitzer Prize–winning playwright George S. Kaufman signs on to direct the play. Gypsy hopes Mike will give her the lead, but he has someone else in mind: the movie star Joan Blondell.

A marquee name, Gypsy has to admit, and she understands Joan instinctively just as she understands Mike. Their ambitions grow from the same restless place, tick to the same frenzied clock. Joan's parents trouped the vaudeville circuits she remembers all too well, tucking their daughter into a stage trunk instead of a crib, telling her the road

was education enough. When vaudeville died she turned not to burlesque but to beauty pageants, winning the 1926 Miss Dallas crown
under the stage name Rosebud Blondell. Three years later, back to
being Joan, she scored her break in the movie *Penny Arcade* and went on
to star in twenty-seven films in thirty-six months. She calls herself "the
fizz on the soda," a nickname that is as fitting offscreen as on. Stories
abound about catfights backstage—cursing, hair pulling, choking, head
banging, all of it—and she once bashed a producer with a silver hand
mirror. But she has four key things Gypsy lacks: blond ringlets, a large
bust, blue eyes that dominate a petite kitten face, and acting talent.
Gypsy soothes herself the best way she knows how, by imagining the
size of her royalty checks.

Rehearsals begin in August 1943, at the old Maxine Elliott's Theatre
on 39th Street, and at first all of the principals are in good spirits. Joan
looks ravishing if somewhat incongruous, like an amorous kewpie doll.
Kaufman has doctored the script—it's less of a collaboration than
Gypsy would have liked, but who is she to argue with the master?—and
on paper, *The Naked Genius* works.

But the lines, spoken aloud, seem twice removed from dialogue that
might occur in real life; the plot more Dalí than Eugene O'Neill. Kaufman sits in the front row, grinning oddly—a nervous muscular reaction,
it turns out, rather than an expression of pleasure or approval. Gypsy
tries to be positive, praising Joan's ebullient delivery and Kaufman's
sure-handed direction, but each rehearsal is worse than the last. It is a
slow-motion unraveling that recalls the worst phase of her life, the un-
speakable stretch of time before she broke away from Mother, those
lost days when she went places and did things that no one associates
with Gypsy Rose Lee, slippery memories she can't bear to relive. . . .

One morning Gypsy wakes up and decides not to return to the theater.

Mademoiselle Fifi, another of Billy Minsky's brilliant creations.

Chapter Eighteen

When a burlesque producer is asked in court about the morals of his workers, the answer always is, "Some virgins, no professionals."

—JOSEPH MITCHELL

New York City, 1925–1928

It was true that a certain sect of uptown snubbed the Minskys, and that certain detractors gleefully reported that their "bold invasion of Broadway is all over," but as soon as the Hawaiian octet disbanded and the uncharacteristically svelte chorines shuffled away, the brothers turned out the lights on the Park Music Hall and found a rightful home north of 14th Street. Billy Minsky was eager to open as soon as possible; mourning his failures merely got in the way of learning from them. The experiment at Columbus Circle would neither define nor destroy his name.

This latest venture of *"les frères* Minsky," as the press dubbed the brothers, was called Minsky's Apollo (not to be confused with *the* Apollo, which had yet to debut). Located in Harlem on 125th Street between Seventh and Eighth Avenues, Minsky's Apollo shared the block with Brecher's Opera House, where Fanny Brice and Sophie Tucker often ruled the stage, and another burlesque palace, Hurtig & Seamon's, a venue exclusively serving the Columbia Wheel.

One soup-thick afternoon in August, Billy stood outside surveying his new building, eager to tell his main investor, Joseph Weinstock, about his plans for Minsky's Apollo. Like Billy, Weinstock was a cunning opportunist, once having bid $50 at an auction for a vacant seat on the New York Stock Exchange—and winning it. Several plainclothes officers and uniformed members of the exchange had to guard its doors to prevent Weinstock from entering until a judge finally deemed the price "grossly inadequate." After the debacle on Broadway, Weinstock was taking a risk by backing the Minskys, and Billy wanted to soothe any lingering misgivings.

He felt a tap on his shoulder. This time he wasn't in Lee Shubert's neighborhood, and Billy expected to find one of two people when he turned around: the Columbia Wheel producers, Jules Hurtig or Harry Seamon.

"You won't last four weeks," Hurtig warned.

Billy smiled through a gauzy hoop of cigar smoke and let the old man believe he was right.

When time permitted, Billy explored the local streets, strolling past Harlem Hospital and the twenty-cent-shave corner barbershops, the thrift stores and cheap Chinese restaurants, the pet shop where a monkey had escaped and killed a flock of canaries. There was serious talk, finally, of a triborough bridge that would link together Queens, the Bronx, and Manhattan. Clearly it would take years to open—some things even New York couldn't hurry along—but he expected it to boost patronage at Minsky's Apollo when that day finally came. He'd picked a bustling block in a diverse neighborhood—Jewish between 110th and 125th Streets and black further north, with Jungle Alley along 133rd Street between Lenox and Seventh Avenues. The area boasted the densest concentration of nightclubs and cabarets in New York, luring the sort of people who shaped the city's ethos and manipulated its mood, the very folks whose business Billy courted and whose accolades he craved.

If the rules had been rewritten at the end of the Great War, they were now abandoned altogether. Mores were discarded and manners dismissed at every level of society. New York's cultural arbiters no longer hailed from the Social Register or the Four Hundred; nightlife had turned fluid and democratic. Closed circles cracked open and made room. "There's no such thing as a set anymore," Carl Van Vechten wrote in his novel *Parties*. "Everybody goes everywhere."

They went to side streets around Jungle Alley to buy cocaine and marijuana, ten joints for a dollar, and to basement speakeasies where a silent man granted entry by yanking a long chain attached to the door. Down a steep flight of stairs elite uptowners and Greenwich Village bohemians and blacks crowded together at wood tables and sipped bootleg liquor with street names like "smoke" and "lightning." They climbed upstairs to rent parties, where jazz musicians and piano "professors" raised money to help friends pay their landlords; marveled at the Clam House's lesbian headliner, a 250-pound crooner clad in a top hat and tuxedo; and were charmed by A'Lelia Walker, Harlem's foremost hostess and heiress, the daughter of the first black female self-made millionaire. They ran into an infamous character called "Money," a hunchback who served as an unofficial tour guide for white interlopers. The final stop, invariably, was a dive run by Sewing Machine Bertha, who showed pornographic films as a preview to an after-hours live sex show featuring actors of all races.

Whites also went to clubs meant for them and them alone, Connie's Inn and Small's Paradise and the Cotton Club, the last the most exclusive destination of all. There the gangster Owney Madden sold his personal brand of beer, Madden's No. 1, and denied blacks entry unless they were light enough to pass. He hired Duke Ellington and Cab Calloway and produced every kind of black show that whites might want to see: the smiling black, the shuffling black, the blackface black, and a mandatory jungle number where a line of chorus girls, no darker than "high yellow," shimmied until their costumes slipped off.

Billy knew Minsky's Apollo would have to distinguish itself in order to siphon customers from the more established clubs; the Minsky name was still unproven in this part of town. Hurtig & Seamon's did a few things right, catering to the neighborhood with a mixed-race production called *Super Black and White Sensation* featuring "70½ People: 35

Whites and 35½ Blacks," and an all-colored company, Lucky Sambo. At Minsky's Apollo, black performers and customers would be just as welcome as whites, and he'd encourage them to interact and play off each other, just as they did at the National Winter Garden.

The brothers placed ads for chorines, coochers, comedians. One comic, a young man named Joey Faye, had some of the freshest sketches Billy had seen in a very long time.

"You got any more material?" Billy asked.

"I got a lot of material," Faye said, "but it's all stolen—most of it, anyway."

"Stolen?" Billy asked, smiling.

"From the *First Little Show,* from the *Second Little Show,* George White's *Scandals,* Ziegfeld's *Follies,* the Palace Theatre, the Greenwich Village *Follies*—all the shows around."

"Well, let me see some of the stuff," Billy prodded, and the comedian obliged.

"Can you put one of these on for Friday?" Billy asked. "For every sketch you put on, I'll give you twenty-five extra bucks in addition to your salary."

"Won't you get sued? After all, it's not our material."

Billy leaned in close. "How can I get sued?" he reasoned. "We open on a Friday. We do the show Saturday and Sunday. They can't sue me until Monday. Tuesday I go to my lawyer. By Wednesday, we answer the suit, Thursday the show is finished, and Friday we put on a new one. No show, no suit."

Faye finally understood, and smiled back.

───

For his chef d'oeuvre Billy discovered a stripteaser working at the Olympic theater, and lured her away. He intended to rotate her appearances between the Apollo and the National Winter Garden and began remaking her into his own creation. By the time he finished she was no longer Mary Dawson from Philadelphia, born to a devout Catholic mother and Quaker father who worked, improbably, as a cop. Instead she was Mademoiselle Fifi, late of Paris, "an Oriental dancer" of astonishing magnificence and skill. Billy held full-scale press conferences to introduce his exotic star, instructing reporters to direct all questions to him.

"Mademoiselle Fifi," Billy explained haughtily, his arm wrapped around the girl's waist, "does not speak so good the English. So I will be her spokesperson."

Next he placed cryptic signs in the subway—SHE DANCES TONIGHT—WHO?—FIFI—and mailed a perfumed letter to every business owner in Harlem. He penned each word himself in delicate, looping cursive:

Dear Sir:
    You being a man about town, we are taking the liberty of sending you a season pass for the Apollo Burlesque Theatre on 125th Street, West Side. You will agree there is no greater thrill than to watch a fast, good-looking, perfectly formed chorus of young beautiful girls. We've got all of that, and lots more. . . .
                    Yours for a good time,
                    Mlle. Fifi

On the Apollo's opening night, the promise of Mademoiselle Fifi's splendor had customers lining up around the block, a queue that reached as far as Hurtig & Seamon's marquee. Mademoiselle Fifi delivered her finest performance to date, stepping onstage in her "gorgeous golden cape" only to drop it at the first note of her song. No union suit covered her flesh. She gave the crowd spins and kicks "with a few cooch movements thrown in," cooch movements so brazen and raw that policemen began filing up the aisle, no doubt summoned by John Sumner and his cadre of prudes.

Billy had always shared his city's intolerance of timidity and hesitation, the belief that pausing to consider your place meant you were already far behind. During the Jazz Age the pace was doubled, the challenges amplified. He'd expected reformers at the Apollo's debut but declined to activate Herbert's red-light warning system—a tactical decision he hoped would pay off, yielding a just reward for being as bold and quick as the era demanded.

The furor over Mademoiselle Fifi only lasted long enough for Billy to make his point: nudity on his stage was no more offensive or illegal than on Broadway. The rules should not change for burlesque, be it north or south of 14th Street. Recalling one critic's assessment of the Apollo's debut—"burlesque red hot off the grid and well-spiced with double en-tendre sufficiently suggestive to be understood by the blind and the deaf and dumb alike"—he decided to make his point again, this time with such theatrics and disdain for subtlety that no one would ever for-get it, a plot worthy not only of New York's attention, but also of its his-tory.

———

*A*s the Minskys told the story and as it thereafter told itself, the trou-ble began with the member of the Minsky family least likely—at least at that point in time—to invite it. On Monday, April 20, 1925, Louis Min-sky, who had maintained a careful distance from his sons' burlesque en-terprise, received a strange letter in the mail:

> I address you, sir, not as principal of the Minsky Realty Company,
> but as proprietor of the National Winter Garden Theatre, on which
> premises "burlesque" shows are produced. . . .
>
> On Monday the 13th I purchased a ticket to the balcony of the
> National Winter Garden and witnessed the show advertised to be
> "Burlesque As You Like It." I did not like it. In particular I did not
> like the so-called "comedy sketches." Specifically, I did not like the
> sketches entitled "Antony and Cleopatra" and "Desire Under the El."
> I found them to be lewd, obscene, contributory to immoral con-
> duct, and in gross violation of Section 1140-A of the Penal Law. . . .
>
> Might I suggest, sir, that your "comic" actors follow the suit of
> the singing and dancing young ladies of your company, who disport
> themselves with great jest and jollity, with no resort to unseemly ac-
> tions. . . . I might go so far, sir, as to cite the Oriental shimmy-ballet
> of Mlle. Fifi as an exemplary model of popular entertainment. A
> certain tolerance may be observed in the case of the French-born
> performer such as this young artist.

I shall purchase a ticket and be in attendance at the National Winter Garden on the evening of April 20th. If I find that the comedy sketches are still in violation of the law and public taste, I shall not hesitate to have your performance stopped. I shall summon the police and you will be served with my complaint flagrante delicto.

—John Sumner, Secretary
New York Society for the
Suppression of Vice

Louis Minsky wasn't quite sure who Sumner was or what he was talking about. He didn't know the allegedly distasteful sketch was called "Anatomy"—not "Antony"—"and Cleopatra" (and that it had a subtitle: "Shakespeare Shimmies in His Grave"). He also failed to connect "Desire Under the El "with *Desire Under the Elms,* the Eugene O'Neill play currently on Broadway. He didn't even realize the absurdity of lauding Mademoiselle Fifi as a paragon of virtuous entertainment, considering she had already spurred a raid at the Apollo. But like his sons, Louis recognized a prime opportunity when he saw one: if he kept the letter to himself, and if the National Winter Garden were raided, his boys might be delivered back into a decent world.

Louis tucked the letter into his vest pocket. What will be will be. God would handle Abe, Billy, Herbert, and Morton, even if both he and Mr. Sumner failed.

*U*nbeknown to Louis Minsky or John Sumner, the brothers had ordered a "Boston" version of all performances on the night of April 20. They feared a visit not from John Sumner but from Mary Minsky, who had declared her intention to finally spend an evening at the National Winter Garden (and who suspected that Billy's interest in Mademoiselle Fifi extended beyond the professional). As a good and loyal wife, wasn't it high time she met the people Billy called his "other family"? Besides, if the shows were truly as decent and respectable as Billy said, why would he object?

Billy knew he must agree to Mary's plan or risk wrath and headache at home. For that night, he and Morton would join Abe and Herbert downtown and let their team of managers run Minsky's Apollo. As a precaution, Billy sent out word to his chorines that, for that performance only, "brassieres will be worn at all times." Comedy personnel will not deliver unrehearsed lines in Yiddish. There will be no talking or fraternizing with the audience during scenes. He thanked them for their "splendid cooperation" and believed the situation was under control.

Billy waved to Mary, sitting with her brother high up in the last row of the orchestra, but missed John Sumner settling into a prime spot next to the runway, where the acoustics would amplify each crude double entendre and odious joke. For camouflage Sumner bought a hot dog, a box of Cracker Jack, and a bottle of celery tonic, but kept a notepad, pencil, and a paraffin whistle tucked inside his jacket pocket.

He sat, pencil poised, as the Minsky band leader simultaneously lifted his baton and tapped a buzzer on the podium with his toe, alerting the doorman six floors below to hustle in the latecomers. The reformer winced through the faux-romantic overture, the sobbing saxophones and moaning violins, and shifted away from the patron sitting next to him, a man reeking of garlic and home-brewed beer. Next came Tom Bundy, the Minsky's top comic and master of ceremonies, announcing the chorines in his bullhorn voice ("Presenting the fair, the fragrant, the fabulous, blushing, beauteous—*Roses of Minsky Land!*") and now the girls themselves, sidling down the runway, one dozen kicking west toward the Bowery and the other dozen east toward Chrystie Street, the muted magenta spotlights rouging the skin of their thighs.

He endured a tiresome sketch called "A Quiet Game of Cards," which involved thick rolls of play money, hatchets, cudgels, pistols, a bladder, the occasional cannon, and the following dialogue:

COMIC NO. 1: "My friend, that's a terrible cold you have there, terrible! Didn't you say you always slept in a nice, warm bed? How come you caught a cold?"

COMIC NO. 2: "Last night her husband showed up and I had to get
up out of the nice, warm bed and go home."

He watched "Desire Under the El" (during which the fellow next to
Sumner complained about the "good parts" being edited out), and
"Anatomy and Cleopatra," which featured balloon bosoms, a prop phal-
lus, and tasteless jokes about rigor mortis. Sumner didn't know whether
to be relieved or disappointed by the puerile splendor of it all. In the
back of the house six of his detectives fixed their eyes upon him, watching for the crook of his finger, the invitation to charge forward.

He had one last hurdle, or hope—however he chose to view it—and
he waited for Mademoiselle Fifi to take the stage.

———

So far so good, Billy thought, although he could sense that the regulars were annoyed and antsy and would probably demand a refund. He
gazed upward at Mary, who was clinging to her brother and slicing her
hand through the cigar smoke; how she hated the musky smell, the
sting to her eyes. But the show had been clean enough to keep her in
her seat and out of his business, which was all that mattered. Wait—
was that Joseph Weinstock, his principal investor, sitting nearby? Billy
felt something like a tuning fork churning in his gut. Weinstock was a
rash, brash, temperamental man, and if he sensed that Billy was taming
down the shows, he would rescind his partnership. Billy could take a
Philly girl and transform her into a *fille de joie,* but he couldn't produce
burlesque on Minsky money alone.

He found Mademoiselle Fifi in the wings. Her sheath of black netting made a grid of her skin, arms and legs and torso delineated into
fleshy pink squares. She wore a scarlet cape studded with rhinestones
and a matching headband topped with a towering exclamation point of
feathers. She looked at Billy as if she couldn't take a step without his
personally positioning her feet. He had time for only a few words, so he
chose them as judiciously as possible.

"This is it, Feef," he said. "The whole ante's riding on you." He hoped she understood. He coasted a hand toward her shoulder, intending to give her an encouraging push, but instead his fingers brushed her breast. That look again, and then she said, softly, "You do love me, don't you, Billy?"

He couldn't hear. The music soared from the pit. From somewhere in the distance a candy butcher hollered about chocolate bonbons and girlie cartoons. Beyond the velvet curtain the audience waited, expectations pacing like caged animals in their minds.

"God love you," Billy said, and then there was no barrier between his star and the audience.

He watched her dance. She was graceful as always but distracted, her angles lazy, her limbs sluggish. This was no time for artistry, the pirouettes and the arabesques, the coquettish dipping of her chin. The audience wanted bare flesh, and now. He began to mime directions: grinding his jowls and thrusting his hips and cupping imaginary Amazonian breasts in his hands. Fifi spun back toward the wings, her cape billowing behind her, and it came to her that for once she held the power in the relationship; she had Billy Minsky precisely where she wanted him. She froze, her torso bent, leg held aloft and curled behind her back.

"Billy," she whispered. "Tell me you love me."

"Feef! I'm trying to tell you—cut the ballet! Go to the cooch! The cooch!"

"Are you going to say it, Billy?"

He was apoplectic now. "Feef!" His spittle sprayed her face. "You goofy kid! Go to the cooch!"

She twirled away and back again.

"Say it, Billy!" she said, stretching toward him. "Say, 'I'm in love with you, Fifi.'"

He could no longer control his hands. One reached out and coiled like a tentacle around her wrist. She lost her balance and fell against him.

"Get this straight, kid," he said. "I am not in love with you. Have you got that? Now get the hell into your cooch."

He let her go and she let herself go, spinning into a haze, her feet so brisk against the runway they seemed to whip up tendrils of smoke. The orchestra heaved and flailed, a medley of Puccini, Joplin, and Of-

Minsky "Rosebuds" have their day in court.

fenbach's *Gaité Parisienne,* and even after Mademoiselle Fifi shed her cape and netting and brassiere, she did not stop spinning.

Beneath the crash of cymbals John Sumner's paraffin whistle blew meekly.

 $\mathscr{S}$ ince it was a Minsky story—and an entirely fabricated Minsky story, at that—the details of the fictitious raid grew bolder and more absurd with each retelling, skipping over all the inconveniences that littered up their path. No one questioned why this incident, so notorious it inspired a 1968 movie starring Jason Robards and Bert Lahr titled *The Night They Raided Minsky's,* was never reported in any trade or mainstream or tabloid newspapers of the time. Or why John Sumner, a prodigious keeper of his own records, felt compelled to throw away his letter to Louis Minsky. Or the true whereabouts of Mademoiselle Fifi on that night, when she claimed to be attending a dinner at the

Waldorf-Astoria for the American Medical Association, three miles and a world away from the National Winter Garden.

Instead they recalled how Fifi, devastated by Billy's rejection, bit her lip and stripped with blood beading down her chin, a burlesque of a sacrifice, a cooch dancer scorned. And how, at the inevitable trial, the judge, an old family friend of the Minskys, asked Sumner to demonstrate Mademoiselle Fifi's "pelvic contortions."

"Your honor," Sumner reportedly said, "it would be very difficult without musical accompaniment." Four Minsky employees hummed a tune, the judge waved his gavel, and Sumner's hips rotated with all the fluidity of a rusty wheel.

"That poor man!" Mademoiselle Fifi cried. She veiled her eyes with a graceful hand. "They mustn't make him do that."

"Mr. Minsky," the judge said. He nodded toward Sumner, who had collapsed, breathless, in his seat. "Would you as proprietor of the National Winter Garden hire this dancer for your show?"

"Your honor," Billy answered, "I wouldn't wish this dancer to waltz on the grave of my own worst enemy."

But the finale of the most famous burlesque raid in New York history remained the same: the trial lasted for seven weeks, and the Minskys always won.

Chapter Nineteen

The only time I'd ever marry again is if someone beat
on my door and said, "I have $27 million and I'll live
elsewhere."

—JOAN BLONDELL

On and Off the Set of *The Naked Genius*, 1943

Gypsy reappears in Boston on September 27, when *The Naked Genius* premieres at the Wilbur Theatre, a plain but handsome redbrick building on Tremont Street. Mike gnaws on his cigar and keeps his face free from expression. Kaufman grins his excruciating grin. She can barely stand to peek through her fingers at the stage and focuses instead on the critics' section, watching them scribble and cringe, listening for their groans. They hate every facet of the play except for Joan, which doesn't stop the actress from cornering one reviewer and screeching until his ears "smarted." The notices are so bad, in fact, that Mike sends a personal gift to each critic, thanking them for the constructive criticism, although he intends to ignore every bit of it. In truth, he confides to Gypsy, he doesn't much care about the reviews—just that the play makes money.

"It is not a critic's play," he explains. "It is a premeditated crime of box office. I knew exactly what I was doing."

Nevertheless, at Gypsy's and Kaufman's insistence, they head back to New York for a major overhaul, junking the first act and rewriting it entirely. The protagonist is no longer called "Gypsy" but "Honey Bee Carroll," whose moneygrubbing mother, "Pansy," carries a chicken under her arm and issues this command: "Just make it out to cash." (Rose, true to form, takes grave offense at this portrayal, and threatens to file a suit claiming the play violates her civil rights.) Joan Blondell now wears a diaphanous nightgown instead of a bathrobe and performs several burlesque routines reminiscent of Gypsy's, with powder puffs and an Adam-and-Eve costume adorned with leaves. Mike adds a mantelpiece clock that suffers a seizure each time it strikes the hour, a nod to William Saroyan's fantastic pinball machine in *The Time of Your Life*. The top lifts and lets loose a gush of water, in which a school of fat plastic cherubs float and dip and dive. "A waterfall gets 'em every time," Mike reasons, although Gypsy points out that Saroyan's contraption works only because his play does as well. Borrowing again from Gypsy's past, Mike also recruits several feathered and furry costars to join the cast, including seven dogs, one rooster, and a rhesus monkey named Herman. They begin fighting again, vehement clashes backstage and on the phone, and Mike tells her it would be best that she stop attending rehearsals.

By the time they arrive in Pittsburgh on October 11, Gypsy can't even look at him. "Mike," she writes,

> I blame you for your not allowing me to be at rehearsals. For not allowing me a word as to the changes. For constantly belittling my efforts . . . you say you're glad to break up the 'Boy Genius' myth. I'm only sorry you are pleased about breaking it with a play I bled over for many months, yes, years. You say you can razzle dazzle it. . . .
> Can you blame me for wishing that the play could stand on its own without a razzle dazzle?

She also vents to the press. *The Naked Genius*, she quips, is neither naked nor displays any genius. "Every time I see that show," she adds, "I get a new fever blister on my upper lip." After the Pittsburgh reviews, Gypsy and Kaufman join forces and corner Mike.

"The critics will slaughter us," Gypsy says. "Fold it, Mike."

"I'm taking it to New York," he replies, and that is that. She knows the source of his obstinance, and that it would be hypocritical to insist it doesn't matter: money. Without at least a three-week Broadway run, his pending $350,000 deal with 20th Century–Fox will collapse.

Fine, then, she tells him—change her credit to read "Written by Louise Hovick." This mess will not be blamed on Gypsy Rose Lee. Kaufman finds a scapegoat of his own, a colleague and avowed nemesis. "Mr. Todd," he requests, "change my credit to 'directed by Jed Harris.' "

On the night of the October 21 opening, Gypsy strolls into the Plymouth Theatre on 45th Street, her hair pulled into a sweet coiffure, like a dollop of ice cream, her cape hugging her shoulders, her cigarettes close at hand. Mike sits nearby with his prizefighter's face, bracing for the punch. It's the first time in twenty-five years on Broadway that Kaufman skips the opening night of one of his shows. "I can sort of understand why Gypsy Rose Lee and George Kaufman wanted *The Naked Genius* to close last week on the road," writes critic Louis Kronenberger. "What I can't understand is why they didn't get out an injunction or mutilate the scenery or shanghai the cast."

Every word of it expected, but Mike saves two surprises just for her. After the curtain's merciful drop, after the Saroyan-inspired clock stops seizing, after Joan accepts the only sincere applause of the evening, he helps Gypsy into the back of his limousine and directs the driver to the "21" Club, where even the phalanx of lawn jockeys seems to pass mute judgment. They take a booth near the kitchen where Ernest Hemingway once seduced a gangster's wife. He kisses Gypsy chastely on the cheek and presents her with a small box. A gleaming gold compact from Cartier lies inside. It is her opening-night present, he tells her. She deserves it.

Mike also tells her that he produced *The Naked Genius* just for Joan Blondell, and that she returned to Broadway after twelve years in Hollywood to be with him. He tells her he is determined to keep the play open, not because it's Gypsy's work but because he wants Joan to stay. He tells her he is in love with Joan, and plans to marry her as soon as he can.

Gypsy listens to him, a howling silence in her ears. An emergency brake slams throughout the room. All around her laughter slurs to a halt, legs pause midstep, cigarette smoke thickens and clots. The moment splices itself in two, and she holds both parts up to the light. She could be her mother, dissolve into a cyclone of furious weeping, shade the feeling even blacker than it really is. Or she could be Gypsy Rose Lee, who knows when to let Louise Hovick meet her gaze, and tell her she has already given too much away.

She stands and walks away without a word, leaving the gold compact on the table. She adds Mike to the list of things Joan has that she doesn't, to the long list of things she's never had at all.

Chapter Twenty

The first hundred stares are the hardest.

—GYPSY ROSE LEE

On the Vaudeville and Burlesque Circuits, 1928–1930

Mother and daughter headed back to Seattle, the frosted windows of the Studebaker making the old neighborhood look softer than Louise remembered it. Her childhood resurrected itself in a lingering slide show: the squat clapboard house where Mother gave birth to her—the original Ellen June—and then took away her name; the lodge halls where Louise realized her sister had something she never would; the sight of Grandpa Thompson waiting on his front porch for any or all of the Hovick women to return to him, at long last.

Mother told her a story about Grandpa Thompson on the long drive home, while sleet stabbed the windshield and the darkness closed in around them. When Grandpa was a little boy, Rose began, he went to live for a time with his aunt and uncle on their farm in North Dakota. It was a desolate place, the closest neighbors miles away. The winters were so brutal they had to crack the ice on the water pitchers just to wash their faces in the morning.

Grandpa's uncle was a kind man, but his aunt was volatile and cruel. She hated the isolation and repetition, her life nothing more than the relentless accumulation of the same empty day. She decided to escape.

She gathered her five children and Grandpa Thompson, piled them into a big wooden sled, hitched up the horses, and set off.

The six children huddled close and buried themselves beneath blankets. Grandpa Thompson watched his aunt stand up, cracking the whip like a man, her long black hair lashing back at the wind. Then he heard the howling of wolves. The pack chased the wagon, lunging at the horses' hooves, leaping at their throats. The children cried, and the oldest, a boy Grandpa's age, climbed in the front seat to protect his mother.

With one swift movement she pushed the boy down into the wolves' waiting mouths, and for a few moments they stopped chasing her. When the animals came back, she reached back for her other children and dropped them to the wolves, one by one. Grandpa Thompson clamped his hands over his ears to drown out the shrieks. By the time she returned to the farm, only the baby and Grandpa Thompson were left.

Louise let the story replay in her mind and shut her eyes tight.

"Mother," she said, "they weren't related to us, were they?" The answer was very important; she didn't want that black-haired woman to be any part of her.

"Yes, they were," Rose said.

And then they were home, Grandpa Thompson waiting on the porch, right where he belonged.

Grandpa was at a crossroads as well, having tired, finally, of Big Lady's fanciful excursions. He had begun an affair with a woman who lived nearby. One of these days, when Big Lady graced their little house with her formidable presence, he would slide the divorce papers across the table. She would treat them as she treated everything about their marriage, with no consideration or attention at all, and sign without reading a word. Out of pure, blind fear, he would continue to live under the same roof with Big Lady, never telling her she was no longer his wife. When Big Lady discovered the truth, she turned to the daughter who best understood the importance of having the last word.

"He can't do this, Rose!" she raged. "I've given him the best years of my life. And now he thinks he's going to marry her? And when he dies, she'll get his pension? Oh, no, he isn't going to get away with this!"

Charlie Thompson, like every man involved with a Hovick woman, didn't get away with anything. Six years later, in January 1934, he still hadn't mustered up the courage to marry his girlfriend and was still living with Big Lady. One day they went out for a drive, and their car was struck by a railroad switch engine at Colorado Avenue and Spokane Street. Grandpa Thompson suffered severe spinal cord injuries and died five days later. Big Lady sustained minor head injuries and began collecting his pension.

———

*A*t the moment, Grandpa Thompson was comforted to see his daughter and at least one of his granddaughters. Taking Rose in his arms, he said it was fine to cry over June and the demise of the act, but not in front of the neighbors. No sense letting the past yank her back when she needed to plot a future. Rose dried her eyes and agreed. Then she got to work.

First things first: no boys in the act this time—too untrustworthy and temperamental. Girls were much easier to handle. "We'll comb the city of Seattle for talent," Rose announced. "We'll cover every dancing school, every amateur contest. We'll get the cream of the city's crop." Her optimism waned, however, when she began making the rounds. Not one of them was as talented as June, and their looks failed to compensate. Even Grandpa Thompson was skeptical, musing that if this was the cream of the city, someone had scooped the top layer off the bottle.

But Rose forged ahead, holding rehearsals in the basement of a local lodge hall. Louise set up her sewing machine in the corner and began work on the costumes: cretonne and organdy, with ruffled bloomers and oversized matching hair bows. She designed a black velvet trouser suit for herself since she was the "tailored type," as Mother put it, which she took to mean that her weight was still a problem. The costumes fit Mother's criteria: girlish and cheap.

The act consisted of Louise and seven other girls: Madeline, Ruby, two Lillians, Dorothy, Mae, and Vanna. They would be called, alternately, "Madam Rose's Debutantes" and "Madame Rose and Her Dancing Daughters." For branding purposes, Rose decided each of them should take her name as a surname: Madeline Rose, Ruby Rose, and so on; even Louise would perform as "Louise Rose." Mother sketched out prospective routines and personas: the "tuff" girl, the Hula Girl, the "rube" girl, a "Wop" number, a "Daddy song," and a dance in which they used oversized mechanical baby dolls as partners. The freakishly flexible Ruby Rose, still petite enough to pass as a "wee tot," did a contortionist routine. Louise adorned Ruby Rose's brassiere with layers of filmy ruffles, so her "two tiny swellings" were concealed when she sank into her backbends. Since Rose didn't take her dreams and omens lightly, she decided that Susie the Dancing Cow would be spared retirement. Grandpa Thompson helped them pack up the Studebaker, affixing the scenery to the roof, the cow head on the trunk rack, and makeup and shoes wedged along the running boards. Rose's dogs and Louise's new monkey, Woolly Face, crammed inside.

Bookings were difficult at first. In El Paso, Texas, they served as the Tuesday-night entertainment for the local newspaper's fourteenth annual Cooking and Better Homes Exposition. No admission charge and no payday, but Rose worked the press as only she could, promising "a kaleidoscopic pageant, differing in its whimsical phases, specialties and climaxing in a beautiful finale." On to Tucson, where the Dancing Daughters were billed under the new Conrad Nagel talkie *Let's Make Whoopee.* Just to shake things up a bit, Rose gave herself a number in the act, singing "Mother Machree":

> *There's a place in my memory, my life, that you fill.*
> *No other can take it, no one ever will.*

For this performance, out of both habit and heartache, Rose submitted to the newspapers an old photograph of June.

Three months now, and not a word from the Baby.

Rose had no idea her daughter was living, as June herself put it, "in the shadow of the real world" on the dance marathon circuit, swaying on her feet for weeks at a time with only ten-minute intervals for rest, growing calluses on top of calluses, watching her fellow "horses" go squirrely from lack of sleep. The assistant surgeon general issued a graphic warning about the fad: "It's the same as putting a five-ton load on a one-ton truck. Something must give. No nervous system, no matter how strong, can stand seventy hours of dancing without ill effects. It may result in overstrained heart, rupture the muscles, or cause serious injury to the nerves of the body. The dancers may not notice it for months but the strain they put on their bodies is certain to tell."

One teenage girl had visions of Jesus. Another disrobed in the middle of the dance floor and went through the motions of taking a shower. A young man gnawed off the tops of potted palms, believing they were fried eggs. Some talked to imaginary friends or snatched nonexistent objects from the air. A twenty-seven-year-old dancer named Homer Morehouse dropped dead of heart failure as he left the floor.

But June, used to working herself past exhaustion, knew she could survive—and that this job was temporary. Every hour with Bobby on the dance floor was spent plotting her return back to both the stage and to Mother, this time following her own schedule, writing her own script.

———

With Gordon's negotiating skills in mind, Louise devised a plan: if they offered one free night, the managers might be persuaded to book them for a week or two. It worked. The Lyric Theatre in Yuma, Arizona, professed to host a "complete Orpheum Circuit," but its advertisements blared pure burlesque:

Attraction Extraordinary
GIRLS—GIRLS—GIRLS
And Then Some More
Madame Rose
—and—
Her Dancing Daughters
Vaudeville's Most Beautiful Production
Watta Show! Watta Show!

The Dancing Daughters were actually headlining this time, their name strung up in blinking lights—so what if the orchestra was inadequate, with the town butcher moonlighting as the violinist and the manager's teenage nephew working part-time as the drummer? If only a stagehand hadn't nailed their scenery to the back wall, thereby making it impossible to enter and exit fluidly, a misstep that sent every girl but Louise into nervous hysterics. One of them refused to do her number with Porky, the baby pig Rose picked up at a roadside farm along the way. The contortionist's shoulder strap broke as her dusty, stockinged feet brushed against her forehead, dropping her leotard and exposing her breasts. She quickly righted herself and fled the stage in tears. During the new military number, the backs of the uniforms were supposed to spell out DANCING DAUGHTERS in radium, a radioactive chemical (and, as it turned out, carcinogenic besides) used in luminous paints. Some of the girls were out of order, some sobbed in the wings, and the rest were too paralyzed to turn around. The audience tittered and offered a timid patter of applause.

After the show Louise found Rose in their hotel room, consoling the girls. She could either join them and wait for her mother's moods to turn, from sympathy to despair to outrage and back again, or she could step in and direct the action, sure as a conductor waving his wand.

"Look at us, Mother," Louise said. "You're pretending we're little girls and that's what's wrong. We aren't little girls anymore. We're almost grown up. Then why not make us look really grown up? Have us wear make-up and high heels—"

Rose stood. "Stop that yelling and shouting," she said. "You'll wake up everybody in the hotel. High heels? Have you lost your mind? High heels, on these *children*?"

"That's just it!" Louise stepped closer to her mother. "We're not children anymore. We're not anything. We have to make ourselves into something. Just think how much better we'd look if we were blondes!"

Rose's eyebrows leapt, and she clamped a hand over her mouth. After a moment her expression relaxed. "The girls might be very pretty as blondes," she conceded. "Yes, I'm sure they would. And we could change the name of the act to "Madam Rose's Baby Blondes.""

"No, Mother," Louise said. "I have a better idea. We'll change the name to Rose Louise and Her Hollywood Blondes, and I'll be the only brunette."

Rose relented. She watched as Louise poured peroxide over every head but her own, and agreed that the change called for new press photos. Arranged in ascending order of height, the girls flashed full-tooth grins for the camera, peering over pale, bare shoulders—all but Louise, who dipped her head coyly away from the others and allowed the corners of her lips only the slightest upturn. For the first time her face found a mask that fit: sultry, sly, and suggestive, with no trace of Plug, Hard-boiled Rose, or even Louise.

———————

$\mathcal{R}$ose did her part updating the publicity materials, calling the Blondes "Seven Sunkist Sirens of Song & Dance" who were "really and truly from Hollywood" and scheduled to appear in "a number of the larger cities." Despite their newly saucy appearance and the more suggestive phrasing of their ads, the act remained the same: the dancing cow, the mechanical dolls, the skit with Porky the Pig, the perennial "Hard-boiled Rose." She secured them bookings at knock-off Orpheum Theaters in places like Marion, Illinois—theaters that weren't on Martin Beck's once-prestigious circuit but clung to the vestiges of his glory. The Orpheum Circuit didn't even exist anymore, technically, having merged with the equally formidable B. F. Keith–Albee Vaudeville Exchange. Edward F. Albee, who once boasted "I am vaudeville," was also ruined; his most trusted associate betrayed him by selling all of his Keith-Albee-Orpheum stock to one Joseph Kennedy, father of the future president.

Kennedy announced that the longtime vaudeville producer was "washed up," dropped Albee's name, and combined the company with RCA and the Film Booking Offices of America to create Radio-Keith-Orpheum. RKO quickly came to dominate the market, producing radio programming and movies in a theater chain that reached every corner of the country. By the time Louise christened her Hollywood Blondes, only five straight vaudeville theaters remained nationwide. Getting booked was now more a game of musical chairs than a matter of talent or reputation. Acts trouped the same sad string of cities again and again, hoping to be in the right place when the melody stopped.

Which was why Rose Louise and Her Hollywood Blondes once again found themselves in El Paso, this time for a gig at the Colón Theatre, situated in a neighborhood populated by Mexican immigrants who'd fled during Pancho Villa's reign. An alley along the back of the theater served as a roving red carpet for prostitutes, pimps, and johns. The Colón's manager placed Spanish-language ads in the *El Paso Times*, promising that Rose Louise and Her Hollywood Blondes would deliver "deliciosos" and "sugestivos" numbers "in the style of New York, Paris, London, or Mexico City." Mildew coated the walls and the air reeked of sweat, but the shows were fantastic, unlike any Louise had ever seen: a strange, frenetic mosaic of sequins and spangles and feathers and heels with dangerous spikes. Bare torsos swelled and rolled like sleek olive waves. One comic bit a leading lady's behind, another peered down his pants as if stunned and delighted by what he found there. Every word was in Spanish; even the audience's laughter sounded foreign and surreal, a Dalí painting in audio.

"They'd never get our comedy lines," Rose whispered to Louise. She did not approve of the biting and leering, but the Colón had booked them for a full week at $35 per day. "We'd have to learn the act in Spanish."

"The whole act?" Louise asked.

"Of course not. Just the key words."

Rose found a stagehand who spoke passable English to translate a few of their numbers, "I Have a Cow," "Vamp a Little Lady," and "I'm a Hard-boiled Rose." The last song proved particularly difficult, however, and when Louise launched into her refrain, talk-singing *"Yo soy una gancha,"* the audience roared. Only later did she realize what she actually said: "I am a hooker."

It was their most successful performance to date.

———

*E*ven on the road, a dull, muted sameness pervaded their days. The girls ate the same meals when they ate at all: sardines on graham crackers, gingersnaps, candy bars, and, during truly desperate times, dog food. They piled into the Studebaker in the same cramped order, sleeping upright on the night trips, animals tucked between limbs. They removed their makeup with the same cheap tub of Crisco, which Rose insisted was "purer" than cold cream. They listened to her daily complaints about money and why the grouch bag was skimpy. "A dime here, a quarter there," she always said. "It all adds up, you know. Next time your parents send you spending money you must keep notes on how much you spend." They abided her obsession with daily expenses: a quarter for a hat, $10 for a week's rent, shoes for $3.60, a dollar for "eats." They humored her insistence that vaudeville would survive, that "nothing will ever take the place of flesh." They felt the same flutter of panic after each performance, knowing it might be the last time they were standing behind the curtain when it fell.

They made it to Kansas City, Missouri, where they hoped to get work at some theater, any theater, even though the town hadn't put on vaudeville in months. While Louise and the Blondes struck poses, Rose regaled a local agent, Sam Middleton, with stories about their successful (and wholly fictitious) show in Mexico City, making up the details as she went along. Gorgeous theaters, she exclaimed, with revolving stages and orchestra pits that rode up and down on elevators. The Mexicans couldn't stop gaping at all that blond hair. Anyone who thought vaudeville was dead should take its temperature south of the border. "If it weren't for that terrible revolution," Rose added, "we'd be there right now." She took no notice of the *Variety* on the agent's desk, nor of what would become its most famous headline: WALL ST. LAYS AN EGG. The agent shook Rose's hand, told her he'd be in touch if anything came up.

In the meantime, they holed up in a hotel room in downtown Kansas City. A brief engagement at a nightclub called the Cuban Gardens—which was neither Cuban nor a garden, Louise noted—ended when one of its investors was shot dead over a dog-racing dispute. It was just as well, since the place was clearly disreputable, what with a master of ceremonies who called himself "Happy Vic Allen, the Kansas City Joy Boy." Louise's nineteenth birthday (sixteenth, according to Mother's math) fell on the night they closed, and with only $82 left in the grouch bag they had to cancel the customary Chinese dinner. When the agent finally called a few days later, Rose tried to sound nonchalant and didn't mention the Cuban Gardens debacle at all.

"Now here's the deal, Rose," he said, his voice so shrill Louise could hear it from across the room. "It's for a full week, right here in the city, two shows a day—"

"What is the salary?" Rose asked.

"Three hundred."

"As a personal favor to you, Sam," Rose said, struggling to keep her voice calm, "we'll take it."

The Gayety Theater was a sprawling structure on the southeast corner of 12th and Wyandotte Streets, with a gingerbread-colored brick facade and ornate white moldings outlining the windows. A lattice of steel rose from the roof, supporting a vertical string of letters, each as tall as a door: BURLESQUE, the sign read, a saucy constellation winking against the sky. Just for good measure, a canvas banner unfurled beneath the marquee:

40 GIRLS 40. BURLESQUE AS YOU LIKE IT.
40 GIRLS 40.

Rose stopped in the middle of the street. "Burlesque!" she whispered, as if the word felt lewd inside her mouth. "Sam wouldn't dare do a thing like this to us."

She stormed inside the theater, angry now. Louise understood her mother's reaction; respectable vaudevillians never stooped to burlesque unless they had to, and even then they kept the transgression to themselves. But there was no rule for what vaudevillians should do when burlesque was the only option left.

Louise and the girls waited in the lobby. Years later, when she wrote the story of how she became Gypsy Rose Lee, she crafted this memory carefully and with great detail, as if it picked up color and dimension with each recalling. She remembered the life-sized cardboard cutout of a blonde looming over everyone, the tiny triangle patch covering the area where panties should have been, the two tassels affixed to either side of her brassiere, the way a breeze from a strategically placed fan pinwheeled the fringe. She gave this performer (likely a composite sketch of several burlesque mentors) a name, TESSIE THE TASSEL TWIRLER, and made her a cornerstone of the fable her life would soon become.

Mother came huffing out, Sam following and grabbing at her arm.

"Don't touch me!" Rose said. "There are laws to protect innocent women and children against fiends like you!"

"Let's go inside and talk it over," he said.

"Never! I'd rather starve first."

Louise stepped forward and faced her mother. "Well, I wouldn't," she said. "I'm tired of starving to death. That's all we've been doing for years. We have eleven dollars after the garage and hotel bill are paid. Where can we go on that?"

"Don't say that, Louise," Rose said. She shushed at the sobbing Hollywood Blondes. "Something will turn up. It always has, and it always will."

"It already has turned up. This is it. Nothing better is ever going to turn up for us. There's no place left for us to work anymore, Mother. There is no more vaudeville."

"You gotta roll with the punches," Sam added. "There's a lot of dough to be picked up in burlesque, and what the hell, your life don't go with it."

"Yes, it does." Louise did not say these words so much as hear her lips say them, and she knew they were true without knowing why.

Chapter Twenty-one

How can we explain each other's behavior? How can we love fiercely, and yet comprehend the utter cruelty that's being piled upon us? It hurts so terribly and you feel so helpless, like a butterfly on a pin.

—JUNE HAVOC

New York City, 1943

It has been a stop-time year, all forward motion suspended, a looping refrain with no accompanying song. Every facet of Gypsy's life threads together and pulls tight to restrict her: *The Naked Genius* debacle, her health, her finances, her family, her new home, the end of her relationship with Michael Todd—after which June sends a letter, reminding her of the perils of looking back:

> I am sorry, really I am but I 'spose you have had a million people tell you that it couldn't have worked for Houdini anyway. Now what? Are you going back to the dark alley life? I hope not.

Gypsy heeds the advice and grounds herself, focusing on her home. It is the center of her life and what she hopes will center her; she is thirty-two, now, and has to think that way. She'd bought it at Mike's insistence, a 1917 New York City landmark on East 63rd Street, former property of the Vanderbilts and future property of Spike Lee, for the price of $12,500, a bargain even then.

In the parlance of realtors, the place has beautiful bones: two houses connected by a courtyard, twenty-eight rooms in all, an elevator, a Spanish Mediterranean stucco facade, an arched entryway and balcony, a garage that will soon house a silver-and-maroon Rolls-Royce monogrammed with her initials—used, of course, although she'll claim it was built especially for her. But the basement is a swamp, the elevator cables are missing, the hallways and stairs are slick with grime, the pipes are rotted through, and the old coal-fire furnace is busted beyond repair. Building materials are in short supply due to the war, and even if she cajoles stagehands into doing the work for her, renovations will be costly and drag on for years.

Nevertheless she applies for permits, gets estimates from contractors, signs off on plans to excavate the street and install a new tap in the city main. Details matter, too, and during her rare downtime she scavenges through Upper East Side antique shops. She doesn't believe in spending money on frivolous luxuries—room service, for example—but on investments, pieces that will outlast her, if not her legacy: English Regency painted armchairs, a papier-mâché-and-pearl worktable, bunches of antique glass grapes. For the grand foyer she plans an intricate scrollwork design done entirely in gold leaf, the initials "G.R.L." etched on every door. Picassos and Vertes along the walls, a miniature kitchen in her bedroom, and a professionally painted mural in the dining room—angels lolling on woolly clouds, tufted across the walls and ceiling. She pawns an iron dolphin in exchange for a Victorian bed, and reminds the work crews to preserve the contents of her refrigerator before cutting the electricity. "Of course it goes without saying," Gypsy instructs, "how vitally important it is that food be kept in good condition to prevent any waste."

The requests for money have never stopped and never will; it wouldn't be her family, otherwise. "We know how well we're doing," Gypsy says, speaking for herself and June, "by the number of fan letters we get from needy relatives." Big Lady and Aunt Belle have stacks of unpaid bills, emergency operations, a dossier with the Seattle Welfare Department. Gypsy receives a notice in the mail:

> Dear Miss Hovick, we normally write to the agency to have a worker interview relatives of relief recipients, but we felt that you would appreciate our contacting you personally. A minimum budget of $36.75 per month would be sufficient to keep your relatives off the relief rolls.

The emotional demands are just as exacting, what with the family's constant complaints about Rose's behavior during impromptu visits out west. She was an "insane person," Aunt Belle recalls, stinking drunk, shaking her fists and kicking and bellowing, and it took two people to hold her down and carry her away. "I'd rather put a gun to my head, Louise," Belle says, "than die a slow death trying to live with her." Before leaving the state, Rose ran up more than $100 on Big Lady's credit at the drug and grocery stores. If Gypsy could send just enough to cover those bills, they'd be forever grateful. Gypsy does, although she can guess what the pair will later say in letters to Rose. "I can't imagine why Louise treats you so mean," Big Lady sympathizes with her daughter. "She will find out later that her Mother is her very best and only real friend."

Despite the cadence of their relationship—the whiplash back and forth, the hysteria, the silence, the withdraws and withdrawals—Big Lady is right. Gypsy might have taken to her bed in "a total state of heartache" after the breakup with Mike, but Mother is the love of her life. "They loved each other," June said. "Madly." Theirs is a primal connection that Gypsy is incapable of severing, parallel to love and just as deep but rotten at its root. It is a swooning, fun-house version of love, love concerned with appearances rather than intent, love both deprived and depraved, love that has to glimpse its distorted reflection in the mirror in order to exist at all.

It is why Gypsy acquiesces when Rose asks for a farmhouse on the Hudson River to share with her girlfriend. "Louise dear," she writes, "I

don't ask much of you darling. . . . A beautiful all renevated [*sic*] painted
8 room house. A pipeless heater burns anything—wood, coal, or bodies. Please don't use that last statement for press."

It is why Gypsy forgives her when Rose arrives at domestic relations
court in a chauffeur-driven limousine, her petite frame lost under a
mink coat and piles of jewels, to accuse Gypsy of stopping her allowance. It isn't about the money, Gypsy knows, but about touching
her daughter's life with the heaviest hand she has, about bad attention
being better than no attention at all—the same sort of attention she
herself sought at the *Pal Joey* premiere, when the spotlight was meant
only for June.

It is why Gypsy looks past her lunatic behavior out in California, the
inappropriate pleas to Michael Todd for help ("he loves *his* mother,"
Rose says pointedly), the threats of resurrecting pieces of those dark
alley days: "My life with you," Rose writes,

> was anything but a happy one. Things you made me go through and
> endure in regards to all your stepping stones to your getting where
> you were interested in getting at any cost must now be told to your
> faithful public that do not know you at all.

Now, when Rose suffers serious injuries in a car accident, it is why
Gypsy forgets everything that came before and yanks her mother close,
even lets her see her fear. She confides in Rose about her own bad
health, the pending operation to remove "every tooth in my head," the
duodenal ulcer that makes her vomit blood. She shares her disappointment about *The Naked Genius,* knits Rose a sweater, advises her to "be
brave and try to rise above the pain."

When she decides to leave for Hollywood—just one movie, this
time, and under her proper name—she gives her mother a sincere
good-bye, one that signals they will talk again, sooner rather than later.
"This isn't a pleasure trip for me," Gypsy writes.

> I'm on a job, I will have no time to entertain anyone. You have the
> farm, and gawd knows I could scarcely afford to see that you kept it.

Now you must try and work out some happiness for yourself. I have a tough job ahead of me, it isn't a cinch at my age to start all over, but that is what I am trying to do.

Gypsy has two tasks in mind but keeps quiet about the second, a secret plot that blooms sweetly inside her mind—a plan to change her life for good and, hopefully, for the better, a plan even Mother will understand.

Chapter Twenty-two

Viewed in retrospect, after the sobering years which
have intervened, the dead-pan thrill-seeking of the
self-styled "lost generation," the senseless cavortings
of "flaming youth," the determined squandering and
guzzling and wenching of the newly rich, combine to
form a lurid picture of a race of monsters outrageously
at play.

—POLLY ADLER, NEW YORK'S PREEMINENT MADAM

New York City, 1928–1930

Just like that, from one year to the next, it changed. The National Winter Garden was no longer a haven for slummers, the ironic last stop
after a night that would soon and best be forgotten, but a premiere destination, the place where things began.

On the first night of the new season, Morton and Herbert Minsky
stood in the lobby, waiting for the clock to strike eight. Riotous bouquets of flowers sweetened the air, and a floral horseshoe made of
roses bowed over the brothers' heads. Together they watched the luminaries arrive, counting them the way brother Billy counted money.
There were the members of the Algonquin Round Table: Robert

Mayor Jimmy Walker with his mistress, Betty Compton.

Benchley and Heywood Broun, Alexander Woollcott and Harold Ross, Marc Connelly and George and Beatrice Kaufman. Dorothy Parker, party hopping in Paris with Ernest Hemingway, just missed the occasion, unfortunately; the woman knew how to make a grand entrance. Tiny and fragile but fierce, not quite five feet tall, wearing all black and an embroidered hat too large for her head, dark brown hair tucked primly underneath, she'd inquire, "What fresh hell is this?" when the door swung open to let her inside.

Next came Walter Winchell and opera legend Feodor Chaliapin, actress Mary Pickford and critic Brooks Atkinson, publisher Condé Nast and *Vanity Fair* editor Frank Crowninshield, artist Reginald Marsh and writer Edmund Wilson (who lamented the National Winter Garden's newfound respectability), financier Otto Kahn and poet Hart Crane, who, in "The Bridge," his epic celebration of New York, devoted a passage to his favorite house of burlesque:

> *Outspoken buttocks in pink beads*
> *Invite the necessary cloudy clinch*
> *Of bandy eyes . . . no extra mufflings here:*
> *The world's one flagrant, sweating cinch*
> *And while legs awaken salads in the brain*
> *Lead to ecstatic nights of passion elsewhere as*
> *You pick your blonde out neatly through the smoke.*
> *Always you wait for someone else though, always*
> *(Then rush the nearest exit through the smoke.)*

Last but not least, in sauntered Mayor James J. Walker, pointing a greeting at the Minskys with a walking stick, his showgirl mistress, Betty Compton, on his arm. Everyone raised a glass to toast "Beau Jimmy," the "Night Mayor," the "Jazz Mayor," favorite son of Tammany Hall, a Democrat's Democrat and a New Yorker's New Yorker, as ambitious and clever and flawed as the city that raised him. They thudded Walker's bony back as he strolled to his seat, stretched to pump his little hand, tossed admiring questions and unstinting praise. Look at that suit—his entire wardrobe was custom-made: a hundred ties with a hundred matching handkerchiefs, dozens of pairs of two-toned shoes, an entire closetful of spats. Did he really plan to slip an illuminated wrist-watch upon the Statue of Liberty's upraised arm? Would he throw his perfect first pitch at the Yankees, Giants, or Dodgers game? Which first night on Broadway had he enjoyed most—Noël Coward in *The Vortex*, Humphrey Bogart in *The Cradle Snatchers*, George S. Kaufman's *Strike Up the Band*? What other mayor would activate the siren of his limousine so he could scythe through Times Square traffic? Who else could speak cordially with Governor Roosevelt one minute and underworld kingpin Arnold Rothstein the next? How brazen that he called the gangster Owney Madden's nightclub, the Central Park Casino, "Jimmy Walker's Versailles," and how apt that he was more productive there than at City Hall. When were he and Betty taking their next romantic rendezvous to Florida? Oh, and how they loved Walker's retort when Congressman Fiorello La Guardia attacked him for raising his own salary by $15,000. "Why, that's cheap!" the mayor said. "Think what it would cost if I worked full-time!"

He belonged to them and to this time, not only a product of the era but its living expression, and nothing in his insouciant grin or jaunty, wing-tipped lope suggested it wouldn't last.

For some National Winter Garden regulars, especially the ever-evolving membership of the Algonquin Round Table, the night could end only at Polly Adler's place, New York's finest brothel. Madam Polly modeled her house—not a home, she always clarified—after the long-defunct Everleigh Club of Chicago. Aside from the traditional whore-house decor—gilded mirrors and oil nudes, Louis Quinze competing with Louis Seize—Madam Polly had a few signature pieces, including a Chinese Room where guests could play mah-jongg, a bar built to resemble the recently excavated King Tut's tomb, and a library stocked with classic and contemporary works, compliments of Dorothy Parker and Robert Benchley, two of her most devoted patrons. The late-night revelers sipped champagne and traded tales of Minsky antics: the obscenity trial the brothers treated like an opening night, inviting Lady Astor and Mrs. Charles Dana Gibson to sit in the front row; the time Billy Minsky ordered a chorus girl to drink a vial of poison—the real thing, it was said—in homage to Rudolph Valentino's death; and the bevy of "horizontal coochers," whose onstage gyrations would make even Madam Polly's courtesans blush.

———

$\mathcal{B}$ut such success fostered distrust and resentment among the brothers. The rift happened slowly, imperceptibly, a fault line sliding by inches until the halves no longer met. One day Abe woke up and would not speak to Billy. He forbade his wife, two children, and extended family to mention Billy's name in his presence.

Fine, Billy thought. If that was how Abe wanted to behave, he wouldn't stop him. His work schedule didn't leave him with any time to care.

It was jealousy, of course—it couldn't be easy for Abe to realize he was no longer the brains behind the Minsky empire, the family wunderkind. For all of the apocryphal stories about the invention of striptease, Billy truly was marking new territory. He believed that the way a slinger shed her clothing mattered, that the means to the end should be as enticing as the end itself. What he offered was an art form, one as vital and uniquely American as baseball and jazz, not a mere naked bump and grind but characters, *honed* characters, each with a personal history, all of them capable of telling stories rawer and more intimate than anything offered on Broadway.

Each new girl who entered the industry now did so with a challenge: find someone to be and then become her, never once looking back. The savvier stripteasers developed personalities that had nothing to do with who they once were, filling in their pasts with high adventures and charming lies, all the glorious or sardonic reasons why their names belonged in lights. And each girl understood, as well as Billy himself, that the encore should end only when she had nothing left to strip. These days, when shocking behavior rose in inverse proportion to one's ability to be shocked, patrons could not live by stylized routines and imaginative pedigrees alone.

It didn't matter if John Sumner was tucked away in the back row, that silly whistle hovering at his lips. Everything the reformers did, or were thought to have done, ended up being a boon for burlesque: the spectacular, fictitious raid at the National Winter Garden; the real raids at the National Winter Garden; the occasional restriction Sumner and his vice goons managed to coax from elected officials.

Shuttered theaters reopened to sellout crowds. Police who made the arrests skipped the court proceedings, thanks, in part, to the Minskys' generous "presents" to certain members of the force. And the city, by and large, had little use for Sumner and his squad of self-appointed moralists. New Yorkers did not tolerate the spineless or prudish, let alone limits on popular culture from those ill equipped to judge it. The only true crimes were poverty and earnestness, the need to believe in a world beyond the immediate and ephemeral, past the next drink or joke or thrill. New York glided along the glib, shiny surface of things, the rest of the country following closely behind, all content to ignore the growing rot beneath.

Billy Minsky was at the head of the pack, tending to ambition as if it alone kept him alive, surging blood through his veins and propelling the pulse of his heart. He never listened to Morton, who still spoke of their dear, now-departed mother in the present tense: "Remember what Mama says, Billy," his little brother warned. "A wise man does not put his head into a tiger's mouth to prove the tiger roars." Billy still dreamt of Broadway, determined to prove that his failure at the Park Music Hall was an aberration. His weekly windfall from Minsky's Apollo went directly into the stock market.

Billy wasn't alone in his orgy of speculation; investing had become a national sport. Everyone from the barber to the street conductor to the mailman boasted about being "in the market"—called the "Hoover market" when particularly bullish—and even those safe on the sidelines kept a daily tally of its dizzying surges and temporary plummets. Everyone had a friend-of-a-friend story detailing a lucky take. Brokerage offices sprang up around the country. Most outfits had direct wire connections to New York and appeared outwardly respectable. Others, called "bucket shops" and "boiler factories," operated out of vacant storefronts or hotel suites. Confidence men barked into rented telephones, convincing one sucker after another to invest in unknown, unlisted, and nonexistent securities.

During the third weekend of October 1929, brokers sent out thousands of margin calls. Some customers responded but many didn't or couldn't, and their holdings were dumped on the market. Panicky investors decided to get out while they still could. Billy Minsky was not one of them. "Any day now," he told Morton, "I'm going to sell my holdings out, make a killing, and start the theater." He trusted his sense of timing, and it pulled him back, counseled him to wait.

His mistake was apparent on Monday, when 6 million shares were sold. Six million more on Tuesday, 8 million on Wednesday, prices in wild free fall. *The New York Times* index lost fifteen to twenty points each day. The tickers ran two hours behind. On October 24, what would become known as Black Thursday, United States Steel, General Electric, and RCA all dropped by dozens of points before noon. No one believed the soothing dispatches from Washington and New York about the "fundamental soundness" of the market and the economy. In the span of two months, from the peak of the bull market in September 1929 to October's crash, more than $32 billion worth of equities simply disappeared, Billy Minsky's entire personal fortune included.

He had just turned forty-one years old, and had every reason to believe this was the worst thing that would ever happen to him.

Chapter Twenty-three

I only fucked Gypsy Rose Lee once.

—OTTO PREMINGER

Hollywood and New York City, 1944

She knows him when she sees him. It isn't his looks, although he is not unhandsome. He has a perfect smooth oval head and jewel blue eyes so deeply set they seem to await excavation. His lips purse in a permanent half smile that never bares teeth, an expression that both mocks and charms. He has a presence that makes an empty room feel unbearably crowded and a voice that slaps the air: "You always louse things up, don't you? Lousing things up and getting in the way is your particular specialty, isn't it?" He is a terror, a tyrant, and a talent—in short, perfect. Technically she's still married to Bill Kirkland, but he is hardly the man for this job. As she told her sister years ago, "I'm going to have a baby someday, June, but I'm not going to just have a baby. I am going to pick the toughest, meanest son of a bitch I can find, somebody who's ruthless, and my child will rule the world."

Before she knows him she knows of him; Otto Preminger was a theater actor and director in his native Austria. He immigrated to America and is now in preproduction of his noir masterpiece, *Laura*, while Gypsy is filming *Belle of the Yukon*, a Western musical set in the days of the Alaskan Gold Rush. She plays Belle de Valle, a vampy, world-weary showgirl, and looks glorious in every shot: a young Big Lady with a scooped-out waist and legs so long she has her stockings specially made, or so she claims. But on film she appears strangely unable to move, as if her corset stretches the length of her body, and her delivery—that odd, imperious lilt that works so well onstage—stunts even her best comedic lines. "The best thing's to get mad," she says, when asked what heals a broken heart. "Break something. Over the guy's head, if possible." No chance of critical acclaim, she knows, but at least she's billed as Gypsy Rose Lee. She is here on her terms, and ready to set her plan in motion.

Like Michael Todd, Otto is married, but, unlike Mike, he has an arrangement with his wife, Marion, a would-be actress who shares many traits with Gypsy: long legs, glossy dark hair, more ambition than talent, and a penchant for reimagining her past. She transformed her impoverished family into nobility and gave herself a title: the "Hungarian Baroness." As long as Otto dutifully plays host for her parties and promises not to seek a divorce, he is free to do as he wishes.

But Gypsy, unlike Otto's previous conquests, has no interest in his "delectable Viennese manner" or his belief that "sexual pleasure belonged to him" or his (somewhat contradictory) renown as a "good lover." One night, during a party at the home of studio executive William Goetz, Gypsy approaches Otto. She speaks about art and literature and her historic mansion in Manhattan. She spins funny stories about her mother, knowing that Rose, too, has a reputation that precedes her. She brings him home just once, because once is all it will take and she is nothing if not economical. When she leaves Hollywood she does not bother to say good-bye.

She knows that the baby, be it a boy or a girl, will be flecked with little bits of Mother, that Rose Hovick is too potent to be diluted in just one generation. Once again it's time to carve some space away from Rose; Gypsy wants her style of mothering to be entirely her own. She can't tell Rose the news, since saying the words aloud will extend an invitation she can't rescind. Surely Mother will hear anyway from Belle and Big Lady, the latter of whom makes a joke that can be considered witty only in their family: "Louise dear," she writes, "please have a boy. HA HA."

In September, Gypsy sequesters herself in Reno, Nevada, where she finally files for divorce from Bill Kirkland. It takes just over a month for the split to be official. He knows as well as she does the value of maintaining a facade, and agrees to play her game.

"People here ask when the baby's coming," he writes, "and I say Dec. or Jan. and try to look like a proud papa, without talking like one . . . be a good fat girl and get lots of sleep and rest so that everything will be fine and dandy."

June plans a baby shower, inviting twenty of Gypsy's friends, who bring a bassinet, blankets, knitted sweaters with pockets the size of a fingertip. "The cake and tea were good, but not worth the price of admission," Gypsy notes. "Only one or two of the presents are bankable, in case the baby is anything like his grandmother."

By chance Otto Preminger travels to New York in December and calls Gypsy, curious to know why she departed so abruptly. He discovers she is at Woman's Hospital at 110 Street and Amsterdam Avenue, waiting to give birth to his child. She does, prematurely, on December 11. Her son weighs just five and a half pounds and she names him Erik, using the traditional Norwegian spelling; Daddy Jack and his family will be proud. Otto appears by her bedside. "I can support my son myself," she tells him. "I want to bring him up to be my son only." She asks that he keep his paternity a secret, and he agrees.

A radio newscast informs Rose Hovick that she has a grandson. She calls the hospital at once, and the operator refuses to connect her to Gypsy's room. She calls again, to no avail. She weeps and scribbles in her diary: "O please God help her to forget the foolish past and let me be with her again. I am so lonesome to hug and kiss her I am starving to death inside." She tries a third time. Gypsy accepts this call and tells her mother she can see the baby, but only through glass.

Rose arrives at Woman's Hospital and is led to the maternity ward. She waits, pacing, kneading the hem of her fur coat. Gypsy stays in bed where her mother can't see her and imagines the scene, the nurse holding Erik up to the window, close enough for his quarter-sized heel to tap the pane. Mother will see his red-brown hair and long, restless legs and be struck by the resemblance. She will press her palm against the glass and align her skin with his, making contact without touching. He looks just like little Louise, the child whose earliest memory is disappointing her own mother, and Gypsy is grateful for the divide.

Rose Louise Hovick, shortly before becoming Gypsy Rose Lee.

Chapter Twenty-four

I'm really a little prudish, which people may think incongruous. I'm not as broadminded as I sound, with my
boisterous way of talking. I'm not easily shook, but I do
take a prudish point of view on certain films, books,
and trends. Then, I pull myself up short and ask myself
how Gypsy Rose Lee could possibly be this way.

—GYPSY ROSE LEE

On the Burlesque Circuit, 1930–1931

And so here she was, still living with her mother, still a virgin—not even
past her first kiss, at that—learning what had taken the place of vaudeville, the only life she'd ever known. She couldn't yet decide what to
make of the lesson. It wasn't just the dressing room at the Gayety: cigarette butts and greasy towels and body makeup sluiced across the floor,
gnats swarming half-full glasses of warm beer, a sink clogged with dirty
underwear, rhinestones glinting in all directions like pairs of beady eyes.
It wasn't just "Tessie the Tassel Twirler," older and softer and kinder,
somehow, than Louise expected, telling her she "got a certain class about
yourself, in a screwball kind of way. You just got to learn to handle it."
Nor was it the acts: a showgirl dressed in an octopus costume complete
with roving black tentacles, shaking like a wet dog; another emerging

from a seashell, wholly naked save for a strand of faux pearls; Tessie's own rare talent—shared by a famous stripteaser named Carrie Finnell—to make her bare breasts rotate, one at a time, with no other movement or effort at all. It was the realization that she'd found a secret slit in the curtain, one that led far past backstage to another universe altogether, at once spectacular and foul and terrifying, made all the more so by the silent, shameful feeling that she could belong here.

The burlesque folk recognized it, and recognized it inside her, and nudged Louise along in ways both sly and bold. "The quicker you forget what you used to be," Tessie told her, "the better off you'll be. Start thinkin' about what you're goin' to be tomorrow—not what you were yesterday."

For the moment, at least, Louise was still the head of the Hollywood Blondes, the act meant to deter the cops from raids and shutdowns—"a troupe a silly virgins," as Tessie called them. Rose's scorn for burlesque lasted "all of five minutes," according to June. "As long as it brought in the money, she didn't care." The Hollywood Blondes began rehearsing their same old routines, while Sam the agent assured the manager that the girls looked much better with proper lighting and full makeup and short costumes. The manager seemed unconvinced, until one day he took a long look at Louise and asked if the "big one could talk." He was short of talking women, he explained, and Tessie refused to do comedic scenes.

The next thing Louise knew, she was wearing a hula skirt that parted in the front, two frothy bits of fabric over her breasts, a bright red jewel in her navel, and strappy gold high heels—a marked difference from the Hollywood Blondes' customary bobby socks and Mary Janes, and she'd never realized her legs were so long. It came to her that she resembled Big Lady when her grandmother was still young and ravishing, before she missed her chance to flee Seattle for good.

"For a kid, you got a lot of sex in your walk," Tessie said with genuine admiration, and shoved Louise through the slit in the curtain, back to the other side.

"You *are* real!" the comic cried when he spotted her. "You're not an illusion—"

From somewhere in the dark her mother hissed: "Louise! Hold in your stomach!"

She took a deep breath. "I'm real," she murmured, in a voice she'd never heard before. "I'm no illusion—here take my hand, touch me—feel me . . ."

━━━━━

*R*ose Louise and the Hollywood Blondes signed on for a month at the Gayety Theater, all of them—dogs and Porky the Pig and Woolly Face the monkey included—staying at a nearby hotel. They were making $250 a week (about $35 each) in Kansas City, and at the best New York houses—Minsky's National Winter Garden, Minsky's Apollo, and Irving Place—a bottom-billing girl could earn $70 to $125. A lot of big stars worked in burlesque, Rose reasoned, and "it all came under the heading of experience." Mother looked at her differently now, Louise noticed, as if she were one of the forlorn Christmas trees dragged on the train during their vaudeville days—an inferior but acceptable facsimile of the real thing, a place to hang Rose's flickering wishes and filmy dreams until every branch was covered, and no one could tell the difference.

More than a year, now, since June's escape, and Mother had yet to mention her.

In addition to her act with the Blondes, Louise took part in several comedic sketches opposite the straight man, reciting lines like "Meet me round the corner in half an hour" and "Quick, hide, my husband." She found ways to make the jokes funnier than they were, holding the ends of certain words to stretch them out, winking at herself as much as at the audience. In some strange, removed way, she felt as if she were acting.

She knew it wasn't talent, but who needed talent? What did talent get June but broken bones and a broken spirit and a broken life, out there somewhere doing God knows what? Mother was right when she said there was no substitute for flesh, but the axiom applied to burlesque, not vaudeville. Vaudeville, with its sense of sunny, mindless optimism, no longer spoke to the country's mood. Burlesque did, loudly and directly.

The Depression affected female workers to the same degree as men, and thousands of them, out of work and other ideas, applied at burlesque houses across the country: former stenographers and seamstresses and clerks, wives whose husbands had lost their jobs, mothers with children to support, vaudevillians who finally acknowledged the end of the line. Compared to other forms of show business—compared to *any* business—burlesque enjoyed a low rate of unemployment, and 75 percent of performers had no stage experience at all. Pretty girls were finally available at burlesque wages, and the supply equaled the demand.

Burlesque houses from Chicago to Missouri to New York City employed a standard routine. Each applicant endured an interview conducted by the senior chorus girl, who called herself "the Captain." Her first question—"Will you pose?"—was essentially an order: a girl should strip as bare as the boss demanded. Don't worry about the audience, the Captain assured, because no one would be permitted to touch her. "Dance hall girls get handled by those bums," she added. "There's no monkey business in this show." She called the boss over to assess a girl's face, but she herself examined figures: disrobe, she ordered, and turn around, slowly, pausing left, right, back. The women found kinship with the desperate men who came to watch them, performer and spectator equally naked.

Burlesque, like vaudeville, had its own language and rules, an accidental subculture forged by people who never intended to dwell there. For Louise it was as easy as memorizing passages from *Das Kapital* or *Remembrance of Things Past* during those long train rides and layoffs in dreary hotels. She learned that a "skull" is a double-take, delivered by a leering comic, and that G-strings might have been named for the lowest string on a violin. A provocative stripteaser was known as the "snake type," and a voluptuous body was a "swell set-up." When a drummer made a rim shot during a striptease number, he was "catching the bumps." If a girl pulled her G-string aside or discarded it altogether, she was "flashing her knish."

Louise listened to the incessant, cheerful spiels of the candy butchers and marveled at the Gayety's runway, the first she had ever seen. She learned it was taboo to watch other strippers' acts from the wings; everyone worried about rivals copying routines and stealing gimmicks. "If you were caught watching in the wings," one stripper warned, "you got a bloody nose." Backstage, she saw girls rouge their nipples so they turned deep red under the blue spotlights. She encountered the young Jerry Lewis, tagging along with his comedian father and somehow sneaking backstage. "Oh, I like that," the kid said, ogling the naked slingers and scampering from dressing room to dressing room until his father found him. "Jerrrryyy," Dan Lewis called, yanking his son's arm. "Let's go." She listened to the performers lament where they were and boast about where they belonged: in New York, under the direction of the one and only Billy Minsky, the best in the business—on any given night he might be sitting in the audience, waiting to discover them.

She met the "G-string buyer" who offered each girl $5 for her garment; neither he nor his customers were interested unless they were used. She learned how backstage morals varied with time, place, and people. Sometimes the stripteasers and chorines were churchgoing and chaste, but more often prostitution thrived at the stage door. Some of the girls suffered multiple scars from surgeries to remove genital warts, and applied homemade tonics and potions to dull the symptoms of syphilis. Proper treatment for the disease required repeated shots of arsenic compounds alternated with shots of bismuth to reduce the chance of toxic reaction, weekly appointments for more than a year, an ordeal that could cost as much as $1,000. If a girl couldn't afford a complete regimen, she skipped appointments and soon suffered a relapse.

Louise came to understand the bartering system, both crude and intricate, internal and external, that allowed someone to take off her clothes for a living. By prescribing explicit rules and regulations of undress and behavior, the censors actually helped those who were inclined to push the limits; anything that wasn't expressly forbidden was, in effect, sanctioned. The girls knew this, and also that more of their unemployed sisters would be joining burlesque each day. Increased numbers meant fiercer competition, and fiercer competition bullied them into going further than they might otherwise have dared.

Louise realized that the men, too, were familiar with the system, and came to the theaters fully prepared for the "early-bird acts," women kissing their own breasts and crouching on the runway, low down and close enough to touch. When the lights dimmed they pulled a milk bottle from their jacket, stuffed a slab of liver inside, and undid their zipper. As a lark, the house drummer occasionally got in on the act, asking a patron in the first row, "Am I keeping the right rhythm for you? You want me to go any faster?" Some of the more discreet customers brought newspapers to spread across their laps, the rattling progressing within minutes from timid to furious, and Louise wondered what the girls onstage were thinking while all this went on: if they indulged themselves and felt sick inside the moment, if they imagined a kind and distant place, or if they somehow willed their minds to remain empty of all things.

On February 21, 1930, police raided the Gayety, the sergeant in charge complaining of "shocking" displays of anatomy and immoral "parties" where the revelers committed acts not fit for print. Rose, Louise, and the Blondes packed up their animals and costumes and hit the road again. They had a driver now, a friend of one of the Gayety's stagehands. Her name was Murphy and she was, in the words of the stagehand, "as big as a horse, a real good-natured slob," with the "strength of ten men." She had worked as a taxicab driver and a housepainter, and Rose adored her right away.

They ended up in Toledo, Ohio, where they had an engagement at another Gaiety Theater, same pronunciation, different spelling. Louise suggested they camp out instead of wasting money on hotel rooms, and Rose agreed. She unwound the grouch bag from her waist and paid $42.50 for a secondhand tent, a two-burner cook stove, stakes, a box of cooking equipment, and an army cot. Murphy drove the Studebaker past city limits to the most rustic spot she could find, a weedy swath of grass behind a welding shop. They brushed their teeth in a nearby trickle of water, donned flannel nightgowns, and slept in a tight line, the dogs and Porky coiled by their feet, the monkey at Louise's side.

Louise awakened a few hours later to the sound of strange footsteps.

A hobo was wandering around, crunching heavily across the frozen ground. Her mother, sleeping on the cot next to her, sprang up and stared at the slit in the tent, terrified that the man might force himself inside.

"Close the flap," she whispered. "Hurry, Louise." She tunneled a hand beneath her pillow and pulled out her gun. The dogs snarled and yanked at their leashes.

"Stop where you are!" Rose yelled. "Stop or I'll shoot!"

She fired a shot straight through the side wall of the tent, and another and another, until the small space clouded with smoke. There was a sound like bricks smashing, and then a heavy silence. Rose turned back to Louise with a taut, steady look, registering somewhere between an invitation and a command. With that, mother and daughter understood what must be done, and what must never be said.

As Gypsy would later tell it, her mother crawled from the tent to investigate and declared that she had murdered a cow. Rose began to cry. "A poor, defenseless cow," she sobbed. "Oh, why did I do it?"

They had to bury the body quickly, Rose said, before its owner discovered what had happened.

Louise lifted the thick slab of a head, trying not to stare at the face. She nearly fainted from the sour smell of its last escaping breath, the mottled stickiness of blood between her fingers. They dug until dawn, pushed and pulled and rolled the body into the grave, and covered it up with dirt.

"What a waste," Rose said, peering down. "We should have cut off a few steaks before we buried him."

———

With its shabby marquee and parade of lurid photographs along the sidewalk, the Gaiety in Toledo was a demotion from the one in Kansas City. The headlining show was called *Girls from the Follies*, and its producer, Ed Ryan, had descended into panic. His star, Gladys Clark, got drunk and assaulted a hotel manager in Dayton—with an inkwell, of all things. The cops threw Gladys in jail, the rest of the troupe had moved on without her, and now he was desperate for a replacement. A renowned star on the Mutual Wheel, Gladys held nothing back during her strip numbers. "When Miss Clark is showing she's just showing," as one critic put it, "walking around like a queen wondering if the tub is full."

Rose, Louise, and the Hollywood Blondes stood in the lobby, waiting for Ed Ryan to acknowledge them. "There isn't any show without her," he explained to the theater manager. "Where can you find a woman in Toledo who strips, does scenes, and plays five musical instruments?"

In that moment Louise Hovick traded in the last piece of herself, and when she opened her mouth it was Gypsy Rose Lee who spoke. She told Ed Ryan that she could fill in for his missing lead, strip scenes and all, and then she sat before her dressing room mirror and met her creation for the very first time. "I was a star," she thought. "I picked up the lip rouge and rubbed it on my mouth, then I put up my hair behind my ears and gazed at myself for a long time. I was a *star.*" She was an outline now, an exoskeleton on stark display, and she wanted to start adding texture and layers, to shade herself in.

She strolled outside to christen her creation, telling the man stringing her name up in lights that Rose Louise wasn't her name at all. She was Gypsy Rose Lee.

"I happen to be the star of this show," Gypsy said, "and you'll put up *my* name the way *I* want it put up!"

She waited until those three words dominated the marquee and then said them aloud, pleased with the feel of them on her lips, the crisp, assured sound of them as they hit the air.

For the rest of her life she'd tell numerous versions of how she made the transition, her delicate, unclean break from the past. It was Rose, and not she, who looked that producer "straight in the eye" and said her daughter would strip. "I have," Gypsy claimed, "been pushed into everything I've ever done." She had no idea how she came up with "Gypsy"; it was merely a prefix for "Rose Lee," a pseudonym to trick Grandpa Thompson from learning she was in burlesque. She acquired the nickname during her days as a kid in vaudeville, when she wore a bandanna, winter and summer, to keep her hair in place. "Rose Lee" was still too close to her mother's name, and she felt she'd earned the "Gypsy." Because of her "lush, exotic beauty" and "roaming nature," she had *always* had that nickname. Of course "Gypsy" came from her ability to read tea leaves and see the future, what else?

Put together, she liked its cadence: the exotically strange Gypsy, the languorous drum roll of Rose, the cymbal clash of Lee. It worked on many levels: Rose as verb, predicting the future, suggesting ascension; and Rose as noun, the name of her mother, the most stubborn bond to her past. It was a headliner's name, a name that stood on its own, and she no longer needed the Hollywood Blondes. She didn't need anyone, except for the man who would discover her.

━━━━━

For her very first strip she wore a costume she'd made that afternoon, pinned instead of sewed. It had sheer lavender netting with violet buds for the bodice and a full skirt she lifted primly as she pushed through the curtain, as if she were a proper Victorian lady alighting from her carriage. The orchestra launched into "Little Gypsy Sweetheart" and she strolled across the stage, taking her time, just like Tessie and Flossie and the Octopus Girl, hearing her mother's voice beneath the song ("Smile, dear! Hold your stomach in!"), feeling the spotlight's searing focus on her face. One by one she pulled the pins from her side and dropped them into the tuba below. *Plink, plink, plink.* A collective low murmur from the audience; they'd never seen such a trick. Backing up, sweating now, her arms slick, beads sluicing down her back and stinging her eyes, she dropped her shoulder straps and let the lavender netting fall, exposing herself for an interminable second until the curtain swallowed her whole.

For the second number she changed into another homemade costume, sheer red netting festooned with three blooming cotton roses. With prop in hand—a powder puff on a stick, just like the one June used as a kid—she flitted about the audience, talk-singing an old turn-of-the-century whorehouse ditty she learned in Kansas City:

> *Oh, won't you powder my back every morning?*
> *'Cause, honey, there's no one can do it like you.*
> *Oh, won't you powder my back every morning?*

It makes me feel happy when I'm feeling blue.
And if you powder my back every morning,
Then maybe some morning I'll do it for you!

She found a bald man, picked up the lone thatch of hair threading across his pate, and tied a red ribbon around it. Yanking at his coat lapels, she ordered, "Now stand up and show them how pretty you look." When he sank down further, she pulled harder. "But darling," she protested, "I want them to see how pretty you look!" She bent and kissed the man's head, fleeing back to the stage while the applause swelled behind her. "They would always be so embarrassed," she said of her baldheaded targets. "And I was always so panicky, so very panicky."

And that's the way she told the story of her first year in burlesque, the time between Kansas City and New York, before Gypsy Rose Lee filled her up entirely and for good. She merely lifted her skirt, dropped her netting, let a strap slide from her shoulder. "Well," she said, "the shoulder strap led to one thing and another, if you know what I mean, and that's how I started the strip business." It was beneath her to attach details to that "one thing and another," disrespectful to include such memories in her scrapbooks, sacrilege to admit that the singular, legendary Gypsy Rose Lee had begun just like everyone else.

Others, over time, would pick at the thick, vague knot of that missing year. "She was never an ingenue," June said. "She was never 'the ingenue.' And she never just dropped a shoulder strap. Ever." Gypsy's own son wondered about what she had done and seen before she became herself. "There is a year my mother doesn't talk about," he said. "It's blanked out. I'm sure that it was not an easy year . . . there were rough girls, gangsters, prostitution. They had to eat. And she was perhaps forced to do things against her will." But with the aid of time and distance Gypsy Rose Lee could give herself a backstory, adding and subtracting and editing until the myth and the original were one and the same.

Soon after the Hollywood Blondes disbanded and she and Rose set out on their own, Gypsy heard from her long-lost sister. June had just finished a marathon dance in Revere, Massachusetts, and discovered Gypsy was performing nearby. She called the theater and told Gypsy she was on her way.

"Well, don't stay," Gypsy replied. "I don't want you to see the show."

Not enough time had passed for Gypsy to establish the distinction between herself and her creation. She was still lost in the ugly tangle of those murky nights, strange hands touching her, low voices giving orders that dulled her mind.

"Well, my goodness," June said. "Why not?" And she meant it.

June believed that her sister, her clever, brilliant sister—the voracious reader, the haughty Duchess, the greedy collector of lush dreams and exotic words—could somehow get away with being *in* burlesque without being *of* burlesque, without doing any of its dirty work. Maybe Louise just walked out and posed onstage as she often had in vaudeville, making a beautiful picture, the Doll Girl, or a funny one, the Bowery Tough. Maybe she did just drop a shoulder strap, peel off a glove, spin so that her skirt bloomed around her.

Settled in the back row, waiting for her sister to appear, June heard a rustling noise. She turned and a man bent down, leveling his head with hers. "Would you like a cup of coffee?" he asked, each word a rank hiss of breath. She shook her head no and turned away, waiting for the sound of receding footsteps.

Then it came to her: My god, she thought. That was code. He thinks I'm a prostitute, just for being in this theater.

And then Louise stepped out from behind the curtain and she wasn't . . . Louise. June didn't know *who* this girl was, stark naked, thrusting her hips, crouching on the runway, her silhouette stained by sallow light. She watched for as long as her eyes would let her. "I couldn't stand it," June said. "I didn't even go backstage afterwards. I was in horror."

Gypsy watched her leave and thought, How dare June judge her? What does she know, where has she been? What does her marathon audience bring in with them? Picnic baskets, most likely, so they can munch while watching a bunch of rejects have sex standing up and keel over from exhaustion. Her audience was no scabbier or sicker than June's, and one day someone who mattered would be in the front row. Poor naïve June probably didn't even understand the sound of all those rattling newspapers.

June stayed long enough to watch Louise leave too, waiting for the slow, bedraggled scat singing of "Minnie the Moocher" to stop, hiding in the alleyway's shadows. She heard shouting, something about costumes, and then saw bodies tumbling out a side door. There was Mother, furious, indignant, dragging spangled bits of clothing onto the sidewalk and stuffing them, unpacked, into an idling taxi. Louise stood nearby, hugging herself, wearing only a pair of glittering heels. She didn't move until Mother dropped a coat around her shoulders and led her, gently, into the backseat.

——————

*G*ypsy seized control of what she could—her weight, for one. She ate only one meal a day, but every few hours she sipped a vegetable "essence" of her own invention:

three bunches of carrots
six onions
six tomatoes
one bunch of parsley
two bunches of celery
two quarts of water
no seasoning
Simmer for twenty minutes. Pour off the juice, chill it and drink.

It worked. She was still no bombshell; her breasts were small and her rear pear-shaped, but her waist was tiny and her legs epic, two pillars astride the entrance to some secret, exclusive city. Five feet nine and a half inches and 130 well-distributed pounds. Rose delighted in her daughter's new shape and image and name; they were true partners and equals now, complicit in both what had already happened and what was yet to come. In preparation for new press photos, Mother fluffed Gypsy's hair into a soft auburn cloud and painted delicate teardrops in a cascade down her cheeks. She also sent Gypsy flowers each night over the footlights, addressing the cards to "The Fairest of Them All," "My Queen," "Stageland's Loveliest," and "The One and Only Gypsy." She signed them from "a secret admirer." When Gypsy discovered her mother writing one of the cards, she was mortified.

"You should have told me," she said. "It makes me feel like a fool—and unless you want to wind up in jail you'd better stop writing those letters, too. There's a law against that."

"Law?" Rose asked. "Don't make me laugh. A mother's love knows no law!"

Some of the venues were almost respectable, nudging the limits of obscenity statutes without breaking them, and in those places Gypsy felt safe leaving the stage to interact with the audience. At the Latchia Theatre in Cincinnati, she sashayed up to a man in the front row and "gave him a lesson in the art of kissing," in the words of the local newspaper, "such as only a red-haired lady knows how to do." She sewed a few more costumes for her wardrobe, a set of pink pajamas and a dark blue bathing suit among them, and proved a natural at speaking to the press.

"You'd ought to read some of the funny letters I get from fellers who think because I ogle at them from the stage that I have a crush on them," she said. "I received a letter from a drugstore clerk once who enclosed a stick of gum in the letter just to show he wasn't a cheap guy. He promised to buy me a whole box if I would go out with him. Then I received an invitation to go riding from a parachute jumper who enclosed various pictures of himself taken in various poses while he was clinging to a parachute."

Every night, she and Rose huddled together in their hotel room and helped themselves to June's history, appropriating and editing her scrapbooks until they fit the story of Gypsy as a born talent and star. It was she who had been called "Baby June," who had headlined the Orpheum Circuit, who had ventured out to Hollywood to star in pictures with Douglas Fairbanks and Charlie Chaplin. When Gigolo died she had vowed never again to take anything that didn't belong to her, but Louise had made that pact, not Gypsy Rose Lee.

On March 19, 1931, a Thursday night, she performed in a revue at the Empire Theatre in Newark, New Jersey. Called *Wine, Women, and Song,* it was one of her cleaner shows by far, and even the trade magazines seemed relieved by the temporary reprieve from early-bird acts. "No filth," *Zit's Weekly* wrote appreciatively, "just great entertainment and clever performers." The press and audience alike were most enthralled by the "new find" named Gypsy Rose Lee, a "brunette of unusual face and form" with a "charming personality" and "flirty eyes."

By now she knew how to mark herself as different, how to put on as she was taking off. She played the prude who showed her skin almost by accident and always as a lark, a self-professed "daytime person living in a nighttime world." Here she came with her powder puff on a stick, walking the aisle slowly, her long, elegant neck craning left and right, settling on the winner. "Darling! Sweetheart!" she exclaimed. "Where have you been all my life?" She rushed to him, left a bright red imprint on his gleaming skull. He panicked and fled. She shook her head and *tsk-tsk*ed while she watched him go. "Lost him," she murmured, and her eyes swept over the crowd. In the smoky thick of it, chomping on a cigar fat as a baby's arm, stood a short, blocky man whose eyes pinned her down, recognizing not who she was but who he'd make her become.

Chapter Twenty-five

You can become a winner only if you are willing to walk
over the edge.

—DAMON RUNYON

New York City, 1930–1931

When America awakened from the crash its citizens had no idea what
to do with themselves. In the span of one week the blinding clamor and
deafening glare of the past eight years fell silent and dark. Every morning Billy Minsky read of another tragedy, hoping to soothe the sting of
his own. The founder of a coal firm in Providence, Rhode Island, shot
himself in his broker's office while watching the ticker. The president
of the Rochester Gas and Electric Corporation, who lost $1.2 million in
a single month, locked himself in his bathroom and inhaled gas from a
wall jet. The head of a major brokerage firm in St. Louis guzzled poison. A man slit the throats of his wife and seven sons before turning the
knife on himself. The owner of a wholesale produce firm jumped from
a seventh-floor window of the Munson Building on Wall Street. A
Scranton man doused himself with gasoline and struck a match. In the
Bronx, a man who lost his life savings of $30,000 leapt in front of a
Jerome Avenue subway train.

Politicians began finger-pointing and public posturing. Newly elected
New York Governor Franklin Delano Roosevelt decried the "improper

Minsky's Republic, circa 1931.

schemes and questionable methods" that had fed the crisis. Mayor Jimmy Walker urged movie executives to show pictures "that will reinstate courage and hope in the hearts of the American people." More than four hundred leaders representing every branch of industry, commerce, trade, and finance convened in Washington, D.C., to discuss President Herbert Hoover's plans to stimulate and stabilize the economy. The president himself offered one last word of advice: "work."

New York donned a stoic face and obeyed. Brokers, bankers, and clerks filed downtown even on Sundays. Restaurants kept their doors open past normal hours. Tour buses made special trips through the district, pointing out "where all that money was lost." The employees of one brokerage house, which stayed open until anywhere from ten at night to five in the morning, adopted the unusual custom of singing "The Star-Spangled Banner" before heading home, often so loudly that police came to investigate. A sixteen-year-old messenger boy for the New York Stock Exchange did a brisk business in boutonnieres, since proper brokers considered it uncouth to trade without a flower adorning their lapel, no matter the circumstances.

———

Billy Minsky, too, turned his focus toward rebuilding what was lost. He no longer had the capital to buy his own Broadway theater but he still had his investor Joseph Weinstock, who had emerged from the crash with both his bank account and his faith in Billy intact. Weinstock agreed it was time to make another run on Broadway. These days a man couldn't spare $5.50 for legitimate theater, not even if he wanted to, but for just $1.50 he could see pretty women taking off their clothes—prettier, now, than ever before; all of those aspiring actresses who once dreamt of applause on a stage were now settling for whistles along a runway. They should be grateful, Billy thought, just to have anyone, any voice, caring to call for more.

When Billy wasn't busy at the Apollo or checking on his brothers down at the National Winter Garden, he scoured the trade papers, made phone calls, and took long strolls through Times Square. It was clear, already, that the Depression was having a profound effect on

Broadway. The number of productions declined from 239 in 1929–1930 to 187 in 1930–1931, and would continue to drop throughout the decade. "By 1930," wrote one historian, "the boom that had engulfed New York for nearly 30 years was over. . . . [In] no sphere of urban life was the Depression more accurately mirrored than in Times Square, the center of its theater and entertainment world." Billy walked along 42nd Street, past the hot dog stands reeking of rubbery meat, the no-madic pitchmen unloading broken watches and rusty shears, the hobos and migrants shuffling along in a melancholy chorus line. In the lobby of the Hotel Marguery a man could turn a crank and watch a peep show of odalisques.

Billy stopped halfway in between Seventh and Eighth Avenues. Next door Noël Coward's stilted satire *Private Lives* played to a dwindling au-dience, and down the street Fred and Adele Astaire—antiquated relics from an obsolete time—pranced for rows of empty seats. If the legiti-mate houses succumbed entirely and offered themselves up, one by one, to burlesque, Billy would cheer each transformation, each step into Broadway's new and inevitable future. And this, number 209 West 42nd Street, would be the first.

Built in 1900 by Oscar Hammerstein, the Republic Theatre had been home to Broadway's longest-running production, *Abie's Irish Rose,* a sappy, sentimental tale about a nice Jewish boy who marries a Catholic girl. By the time the show closed in October 1927, it had played in New York a record 2,327 times without interruption, nearly double the pre-vious longest run of any production in America. Currently, the Repub-lic was operating as a movie house, showing shorts all day for a quarter admission.

Billy also knew that one of *Abie's Irish Rose*'s principal financiers was none other than gangster Arnold Rothstein, who, one week before the mayoral election between Jimmy Walker and Fiorello La Guardia, had been shot in the groin while leaving a card game at the Park Central Hotel.

Rothstein survived for a week in the hospital, wandering into and out of consciousness, and every time he roused the cops were hovering over his bed, shouting questions.

"Who shot you?" one detective asked.

"Got nothing to say," Rothstein whispered. "Nothing, nothing. Won't talk about it."

On election day, when Franklin D. Roosevelt narrowly beat Al Smith for governor and Jimmy Walker trounced Fiorello La Guardia for mayor, Arnold Rothstein died, his assailant still a mystery.

Billy followed the case closely; his gangster source back from his newspaper days, Beansie Rosenthal, had mentored Rothstein and initiated him into the underworld. But Billy was most interested in Jimmy Walker's reaction to the shooting. On that evening, the mayor had ventured in his chauffeured, silver-trimmed Duesenberg to a nightclub in Westchester. An associate approached and whispered the news into Walker's ear. The mayor called for his car and apologized to the bandleader for leaving so early. It was only just past midnight, but he must return to Manhattan at once.

"Arnold Rothstein has just been shot," Walker explained. "This means trouble from here on."

The mayor surely realized that any investigation into the kingpin's empire and untimely demise would lead to the door of City Hall. Throughout the mayoral campaign La Guardia had done his best to paint Walker as a puppet of Tammany Hall and an advocate of New York's underworld, to no avail; New York still yearned to believe in its mayor and all he represented, the raucous vulgarity and gleeful rapacity of the precrash days. As a son of a former Tammany politician, Billy understood the depth and force of the organization's reach, and how fiercely it would fight to maintain its grip when the wrong sorts of questions were asked; what would happen if Tammany, for once, couldn't dictate the answers? He wondered how the city might look, stripped of its familiar mores and codes, and if it would still have room for the Minskys.

━━━━━━

Billy called Joseph Weinstock, who told him that another burlesque producer, Izzy Herk, was also angling for the Republic's lease. They had no time to waste. Weinstock gathered his money, Billy called the press, and it was official: the Minskys were back on Broadway. The Republic would have a two-a-day policy, he announced, $1 admission for matinees and $1.50 for evenings.

The lease, Billy revealed with relish, was for twenty long years.

In a tacit, and—although Billy would be loath to admit it—nostalgic nod to Abe, the original family Francophile, he decided to model the Republic Theatre after the old music halls of Paris, but with upscale touches lacking at the Apollo or National Winter Garden: an intimate, plush lobby where burgundy curtains pooled on the floor; a velvet drape that circled the hot dog concession like a gilded waterfall; a complimentary gardenia corsage for the ladies; male ushers whisking about imperiously, all dressed in the ornate, braided uniforms of French gendarmes; female ushers costumed in maids' outfits with rigid black skirts and lace stockings, spritzing each patron with perfume as she led him to his seat. At Billy's behest, Herbert installed the standard red-light warning system, a precaution borne more of habit and superstition than genuine fear, and a construction crew removed a hundred seats from the auditorium. There would be not one but two illuminated runways, all the better for intimate interaction between the audience and the girls. Finally, Billy had the Republic's drab facade repainted in a sleek checkerboard pattern, onto which he pasted floor-to-ceiling, near-nude likenesses of his headlining slingers as soon as he found them.

He decided to start with some old favorites, Mae Dix and Carrie Finnell. Dix had left burlesque, briefly, to marry an undertaker and then returned after her divorce. She was bitter and therefore feistier than ever, an attitude that only improved her act. "Three years it took me to learn his business," she grumbled, "then the sonovabitch gets jealous because I'm a better embalmer than he is."

Finnell's remarkable pectoral muscles had only grown stronger and more agile, or perhaps they were aided by a new burlesque trick: fish swivels affixed to her pasties. The mechanism allowed Finnell to pinwheel her tassels in any direction, from any position, at any speed, so effortlessly that she began billing herself as the "Remote Control Girl." As she stood perfectly still, the tassel on one breast began to rotate slowly, then faster, then furiously, the other dangling limp and forgotten. One smooth, deft pop and it sprang to life, catching up with the first, the two of them propelling with such vigor she resembled a twin-engine bomber. For her grand finale, Finnell lowered herself to the ground—back first, limbo style—and even when she was fully supine both tassels spun at maximum power. "She has trained each generous bust," raved one critic, "to twitch on cue, jump to attention, and do just about everything except sing 'April Showers' in Swahili."

———————

Mayor Jimmy Walker might not have made it to his office in City Hall on the day of February 12, 1931, but that night he was among a thousand patrons congratulating Billy Minsky on the new Republic Theatre. Men in tuxedos and women in evening gowns clustered inside the lobby, praising one another's fine looks, exposing their necks for a squirt of perfume, wondering what they might expect from a production entitled *Fanny Fortsin from France,* thankful that this odd little venue, with its downtown roots and bourgeois ambition, offered a respite, no matter how brief, from what the world had become.

They watched the horizontal coochers strut to the end of the runways, spacing themselves evenly under the lights. Slowly, gently, as if preparing for bedtime, the girls lay down on their backs and then executed moves never before seen on a Broadway stage: a shimmying and grinding and thrusting of hips that evoked, equally, sexual intercourse and an epileptic seizure. It was daring and brilliant and raw, and the audience was rapt, motionless, unsure if they should laugh or applaud or try, futilely, to avert their eyes. Billy anticipated the critics' responses—the usual ho-hum complaints about the humorless comedy, the raunchiness of the stripteasers, the heavy, sea-lion waddle of the chorus girls—but his audience recognized the show for what it was: entertainment for a fair price, with the appropriate mood for a specific time; a show meant not for the Broadway of old but for the Broadway of the Depression. "The only trouble with the performances," confessed writer L. Sprague de Camp, "was that, when time came to go, standing up presented a problem."

The Republic was at full capacity every night, as many people turned away as admitted, half of them representing the city's political and cultural elite, the other half its most weary and desperate. "In the unnatural blaze of lights over Times Square marquees at eight in the morning," wrote critic Alfred Kazin, "there were already lines of men waiting outside the burlesque houses . . . people sat glued together in a strange suspension, not exactly aware of each other, but depending on each other's presence." The legitimate producers seethed, watching their rightful slice of New York invaded by swarms of the undesired and the uncouth, and Billy, at every opportunity, claimed another inch for himself.

Directly across the street, Earl Carroll presented a new edition of *Vanities,* his long-running "dazzling and superabundant revue," this time with a twist: in *Murder at the Vanities,* a young woman is killed backstage in the midst of a conventional musical. It was a curious amalgamation of comedy and mystery, with the occasional "nasty innuendo" and parade of "Minsky-ized" beauties, and Billy responded by dangling a two-story banner from the Republic's roof that read SLAUGHTER AT MINSKY'S. Earl Carroll was not amused.

Neither was George White, the esteemed producer who had discovered Ethel Merman, W. C. Fields, and the Three Stooges. White always took the same route to work, and one afternoon, Billy stood directly in his path. Billy gave him a slow, wolfy smile, unwrapping the expression as if it were a gift, a sweet, mock lament for the fact that no one was paying $5.50 to see his rusty old *Scandals,* now twelve years in the running.

The producer came at him fast and with purpose. Billy saw the flash of White's fist, his fat, pale fingers aligned like the slats of a miniature picket fence. There was a popping, shallow explosion in his head, and the absurd, horrifying feeling that his nose had collapsed against his face.

In the end he was just bloodied and swollen, no major damage done. In fact, the encounter was a gift, a New York–style rite of initiation into the big time, proof that Minsky's burlesque was finally being taken seriously not only as entertainment, but as a threat.

———

$\mathscr{B}$illy decided to celebrate by finding a new crop of slingers, girls who would elevate him even higher in the ranks of Broadway producers, girls who would make Ziegfeld want to break his legs and the Shuberts to wring his neck. He ventured ninety-nine miles south to the Trocadero Theatre in Philadelphia and took a seat, waiting through the stale comics and lumbering, thundering chorines until the emcee announced the headliner, a girl named Georgia Sothern, who stood no more than five feet tall.

She didn't have a gimmick so much as a double-jointed torso that was able to, in the words of one observer, "bump so vigorously and incessantly and speedily that her act transcended the boundaries of obscenity into the domain of unmannered eccentricity." Another fan marveled that she "strips like she just had dynamite for lunch"; she even fainted during one particularly frantic convulsion. Billy knew Georgia was just starting out, another child vaudevillian who turned to burlesque when the Orpheum Circuit died, leaving behind her real name and "Hazel Anderson" for good. An Atlanta native, she began calling herself "Georgia Sothern," after her home state and region. She scrawled her name so quickly on her first burlesque contract that she omitted the "u" in "Sothern." If she took too long to sign, she feared, the manager might change his mind.

Billy offered Georgia double her current salary, and she became his. It was the highest salary Billy had ever granted a female performer, but Philadelphia prices were not New York prices, and he expected, sooner or later, to find someone worth even more.

And he did.

On March 19, 1931, Billy caught a revue at the Empire Theatre in Newark, New Jersey, called *Wine, Women, and Song.* The headliner took her time emerging from behind the curtain, peering out as if slightly wary about what she might find, and with her first step, even before she said a word, she made it clear to Billy Minsky that he had never seen anyone like her and never would again.

She didn't strut or skip or move in any of the usual ways but sashayed, rather, with leisurely grace, and when she acknowledged the audience it was with faint surprise, as if she were rustled from some deep and intimate solitude and had expected to remain alone.

Then she began to talk.

Clearly she was shy—ironically, most of the slingers were—but this girl had a way of teasing her own trepidation, mocking it, turning it inside out like the fingers of a glove. Stripteasers rarely spoke two syllables on stage, but this one couldn't *not* talk, as if each twirl of the wrists, every stride of those legs, deserved narration. She wielded a powder puff on a stick and swiveled her strangely exquisite neck like a periscope, seeking a secret hidden somewhere in the crowd. "Darling! Sweetheart!" she exclaimed. "Where have you been all my life?"

She wasn't addressing him, but those words, and the girl who spoke them, were already his. The name on the marquee outside read GYPSY ROSE LEE, but she was nobody until Billy Minsky said so.

Chapter *Twenty-six*

Once I chided her, "Mother, don't you trust anyone?"

She snapped, "Trust in God, but get it in writing!"

—GYPSY ROSE LEE

England, 1952

Before Gypsy Rose Lee performs her famous routine for the very last time, but long after she has begun to tire of it, she finds herself, one day, facing the task of writing a letter to her sister that no sibling would ever wish to send. She thinks about their strange, peripatetic childhood, those days when June felt loved—by strangers, if not their mother— and Gypsy felt happiest alone. They have been distant, in both miles and affection, and then reunited, regarding each other with cagey eyes and pricked senses; this dance of rancor and reconciliation will continue for the rest of their lives, and even beyond.

For too long Mother was their lone common denominator. Over the years she dipped in and out of their lives, advancing and receding like a wave, ferocious when she flowed and pitiful when she ebbed but exhausting either way. They took turns fielding her requests and enduring her intrusions. During June's run in *Pal Joey* Mother stormed the office of director George Abbott, stinking drunk, with a "big lesbo" by her side. No charming damsel in distress this time, but a fierce and furious vortex, heard clear through every wall and floor.

Oh, how she loved her girls, she cried, and yet those ungrateful "heels" were "starving" her. Would Mr. Abbott mind getting her something to eat and, perhaps, two tickets for the show? He did, just to be rid of her.

"I hate like hell to give that dreadful person a cent," June wrote to Gypsy. "Jeepers that old bag ought to go to work—not at the job she picked out for us naturally . . . she's too old. But something like digging ditches . . . she is such an Amazon it would be like playing marbles for her."

Gypsy advised June to hire a lawyer, and to communicate with Mother in that way as much as possible, for as long as possible.

Once Gypsy and June gathered some distance from Rose they could make room for each other, and for the first time the present superseded the past. In the early 1940s, Gypsy invited June to live at the house on 63rd Street and to take a trip around the world. "I'd like you even if we weren't sisters," Gypsy told her, a confidence June cherished even as she struggled to believe it. Now, ten years later, they speak often about their husbands, Julio De Diego (Gypsy's third and favorite, an acclaimed Spanish painter she married four years after divorcing Bill Kirkland) and Bill Spier (June's third, and true love); about their children, Erik and April; about work or the lack thereof; about Gypsy's ever-growing menagerie of pets, especially her Chinese crested hairless dogs; about anything at all as long as their words have sweetly dull edges, and don't threaten this fragile thing they've made.

At the moment, Gypsy is across the Atlantic on an extended European tour, and June has tentative plans to join her. She will be good company during this old grind, night after night of applying body makeup from neck to feet and gluing black lace bows to her breasts, seven-year-old Erik watching while she primps without a stitch of clothing on. She tells everyone who questions his presence that she believes a child belongs with his mother, and that Erik has been her constant companion on the road since he was six months old. Of course he receives an education; he's enrolled at the prestigious Professional Children's School, designed for children in the performing arts, which permits students to complete lessons by correspondence while on the road. He counts the future star Christopher Walken among his classmates. Sure, there is trouble occasionally, like the time Erik swallowed one of her straight pins while she was onstage and had to be rushed to the hospital. She was furious and never played that theater again, nor did she thank the owner for saving him.

But Erik is mostly an asset, a constant and reliable piece of her life, and as soon as he is capable of holding a camera or helping her change between acts, Gypsy plans to put him to work. He already does his share, in a way. Any problem—a contract dispute, inadequate advertising, a mechanic who insists he can't fix her Rolls—and she grabs Erik's hand to pull him close; he is the evidence that wins every case. "I'm a woman alone in the world with a child," she says, hearing her mother inside each word, "and I'll do whatever I must to survive."

They spend at least six months of every year on the road—the house on 63rd Street has become little more than a place to do laundry—and she enjoys the tours, especially abroad. She scores the loveliest souvenirs, another skill inherited from Rose, "liberating" ashtrays and keys from her favorite restaurants and hotels, slipping them into her Vuitton handbag when no one is looking. And overseas, at least, she can avoid the graying men who insist they skipped high school to see her shows at Minsky's, to which she always replies, archly, "Honey, I wasn't even *born* when you were in high school."

But Europe presents its own challenges. She has to smuggle her cats into hotels. There are too many drunks on the roads. She loathes Liverpool, where someone hurls a rock through her dressing room window. In Pompeii she half expects to be murdered in her bed. Each night she retreats to her hotel room and vents in her diary: "Rehearsal in three languages is something. One girl speaks only Spanish. 2 Swedes speak only Swedish . . . it is a riot. Leader is a cold fish if I ever saw one. Signs backstage 'no smoking' in five languages. No running water in dressing rooms. . . . Oh Gawd I'm tired." Her show at the New China Theater in Stockholm, in particular, is a catastrophe. The producers bill her as a sexy American stripper, a surefire strategy for failure. Not a female face in the audience, and the men expect a sex show.

"Have decided," Gypsy writes, "that everyone who speaks English has seen the show. Audiences watch me with their mouths wide open, but not laughing. After all, they seem to be saying, 'We show more than this on the beach,' and indeed, with mixed nude bathing, they certainly do." How she dreads facing rows of "bewildered, disappointed, leering faces."

And in London, where she is scheduled to appear at the Finsbury Empire Theatre, the county council suffers an untimely bout of prudery, outlawing stripteasing and ordering her show closed by January. A pity for the Brits, but she does wangle some publicity from the decision, calling the council members "fuddy-duddies" and explaining to the wire services why she isn't a stripteaser at all. "A stripteaser," she says, "is a woman who puts on an exotic sexual spectacle. My act is straight comedy and boy, they love it."

She leaves London and settles in a small city nearby—they all blur together after a while—staying in her usual choice of hotel: any place cheap, with a kitchen, and located close to work. An entire ocean between them, and still Mother can get to her. She rolls a piece of paper into her typewriter, next to which sits an ashtray overflowing with menthol cigarettes smoked to the nub and a mug of hot tea, plenty of cream and sugar. The occasion truly calls for her old favorite standby, coffee with brandy, emphasis on the latter, but alcohol is the lone pleasure she's agreed to give up.

Gypsy begins to type:

Dear June:

I hate like hell to have to write you this letter . . . it's so awful. Mother has cancer of the rectum. They are operating Wednesday . . . if the operation is successful it means that she has to wear a container . . . they remove the entire colon. It means weeks of hospitalization, two nurses and a nurse at home even when she leaves the hospital. . . .

They've been giving her blood transfusions and have already postponed the operation. Some drunken lesbian is causing a lot of trouble with the newspapers—the *Mirror* told me about the entire thing! They didn't call me at home or call Julio—but they called the *Mirror*. Terrible people. But even if she were a total stranger she's in great pain and with an operation like this the chances are fifty fifty. She's at the Good Samaritan Hospital in Suffern New York. Please let me know as soon as you can how much financial help you can give me. I've already had to put out two hundred and fifty . . . and with nothing booked ahead and a year and a half of nothing behind me I'm in a bad way for this great monstrous expense. Up until today the shows were going fine . . . but my God I can't concentrate on my work with this hanging over my head. Between the newspapers, the drunken bitch, and the general horror of it all I'm almost out of my mind. Please let me hear from you as soon as you can make it.

She types the word "Love," signs "Gypsy," and realizes that the beginning of Mother's end is also, somehow, her own.

Gypsy Rose Lee, headliner at the Republic, circa 1931.

Chapter Twenty-seven

It was all too discouraging not learning to sing
Until the messrs Minsky took me under their wing
They put my name on Broadway in electric lights
Below it said wrestling, Thursday nights.

—GYPSY ROSE LEE

New York City, 1931–1932

The city felt different from Gypsy's time there as a child, back when she toted Gigolo on her shoulder and slunk through the streets with a fur-clad June, the two of them such an odd spectacle that even New Yorkers stopped to stare. Now it seemed as if someone had uprooted an expanse of color and noise and in its place laid tracks of fervent desperation. The street vendors hawked Tijuana Bibles—pornographic comic books featuring crude couplings between Minnie Mouse and Donald Duck and other celebrities, real or cartoon. Police arrested the "singing beggar" of Broadway for the twenty-ninth time. Flappers were extinct, and once again hemlines grazed ankles. Homeless men loitered in front of Hubert's Flea Museum, where fleas "juggled" balls coated in citronella. Two and a half miles north, a "Hooverville" of shacks sloped along the emptied Central Park Reservoir, sandwiched between several new luxury apartment buildings on Fifth Avenue and Central Park

West. The air smelled of old hot dogs and fresh perm solution, and the lights fell hot and merciless on Gypsy's face.

In one particular house on 42nd Street, New York wasn't New York at all but a miniature corner of Paris—how else to explain the doorman's curlicue mustache and red-lined cape; the female ushers wielding perfume atomizers; and, of course, the Napoleon Bonaparte doppelgänger who called himself Billy Minsky, a century removed from the original but equally in command of his empire. He met Gypsy and her mother at the Republic's stage door and told them to follow him to their dressing room, up one flight of iron stairs. Not the largest room, but still a decent size, with a clear view of the stage. Once she was settled, Gypsy planned to bring Woolly Face in to keep her company.

Billy Minsky was shorter than both Gypsy and Rose, and he stared up at them through thick glasses. As soon as they'd received his telegram, not so much requesting but ordering Gypsy to work at the Republic, Rose began packing their bags. "He wants us!" she gasped, skipping around their room. "This is it, Louise. This is the break we've been waiting for! The Republic Theatre is the showcase of Broadway. Billy Minsky said so himself. Why, burlesque is the womb that has borne great big stars, and the *Ziegfeld Follies* at the Winter Garden is no different in any way from *Ada Onion from Bermuda* at Minsky's!"

Gypsy remembered the gossip on the circuit about the so-called inventor of modern burlesque and his brother-partners, two of whom hovered behind Billy now. Herbert was thin, with greased hair and a mustache so tidy and trim it looked like a set of false eyelashes blinking over his lip. The youngest, Morton, was plump and disheveled, the bow tie on his tuxedo askew, his glasses tilted on the bridge of his nose. He seemed in awe of Gypsy, afraid to look at her directly but unable to shift his eyes. She knew Billy had fallen out with the eldest and original burlesque mastermind, Abe, and a part of her couldn't help but wonder which sibling would win.

Billy had a quick but precise manner about him, and he spoke as if he first ran his words through a blender.

"How old are you?" he asked.

If Gypsy had to guess, she'd say sixteen; in truth she was twenty.

"Just eighteen," Rose said, quickly.

"That's all right, then," he said. "I can't take any chances with mi-nors."

She felt him appraise her. He let his eyes take their time. She was wearing a heavy tweed coat over a dress with a frilly Peter Pan collar. She covered one glove with the other so Billy wouldn't notice the rip in the finger. His stare stopped at her head, which bore a gray felt hat atop a mound of fuzzy curls.

"Do you wear your hair like that on stage?" he asked.

"Of course she does," Rose said, impatient now. "Didn't you see her work?"

He ignored her and dragged a chair from the makeup shelf. Gypsy followed his silent command and sat down. His pulled off her hat and used his fat fingers as a vise, holding her hair flat against both sides of her head.

"Wear your hair like that," he said. "It's more ladylike."

Even though the straight hair made her look like Rose Louise again, Gypsy decided to take Billy Minsky's advice. There were certain people in this business whose requests should be honored, and she sensed that he was one of them.

———

$\mathcal{E}$very day she rehearsed on the rooftop of the Republic Theatre. A line of Minsky Rosebuds danced a frenzied Charleston, and then parted to let the star take her place. Gypsy wore a mink stole and tight dress, sheer enough to show the sharp outline of each rib. Strutting slowly forward, she unhooked the pins along one side until a sliver of hip was exposed. She spun and walked away, letting the dress fall down to the dip of her back. Another spin and her hands made a choker around her neck, elbows just covering her nipples. She imagined someone in the audience begging her to let her arms fall, just long enough for a look.

"Oh, no," Gypsy answered out loud, smiling and shaking her head. "I couldn't do that."

She turned her back to the imaginary crowd again, shrugged the stole from her shoulders, and when she twirled again she held the fur across her breasts.

Again they begged to see her, as much of herself as she could spare. "Oh, no," and she laughed, harder this time. "I couldn't do *that*."

The Minsky Rosebuds ran and clustered around her, half pretending to strip her, half fighting to cover her up.

On Monday, March 30, Gypsy paced the wings of the Republic. This was it, the first real step from her past, her ignominious beginnings. She could hear the barker's singsong bellow: "Come in and see her take it off! Gypsy Rose Lee, the one and only! Like a banana, watch her peel! Watch Gypsy Rose Lee take it off, right down to the fruit!" An hour earlier, per the Minsky brothers' orders, she'd dipped a sponge in a cosmetic called Stage White, which made skin shine like satin under the spotlights, and painted every inch of her body. Rose helpfully pointed out any missed spots and kept her company as she waited for it to dry, stark naked and spread-eagled.

Afterward she attached her pasties and G-string in a complicated, two-stage process of her own invention. With a dab of spirit gum, she affixed tiny circles of flesh-colored net to her nipples, just large enough to pin on two lacy black bows. She placed another strip of net, lined with hand-sewn snaps, so that it just covered her bikini area and bottom, and then fastened her black G-string over it. She never allowed anyone to stand behind her while she did her act—not only because she was more naked in back than she was in front but because she was a magician of sorts, and she wanted no one to decipher the illusion.

She stepped into a fitted red velvet gown that flared like an open flower below her knees. "Breasts more like molehills than mountains," Morton Minsky assessed, but she looked stunning, even with her hair straightened the way Billy had ordered. Black silk stockings, a red garter, gloves that climbed past her elbows, and she was ready for her year—hell, her decade—to begin.

June was in the audience. Apparently she and Bobby had tired, finally, of marathon dancing, and wanted to try their luck as legitimate performers in New York. She had written to Gypsy and Mother to explain the situation and asked, plainly, if she could see them. It was a mature letter, Gypsy thought, devoid of any mention of the way things had ended, and in turn Rose penned a thoughtful response. "This is the only place left for real show business," she wrote. "Come here. We're living right around the corner from Times Square—we can be together again and you can book all the dates you want from the agents who know who you really are. . . . Louise is starring in a big musical comedy right on 42nd Street and Broadway . . . she's the talk of the town and the most beautiful girl in the United States."

Gypsy had not seen June since that night in New Bedford when she was shaking in time to the rattle of those newspapers, and she wanted her sister to understand that everything was different now; *she* was different now, as different as if she'd willfully rearranged her cells beneath her skin. When Gypsy took her sister's hand, she dug in with three-inch crimson nails and let her painted lips graze the air by June's cheek. She could tell June barely recognized her, which was the biggest compliment of all. "Louise wasn't a woman yet," June said, "but she definitely was no longer a child. She was in the middle of the fight, and she was fighting hard."

"I'm sorry I'm so busy, darling," Gypsy cooed, "but it's just one thing after another. It's exciting and I love it, but it is exhausting."

She told June there would be tickets waiting for her at the Republic's box office—complimentary, of course. She insisted; it was the least she could do for June after all the hardship and humiliation she'd been through.

Now the curtain lifted on the "cowboy production number," as the Minskys called it, and Gypsy watched the chorus girls square off, some dressed as cowboys and others as Indians, wearing bows and paper arrows and brandishing pop guns that hurled cotton bullets into the audience. For the grand finale, the curtains spread to reveal two white geldings—billed as stallions—prancing on a rotating platform as the orchestra struggled through the *Poet and Peasant Overture.* Two starlets, naked from the waist up, rode bareback, while the rest of the cast danced and whooped from behind. The audience greeted this spectacle with ho-hum indifference until one of the horses had an accident, at which point they broke into wild applause—that is, until the platform rotated once again and faced upstage. The first five rows were doused with manure, the girls clung to the terrified animals for dear life, and the velvet curtain dropped so the stage could be cleared, quickly, for the next performer, the headliner.

"And now, ladies and gentlemen," the announcer called, "the girl of the year! The unforgettable, the fabulous, Gypsy Rose Lee!"

By now the applause was part of her, as vital and necessary as a muscle, a thing to flex and stretch and use to climb higher. It was what she'd remember most about that night, the way it leapt after her as she worked the stage, unfurling her gloves, shedding her dress one pin at a time, pausing with each muted *plink* inside the tuba. She had coached the tuba player during rehearsals, telling him exactly where to stand and how to position his instrument, a meticulous, private ritual between the two of them. At the finish, when other slingers invited the audience to come closer, Gypsy pulled away and looked down, as if shocked to see so much of her own skin. "How did this happen?" she seemed to ask; proper Gibson Girls, even those living well into the twentieth century, do not end up on New York stages wearing nothing but an open dress and sheer net panties. Backing up against the curtain, standing tall and regal and unobtainable, she gripped its velvet edge and made herself a cape. "And suddenly," she whispered, like the end to a fairy tale, "I take the last . . . thing . . . off!" She hurled her dress into the air, a vivid velvet flag of surrender. A female plant in the audience screamed, the laughter crested over the stage, and the clapping galloped faster than her heartbeat.

"Seven minutes of sheer art," Billy Minsky told her, and the rest of New York agreed with him. Maybe not the most beautiful girl in the world, but oddly striking, her large, lush features a refreshing contrast to the chiseled precision of the *Follies* girls. More than that, she was *funny*, with flawless comedic timing—how many strippers could make that claim? "Gypsy Lee was a riot with her specialty," one critic raved. "She has a style all her own. She knows what to do and when to do it."

She matched Billy Minsky's publicity prowess and began lamenting her "fan trouble." Within five weeks of starring at the Republic, she received six proposals of marriage, one live bunny, a dozen bouquets of American Beauties, numerous boxes of candy, forty-four mash notes, and a case of ginger ale. On the afternoon of April 10, when a complaint by John Sumner prompted a raid on the Republic, Gypsy was one of six arrested for giving an "indecent performance." But only she had a ready quip: "I wasn't naked," she insisted. "I was completely covered by a blue spotlight. Just ask my mother, who is always with me."

She had another when they carted her off to jail and tossed a blanket at her in the cell: "Help!" she cried. "I've been draped!" Rose loved the rides in the paddy wagon, the screaming headlines in the *Police Gazette;* even in June's best years show business had never been so thrilling. "My baby," Rose insisted, "is innocent and pure." She clenched Gypsy's hand and gave her daughter her brightest, loveliest smile, as if to seal a pact that they were in this together, and Rose would always come along for the ride.

The postraid fan mail kept coming, countless telegrams all pledging devotion and support:

```
GYPSY ROSE LEE=REPUBLIC THEATRE=
YOU DON'T DESERVE THE CHEAP PUBLICITY BUT PAY NO ATTEN-
TION WISH I COULD HELP=
ADMIRER.
```

```
GYPSY ROSE LEE=REPUBLIC THEATRE=
NEVER MIND GYPSY YOUR [SIC] A LILY AMONG WEEDS ONE OF
MANY ADMIRERS=GOOD LUCK.
```

```
GYPSY ROSE LEE=REPUBLIC THEATRE=
OFFER MY SERVICES FOR FRIENDLY OR FINANCIAL AID DIRTY
TRICK TO PLAY ON YOU YOUR [SIC] ADORABLE GLADLY HELP
YOU. SIGNED, F. SHANLIN.
```

And two notes scrawled on business-size, heavyweight blank cards, accompanied by flowers:

```
YOU NEED A PROTECTOR MISS LEE. DON'T WORRY YOUR [SIC]
100% WONDERFUL AT DOOR TONIGHT.
QUEEN OF ALL. ANSWER WITH A SMILE AND A CIGARETTE
TONIGHT. 3RD ROOM LEFT. YOUR [SIC] GORGEOUS.
```

Every week the name of the show changed—*Yetta Lostit from Bowling, Lotta Schmaltz from Greece, Iva Schnozzle from Red Hook*—but Gypsy's name was always on top. She earned every cent of her weekly $900 salary, 25 percent of which was paid in IOUs; she stuffed the squares of paper up the rat holes in her dressing room. It was an astronomical sum (about $40,000 in today's dollars), yet she and Rose lived as simply and cheaply as possible, renting a small room with a kitchenette at the Cameo Apartments, across from the Republic, for just $12.50 a week. They spent their late nights huddled together, whispering beneath the sheets, speaking ill of the past and gloriously of the future.

Gypsy accelerated her dieting efforts, temporarily forgoing her essence mix to try every popular fad, eating nothing but lamb chops and pineapple one day, bananas, sauerkraut juice, and lettuce the next. Every night she pressed her thumb against her teeth because Mother told her it would help straighten them. When the big, legitimate Broadway boys came in, Florenz Ziegfeld or Lee Shubert or George White or Earl Carroll, Gypsy would be ready. "I wish she was in another sort of show," June told Bobby, but she never said a word to her sister. Gypsy could hear June's voice anyway, a silent judgment that flogged her ears raw: she might be making burlesque better, but she was better than burlesque.

━━━━━

Although Billy Minsky didn't like Rose and her meddlesome, nitpicky ways, he let her accompany Gypsy to rehearsals and hide out (along with Woolly Face) in the dressing room, a heady clutter of rhinestones and feathers, spirit gum and Sterno, stale coffee and spilled brandy, cigarette butts and sweat and the musk of dirty stockings. Rose made it clear that Gypsy still needed her; who else would warn the girl about developing friendships and fraternizing with other performers on the bill? Who else would have protected her from that unscrupulous, craven Tade Styka, who wanted to paint Gypsy in the nude? Rose made such a scene that three Minsky stagehands rushed in and tossed the artist out. "You know," she told Gypsy, "I'm a good judge of character."

Her daughter could trust her and no one else. That's how it had always been, and always would be.

Under Rose's watchful eye and with her grudging consent, Gypsy discovered she loved the way a cigarette felt cradled between her fingers and clamped between her lips, the wispy frame of smoke around her face. A Minsky comic named Rags Ragland became her benefactor behind the stage. He, too, had chronic dental ailments: a full set of lowers but just two teeth on top, one long incisor on each side. He kept his false upper plate not in his mouth but in a wad of newspaper, stashed away inside the cash register of a Third Avenue bar. He was rumored to be well endowed and a chronic womanizer, methodically making his way through the Minsky Rosebuds and a few select slingers.

Rags taught her how to drink, spiking her coffee with brandy in the morning and filling her flask at night. "Gypsy could really put it away," Morton Minsky noted, "and she often did, even between her acts . . . according to everyone who knew her, she used every form of chemical stimulation on earth, not the least of it champagne." She tried smoking marijuana a few times but found it "revolting," mostly because it made her too passive. "I'm not giving anything away," she reasoned. "I'm selling it. Sweet? Submissive? May as well be a housewife . . . it dims my luster, makes me resemble others—that's the worst thing that could happen." Cocaine was next, and the buzz was more to her liking. At one party she accidentally spilled her lines on the rug, a faux pas quickly forgiven by her host and fellow guests; she was the absent-minded stripper, after all, whose whimsical, choreographed mistakes were as anticipated as the slow, deliberate peeling of her gloves.

She eavesdropped on the stripteasers' chatter in the dressing rooms; of course their theories on men and sex contradicted everything Mother had taught her. Every once in a while the house doctor stopped by to ask the girls if anything hurt or itched. No one could afford to get married these days—the marriage rate had dropped by 22 percent since the onset of the Depression—but seven out of ten single men and women were sexually active. It was illegal to advertise birth control products, so the girls perused women's magazines and read between the lines: various jellies, powders, liquids, suppositories, foaming tablets, and even Lysol addressed "feminine hygiene" and "marriage hygiene" issues. If all else failed, they could try the newly developed, pontiff-sanctioned rhythm method, or insert a 14-karat gold button into the uterus to serve as an IUD.

Gypsy made one enemy: a stripteaser who called herself Electra but whose real name was Goldie Grey. Five feet tall, with blond hair that curled like commas about her head, Electra wore a small pouch around her waist stuffed with batteries. With a flick of her finger, she controlled clusters of blinking lights that covered her breasts and bottom, a gimmick she used on the burlesque circuits for seventy-two straight months (and that would make her famous as a character in the musical *Gypsy*). She, too, was friendly with Rags Ragland, and when he needed a talking woman for one of his comedy sketches, she and Gypsy competed for the job. As much as Rags liked Gypsy, she was too tall for the part, and so began a feud that lasted as long as they were both in the business.

But, despite Mother's warnings, Gypsy befriended a few of the girls, particularly the redhead who hailed from Atlanta and called herself Georgia Sothern. When Gypsy met her at Minsky's Republic, Georgia Sothern was just fourteen years old, and she told Gypsy what had happened the day Billy Minsky learned her true age.

The boss collapsed into his office chair and sank his head into splayed hands. *"Fourteen?"* he moaned. "FOURTEEN! Four-TEEN! This kid is only fourteen years old!" Georgia soothed him by producing an official-looking birth certificate that made her eighteen, drawn up specially by her Uncle Virgil, who used to thwart suspicion by telling people she was a midget.

"I'll put this in the file with your contract," Billy decided. "If anybody ever asks me questions, I'll tell them I didn't know your age when I hired you and that you gave me this as proof that you were old enough. I'll swear I never heard what you just told me today."

The forged papers were sufficiently authentic to facilitate Georgia's marriage to one of the Republic's straight men, who, she said, attacked her "like an animal" on their wedding night. She reported to Billy's office the following afternoon to explain what had happened. He took one look at her blackened eye, her mottled, bruised peach of a face, and decided the only way to overcome the situation was to exploit it. He ordered his wardrobe woman to sew a custom eye patch flecked with rhinestones and called a press conference. The demand was such that Billy booked four extra shows. The audience was more eager to see Georgia's eye than any other part of her body, and for her encore she removed the patch and lifted her face to the lights.

Gypsy came to trust Georgia implicitly. The girl's opinions were as forceful and blunt as her onstage antics, and, most important, she did not try to copy Gypsy's technique. "Gypsy had a style far removed from mine," Georgia said. "She did nothing but walk sedately back and forth

Georgia Sothern.

across stage in time to the music as she removed her costume. It was stripping in its simplest form and a gimmick without really being a gimmick at all. Her act was a complete contrast to my fast strip, and because of it we were both able to appear on the same stage as stars. Together we packed the Republic to the rafters."

In between performances, Gypsy played pinochle with the Minsky comedians (including one "Lew Costello"), who had a game running for months. They kept score on the dressing room walls, and the numbers stretched out into the hallway. Georgia felt indebted to Billy, but Gypsy learned that most of the Minsky employees despised the brothers. One comic boasted about a trick he had taught his dog. Hanging an old coat on the wall, he yelled "Minsky!" and praised the animal when it lunged and tore the garment to shreds. The Minsky Rosebuds complained about the lousy pay, just $21 for an eighty-hour workweek—plus they had to supply their own G-strings. Billy called his policy tradition, a necessary stepping-stone, since most of the big burlesque stars began their careers as chorus girls.

"No actor should join a union," Billy told Gypsy one day. She could have rested her elbow on his head, and he had to forcefully launch his words upward in her direction. "It isn't artistic. Unions are for laborers, people who dig ditches. You're an artiste. You should have stardust in your eyes and music in your heart." He even used his thriftiness as a publicity stunt, advertising that his chorines were "good girls" because they were too exhausted to misbehave. One of them confided the truth of this theory to Gypsy. "It takes time to be bad," she reasoned, "and who the hell's got time?"

Gypsy despised Billy's rationale, even though it was one that had defined her childhood, with Mother always refusing to pay the Newsboy Songsters or the Hollywood Blondes when times were tight, reasoning that the experience on the road was compensation enough. She made notes of every missed paycheck and indignity suffered by her burlesque colleagues. "Seven days a week four shows a day," she wrote, "forty-five hours of rehearsals a week for fifteen dollars. No contracts, no security bond, supply your own shoes and keep smiling. . . . Who wants to know from stardust in your eyes when your feet hurt?" She vowed that no one would ever take such advantage of her, especially once she knew exactly who Gypsy Rose Lee was, and what she was worth.

Luckily she could perpetrate her sleuthing with relative ease, since Billy seemed unusually distracted of late, conferring in hushed tones with Morton and Herbert or retreating to his office carrying the latest issue of every newspaper, the stack so tall it obscured half of his face. Gypsy overheard enough to know that business had declined at the Minskys' flagship burlesque house, the National Winter Garden, and that the brothers were casting about for people and circumstances to blame. It was the fault of Abe, the oldest, having vanished into his private cache of resentment or jealousy or whatever angry sentiment he'd clenched in his small, silly mind. It was "all those down-and-outers," as Morton put it, loitering around the plazas at Allen Street and Second Avenue. It was the fault of other cheap forms of entertainment— talkies and the radio, the same forces that had destroyed vaudeville.

Gypsy read the same daily newspapers as Billy, mostly skimming for gossip and book reviews, but she understood how the page-one headlines might unravel his nerves. Gangster Arnold Rothstein's murder was still officially "unsolved," but everyone knew the true meaning of that classification: the city's police, courts, and prosecutors were all either on the take or looking the other way, stalling in an attempt to keep the wrong pair of eyes from peering too deeply into Mayor Walker's administration. Those eyes belonged to a patrician, pedantic, courtly judge named Samuel Seabury, who, in August 1930, was appointed by the New York State Supreme Court to head what was—and still is—the largest investigation of municipal corruption in American history.

Franklin Delano Roosevelt had approved Seabury's appointment and would be expecting regular updates; the case was major national news, and the governor's political future depended on its outcome. Roosevelt hadn't forgotten how Mayor Walker stood by him and rallied the faithful for his gubernatorial campaign, yet now here he was, monitoring an investigation that threatened to expose corruption at every level of the vaunted Tammany organization. A New York governor with presidential aspirations had to be mindful not only of who helped him along the way but also of how those associations could be interpreted across the country. To become the thirty-second president of the United States, he had to prove himself capable of independent action without provoking Tammany Hall to work against him. "When you're in politics," Roosevelt reasoned, "you've got to play the game."

With that in mind, Roosevelt drew upon his legal training and adopted a pragmatic, indifferent stance toward the investigation. The State Supreme Court, he reasoned, was well within its rights to order the inquiry, and "by virtue of the Constitution and statutes of our state," Roosevelt felt compelled to sanction it. Judge Seabury was free to turn out the pockets of Manhattan's denizens and examine their contents in unstinting detail, even if the process indelibly changed the character of New York City itself.

———————

*W*ithout asking Gypsy or even telling her, Rose dipped into their savings and bought a house out in Rego Park, Queens. It was the end unit in a development done in neo-Flemish style, a tall, slim home with spires and a doorbell that chimed the first few notes of "Ave Maria." It cost $8,888, a significant leap from their little room at the Cameo Apartments, and they had not one piece of furniture to put in it. They did, however, have an 8mm projector and a trunkful of blue movies, which Rose watched as if they were soap operas. Lounging on a blanket in front of the screen, her hand buried in a deep bowl of popcorn, she laughed softly to herself at the "funny parts."

One night, when Rose was home alone, Gypsy lost her virginity to a man named Ed Grimble. She'd worried that she was such "a great big sex star" that no one would ever make a pass at her—"I'm going to have to rape somebody," she moaned—but Ed saved her the trouble. Not particularly handsome, but wealthy and connected on Broadway and in literary circles, he was friendly with people she wanted to know, familiar with places she longed to see. "She *had* to get rid of her virginity," June said, "because she was moving in very fast company." Next she fell into a fling with her friend and drinking buddy Rags Ragland, who taught her how to kiss as if the man weren't a stranger. He called Gypsy "pumpkin" and sent her love letters in verse: "I would like to kiss you if

I could because you have been so very good." She moved on to faster company, a crooked Broadway cop—perhaps the would-be "protector" from her fan telegrams—and then to one of New York's most notorious and dangerous criminals.

Waxey Gordon was forty-three years old, short and plump, with just enough coarse gray hair to disqualify him from true "baldhead" status. He wore a heavy gray suit that encased his girth like cement and a coil of diamonds around his thick wrist. He seldom smiled and when he did it was effortful, as if the corners of his lips were lifting heavy weights, and he was free and careless with his gun.

One night, after the Republic's final show, Waxey arrived at a speakeasy on Eighth Avenue. He was flanked by four bodyguards wearing green fedoras slouched down, shadowing their faces. Gypsy thought he looked more like a booking agent than a gangster, but everyone knew who and what he was and how he'd begun: little Irving Wexler from the slums of the Lower East Side, so skilled at filching wallets from pockets it was as if they were covered with wax; hence the nickname.

During the early days of Prohibition, Waxey connected with the now-deceased racketeer Arnold Rothstein and worked alongside such underworld luminaries as Charles "Lucky" Luciano and Owney Madden. Rothstein had been the master of New York City's illegal liquor trade—the largest operation in the country, with an estimated 32,000 speakeasies—and he taught his protégés everything: the connections to the purchasing rings in Canada, England, and the West Indies; the number of speedboats they had at their disposal for smuggling purposes; the locations of every one of their storage warehouses. At the height of Rothstein's operation, 80 percent of the liquor distilled in Canada found its way to the United States, and the Bahamas' export of whiskey increased 425-fold. Patrons of both the city's exclusive clubs and Bowery dives unwittingly drank alcohol laced with antifreeze, ether, or Jamaica ginger extract—the last of which, when adulterated with a plasticizer, caused a paralytic condition known as "jake leg." Everyone thought of the "jake leg blues" as an affliction of poor southerners, but New York City had its share of victims, roaming Harlem and the Bowery in their trademark dismal march, knees lifted high and feet slapping the pavement, *toe* heel, *toe* heel, the heel forever incapable of landing first.

Determined to take over a number of breweries in New Jersey, Waxey began warring with the Irish gang that controlled them, murdering its members one by one. The breweries were technically legal since they manufactured "near beer"; their authentic stuff was produced and transported to bottling and barreling facilities via an intricate, elaborate system of underground pipes. During one raid, federal authorities discovered a 6,000-foot beer pipeline running through the Yonkers sewer system. In Manhattan, Waxey's web of contacts set up neighborhood cordial shops with "importer" or "broker" plates nailed to the door, a clear signal that they were "in the know." To pick up business, these clever proprietors also slipped flyers under windshields and apartment doors, offered free samples and home delivery, took telephone orders, and urged customers to "ask for anything you may not find" on the menu. For the weekend warriors, steamship lines operating out of New York introduced cruises with no destination at all but the "freedom of the seas."

There were signs the party might be nearing its end. That summer, a five-year-old boy was killed by a stray bullet on East 107th Street, and Governor Roosevelt vowed a crackdown on organized crime. In the meantime, Waxey lived exactly the way Gypsy wished she could, watching the money go out while confident it would come back in. He kept his wife and three children in a ten-room, four-bath apartment at 590 West End Avenue (paying $6,000 per year in rent at a time the average annual salary was $1,850), decorated with the help of professionals, including a woodsmith who custom-built a $2,200 bookcase. Five servants catered to their every whim. His children attended private schools, took daily horseback-riding lessons in Central Park, and spent summers at their house in Bradley Beach, New Jersey. He owned three cars, bought $10 pairs of underwear by the dozen, and stocked his closets with $225 suits tailor-made for him by the same haberdasher who outfitted Al Capone. In 1930, Waxey made nearly $1.5 million and paid the U.S. government just $10.76 in taxes.

And now, in this Eighth Avenue speakeasy, Gypsy watched Waxey Gordon watching her, his eyes fixed with purpose as he summoned a waiter and whispered into his ear. He watched as the waiter approached her table, hoisting four bottles of champagne high in the air, and setting them down, saying crisply, "Compliments of Mr. W." Waxey watched

Gypsy sip the champagne and noted the realization passing across her face: accepting his gift was as much an invitation as a courtesy, an implicit agreement that he would open doors she'd be obliged to step through, locking them tight behind her, no matter what she might find on the other side.

"Thank you for the champagne," she told Waxey when he strode over to her table, the bodyguards lined up like ducklings behind him.

He nodded and said, "You can't tell when you'll run into me again," although she did, indirectly, on the phone the following morning.

The ringing awakened her and Mother, who strained to listen to the voice on the other line. "No names," the voice barked at Gypsy. "I'm calling for the friend you met last night." Mr. Gordon, the voice said, wanted her to visit a certain dentist at 49th and Broadway. She had an appointment the following morning to get her teeth straightened.

The dial tone droned in her ear.

"I never heard of such a thing," Rose said indignantly, and they skipped the appointment.

That night, as Gypsy primped in her dressing room at the Republic, Georgia Sothern's reflection appeared in her mirror.

"Gyps," she whispered, holding her friend's gaze in the glass, "Waxey's very hurt that you didn't see his dentist. He's got you another appointment for the same time tomorrow. You'd better go. Waxey's all right . . . it don't pay to turn up your nose at him."

Gypsy remembered Georgia's warning when the strange man called again, after the show. This time Rose took the call. "I don't understand this," she said, "but I don't like it. My daughter isn't going to any dentist we never heard of and can't afford to pay."

The voice urged them not to worry about paying, since the doctor owed the "boss" plenty. And if the boss wanted Gypsy Rose Lee to get her teeth straightened, she would do it—if she knew what was good for her.

———————

The new caps were beautiful, Gypsy thought, and looked like real teeth—no matter that she could no longer eat corn on the cob, or that they felt like pins lodged deep in her gums. Waxey Gordon was another member of her new world, and she was still learning its language, cracking its code. The people inside it knew nothing of Rose Louise or the bleak, endless days she'd spent running from her, and she rewarded their ignorance by letting them assist in the invention of Gypsy Rose Lee. When Waxey told her to keep her new teeth "brushed good," she did, meticulously and obsessively. When he invited her to perform at a benefit for the inmates of Comstock Prison, at which Florenz Ziegfeld was expected to be a guest, she signed on right away (although her appearance was canceled when wardens worried that she might corrupt prisoners' morals). When Waxey told her he wanted to give her a dining room set for her new home, she could not have been more thankful for the gesture. When Waxey wanted her to appear on his arm or in his bed she complied, learning to take more than she gave without anyone sensing the difference.

She ventured deeper into Waxey's circle, meeting his people's people, noting everyone who floated along the edges. When a man named Vick Mizzy asked her to accompany him home, she assessed carefully, coolly, exactly what he might do for her. He was in the music industry, a person of prominence and power, and she yearned to collect people like him, people who could help develop her creation. Once the door closed behind them, she took off all of her clothes, dropped onto his bed, and said, "You can fuck or suck whatever you want, I'm going to sleep."

For now, at least, she was theirs to admire and to stroke, to turn off and on, to beckon and send away.

"She was very involved in the underworld," June said. "She was one of their pets, just like Sinatra . . . it guaranteed things, the kind of things she wanted."

June happened to be in New York the night Waxey Gordon's stolen furniture was scheduled for delivery. She'd divorced Bobby and rejoined the marathon circuit, spending 3,600 hours on her feet in a recent contest, and was more desperate than ever to find work in a legitimate theater. She subsisted on a hot dog with sauerkraut for breakfast and a jelly doughnut for dinner and spent her days taking acting classes, rushing from call to call, hoping to step onto the right stage at the right time.

Mother wouldn't help her, she was certain, but her sister might—Louise was highly sophisticated now, after all, and she could fill June's pocket with all the right names.

She arrived at the Rego Park house and found her mother wrapped in a bathrobe, popcorn in hand, watching a movie. The projector rattled and hummed and a naked woman appeared on the screen. She lowered herself into a tub, and then a man appeared behind her. He urinated over her shoulder as she soaped herself clean.

Laughing softly, her mouth full of popcorn, Rose told June that her sister was upstairs. "Plenty of popcorn, dear," she added. "Come back and make comfy at the movies."

At the top of the stairs, a short hallway led to a bathroom. June found her sister facedown on the floor. She turned her body over—Louise had gotten so lithe, so slim—and smoothed her hair away from her face. Smeared makeup made her skin look sallow and bruised, and a line of lipstick ran jagged across—what were these?—new teeth, thick and strangely white, still slightly bucked. A flask of brandy stood like a miniature tombstone behind her head. An old memory took shape, frame by frame: her on the bathroom floor, recovering from that last fight with Mother; Louise closing the door and sitting close enough to touch her; a furtive confidence shared, both of them low and lost.

June tried to hoist her sister up.

"Let go of me, June—let go!" she yelled, pushing June away. She pulled herself up and began retching into the toilet. When she finished she leaned back against the tub, making herself as tall as she could, managing even under the circumstances to look imperious and regal.

"What the hell are you doing here? This is a private lesson."

June boggled at her. "Lesson?"

"A lesson in social amenities. I happen to be moving in a very special set of people, and I've got a lot to learn."

Closing her eyes, she took a long swallow of brandy.

"Louise—" June said.

"I'm not Louise," Gypsy insisted. "I'll never be Louise again. Didn't Mother tell you? My stage name is who I am from now on. Gypsy Rose Lee. That's who I am for good. You call me that—Gypsy, I mean. We'll all get used to it."

"But wasn't that name just temporary? Besides, you're not a gypsy."

"And you weren't dainty, either," Gypsy retorted and then gave her sister the help she sought, telling her to "smarten up" and stop playing those "dance marathon games." How unbright did June have to be, thinking she'd get into a chorus line, with those skimpy eyebrows and bumpy knees? And what had happened to becoming a real actress?

As for men, June should know that all of them are married and merely want a "pretty little ornament." Such dalliances were ephemeral, little snatches of phantom lives, and only June could give herself anything lasting or real. Did June even know what or who she was? She had no idea, had she? Well, whatever it was, and no matter how hopeless it sounded to her ears, she needed to pin it down and made a solid vow to it—and not let hell or high water get in her way.

"Believe me, June," Gypsy said. "Nobody—I mean nobody—is going to be a roadblock for Gypsy Rose Lee."

Mother's voice came bounding up the stairs. "Gypsy! Gypsy, they're here. The truck is here with the furniture! Right on the dot . . . it's 4 A.M., dear."

Gypsy sent June downstairs; she needed to fix her face and brush her new teeth. June and Rose waited at the door, watching a team of burly men lug in a long, carved oak table and thirty ornate matching chairs, the grandest dining set they had ever seen. Another man followed, well groomed and smartly dressed, and his very presence crowded the room. His eyes turned toward the stairs, waiting, and Gypsy descended, pointing her toes and accentuating each step, an entrance meant for Waxey Gordon alone.

"I'm sorry I took so long," she told Waxey, and then directed his men to the dining room.

Rose turned to Waxey, looking at him through lowered eyes. She smiled and spoke softly. "Well, son," she said, "I am the mother of Gypsy Rose Lee."

"Pleased to meet you," Waxey said.

She pointed a finger at June. "And this is my baby. She used to be somebody, too."

When Waxey left, Gypsy said good-bye, calling him "Mr. Gordon" and shaking his hand. He called her "kid." Rose sighed and said, "Class.

Class. No pretense, just honesty himself. In this world of stinkers, just give me a straightforward, true-blue gangster every time."

Gypsy walked June to the door, told her not to worry. Mother had always loved June best; it was just difficult for her to say so. "Don't forget what I said, and good luck," she added. She promised to help June whenever and however she could.

━━━━━━

*B*efore long June took her up on the offer. She needed work, any work, and she recalled what Bobby had said to her when they first saw Gypsy perform at the Republic: What's the difference between the naked dames in this one and the naked dames in the Broadway shows? June thought, Rayon or silk, they're both shiny, aren't they? But when Gypsy offered to talk to Billy Minsky on her behalf, she thanked her sister and waited for word.

Gypsy didn't disappoint. She had more power and pull than June had imagined, securing her a six-to-eight-week contract sight unseen. June expected to be a chorus girl, dancing in the first-act finale just before the horses, but it was clear the Minsky brothers expected another Gypsy Rose Lee. "Gypsy assured us she'd show her sister the ropes," Morton said. "Maybe she did and maybe she didn't. Maybe she didn't want her sister competing with her, although I really think the fact was that as far as stripping was concerned, Gypsy had a certain instinct for it and June didn't."

June both wouldn't and couldn't do it. She hadn't Gypsy's sophisticated presence, but she did have shame. She couldn't say that to her sister, of course, since Gypsy was this "big important person, and I was picking up pennies from the street." In the middle of the first week Billy explained, kindly, that they had to let her go due to "fast turnover," although they would pay her in full. Gypsy helped her sister pack her few things in the dressing room and walked her to the Republic's door. She watched June's slow retreat down Broadway, her lips pulled into a faint, stingy smile, thinking how she'd won a bet wagered only in her mind.

But June sensed another chance when Gypsy met her in Manhattan one night and told her there was someplace she needed to go. June agreed; something might turn up if she slipped into Gypsy's world for another moment to have a look around.

Gypsy held out a plain white card. It looked like a business card save for the fact that an address was the only thing printed across it, in un-embellished black lettering. She weighed her motives for saying what she was about to say. It *would* help June, the same way it had helped her. It would shock June, strip off another layer of her cumbersome naïveté. And, in a silent yet unmistakable way, it would dare June to judge her once again.

She pressed the card into June's hand, curled her sister's slim fingers around the edges.

"There are a lot of influential people here, show business and other-wise," Gypsy said. "And if you behave well, and as expected, it'll do you good."

June thanked her sister and began counting down the streets to her destination.

She couldn't recall, decades later, exactly where the party was or what sort of building she entered to find it—a private apartment, maybe, or the secret floor of a nightclub. There was a garland of smoke and chatter around the room's periphery, and a complicit silence at its core. She made her way through the tangle of the crowd, the vivid Flo-rentine hats and subdued felt fedoras, the hands gripping tumblers of Scotch and gin, and found the party's engine, what was making it go. It was a circus party—she learned the term later—an old backroom tradi-tion. A public display of sex as if it were competition, both participants and spectators keeping score: men with unnatural desires and women who fulfilled them, blowing cigarette smoke rings with their privates, feasting on themselves and each other, forcing animals into their vulgar games. One man in particular made his way around the circle, never sated, never tired, all of them working and being worked with grim focus and fierce intent, outdoing the others or their own personal bests.

Did the crowd know who June was, and who had referred her? Did they expect June to *be* Gypsy Rose Lee?

"It was a society," June later said, "and she felt that she had to—she had no shame."

Before June saw anything else she turned and fled. She left her hat on the rack. She never voiced the thought she held the rest of her life: if Gypsy could send her baby sister to such a place, she didn't really love her. She might not be capable of any love—outside of herself—at all.

Gypsy herself recognized the truth in that, at least in this unholy limbo, caught between the Gypsy Rose Lee she currently presented and the ideal version that still lived exclusively in her head, the one who would never barter her pride in exchange for security and success. In the interim she would box up her shame and tuck it away, somewhere high and deep and unreachable, where no one but she even knew it existed. And she would be perceptive enough to mock her own ambition, to realize that she would inhabit this perfect world—this perfect self— only by admitting she didn't belong.

Chapter Twenty-eight

There are three things a man must do alone. Be born, die, and testify.

—MAYOR JIMMY WALKER

New York City, 1931–1932

On her first day Gypsy Rose Lee stood in Billy Minsky's office, peering down at him. Beneath her cheap tweed coat and tattered gloves she was blank and shapeless, and she bowed down to accept his hands upon her head.

He pressed her hair against the sides of her face, framing it, and then leaned back to judge what he had done.

Billy could feel the girl's mother's eyes on him—not on Herbert or Morton, just him—and sense the huffy indignation that pooled around her silence. She had to be nearing forty, Billy assessed, young enough to remember how to use what she had but old enough to recognize its limits. Fifteen, twenty years ago, he might've gone for those fierce, ravenous eyes and deftly carved bones, but such fanciful speculation ceased the moment she opened her mouth. "Where is the green room?" she asked snidely, and seemed pleased and triumphant that he didn't know what a green room was.

He raised his hands from Gypsy's face and her hair released itself, springing back into a mass of frizz. The mother's presence closed in on

him again, but when he turned to face her those flinty eyes shifted side-
ways, as if she couldn't decide whether to act as predator or prey. When
Billy spoke he pointed his words directly at Rose.

"Remember now," he said, "anything you need just come to me."

━━━━━━

How could he market this Gypsy Rose Lee and her singular, cerebral
act, this Dorothy Parker in a G-string and her burlesque of burlesque?
She needed an unprecedented publicity campaign, one as innovative
and original as her persona itself. No matter that her body was more
Ziegfeld than Minsky—a flat bust, but long and sleek as a panther—
because her body, ironically, was almost beside the point. "She had mastered the art of the tease to such an extent that no one minded," as
Morton put it. "Her costumes were suggestive and seductive rather
than the flowery, pseudo-virginal frocks assumed by the less imaginative. She used black silk stockings, lace panties, red garters, and mesh
netting. In a manner new to burlesque, she turned her essentially shy
feelings about disrobing onstage into a mocking, spoofing jest." She
could take a full fifteen minutes to peel off a single glove, and such was
her hold over the audience that they would gladly have granted her fifteen more.

Billy declared that every year the Republic would showcase a new
girl, and the theater's inaugural year belonged to her. GYPSY ROSE LEE,
read the banner from the marquee, THE MOST BEAUTIFUL GIRL IN THE
WORLD! For the first time in burlesque history a stripteaser—not a
comic—would have top billing. Gypsy Rose Lee would perform directly before the Act I and Act II finales—the surest way to incite anticipation, to make the audience beg before giving it to them. He told the
press about his latest find, a Miss Seattle beauty contest winner who
was also a gifted painter, having completed portraits of Fanny Brice,
speakeasy proprietress Texas Guinan, and notorious serial wife and actress Peggy Hopkins Joyce. This refined lady undresses using pins, a
practice heretofore unheard of in stripteasing, and anyone lucky
enough to catch one can redeem it for future free admission.

The city fairly shouted her name. An unemployed ex-vaudevillian climbed onto seventeen-foot stilts and wore an illuminated shirtfront announcing the coming of Gypsy Rose Lee. He was joined by a "mechanical man" named Jose Lisso who discovered, quite by accident, that he had a gift for holding rigid poses over long periods of time. Wearing a monocle, Eustace Tilley style, over one blind but staring eye, he jerked his body down Broadway, paused, jerked some more, and stopped before the Republic's front door. Some of the gawking crowd followed him in and bought tickets to see Gypsy Rose Lee, which, of course, was the point. One afternoon a curious spectator crept up and sank a straight pin into Lisso's skin, and still he didn't flinch. "I stuck a pin into you," the man said. "Didn't you notice it?" For the first and only time, the Minskys' mechanical man broke character. "I noticed it," he replied, "and if you do it again, I'll knock your block off."

Overhead, a plane seared across the Manhattan skyline, trailing a banner bearing GYPSY ROSE LEE in letters bold enough to be read from every corner of the city. And for his most daring scheme of all Billy brought striptease outside, setting up a sidewalk cooch show that hinted at the raunchy splendor beyond the Republic's doors.

Gypsy seemed to appreciate the efforts, following the stilt walker down 42nd Street, gaping at her name chiseled in bold yellow bulbs across the marquee. But most of the time she holed up with her mother in her dressing room. None of the Minskys knew what to make of Rose, who was alternately haughty and prim and coarse and vindictive.

One night Gypsy's act was followed by sixteen chorus girls dressed in silver wings and glittering G-strings, their breasts fully exposed, hands clasped in prayer, eyes turned piously skyward. The angels had just started to shimmy when Rose came bounding downstairs into Billy's office. He looked up from his desk to find her standing in the doorway, slight shoulders heaving, violet eyes flattened to slits, pink slash of a mouth trembling in fury.

"No religious act is following my daughter's specialty," she said, and the words, in both depth of tone and sureness of delivery, seemed to come from someone twice her size. "Take out the number or we'll quit."

Billy puffed a ring of smoke in Rose's direction and considered her threat.

No, he told her. The angel bit stays.

Rose shot him a look of raw, skinless crazy. She spun on her heel and stomped back upstairs, but Billy was sure that wasn't the end of it.

It wasn't. The following day he got a call from Walter Winchell. Did Mr. Minsky know, asked the columnist, that a number of churchgoing Republic patrons (apparently the two weren't mutually exclusive) were threatening a citywide boycott of the theater if Billy didn't take out a certain number featuring nude angels? Did Mr. Minsky have any comment?

Billy didn't believe the citywide boycott extended beyond Rose Hovick, but the angel bit wasn't as important to him as his new star slinger. Besides, he would put nothing past Rose. Morton had it dead right when he said that woman's "river did not run to the sea." Sighing, Billy told Winchell the number would be eliminated by the next show.

When he saw Rose again she caught him in her searchlight beam of a smile, and he couldn't decide if she was more disturbing—and disturbed—when she was angry or pleased.

———

$\mathscr{P}$rivately, the brothers wondered what sort of toll a mother like that could take on a young girl. Gypsy was incredibly bright, no doubt about that, but, as Morton noted, she "had her idiosyncrasies." Her personality skipped like a damaged record, stuck by chance on notes high or low, struggling to find the place where the song should resume.

Her sly sophistication onstage belied her barbaric behavior off. "She used foul words all of the time," observed fellow stripteaser and Minsky relative Dardy Minsky. "And for no reason. She would talk about 'that effing chair.' She had a very un-lady-like manner about her, very crude." A day riding the Ferris wheel at Coney Island with Georgia Sothern was followed by a night in the most sordid corners of Manhattan. No one could miss her talk about those "circus parties," featuring strippers with forty-six-inch bosoms and a man who never got tired. "He could keep a hard-on for hours—do all those acrobatic sex gigs, and still go on and on," Gypsy reported. "But was he satisfied? Oh, no! He had to go and get that damned silicone pumped into his penis, so he could be even more spectacular."

Then there was her monkey, Woolly Face, who followed her every-where, swigging brandy from her flask and sitting on her bare lap while she primped at her dressing room mirror. One day Morton—perhaps inadvertently, perhaps not—walked in on Gypsy conducting a strangely intimate routine with the animal. "She had a monkey," he said, "trained to do things that would have driven any of our license commissioners up the wall. However, she decided not to use that material in her act."

In one area, at least, their new star was remarkably consistent. With every raid, every ride in the paddy wagon, every witty quip to the gos-sip columnists, Billy realized he had never before met someone like Gypsy, whose natural ability for getting and shaping attention—*any* kind of attention—matched his own.

———

*M*ore than eleven thousand people a week came to see Gypsy Rose Lee and her elegant, brainy joke of a strip. Clearly burlesque was thriv-ing on Broadway—not only at the Republic but at the Eltinge, across the street—and Billy figured the Great White Way could make room for one more Minsky theater. He had Joseph Weinstock buy out the Shubert brothers' lease on the Central Theatre at 48th and Broadway, another white flag of surrender from the beleaguered legitimate crowd. The depression that afflicted the rest of the country only buoyed the business of burlesque, no longer relegated to the alleyways of fringe neighborhoods but in demand on the greatest street in the world. Billy offered the simplest explanation, which also served as his personal formula: burlesque gave the people something else to think about. He was so focused on expanding his Broadway presence that he didn't even attend the final night of the National Winter Garden on September 19, 1931, when the curtain fell—finally, officially—on the last sweet memory he shared with his brother Abe.

With both the Columbia and Mutual Wheels officially dead, Billy en-tertained visions of a "Minsky American Wheel," his specific brand of stock burlesque in thirty theaters from New York to Chicago. Nothing and no one could stop him now. He would expand into Brooklyn. He would form an international burlesque company to compete with the

Moulin Rouge and the Folies Bergère, those same iconic institutions he had once aspired to imitate. He contemplated taking over the Metropolitan Opera House for a season of burlesque, and was so enthralled with the idea that he sent his attorney to begin negotiations straight away. And in the spring of 1932 the following ad ran in the personals section of the *Times:*

To Whom It May Concern:

It is not true that Billy Minsky has acquired the lease to the New York Public Library, corner of 5th Avenue and 42nd Street. Signed:

A Friend of the People.

Billy neither admitted placing the ad, nor denied that the idea hadn't crossed his mind.

━━━━━━━

*I*n his little black notebook John Sumner documented all of Billy's rumors and stunts and schemes. He took note when no less vaunted a publication than *The New Yorker* christened a certain section of Times Square "Minskyville." This burgeoning New York neighborhood, the magazine declared, ran from 52nd to 42nd Streets on Broadway, and from Sixth to Eighth Avenues on 42nd Street. One couldn't tour Minskyville without encountering all manner of creative hucksters and moral poison: Indian herb doctors and Gypsy seeresses (both reeking of gin and skilled at picking pockets); divulgers of "golden medical secrets"; strongmen and living statuary; amateur phrenologists who offered to examine people's heads, looking for certain bumps and lumps that indicated sex drive; bums making obscene overtures to female pedestrians; and, of course, the main attraction, Hubert's Flea Museum, featuring its two-headed suckling pig and acrobatic insects. Minskyville, in short, had more in common with Coney Island than Manhattan. "Lose a few hundred infants in Minskyville," *The New Yorker* concluded, "scatter broken glass around to cut your feet on, and you might easily confuse the one with the other."

Manhattan's leading citizens were disturbed by what had become of "the crossroads of the world." Burlesque and its accompanying detritus could flourish down on the Lower East Side, but not under the bright lights of Broadway. The Forty Second Street Property Owners' and Merchants' Association, concerned about declining real estate values, also objected to burlesque in its backyard. Without prompt and decisive action, the indecent and unseemly pockets of the city threatened to invade every street and avenue.

John Sumner monitored these latest developments with keen interest and smug delight. He'd been waiting for such a convergence of forces, for respectable and respected New Yorkers to lend a voice to his cause. During his entire tenure, Jimmy Walker had been aiming disparaging comments at Sumner, like "I have never yet heard of a girl being ruined by a book" and "a reformer is a guy who rides through a sewer in a glass-bottomed boat." Now the embattled mayor would be put on the defensive, forced to speak beyond his usual pithy jokes and glib talk. An old, forgotten official known as the license commissioner was thawed out and dusted off, and he vowed to launch a round of hearings on burlesque—especially Minsky burlesque.

The mayor, meanwhile, prepared to answer to another force for decency and righteousness, the Honorable Judge Samuel Seabury, whose corruption probe had developed into a rollicking farce worthy of Broadway itself.

———

On a Friday night in early May 1932, Billy was standing near the protruding edge of the stage—the apron, it was called—when the rig of a traveler curtain wiggled loose and came crashing down. Startled, he lurched backward into the orchestra pit and landed awkwardly, his left leg splayed beneath him in a limp, unnatural angle. He heard himself make a strange noise, a coarse, primitive gargle, and looked up to see a semicircle of faces fanned around him, mouths screaming noiseless words, arms beckoning to someone or something just out of his sight. He tried to speak. His leg. Yes, his leg hurt, but his *shoulder* . . . goddammit, his shoulder . . . this was all he needed after the week he'd had, what with his star stripteaser up and quitting without any notice, making a liar out of his marquee. You'll be back, he'd told Gypsy. She didn't know how good she had it with the Minsky brothers.

"Do you think anything's broken?" he managed to ask. No one could say. Morton and Herbert carried him to his car, lowering him like a sleeping child into the backseat. Mary heard the car pull up and met her husband at the door, wondering why he was home so early. She summoned a doctor for an emergency house call. No broken bones, he said, just a "pulled muscle" in the leg and "probably a bruise" on the shoulder. He gave Billy a sedative and ordered him to lie flat.

Billy obeyed until the sun seared through the window and poked him awake. He hopped to the car on one leg and drove himself back to Manhattan in time for rehearsals at the Republic. He scavenged through the prop room until he found a cane, and hobbled about on that until it became tiresome. He developed a lurching Quasimodo walk, *stomp* drag *stomp* drag, that folded him into half of his already Lilliputian size. The leg he could handle, but it felt like someone had exploded a bomb inside his shoulder. He told himself it would go away if he ignored it long enough.

━━━━

$\mathcal{C}$olloquially known as the "Tweed Courthouse," owing to Boss Tweed's embezzlement of large sums of money during its construction, the building at 52 Chambers Street was one of Manhattan's most majestic structures, with Corinthian pillars that bowed into graceful archways and an octagonal rotunda awash in brilliant sheaths of light. Judge Samuel Seabury appreciated the irony of trying the Walker administration—the last in the old Tammany Hall tradition, if he handled the case properly—in a venue named for its most notorious and reviled leader.

Serious implications aside, the corruption trial was improbably entertaining—so much so that portions of testimony would inspire the Pulitzer Prize–winning 1959 Broadway musical *Fiorello!* Take, for instance, Seabury's questioning of a New York County sheriff and member of Tammany Hall who had somehow managed to accumulate nearly a half-million dollars in six years on an annual salary of $8,500:

Q: Where did you keep these moneys that you had saved?

A: In a safe-deposit box at home in the house.

Q: Whereabouts at home in the house did you keep this money that you had saved?

A: In the safe.

Q: In a safe?

A: Yes.

Q: In a little box in a safe?

A: A big safe.

Q: But a little box in a big safe?

A: In a big box in a big safe.

Q: Giving you the benefit of every doubt on sums from your official vocation and other gainful pursuits, the $83,000 extra you deposited in 1929 came from the same source that the other money came from?

A: Yes.

Q: Same tin box, is that right?

A: That is right.

Q: Now, in 1930, where did the extra cash come from, Sheriff?

A: Well, that came from the good box I had. [*Laughter*]

Q: Kind of a magic box.

A: It was a wonderful box.

Q: A wonderful box. [*Laughter*] What did you have to do—rub the lock with a little gold, and open it in order to find more money?

A: I wish I could.

Ten days later, the mayor arrived at the Tweed Courthouse, his haberdashery impeccably, if ostentatiously, coordinated: shirt, tie, pocket handkerchief, socks, one-button, double-breasted suit, and the stone in his pinky ring all complementary shades of blue. Five thousand spectators lunged to touch the sleeve of his coat, strained to see him wink beneath the cerulean brim of his fedora. Some wore shirts with BEER FOR PROSPERITY stitched across the front, and they hiccupped and belched in between shouts of "Atta boy, Jimmy!" and "You tell 'em, Jimmy!" A dozen women stationed by the entrance doused him with fresh rose petals, and swooned when he disappeared behind the door.

One week after the fall Billy's condition had worsened. He could hob-
ble on his leg but his shoulder was a throbbing knot of pain. It hurt just
to turn over in bed. No one could even guess at the cause; surely any injuries sustained from his fall should have been healed by now. He worried about the theaters and got angry whenever Morton or Herbert
appeared at his bedside. "Who's minding the store, brothers?" he asked,
and ordered them to get back to work.

The West Side Court, on 54th Street near Ninth Avenue, was a dour,
plain block of a building, as dingy as the Tweed Courthouse was stunning. Morton and Herbert arrived for their hearing indignant and
angry, tired of John Sumner's class-based rhetoric, the accusation that
the Minskys catered to perverts and degenerates indigenous to the
Lower East Side, the implication that the brothers were no better themselves. They listened to a stream of government witnesses natter on
senselessly. The secretary of Franklin Savings Bank insisted that he
would not recommend a loan on any parcel of real estate near Minsky's
Republic. A prominent rabbi condemned "the commercialization of
filth and sex depravity by Jews" (a comment that made Morton long to
retort, out loud, "Presumably by a goy it was okay").

The commissioner decided he would return their license on one condition: stripteasers would have to wear brassieres—an absurd, unten-
able mandate, the Minskys knew, in both letter and spirit. A girl and her
audience existed together alone, negotiating and compromising, both
pretending to offer more than they claimed.

How surreal, how ironically and cruelly odd, for Billy to be onstage
like this—the performer for once, under scrutiny and awaiting judgment. Morton wondered if his brother sensed the heat of staring eyes,
the rush of focused light. They kept their voices soft now, tepid and re-

ceding, and no longer spoke words Billy refused to hear. Paget's disease, the doctors said, a bone malignancy for which there was no cure, but no one quite understood the how or why or when; perhaps it had lain dormant inside his body and been rattled to life by his fall. Morton studied what was left of his brother, imagined what Billy felt: the illness trudging with bleak purpose across the map of his small body, detouring to command every inch, until his body collapsed inside him and pain was all that was left.

Billy turned in his bed to look at each one of them, matching dulcet, blurry words with faces—father Louis, wife Mary, son Irving, brother Herbert—and then settling, finally, on Morton. There was an empty chair where Abe, the first and once Billy's best brother, should have been. Billy hated empty seats more than anything else in the world; they inserted absence into the fullest experience, marred the symmetry of the flawless. For the first time in his life Billy couldn't tell what the audience wanted, comedy or tragedy, and because he was Billy and because he was a pro, he decided to give them both.

"Never work north of Fourteenth Street, right, Papa?" he asked, and somehow his shrunken gargle of a voice carried to all of their ears. They smiled at him, and Morton prepared himself to watch the final act. Their words grew duller around Billy, flat and blunted around the edges, compressed into one listless, monotonous drone. Quiet crept in, stealthy, taking its time, turning down the volume and unfurling the curtain, lowering it by inches, until the velvet hem teased the floor and the darkness seized his eyes.

Chapter Twenty-nine

I am going to give you back to God, Louise, for him to manage you. He will untangle this whole unhappy affair. In the meantime, I am going to know that you will and must love me. Because Louise, without me you are lost, dear. I will always be waiting for you to come to me.

—ROSE THOMPSON HOVICK

New York City and Nyack, New York, Winter 1953–1954

Rose Hovick's deterioration from cancer begins almost imperceptibly, as if her body wants to confront, stage by stage, the thing that dares to kill it. One pound at a time her figure whittles away, the tissue-paper skin of her face fuses to bone, her eyes exchange their quick, bold cunning for fear and rage—the former difficult for her to convey, the latter impossible to suppress.

Her fierce energy burns a shade dimmer, nearly extinguished, and flares again without warning. "Who is paying for that woman out there?" she whisper-screams, eyeing her nurse. "Gypsy! I don't need to pay anyone for living in my house, eating my food, and drinking my beer. Taking advantage because I'm down—well, I'm not that down!" That nurse quits and Gypsy finds another, an older woman who shuts

Rose Thompson Hovick's unmarked grave, Oak Hill Cemetery, Nyack, New York.

off her hearing aid when Rose's voice booms. One night, while tucking her patient into bed, the nurse hears a feeble plea: "Closer, please." She leans forward. Rose slams a metal water pitcher against her face with such force she dislodges the nurse's bridgework.

Dealing with Mother is another full-time job, one that doesn't pay. Gypsy can't eat. Sleep is elusive. Her stomach feels like a clenched fist; it is just a matter of time before her ulcer lights a fire in her core. In lucid moments Mother toys with her and June, sending them on scavenger hunts in the backyard storage shed, knowing full well what they'll find: a dozen radios, eight television sets, boxes of electric blankets, shopping bags overflowing with watches, rings, underwear, fur coats—artifacts from a lifetime spent bilking them both. Rose Hovick is now sixty-two, but for Gypsy the whole ordeal is like having another child, and ten-year-old Erik causes trouble enough. He's been stealing money from her purse since he turned five, $25 here and there, running up charges in neighborhood stores. It's been sixteen years since Gypsy started communicating with Mother through a lawyer—off and on, anyway—and she has done her best to keep Rose away from Erik, from seeping into him. She succeeded for a long time, but Mother found her ways, as she always did, like the afternoon she appeared at the front door of the house on 63rd Street.

Erik was five at the time, a precocious little boy wearing short pants and cowboy boots, and it was his job to greet company. He looked up to see an unfamiliar woman in a ruffled dress, with dark, curly hair sheared close to her head. She had a clown's smile, overbright and vaguely menacing, wide enough to show every perfect white tooth. She bent down to his level.

"Is your mother home?" she asked.

"Whom shall I say is calling?"

"Tell her it's her mother."

Erik knew the house rule: if you don't know a visitor, ask her to wait outside. But this was an exception, Erik thought, his mother's mother, and he swung open the door. The woman stepped inside, and Erik scuttled up the stairs to find Gypsy.

"Your mother's downstairs," he said, "and would like to see you."

Gypsy looked up from her work. She was preparing for her Royal

American Show, the largest traveling carnival of the day, a grueling but lucrative thirty-nine weeks. The company provided the tent and the carneys, she provided the entertainment, and her husband, Julio, had designed a "peep show"—a secondary act titled "What Are Your Dreams?" featuring nearly naked women posing in still-life tableaus— an homage, with Freudian underpinnings, to the *Ziegfeld Follies* and Minsky's interpretation thereof.

"Did you let her in the house?" she asked.

"Yes."

She should handle it, she knew, but she didn't have the time. Besides, Erik had to learn to deal with people like Mother if he were going to rule the world.

"For god's sake," Gypsy said, and sighed. "Hurry up and make sure she hasn't clipped the Picasso."

He ran downstairs and found his grandmother in the foyer.

"I'm sorry," he said, "but my mother's very busy right now and she can't see you."

He waited for her to leave, but instead she sat down on the sofa and patted the spot next to her.

"Sit down and talk to me," she said. "You must be Erik."

He sat and she leaned in closer, whispered into his ear.

"I bet you like guns, don't you?"

She opened her purse and pulled out a Colt .45. She placed the gun in his hands, so heavy he could barely lift it. It took all his strength to climb back upstairs to show his mother his prize, only to have her confiscate it immediately. That particular gun hadn't killed anyone in their past, but Gypsy understood the meaning behind the gesture, felt the panic of that time lodge deeper inside her memory. Mother loved to remind her of what they once had been, both alone and together.

Now, five years later, Gypsy can't believe their sick, sweet game is nearing its final play. She admits Rose to a place called Tender Elms, paying for ten days in advance. "So very elegant," Gypsy notes in her diary. "Expensive but wonderful." She dares to think the matter settled, but two weeks later, after dinner at June's house, she learns Mother went on a rampage and is no longer welcome at Tender Elms. It takes two full days to find another home that will accept her. "I hope this is for the good of all concerned," Gypsy writes, "but I know there is more to come."

And so there is. One day the phone rings and Erik picks up, answering "Miss Lee's residence," just as he's been taught. "Who may I say is calling?"

He listens.

"It's your mother's nurse," Erik calls up the stairs to Gypsy.

"I can't be bothered," Gypsy answers.

"My mother is busy right now," Erik reports.

"Tell her her mother is dying."

Erik relays the message.

"My mother is *always* dying," Gypsy says.

"Tell her it's real this time," the nurse replies, and Erik does.

The remainder of Gypsy's 1953 diary is sparse and quotidian—hairdresser appointments, bill tallies for food and cigarettes, an interview for *American Weekly*—and then the notations stop altogether, until the last week of the first month of the new year. The entry for January 28 reads, simply, "Mother died at 6:30."

She does not write what came before, how Mother got her final wish, the one they'd denied her for years: the three of them together again in one room, close as they could be. June stands at the window. Outside a light snow falls, frost speckling the glass, the only movement among them for a long time. Gypsy sits at the foot of Mother's bed, watching her breathe, the timid sinking and swelling of her chest. She has braced herself for this, practiced her stance and stoic face, her posture of defense. The violet eyes flip open, and Mother pulls herself up on her elbows, grunting with the effort, veins twitching, tiny exposed wires beneath translucent skin. She shimmies toward the end of the bed, toward Gypsy, her breath now coming in dry rasps. "I know about you," she says, a catch between the words, making each stand on its own. "Greedy, selfish! You want me to die. I'm the only one who knows all about you."

One mottled leg slides from the mattress, hangs limply over the side. Her nightgown gapes open. Her old suede grouch bag, still strung around her waist after all these years, now dangles next to a colostomy bag. The sight brings to mind Gypsy's favorite piece of family lore, the

great-great-grandmother and her sash of "horsemeat," waiting for everyone around her to die. Rose clutches at the money bag and teeters, losing her balance.

"You'll fall," Gypsy says and reaches to steady her.

"No! You can't have anything back! Just because I'm letting go—it's
mine! My house, my jewelry . . ." Her body sways from the force of her
voice. Gypsy tries to lower her gently, as if putting her down for a nap.
Rose grips her daughter's forearm and kicks beneath her, torso
writhing, spittle collecting in the corners of her mouth. There is a sudden shift in power, and Rose twists and heaves herself upward. Gypsy
lets her body wilt, allows her mother to take the lead. Gypsy lies on her
back now, the headboard knocking hard against the curve of her skull,
swatches of her hair captured in Rose's fists. For the first time she turns
toward June, who has been watching, wordlessly and utterly still. Now
June rushes at her.

"No," Gypsy says, and means it. "Don't. No."

June had her showdown with Mother twenty-five years ago. It is
Gypsy's turn now, at long last.

For several moments mother and daughter lie together, perfectly
aligned, symmetrical, limbs twining, eye to eye, chest against chest,
breath blowing hot on skin, addressing each other in a language only
they understand. She owes Mother one last moment like this, when no
one else clamors for attention or even exists, when the person Gypsy
loved first—unconditionally, without knowing the consequences—is
the one she still loves best. She damaged this woman back when she
was young, when the original Ellen June, weighing in at twelve pounds
but without an ounce of talent, left her body and the one became two.
That was forty-three years ago, and now it is Mother's turn as much as
it is hers.

When Rose speaks this time, her cadence is steady, a soft, unbroken
moan.

"You'll never forget," she says, "how I'm holding you right this
minute, Louise, holding you as strongly as I can, wishing with all my
heart I could take you all the way with me—all the way down!"

Gypsy doesn't move. She waits, and waits, until the bony fingers un-
coil from her hair and the breath stops tickling her cheek, until their

bodies separate for the very last time. The violet eyes close again, stripping Mother's face of any color or life. She seems to relax, then, sinking into herself, the foundation of an old house settling. Another stretch of quiet, and Rose Hovick hisses the last words Gypsy will hear her say:

"This isn't the end. Wherever you go, as long as either of you lives, I'll be right there. . . . So go on, Louise, tell all your classy friends how funny I was, how much smarter you were than me. When you get your own private kick in the ass, just remember: it's a present from me to you."

Gypsy and one of Rose's neighbors are the only ones to attend her funeral Mass, held at St. Ann's Catholic Church in Nyack, New York. After the service, Gypsy tucks a few dollars into the collection box and slips quietly out the door. Neither she nor June attends the burial at Oak Hill Cemetery, where Rose is laid to rest without any marker bearing her name.

Chapter Thirty

H. L. Mencken called me an ecdysiast. I have also
been described as deciduous. The French call me a
déshabilleuse. In less-refined circles I'm known as a
strip teaser.

—GYPSY ROSE LEE

New York City, 1932–1936

We take great pride in presenting the star of our show, the one and only Miss Gypsy . . . Rose . . . Lee!

The brazen swing of the spotlight rendered the audience unseen, but she could picture their faces—so many faces!—shining like tangles of jewelry. How hard she'd worked to collect them: publishing mogul Condé Nast, playwright George S. Kaufman, the bisexual bon vivant Tallulah Bankhead. Writers and critics and cultural arbiters gleamed from every corner of the Irving Place Theatre: William Saroyan and Edmund Wilson, Carl Van Doren and Carl Van Vechten (the latter of whom once derided burlesque audiences as "childishly leering"), Leonard Lyons and Brooks Atkinson, H. L. Mencken (who would coin the word "ecdysiast" in her honor) and George Jean Nathan (who called her a "kimonophobe"), and a representative from *The New Yorker*, who admitted he "went for Miss Lee, so to speak." Over there sat Jean Cocteau, visiting from Paris, who took one look at Gypsy and murmured, "How vital!" and the pseudonymous Squimpfenhuppels, a New York society couple whose blood, according to one insider, was "three stains bluer than a Duke Ellington rhythm." All Gypsy's personal baubles to flaunt and to flash, and she never felt so pretty as when they were covering her.

Wearing a chartreuse costume adorned with flittered leaves, she swanned languidly across the stage, as though on her way to see *La Traviata* at the Met. In one hand she held a ripe apple aloft, and the orchestra began the sweet soft strains of her song. She talk-sang her words, pinning their ends between her lips, a humming effect she had learned from her prestigious new friends:

> *I'm a lonesome little Eve*
> *Looking for an Adam*
> *Gee I wish I had him*
> *Cuddling me, 'neath the shade of a tree*
> *And in our garden we would be so happy.*

Gypsy recognized the pattern she'd come to establish, at once buoyant and hopeless: exchanging every certain triumph for an unobtainable dream.

She quit the Republic just before her original benefactor, Billy Minsky, died unexpectedly. He'd been furious, especially after all he'd done, discovering and rescuing her from those backwoods burlesque venues, molding her into an American icon. He'd predicted she'd return to Minsky's—for the money, if not the glory—and he knew that, despite himself, he'd happily take her back.

She left for her old gangster benefactor, Waxey Gordon, who'd secured her a spot in a Florenz Ziegfeld show called *Laid in Mexico*. Finally, here was her chance to join a Ziegfeld show—a real, legitimate Broadway show—but *Laid in Mexico* was hardly the *Follies*. The Depression had broken the producer, both financially and literally; Ziegfeld was deathly ill from pneumonia and resigned to borrowing money from Waxey and other gangsters. "Don't ask questions," Waxey ordered Gypsy. "Just do as you're told."

Rose hoped they would change the title of *Laid in Mexico,* which sounded too "Minskyish," and Ziegfeld coincidentally obliged. *Hot-Cha!* was a full-scale musical production, with Ziegfeld's customary barbaric bombast and splendor. When the choreographer asked for her name, Gypsy hesitated, and then confessed, "Rose Louise."

"The moment I said it I was sorry," Gypsy admitted. "He knew who I was, and he'd think I was ashamed of my burlesque name. I wanted to take it back but I didn't. I *was* ashamed and the realization made it worse." She was given the role of "Girl in Compartment," a weekly salary of $60—$840 less than at Minsky's Republic—and no solo introduction as Gypsy Rose Lee.

Hot-Cha! closed after only twelve weeks, a flop blamed on the "depressing times." She wasted weeks, in her mother's words, scouring Broadway for another role before she headed back to the money at Minsky's. Herbert and Morton were now in charge of the Republic. Like Billy, the younger Minsky brothers hadn't been too happy when she left, but they let her make her case to rejoin the fold. What, they asked, made her so popular among the Minsky audience? Why was she considered the best stripteaser in the business?

"I don't know myself what it is," she replied. "I don't feel any spark of genius *here.*" She splayed her hands over her breasts. Morton laughed. Okay, okay—she could have her old job back. "Let's see now," he said. "You were getting $60 up with those big shots; we'll give you $90." She had no choice but to take it, even though it was a 93 percent pay cut from her original Minsky salary.

*S*he glided back toward the wings of the stage, pouting now, the spotlight's thin finger grazing her face:

> *I'm a lonesome little Eve.*
> *All I do is sit and grieve.*
> *Like Eve I carry round this apple every night*
> *Looking for an Adam with an appetite*

Soon after Gypsy's return to the Republic she lost the Rego Park house. All of her furniture was repossessed save for Waxey's dining room set, which Rose shipped to a large, ramshackle apartment on West End Avenue, leased under Aunt Belle's name. A taxi arrived at midnight, and Rose quickly tied to the roof all the relics of their past: the cow head, tent, dancing dolls, gilded guns. Gypsy debated asking Waxey Gordon for a loan, but, in an unfortunate bit of timing, the FBI declared the bootlegger "Public Enemy Number One" and arrested him on charges of tax evasion.

Waxey sent a letter: could she do her old friend a favor, and come visit him at Northeastern Penitentiary? It would so impress his fellow inmates. She agreed, but how she dreaded the slow walk to his table in the visiting room, the amplified whistles inside those thin tight walls, the leers that clawed at her back. It was a runway leading to a place out of her control, with no reward at the end. After two visits, she decided she would never go back. "It made me uncomfortable," she said, "being on display that way."

The Minskys finally relented and restored her old salary, but once again she left burlesque—this time for a role in *Melody*, the new production by George White, of *Scandals* fame. Another drastic pay cut, to just $100 per week. "I guess I wasn't used to so much money," she said of burlesque, "because the more I got the more ambitious I became to land on Broadway." She had just six lines but padded her part by exclaiming "Ouch!" when her bustle caught in the door. Her salary dropped to $50 during the national bank moratorium, and when the show closed in April 1933, her funds were once again depleted.

Down the circular staircase now, slowly, long legs taking their time, her shoes precisely matching her skin—all the better to camouflage her large feet. Her eyes coasted to a bald man in the second row, and she strolled toward him, offering the apple, letting his imagination fill the pauses in her refrain.

> *Would you . . . for a big red apple?*
> *Would you . . . for my peace of mind?*
> *Would you . . . for a big red apple,*
> *Give me what I'm trying to find—*

Of course the Minskys welcomed her back, their Prodigal Strip-peuse. They dubbed her the "Queen of Women" and booked her solid at three of their theaters: the Republic, Billy Minsky's Brooklyn, and the new Park Theatre in Boston, where the overarching philosophy was described as "burlesque moderne." She accompanied Herbert and Morton to a celebratory luncheon at the Hotel Touraine and posed for pictures, the brothers' arms linked around her back. The Minskys vowed to provide work for a "sizable group" of Boston's unemployed while honoring the city's puritanical roots; their show would attract the "limousine trade" and be fit for "your wife, sweetheart, or aunt from Dubuque." Gypsy would even wear a rhinestone in her navel.

Boston's censor nevertheless denounced such Minsky productions as *Wander Over from Back Bay* and *Irma Fish from Brookline,* but audiences were enthralled, especially by Gypsy Rose Lee. Every evening, before she strolled onto the stage, she instructed the stage manager to shush the crowd. It always obeyed. She repaid the Minsky brothers for their loyalty, defending them in the press. "Burlesque pays well," she reasoned. "I'd rather work for good dough in burlesque than sit around waiting for something to come up . . . and the dears who reveal their peeled forms at Minsky's are never within reach of the audience as they are in popular Broadway floor shows, where the drunks paw you, and you don't have to sit with customers who get gay."

This was the part of her Eve routine that the men, bald or hirsute, waited for—the slinky, torturously slow strut, the apple balanced in the elegant curve of her palm, the fruit rolling forward along her fingertips, stopped by a pair of puckered lips. The first man took a bite and then Gypsy backed away, scanning the crowd. Who was worthy of the second, the third, the bite that would strip it to its core?

Despite her speech in Boston, Gypsy once again left burlesque, partly because her prescient, pragmatic, ever-resourceful mind told her burlesque might not always be there to take her back. After Mayor Jimmy Walker resigned from City Hall, his old nemesis—and complete political antithesis—took over in 1934. Fiorello La Guardia would not roll dice with the neighborhood boys, or take appointments at an underworld nightclub in Central Park, or shake hands and propose toasts at Minsky's Republic on opening nights. Instead he was busy turning New York inside out, ordering, within one minute of his official swearing-in, the arrest of gangster Lucky Luciano, followed up by a threat to the entire police department to "Drive out the racketeers or get out yourselves" and the violent, sledgehammer destruction of hundreds of confiscated slot machines.

Which was all well and good for those who had tired of the old regime—journalist Heywood Broun, for one, declared the city "stands in need of scathing sunlight, fresh air and a fine and rousing wind to cleanse its lungs and vitals"—but there were indications that La Guardia's "rousing wind" would be more akin to a tornado, that he wouldn't reform the city's character so much as raze it completely. From what Gypsy knew of him, he sounded a lot like Mother—volatile and vicious (once telling an underling, "You let them shit all over you and pee all over you and you like it so much you lick it up"); obstinate and unyielding; and strangely, anachronistically prudish, insisting, for instance, that his secretary stay in hotels where residents had a midnight curfew.

Gypsy saw bits of herself, too, in the new mayor, the way he was an outsider in his chosen world: five feet two; disproportionately corpulent; sartorially inept; a mouth that spat words at a frenetic, machine-gun pace; a singular, strangely falsetto voice that, in moments of rage, climbed the scales and slid into a prehistoric screech. One of his own advisers dismissed him as "Half Wop, Half American, Half Republican." La Guardia was intent on reinventing not himself but the city that had made her, and he was well aware of Gypsy's place in it. He insulted her, comparing her unfavorably to an opera singer, boasting that the new airport under construction in Queens "will be to Newark as Kirsten Flagstad is to Gypsy Rose Lee." He made quips about her need to "take her clothes off," to which she had a fast retort: Why, Mr. Mayor, she said, "you know I'd never end a sentence with a preposition." At a roast in City Hall, he even dressed like Gypsy, donning a slinky gown and cape, calling himself "Gypsy Rose Lee Guardia." She was safe enough to satirize, but her industry was a menace to New York; burlesque, La Guardia declared, was "incorporated filth."

So Gypsy left burlesque again while she still could, this time at the behest of another Broadway showman, Billy Rose, then-husband of Fanny Brice, her childhood idol. He needed an emcee for his nightclub on 54th Street, the Casino de Paree, which he described as "the usual 50 showgirls in 49 costumes." She lasted only two months and blamed her dismissal on the night she flubbed her lines, unnerved by Fanny's presence in the audience. *Would Fanny recognize me?* Gypsy wondered. *Would she even remember me?* And then she opened her mouth and said, "And now in Jimmy Savo's opinion, the world's greatest pantomimist, Jimmy Savo," when she meant to say "in Charlie Chaplin's opinion." "Get your money," Billy Rose told her when she returned to the wings. "You're through."

That was that, and once again she returned to burlesque, but not to any house run by the Minskys. She was now the featured performer at their greatest competitor, the Irving Place Theatre, located in Union Square and known (to the Minskys' perpetual ire) as the "Metropolitan Opera of Burlesque." She knew that the owners were, one might say, "connected," and that they paid her highest salary to date, $1,000 a week, and that they'd let her take off for important openings and parties anytime she pleased. Herbert and Morton hated to see her go, but they seemed to understand. Gypsy emphasized it was her, not them. She had to leave the ones who made her what she was in order to become what she was meant to be. It wasn't personal. Then again, she now understood that not much about her was.

$\mathcal{B}$y now the apple was bitten down to the core, and with a grand flourish she tossed it to a man leaning over the railing in the lower box. He lunged for the fruit and fell directly into the orchestra pit. A hushed silence, and then laughter and applause as he sprang up and waved the core in the air, triumphant. Turning to the rest of the audience, she vowed to keep searching for her Adam. And yet she had a confession to make, if this wonderful, darling crowd would be kind enough to listen: what she *really* wanted to do, her dream of dreams, was to perform in the *Follies*. Could a lowly stripteaser, one who'd always been snubbed by the "café girls," be so chosen? If one were mortified by the Minskys, could she be glorified by Ziegfeld?

She continued her soliloquy, at once articulating and ridiculing her ambition, and the orchestra launched into a chorus of "Lullaby of the Leaves." Time to unpin her leaves, one by one, toss them to the audience, slip back behind the curtain, wait for them to roar her name. They never let her down. Peeking out, she protested, "Darlings, please don't ask me to take off any more. I'll catch cold. No, please, I'm embarrassed. No, honestly, I can't. I'm almost shivering now," smiling so they could see every one of her hard-earned teeth. In the end she yielded, as she always did, emerging long enough to unpin the three last, vital leaves, her final figments of control. For one eternal second she stood wholly exposed, without even a layer of innuendo for cover, and then the lights snuffed out, blanketing her.

Once again she stepped out of sight, truly shivering now, needing a brandy, craving a cigarette, feeling her ulcer flare like a lit match, and she puzzled at the moment the mood changed, that subtle, nearly imperceptible shift: did the crowd turn on her, or she on it? Not this night in particular but *every* night, all of those gilded faces melding into one seething mass, a rutting animal so deftly biding its time. All of them— *it*—expected something she was disappointed they wanted, her disappointment compounded by the fact that she had nothing left to give.

―――――

At long last she knew who Gypsy Rose Lee was. She had found someone to assemble her final pieces with calculated care, her whole more polished than each individual part. His name was Edwin Bruns, "Eddy," she called him. He was the youngest member of the New York Stock Exchange and an active participant in the Friars Club, and he would never be seen at one of those backroom "circus parties." Nine years earlier, in 1925, he had married a Miss Margaret Offerman of Brooklyn in the Italian Garden of the Ambassador Hotel, a venue so prestigious and posh it seemed more suited to Monte Carlo than Atlantic City. One journalist investigated his illicit romance with Gypsy to no avail, concluding that Eddy was a "mythical admirer from New Jersey, with a great deal of money, whose identity no one on Broadway really knows." Gypsy, wanting to keep his cover, offered a cryptic explanation: "He's so darned handsome," she said, "that I have to keep him under cover so no one else will go for him." Worth $2 million, he promised to take care of Gypsy so she'd never have to worry about money again, if that were even possible.

Eddy came to matinees only, so as not to arouse the suspicions of his wife, and taught Gypsy where and how to be seen. It wasn't enough to attend the premiere of *Jumbo*, Billy Rose's gaudy circus spectacle at the Hippodrome, or the opening night of the Met. She had to be even more fantastic than the shows, dressed in a floor-length cape made entirely of orchids. At just the right moment she emerged from a limousine and let the cameras douse her with light—"ignoring the others," she noted later, "wearing the same old things." The gossip columnists applauded her ingenuity:

"Among the death watch at first nights recently," wrote O. O. McIntyre in the *Journal-American*,

> has been the long-reigning Queen of Burlesque, Gypsy Rose Lee. She is among the celebrity curiosa that collects at smart soirees. An eyeful in a showy way, but not quite the over carmined type one might expect. . . . Gypsy is of an intelligence belying her calling. Quick on the trigger . . . as she continues her slink through the Park Avenue drawing rooms there are not many who do not angle for her, and in every instance, to those who have not seen her she proved a surprise package. Those who expected to find Miss Lee over rouged and thickly veined with Rabelaisian repartee, discovered instead a self possessed lady with a cough drop voice and a dress suit accent who might have run up from Bryn Mawr for a prom.

One critic, though, dubbed her "the hillbilly's Juliet," which only proved the past still kept too quick a pace behind her.

She was someone who had learned her mother's most useful lessons. A thing worth having was a thing worth stealing, and if you were crafty enough the original owner would believe it should have been yours all along. Such was the case when Eddy escorted her one night to the

Savoy Plaza, the grand Art Deco hotel that lorded over the midtown entrance to Central Park. There in the Café Lounge, Dwight Fiske, an openly gay member of the now-defunct Algonquin Round Table, presided over a piano and talk-sang his salacious ditties.

Gypsy became a regular, sitting at a table by the stage, chain-smoking as she jotted down the lyrics to her favorite songs: "Mrs. Pettibone," which recounted three failed marriages; "Anthony and Cleopatra" (Gypsy especially appreciated the heroine's motto, "Keep them waiting, and they always weaken in the end"); and "Ida, the Wayward Sturgeon," the tale of an adulterous love affair, as told by a fish. From then on, every time she performed one of those songs at Irving Place, dressed in girlish petticoats and bows, Dwight Fiske himself sat in the front row, thinking that no one but Gypsy Rose Lee could have made his jokes her own.

$\mathcal{S}$he was someone who finally lived alone. No more huddling under the sheets with Mother, burying secrets in the safety of the dark, secrets that belonged to Louise Hovick only. She didn't even want Rose to visit her at 81 Irving Place in Gramercy Park, a distinguished brown brick building where gargoyles perched on Romanesque archways and she never had to open her own front door.

She decorated the apartment herself, with just the slightest assistance from the antique dealers on Third Avenue. It was an ebullient mix of periods and styles: blackamoors guarding the front door; a Chippendale sofa; a few chairs covered with her own needlework; Victorian settees upholstered in a muted salmon; crimson satin draperies held back by brass angels in flight. Metal and plaster cherubs kept watch in every corner, and on the walls she hung a smattering of Charles Dana Gibson plates, a collage of her programs and press clippings, a series of Marcel Vertes watercolors (including several portraits of herself), a white elephant from Florenz Ziegfeld, and a hodgepodge of Victorian tattoo designs, all elaborately framed with colored velvet mattings and a wreath of gold leaf. Each piece could prompt a conversation—whether or not nudity was innocent or risqué, whether tattooed skin was naked or concealed, whether societal notions of such matters had advanced or stagnated or regressed. Nothing matched, but it was hers. It was *her*.

To attend to her every need, Gypsy hired a cook and maid, Eva Mor-cur, another of Eddy's brilliant ideas. Every star had one, he told her, and she needed to start behaving as such. A former singer for the Cotton Club in Harlem, Eva too craved publicity and knew how to get it, waiting until the cameras were poised before draping Gypsy with her silk robe. On Friday nights Gypsy threw exclusive soirees, her invitations coveted by those on the social register (including the aforementioned Squimpfenhuppels as well as the Otis Chatfield-Taylors), artists, writers, and gangsters alike. Eva fretted over every detail, preparing several courses of comfort food—roast beef and liver smothered in gravy, platters of vegetables, boiled potatoes, homemade chocolate cake—while Gypsy ran about in a frenzy, wearing nothing but a sheer negligee, three-inch fingernails, and $25,000 worth of jewelry, soon to be stolen during a holdup in her apartment vestibule by six men who apologized and told her, "We're broke or we wouldn't do this, Gyps." She tried to swallow her pear-shaped diamond ring, but one of the thugs punched her so hard she spat out the diamond and loosened a few of her Waxey Gordon–sponsored teeth, as well. She instantly recognized the thugs—old acquaintances from her underworld days—and knew better than to say a word.

After the guests arrived and collected flutes of champagne, the talk turned to art and books and theater and, inevitably, to Gypsy Rose Lee herself. What did she think about *Strip Girl*, the show on Broadway that told the story of a burlesque dancer? Was it based on her life? "I consider that show an insult," Gypsy replied, "not only to me but to the many stars who have been in burlesque. The author should have his eyes opened and his mind washed." Did everyone hear that Mae West called her "Lady Peel"? Gypsy's retort: "Mae West," she said, "is the weakest link in the Vassar daisy chain." When another actress, Carole Landis, criticized "leg art," an informal term for burlesque, Gypsy feigned offense. "Leg art requires no protection from Miss Landis," she purred. "I am sure no one will mind if she does *Salome* in long underwear and a fire helmet." When Yale boys informed Gypsy she placed second to Ann Sheridan in a campus popularity poll, they asked for her opinion of the actress. "I think he was a swell general," she said sweetly. Did everyone see her picture with the Princeton football team, where her position was given as "Right End"? How clever she is, sea-soning her conversation with French—*comment beau, comment special, comment futé*—and to think she had so little formal education. Did they hear Gypsy once attended a publishing party with playwright and pub-lisher John Farrar? She took charge of every conversation, tossing off casual references to Shakespeare and Karl Marx, to Dorothy Parker's *Death and Taxes* and Damon Runyon's *Guys and Dolls,* to the recent au-tobiographies published by Emma Goldman and Lincoln Steffens. Isn't it darling when she tilts her head self-consciously and inquires, "Whither the New Negro?" Have they heard that Gypsy is a drug ad-dict? A lesbian? A damn good female impersonator? Aren't her stories about her mother hilarious—bilking all those lodge men, stealing blan-kets and wigs and entire sketches, shooting at her sister's boyfriend, threatening the late, great Billy Minsky?

And Gypsy relished all of it, standing behind her shiny chrome bar and letting them come to her. On these nights she was incapable of turning herself off, of doing anything that would stifle Gypsy Rose Lee, and the next morning she waited for proof that she was still worthy of her own creation. Drama critic Bernard Sobel sent a letter she pressed into her scrapbook for safekeeping:

Dear, beloved, dazzling Gypsy:

   It was all so wonderful, so cozy, exciting, alcoholic and fascinat-ing that I have decided to forswear parties. No. I will never go to an-other party, for fear of obscuring the glow of yours.

   There they sat in that salle à manger, Heywood Broun, and the engaging Connie, and you—on the floor, I believe; and deliciously sensual Fanny Brice, the pure Semitic passion percolating through the comedy conversation. . . . There they all sat, excepting those who, like Tallulah Bankhead, were standing at the refectory table grabbing a second portion of the hot liver.

   And those, like George Jean Nathan, who were not standing were traipsing around the house; rushing into the kitchen and the ante-chambers; guzzling beer; listening to George Davis; sliding up and down the elevator; studying the Greek frescoes over the mantel-piece; inspecting your well-worn and notably high-brow library;

gossiping about you; chit-chatting about your guests; admiring the African knickknacks in the shadow of the high semi-circular window.

But alas and alack! It's all over now: the memory of the kiss Beatrice Lillie administered as she passed me in the hall; the feel of your rounded, taut breasts; the quality of Claire [*sic*] Luce's personality; the ubiquitous energy of your faithful secretarial Achates; the realization that some of your guests had salad and others did not.

I'm inarticulate with emotion. I'm saddened at my own mendacity because it's all the bunk that I won't go to another party as long as I live. Just ask me; and—of course, keep on loving me.

She was someone unsure of how to fit her family into her new world, if at all. June was tap dancing her way across the country, playing "every ladies' luncheon, bazaar, county fair, or turkey shoot" from Boise to Denver to St. Louis, still hoping for a break. She was pregnant, due in April 1935, and like Gentle Julia in vaudeville all those years ago, she never identified the baby's father. The idea of having her own family moved her to reconnect with her sister. "There was someone other than myself," June thought, "who was aware, indeed wary, of family characteristics. I wasn't alone . . . my sister would understand." (June, ironically, would one day borrow a bit from Rose's old stories, telling her own daughter, April, that her father had died after contracting syphilis, masturbating and then rubbing his eye, through which the disease entered his brain.)

June took a bus to New York and knocked on the door of the West End apartment, where she assumed Gypsy lived with Mother.

"What in hell has happened to you?" Rose asked. "I don't know anyone who can help you. My poor baby." But she let her inside and told her not to expect Gypsy. "Oh, no," Rose said. "She lives in a penthouse downtown. Got a maid that waits on her hand and foot—I'm only allowed in when nobody else is there. You'll be the same."

For a brief time June moved in with Rose, and slowly, cautiously, Gypsy let her sister reenter her life. Once June appeared at her hospital bedside after Gypsy was rushed in an ambulance from Irving Place—after yet another shot from her ulcer. Wires patched to her chest, a heart monitor blinking nearby, Gypsy gave her sister a lingering look of pity. "I'd like to be sure this baby business doesn't ruin all your chances," she told June. "You wearing that big bra? If your breasts droop you're going to be out of luck, that's all. . . . It's too late to try to help you any other way."

Another time, the bell rang during one of Gypsy's parties. She swung open the door to find June, oddly nervous, shifting her weight. Behind her, in the parlor, all her famous friends were smoking pot and laughing like idiots, and Gypsy wished they all would just leave and leave her alone. At least for the night.

"Getting on my nerves," she said, her arm sweeping toward the noise. She wrapped a white mink around her shoulders. "They'll never know I'm gone."

Over an order of yaka mein, still the cheapest dish on the menu, the sisters circled each other warily, wondering what to omit and what to divulge. Gypsy emptied a jigger of brandy into black coffee, lit a Murad cigarette. For reasons both banal and complicated, she felt the need to explain herself.

She reached into her bag and tossed a newspaper on the table. "Look at that," she commanded June. Two curved lines marked the relevant paragraph like black wings.

June read aloud: "Gypsy Rose Lee says her favorite fan sits in the front row at every performance with a lunch box on his lap and his room number printed on his forehead."

"If I keep saying things like that in all those columns," Gypsy said, "I'll be a fad."

"You want to be a fad?"

"I want to be a legend. A fad is just one step along the way." She sipped her coffee and debated telling June her big news: an offer, at long last, to be in the *Ziegfeld Follies*. After Florenz Ziegfeld's death in 1932, the Shubert brothers had taken over the title and offered Gypsy the part previously played by Josephine Baker. They would open in New York at the Winter Garden and then go on the road. The salary was disappointing, just $250 per week, and she would have to cover costumes and travel expenses. But for the first time she'd be a real principal and, even better, work with Fanny Brice. Fanny, too, had fallen in with gangsters and changed her appearance, hiring a Chicago doctor to use "saws, hatchets, chisels, files, and whatever other instruments were necessary" to reshape her nose. She had been able to transform her vaudeville past into a legitimate stage career—a feat even June, with all those lessons and dedication to her craft, had yet to accomplish.

"Think I've got a lovely job coming up, June. It means the road, but you'll be proud of me." She guzzled the rest of her coffee and began reapplying lipstick, waiting for her sister's reaction.

"I'm proud now," June said, surprising her.

They were quiet a moment, studying each other.

"Let's say you're prouder now than you were, huh?" Gypsy said, and they walked together out into the cold. The wind rocked the air and lashed at their faces. A fleet of Packard sedans and boxy Oldsmobiles trudged along Lexington Avenue, keeping them noisy company. Without thinking, Gypsy pulled her sister into her arms.

"I wish to God I didn't worry about you, June," she said, "but you don't make it easy." She sneezed into June's hair. "There. If I catch cold in this frigging wind, it's going to be all your fault!"

June unwrapped herself. "Go on home, go inside," she said. "I'm fine! Don't worry, I'm going to be okay."

Gypsy walked halfway down the street before turning back to shout, "Like hell you are!"

━━━━━━

She worried equally about her mother, but for different reasons. She'd stashed Rose away in that rambling apartment on West End Avenue, where she rented the empty rooms to a bevy of lesbians who found her as charming and irresistible as Murray Gordon had all those years ago. Rose knew they weren't welcome at "normal joints" and took full advantage, sending them on errands and charging them for every measly meal: 75 cents for a plate of spaghetti with no cheese, 15 cents for a cup of coffee. The yelling, the screaming, the all-night brawls culminating in accusations about who was stealing from Rose—Gypsy heard about all of it from June. There were the inevitable reconciliations, too, with Rose sobbing about how she couldn't work because of her asthma and how much she loathed sex. "I gave up marriage years ago because I hate sex, hate hate sex," she'd say, clinging to her pet *du jour*. "Don't I, Kate?" The girl would say, "Yes, Roanie, yes," and squeeze Rose to her chest. And they all knew to comfort Rose when she told tales about her two daughters, the one who had failed her and the one who had forgotten her.

It's true; Gypsy Rose Lee did push Mother away, and remade her in the process. Rose was now a legend in her own right—the punch line to Gypsy's favorite jokes, the antimoral to every parable, the sad, twisted cameo in her act. Gypsy's Irving Place repertoire included a number called "Give Me a Lay!" Henry Miller, on at least one occasion, sat among the nameless men who fanned newspapers across their laps, watching Gypsy shuffle stark naked across the stage, her only prop a Hawaiian lei. She asked if they knew how it felt to get a good lay, how even her mother would be grateful for a lay once in a while. Why, Mother would take a lay on the piano, or on the floor. An old fashioned lay, if need be. A lay any old way, yes sir . . .

"The strippers talk to their customers as they do their stunt," Miller reported.

The coup de grâce comes when, after having divested themselves of every stitch of clothing, there is left only a spangled girdle with a fig leaf dangling in front—sometimes a little monkey beard, which is quite ravishing. As they draw towards the wings they stick their bottoms out and slip the girdle off. Sometimes they darken the stage and give a belly dance in radium paint. It's good to see the belly button glowing like a glowworm, or like a bright half dollar. It's better still to see them holding their boobies, especially when said boobies are full of milk.

Rose knew too much about the mechanics of Gypsy's creation, where the paint might peel and the screws might loosen, the remote corners where the damaged parts were stashed, the lovely lies they invented together to fill in all the gaps. With one dagger word Mother could kill her, a fairy-tale character that couldn't be put together again. The city had become too small for both of them, so Gypsy bought a country house and farm out in Highland Mills, New York, an hour northwest of the city. She named it Witchwood Manor, and there Rose once again collected a harem of willing and faithful servants. They hoed the land, tended to the animals, reroofed the barn, painted the chicken coop, and widened the driveway. Rose paid them nothing for their effort—wasn't part of the fun of living on a farm tending to its upkeep?—and in turn each of them gave Rose $3 per night.

On Fridays, just before Gypsy's parties began, Mother sometimes showed up with her rooster, Solly, tucked under an arm. She did not understand how her elder daughter, the one she'd made her namesake, had become this creature who no longer needed or wanted her. Being cut off from Gypsy was every bit as painful as giving birth to Rose Louise; it was as if her firstborn nearly killed her all over again.

The rift affected them equally but inversely, protecting who Gypsy had become while dismantling who Mother had been—Madame Rose, the "Developer of Children"—and there was no room to give on either side. Rose tried to take what she could, literally pushing at Gypsy's door, Solly squawking and fidgeting as she fought for purchase.

"I guess he's not good enough for such a grand apartment," she yelled, thrusting the rooster at Gypsy. "All we're good for is to work like horses on that farm of yours."

Beyond her daughter's shoulder she heard the clinking glasses and riotous laughter. She glimpsed the sleek fur stoles, the animals' heads still attached, resting on the bodices of empire gowns. She smelled smoke so foreign, so musky sweet, she forgot all about her asthma. For once her words held no self-pity or deceit, and they dropped from her mouth like hail, cold and hard and perfectly formed.

"I," she said, "have as much right to be at this party as you have. And by God, you can't keep me out."

Gypsy clutched her mother's wrists and danced her backward into the elevator.

"Get the hell out of here," she said, "so I can be myself!"

Rose snorted. "Yourself? You mean so you can pretend to be that phony-voiced con artiste with the trick French gags and the filthy jokes, and waltz around half naked with all the flashy jewelry Eddy tosses your way?"

"Out!" Gypsy insisted. "Out, for God's sake, and let me go to work."
Finally Rose relented, and she was gone.

It wasn't over, though; it would never be over. From June she heard
every accusation and complaint: Mother just didn't know why Gypsy
spent every weekend in a hospital, ulcer or no ulcer. She says it's restful?
Fiddle! Why not go in a taxi instead of an ambulance? Gypsy thinks it's
stylish to be exhausted all the time. Here Rose was, a prisoner up in the
country, while Gypsy enjoyed ambulance rides and all that publicity.
Anyway, the illness was all in Gypsy's mind. The girl was scared of her
own shadow, nervous about everything, and it served her right. That's
what she gets for ignoring her own mother, for treating her like a
stranger and a joke, for being an "unnatural child." Her heart was sick
with shame for both her daughters. One day, if Gypsy didn't repent,
everyone would know every detail of her seedy, sordid lost year in burlesque, when she was no more special than anyone else, when she
nearly killed herself in order to live.

On occasion, only when necessary, Gypsy and Rose reunited and remembered how it had been, just a poor single mother and daughter
against an unforgiving world. Such a temporary reconciliation was vital
on the afternoon of November 3, 1936, when Gypsy invited her mother
and sister to meet at her apartment. This time, Rose did not bring Solly
the rooster, and she made sure to arrive before June. She and Gypsy
needed to discuss that morning's *Daily News*—in particular, an article
about an actress calling herself June Havoc: "The world knows of
Gypsy . . . darling of the literati, star of the *Follies*, lily maid of the Minskys, but who knows of her younger sister, June. . . . Her show, *Forbidden Melody,* might not be a hit, but June Havoc, secret sister of Gypsy
Rose Lee, most certainly is. Broadway is still ringing with the applause."

June had finally gotten her break.

Sitting at the table, sipping tea, they remembered the highlights they
had filched from June's career. Child prodigy on the Orpheum Circuit,
earning $1,500 at just seven years of age. Sought in Hollywood by every-
one from Mary Pickford to Charlie Chaplin.

When June arrived, Gypsy was bent over a web of golden thread, her
knitting needles clicking softly. Mother sat at the head of the table. She

cleared her throat, signaling that this was business. "We know you are on dinner break, dear, so I'll be quick," she said. "You know, dear, no one ever expected this freak reappearance of yours. I made this big success for your sister, and of course we needed interesting things for her background—the interviews and all of that—she had to have someone to be, so it was the most natural thing in the world. We used the Baby, then the child-star vaudeville background. It's been very successful. That's what everybody believes, now, so you can see it's too late to try to take any of the stories back, dear."

Gypsy could feel June's eyes on her, but she kept her head down, focusing on the needles. She was thrilled for June, she really was; her sister deserved her own break from the past. But some of the history had been Gypsy's for so long there was no easy way to return it. June didn't need those stories to help her; she could sing and dance and act. It was only fair. And Gypsy was, after all, the original Ellen June.

"You mean," June said, "I can't ever say I was—I am—"

"We never said you weren't there, too, June," Rose explained. "Only, if you are going to actually be back in show business with us, dear, you must find someone else to be. Just find a good story and stick with it. . . . We'll get together, and maybe some part that hasn't been used can be twisted back for you."

They were all at the elevator now. Gypsy propped the door open with her foot. She dropped the golden cap on June's head, the head Mother claimed was once small enough to fit into a teacup. The thread matched her hair color precisely. "There," Gypsy said, satisfied, and the elevator slowly lowered June out of sight. Gypsy felt Rose at her back, the swipe of her breath, the coolness of her skin. At moments like this she remembered. She had never loved anyone like she loved her mother, until Gypsy Rose Lee was born.

$\mathscr{C}$hapter $\mathscr{T}$hirty-one

Whenever La Guardia talks I can't see anything but
his tongue.

—O. O. MCINTYRE

New York City, 1932–1936

Herbert had always preferred to let Billy speak for him, and now, in his brother's overbearing absence, he found it difficult to speak at all. Sitting shiva at Billy's home in Brooklyn, he tried to execute the mechanics of forming words—gathering a gust of breath, pursing his lips—only to have the effort sputter and die, an engine that forgot how to start. Morton became a vortex of activity, as if by moving faster than his grief he could somehow elude it, this cold, still loss of "the biggest influence in my life." He called the stage managers at every Minsky theater, ordered rehearsals to proceed as scheduled, informed all of New York City that it had heard the last from one of its most vibrant citizens. "Billy was dead," Morton wrote. "The burlesque business, the theater, all the wise guys up and down Broadway, the strippers, the comics, the straight men, the stagehands, all knew something had gone out of their lives."

The family was still sitting shiva when he got a call from the stage manager at the Republic.

"I don't know how to tell you this, Mr. Morton," he said, "but I don't think we can work this deal without a Minsky. Things just aren't going right."

Morton sighed. With raised eyebrows he glanced at Herbert, who nodded. It was Billy's last show, and they owed him at least this.

"Okay," Morton said. "Call a full-cast rehearsal after the show on Monday night. We'll work until we get it right. I'll pay time and a half if I have to."

———

Morton crammed work into every moment of his life. When not overseeing rehearsals he tended to minutiae at the Republic. As soon as he arrived at 10:30 A.M., he locked himself in his office, reviewed the mail, checked in with one of Billy's press agents (a man with the improbable name of Georgia Alabama Florida) to discuss the placement and content of ads. He made phone calls about structural changes, prop deliveries, and potential legal problems from John Sumner and his allies. In late afternoon, after the leading Minsky Rosebud conducted her preliminary interview, Morton summoned Herbert and held auditions, watching the girls line up on the stage. With a wave of his hand, the dance director signaled the girls to raise their skirts waist high, and the brothers leaned in for leg inspection. They kept their assessments impersonal and terse, just as Billy had taught them: the words "You're acceptable" or "You're not" sufficed. Agents from across the Midwest, especially Chicago, sent photographs and reviews, hoping to make one of their clients the next star stripteaser at Minsky's Republic, and Morton sifted through them all.

Home at 5 P.M. for dinner and back to the Republic by 7:30. He watched the curtain rise, scanned the audience for famous faces, and invited any attending celebrity to have a drink with him during intermission; in these waning days of Prohibition, people still appreciated a glass or two of superior whiskey. At least three times a week, Morton noticed, Milton Berle slipped into the audience with a pencil and pad, laughing to himself, scribbling down the best sketches and jokes. The brothers didn't mind. Berle was a solo stand-up comedian, not a burlesque star. And besides, every worthwhile Minsky joke had already been stolen at least once. As Abe always said, "Not one new burlesque skit has been written in the last twenty years."

Billy's death had yanked Abe back into their lives. Their private family entanglement became suddenly and rudely public, and all of their eldest brother's furtive plans came tumbling to light. Just one month after Billy was buried, Abe called a press conference to announce that he was splitting, officially, from his family.

It was about time he branched out on his own, Abe said; Billy had held him back all those years, distorting the original Minsky vision. He planned his own theater, operated for and by himself. Minsky's Gaiety at 46th and Broadway would compete with both the Republic and the Central. Abe's comedians would be funnier; his decor, classier; his stripteasers, prettier and more inventive. Furthermore, after the Gaiety got rolling, Abe planned a theater called the New Gotham in Harlem, just up the street from Minsky's Apollo. "I go my own way," Abe said, "and Morton and Herb can do as they please."

Morton considered these words and all of the messy, complicated history laced through them. He tried to align his thinking with Billy's, to conjure up his brother's most likely response: one that would downplay Abe's ambitions without dismissing them outright, and make clear that only Billy's theaters offered the authentic Minsky experience (the definition of which, Morton was beginning to realize, was both subjective and malleable). After consulting with Herbert, Morton called his own friends in the press.

"He thinks he can fill a burlesque house with smart-aleck stuff like George S. Kaufman," Morton said. "It doesn't pay to shoot above their heads. Abe will find that out." He thought for a moment and then added a line he knew would scrape at Abe's considerable ego, a line that technically wasn't true: "We're the originals."

Already Morton could sense how this "battle of burlesque," as the press called it, would evolve. His eldest brother would learn soon enough that Depression-era audiences preferred the obvious over the subtle, cooch over class—the most efficient tools to blunt the edges of their endless, jagged days. When Abe opened the Gaiety and the New Gotham, Morton and Herbert would encourage their girls to shake faster and strip further than they had ever previously dared. It was no longer just a matter of validating Billy's legacy, but of creating and defining their own.

A daring stance, the brothers knew, especially with their old friend Jimmy Walker no longer in City Hall, let alone among the audience at their theaters. Mayor La Guardia was busy overturning time-honored traditions and codes, flinging unmasked contempt at the way things had always been done. "His puritanical streak, that sense of moral outrage," said one observer, "was so highly developed that he could make no distinction between a truly original theatrical genre, only one part of which featured the unadorned female breast, and ordinary prostitution." The Minskys kept close watch on La Guardia's arrests of underworld kingpins, his proclamations against indecent entertainment, and, most disconcerting, his installation of new commissioners, all of whom were regarded as experts in their particular fields (itself a significant change from municipal politics as usual) and one of whom, Paul Moss, would soon turn his attention to a certain burlesque house in Times Square.

━━━━━

Honoring Billy's tradition, the brothers made frequent trips to theaters in neighboring states, discovering, at the Trocadero in Philadelphia, a stripteaser named Margie Hart. An odd amalgamation of hot and demure, Margie kept a Bible tucked under her arm while she pranced across the stage, stopping occasionally to brandish the Good Book and shout, "If I shake it's for my mother's sake!" (a literal defense, as it turned out; once finding success in New York, she imported her entire family from rural Missouri and ensconced them in a sprawling apartment on the Upper West Side). In another act, the one that would make her famous, Margie never took anything off at all.

Wearing a "trick" breakaway dress made of narrow strips of silk, she disturbed the panels with casual flicks of her fingers, exposing a smooth expanse of thigh and waist, and, quite possibly, in the words of Morton Minsky, "that promised land the audience was yearning to see." Yet one couldn't be certain: was she wholly naked, without even the slightest G-string for modest accompaniment? Or was her G-string a trick worthy of Houdini—a Chicago G-string, they called it, made of monkey fur or wool, identical, for all intents and purposes, to a strip of pubic hair?

Even the Minskys were flummoxed, but they never asked Margie the truth. The less they knew, the more difficult it would be for John Sumner or the new puritans in City Hall to harass them. The brothers offered Margie $750 a week to headline the Republic, and the same New Yorkers who hoped to catch one of Gypsy's stray pins debated the true extent of Margie's revelations.

Unlike Gypsy, Margie Hart never developed a taste for booze and smoked only nicotine-free cigarettes, but she, too, understood the value of publicity. She hired her own press agent, who promptly informed Margie's admirers that she was a sweet, pure country girl at heart, and instead of perfumes and furs she preferred cultivators and pigs. Margie received her desired gifts, but other stunts were less successful. A "strip-duel" challenge with swimmer Eleanor Holm (whom Margie accused of padding her bathing suit) was politely declined, and her attempts to join Gypsy in the ranks of the literati proved frustrating and fruitless. Despite her agent's gentle prodding, she couldn't begin to get through Schopenhauer, and Bryn Mawr College saw no reason to establish her proposed "Margie Hart Scholarship for an Ambitious Burlesque Girl." Abandoning her highbrow aspirations altogether, Margie remained friendly with Gypsy but, given the chance, slyly critiqued her style.

"Gypsy Rose Lee's act is too subtle," she said. "You have to bang them in the eye in burlesque."

———

Subtle or not, Gypsy Rose Lee was still the biggest name in the business, and Morton wanted nothing more than for her to return, permanently, to the Minsky fold. But she had moved on, this time for good, to their biggest competitor, the Irving Place Theatre in Union Square. The brothers abhorred the Irving Place, whose owners—unlike the Minskys themselves—were hardly household names, and the infuriating distinction, made by some, that "real" writers (not to be confused with the Minskys' devoted cadre of critics) preferred 14th Street to Broadway.

And it was at the Irving Place in Union Square that Gypsy developed an activist conscience to complement her literary airs, walking through throngs of Communist protestors and getting an earful about proper wages and working conditions, all those topics Billy had outlawed during her early days at the Republic. When burlesque performers demanded their own union—how could they implement President Roosevelt's ideas about fair labor laws without one?—Gypsy got herself named to the executive board. And when, in the fall of 1935, Minsky stagehands, chorus girls, and stripteasers went on strike, it was Gypsy who organized the effort against her former bosses.

"Gypsy called our theater," one stripper remembered, "and asked for some pickets. All of us strippers put robes on over our G-strings and paraded outside the theater flashing passersby and shouting, 'Don't go in there, boys.' "

The Minskys settled that night.

———

One day, while Morton was sitting in his upstairs office at the Republic, "mulling over the vicissitudes of the burlesque business and the characters in it," he heard a forceful rapping on his door. He looked up to find his wife Ruth's Aunt Mae, a proper old dowager married to a renowned astronomy professor. She had an air of hurried concern, and began speaking as soon as she sat across from him.

"Morton," she began, "I have a problem you may be able to help me with. One of my good friends is a Mrs. Mizzy. Her son, Bob, has been courting one of the young ladies in your employ—a certain Miss Gypsy Rose Lee. Do you know anything about her?"

Morton rustled some papers and cleared his throat, stealing a moment to compose his reply. He had never seen this Mizzy boy around the theater when Gypsy worked here, nor sneaking backstage to visit her in between shows. Most likely, Mizzy met her at one of her famous and exclusive parties, where preeminent writers and artists and socialites romped about with strippers and a smattering of shady mobsters. He didn't know anything "really terrible" about Gypsy, just about some of the people and situations she tolerated along her way, the shifting, dubious nature of the steps that had carried her up. "If you elimi-nated Waxey Gordon and his four green-hatted henchmen," he thought to himself, "and the fact that she showed porno movies in her dressing room and encouraged her monkeys in their obscene antics, and the fact that some of her claims to being a great reader and aficionado of the opera were nonsense, I guess she was okay." What he did know was this: if this Mizzy boy, whoever he was, had fallen for Gypsy, nothing he could say would talk him out of it.

Aunt Mae rested her face against her slight, elegant hand, a code ges-ture for growing impatience.

"I can tell you this, Aunt Mae," he said. "Miss Lee is a very intelligent woman."

She clasped her hands together now, clearly relieved, and leaned for-ward. "Oh, Morton! Is she really intelligent? Can I tell Mrs. Mizzy that she's *really* intelligent?"

"She's *really* intelligent, Aunt Mae," he confirmed. "I assure you."

———

*A*fter Aunt Mae left, Morton thought about their exchange and about Gypsy, who, through her publicity and her persona and, let's face it, her mother, had boosted and hindered burlesque in equal measure. A writer named H. M. Alexander, at work on a book about the business, had spent quite a bit of time backstage at the Republic, chatting with slingers and Minsky Rosebuds, noting their habits and probing their backgrounds, and offering his opinion on what had already happened and what was yet to come. "If the striptease is an indecent performance today," he wrote, "it was as much so five years ago. Then, however, the owners, limiting their advertising to word of mouth, tried to avoid attention from the reformers. Their attitude was changed by a cer-tain Mrs. Hovick. She was ambitious; she had a daughter; the child's stage name was Gypsy Rose Lee. When Mrs. Hovick still had to make Gypsy's costumes herself and cook all their meals on an electric plate, she somehow managed a rented limousine, a chauffeur, a body-guard . . . publicity made Gypsy."

Morton remembered the day, four years ago, that he met Gypsy, and the way Billy palmed her face inside his small hands, filling them up. He'd had a gift for finding people who could build his dreams, and arranging them, one by one, in the most lovely, efficient way. His editing was equally deft, adjusting and extracting when necessary, whenever a single part threatened to consume the whole. One of the last things Billy did before he died, Morton would never forget, was to hang signs in every Minsky theater, declaring, in bold lettering:

THE MOTHER OF GYPSY ROSE LEE IS
NOT ALLOWED BACKSTAGE

Clearly Gypsy shared that skill with Billy, the ability to collect and assemble and discard people when necessary, including versions of herself, with such a fluid touch it was as if they'd never grazed her life at all. And it occurred to Morton that he, too, shared something with Gypsy: the terrifying responsibility of carrying out someone else's dreams, and the dank gray fear of what might befall them after you finally make them your own.

Chapter Thirty-two

History is fables agreed upon.

—VOLTAIRE

New York City, 1956–1959

The story of Gypsy's life is a fable before Broadway bills it as such, a myth she wants to sell not only to the public but to herself. Once upon a time there was a girl with many names: Ellen June, Rose Louise, Plug, Hard-boiled Rose, Louise Hovick, and the one she liked best, Gypsy Rose Lee. She would grow up and wear that name as if it were a cape made of orchids, a vision no one had seen before, and try to forget everything she did to make it fit just right.

The story means everything to her, especially since she is no longer living it. On New Year's Eve 1956, a half hour before she is to go onstage at the Cavern in Fort Lauderdale, her hands begin trembling. She sets her straight pins down on the vanity and forces herself to listen to thoughts that have been circling her mind all year.

She is at the height of her fame, "the most publicized woman in the world," in her agent's words, photographed, painted, and interviewed more than any other, and therein lies the heart of her problem: "There is," she concedes, "nothing left for me to show." Her entire act now revolves around the idea of passing the mantle, dressing burgeoning burlesque stars and teaching them the proper etiquette of stripteasing.

Younger audiences who never saw burlesque in the 1930s don't appreciate her satire and parody. She seethes if she doesn't get top billing. To her embarrassment, she finds herself disparaging Josephine Baker to a nightclub manager, calling the expat entertainer moody and difficult, cataloguing her anti-American statements. She of all people should know better, having been named as a Communist sympathizer on the Red Channels a few years earlier, along with Orson Welles, Dorothy Parker, and Leonard Bernstein. "Is a performer justified in rapping another performer under these circumstances?" she writes in her journal, and notes she's broken one of her resolutions: Speak well of all or not at all.

Sitting in her dressing room in Florida, she decides it's over. She says it out loud, making it real. "I've had it," she tells Erik, who has just turned twelve. "I'm forty-two years old. Too old to be taking my clothes off in front of strangers . . . never again." She doesn't even want to consider her more probable age of forty-five. After the curtain falls, she eats twelve grapes at the stroke of midnight, hitches her trailer to the back of the Rolls-Royce, and heads home with her son to New York.

Her usual worries about money amplify. To conserve oil for her furnace, she turns the thermostat off at night and sets it at just 62 degrees during the day. She cancels her newspaper subscriptions, cuts her drunken cleaning lady down to once a week, stops her massages altogether. She frets over the fact that her one-woman show—"A Curious Evening with Gypsy Rose Lee"—is still only a pile of film reel in the corner of her living room. She scolds Erik for asking for new clothes: wasn't he satisfied with the socks and underwear she bought him a few months ago? And if Harry Truman, as president of the United States, had time to wash his own socks and underwear every night, Erik could certainly do the same. "Good God, Erik!" she shouts. "Isn't it obvious? Without the act, I haven't the faintest idea of how we're going to survive." Her sleep is invaded by disconcerting dreams, Freudian and heavy with symbolism. In one, she sits on stage with comedian Jack Paar, opens her mouth to talk, and a long, green mass unfurls from her tongue, twisty and slick as a snake, no end of it in sight.

She always knew she would write a memoir, and now the time has come: Mother is dead and no longer a threat, and Erik sparks her memory with persistent questions: How old was she when Aunt June ran away? Would Grandma have found a place for him in the act, even though he can't sing or dance?

"I couldn't sing or dance, either," Gypsy tells her son, "but she found a place for me."

He thinks about that for a moment. "Your mother must have been a very nice woman," he says.

Gypsy smiles but doesn't respond.

She sequesters herself in her library and drafts the events of her life partly as she remembers them, partly as she wishes they'd been. She and June were comrades and confidantes from the beginning, Mother was eccentric but never cruel, and there was no long, secret black season between then and now.

Harper Brothers has scheduled her memoir's release for May 1, 1957, and she takes charge of the publicity campaign, sending an advance copy and personal note to every entertainment columnist in the country. She won't—can't—let Gypsy fail; the book is her personal monomyth, her chance to study each one of her thousand faces and decide how to best present them to the world.

The book is an instant commercial and critical success—"an honest, unsparing document, extraordinary Americana," proclaims The New York Times—and Gypsy's lawyers begin negotiations for film rights. MGM and Warner Brothers each offer $200,000, but she has a gut feeling about David Merrick, a former lawyer from St. Louis with a roadkill toupee and a gift for publicity. He wants to turn Gypsy into a Broadway musical and is offering $4,000 against a percentage of the box-office gross. A risk, but his energy reminds her of Michael Todd, and business was the one arena in which he'd never been a disappointment.

There is one significant problem: June. She's working on her own book, a gritty and harrowing portrait of Mother, the vaudeville years, and marathon dancing during the Great Depression. For the first time the sisters' intrinsically opposing worldviews are going to be laid out for public consumption and judgment. June objects to the way Gypsy winks at the truth and even rewrites it entirely, how she softens not only Mother's edges but her own.

Gypsy knows she needs June's cooperation, if not her blessing, in order for the memoir to make a successful transition to the stage. She remembers one of the dinners she and June shared nearly twenty years ago. They met at their favorite Chinese restaurant in New York, still awkward, still strangers, and Gypsy wondered, as she always did, what would come next.

"From Hard-boiled Rose to Gypsy Rose," she said. "The story of my life."

"Why don't you aim at that?" June asked. "Writing a story, I mean. Or a book or a play. I'll bet you could do it, Weese."

When the bill came, June stopped Gypsy from opening her wallet.

"I want to pay it," she explained. "I want this to be my night, right down the line. I'll put it in my diary as the night I found a direction in life for my big, fat sister."

June has to understand that this memoir, and everything it can lead to, is at once Gypsy's most legitimate work and greatest gimmick. It will keep her name in lights after she is no longer there to pose beneath them.

Gypsy's lawyer draws up a contract, a letter drafted as if by June's hand, beginning with the words "Dear Gypsy" and ending with a line where June should sign her name. In between lie four pages of legalese that acknowledge, confirm, and consent to release in all forms and media any and all references to June Havoc. "The use of my character," it states, "may include actual incidents involving me, and/or fictitious incidents in connection therewith, or may use incidents which are partially true and partially fictitious."

Gypsy waits, but June never signs. And the sisters never speak of it at all.

Chapter Thirty-three

Nobody ever looked inside her as long as she lived.
They'd say, "She's great, she's marvelous," but they
never knew the struggles and the ugliness that she had
survived, and the cruelty and the ruthlessness she had
to resort to in order to triumph.

—JUNE HAVOC

Hollywood and New York City, 1937–1940

She wanted success in Hollywood more than anything she'd wanted in her life. She wanted it so badly her ulcer raged inside her and she began to vomit blood. She wanted it so badly she had more work done on her teeth, those endlessly troublesome vestiges of a past life. As bad as her teeth had been during childhood they were even worse now, with painful abscesses pooling around her lower left molar during bouts of exhaustion or stress. Waxey Gordon's quack dentist replaced the tooth and then she paid another legitimate dentist to replace it again, with no success. She had her entire mouth redone but the problem persisted. She gargled with salt water and popped antibiotics and clamped ice against her jaw. During a performance one of her new teeth fell out and dropped into a fan's outstretched hand. Her smile sufficed for the the-

Crime scene photo from the death of Ginny Augustin, June 1, 1937, at Gypsy's country home.

ater but wouldn't do for close-ups—the incisors still nudged against her upper lip—so she paid yet another dentist to install yet another set of caps. She couldn't stand for him to inject the Novocain and decided to do it herself, standing in front of a mirror, sinking the needle into her gums, eyes tearing from the pain, her brandy nearby to keep the rest of her body equally numb.

She wanted it so badly she took Gypsy Rose Lee away from everything that mattered. Good-bye to her married lover Eddy and her Gramercy Park apartment and Friday-night salons. Good bye to the *Follies* and Fanny Brice, her roommate when the show went on the road, who called her "kid" and dispensed pills as often as she did advice. Good-bye to burlesque and her dressing room and Georgia Sothern and her fans (one of whom replenished her gem collection with a 69-carat star sapphire ring), to the sight of the airplane streaming her banner and the sound of the barker shouting her name. Good-bye, even, to the Minsky brothers, who opened a new theater called Minsky's Oriental even as Mayor La Guardia threatened to shut them down. As a favor to her old employers, she agreed to attend the opening ceremony and break a bottle of champagne against the box office and, in another publicity-gathering stunt, accepted a Minsky-issued degree, "Doctor of Strip Teasing." Somehow the brothers convinced six professors from New York University to preside over the festivities. They were joined by ten other stripteasers, wearing dainty caps and sheer gowns, who were eligible for lesser honors. It was the least Gypsy could do to repay them as New York politicians raged against burlesque, a backlash that yielded her two favorite headlines to date: "Congress Learns of Gypsy's Art" and "Congressional Hearing Halted for Reverie at Mention of Gypsy Rose Lee."

She said good-bye to June, who was busy raising her daughter and trying to match her success in *Forbidden Melody,* and to Mother, who diligently wrote every week while Gypsy was traveling with the *Follies.* Rose sent recipes and Walter Winchell columns and clippings about the Minsky brothers' troubles, scribbling "Serves them right!" and "Thank God we're out of it, dear" in the margins. If Gypsy got negative reviews—Ed Sullivan, for one, declared that she "lacked the talent" of Fanny Brice—Rose sent soothing letters:

Dear Louise,

   I received your loving letter it made me very unhappy to hear that you are so worried and that your show is not doing what you planed [sic] it would. . . . And all your hard work and terrific expense for no returns. I feel terrible darling and I wish with all my heart I could help you. I don't sleep thinking about you Louise . . . don't worry dear you will find something that is maybe the best thing for you to do. It may be just around the corner waiting for you. <u>Don't worry</u> everything is going to be grand. . . . Please call me as soon as you can. It will make me very very happy. (<u>And keep your chin up.</u>)

Love, Mother

When Rose learned that Hollywood was around the corner for Gypsy, and that 20th Century–Fox president Darryl Zanuck had bought out the *Follies* contract for $20,000, she clipped a two-inch advertisement from one of the New York papers and mailed it off: "Artist Wanted to replace Gypsy Rose Lee in Ziegfeld *Follies*. Experience not necessary."

Rose underlined the words with a red crayon, her only comment.

———

She wanted it so badly she begged Rose to come join her out west. William Hays, president of the Motion Picture Producers and Distributors of America (which was later renamed the Motion Picture Association of America), "frowned" on her contract, and religious groups nationwide sent upward of four thousand letters to 20th Century–Fox, threatening to boycott any film starring Gypsy Rose Lee. The burlesque performer was, in the words of one Catholic Legion of Decency representative, a "headache" that the organization "sought to cure." She had expected star treatment—Zanuck offered her $2,000 per week, and every gossip column bolded her name—but her fellow cast members treated her with wary disdain. One morning, in between takes, Gypsy visited the dressing room of Alice Faye, her costar in her first film, *You Can't Have Everything*. It looked like a secret little alcove of Heaven, a gilded palace of a space with beveled mirrors and pond-deep rugs, and Gypsy couldn't help but ask: How did she get it?

The actress's lips sank into a smirk, her eyes into withering crescents. She said, "I worked for it . . . *honey,*" in a tone that made clear precisely what sort of work she meant.

Gypsy waited until she was back in her own dressing room before she let herself cry. Again she remembered her shameful first year in burlesque and, afterward, the most sacred vow she ever made: Gypsy Rose Lee would never be controlled by desperation or need, or succumb to the force of someone else's will. And now the world around her refused to play along. She cried whenever no one was looking. In each take her face was bloated, her eyes swollen.

Absurd as it sounded, and although she knew she'd regret it, Gypsy Rose Lee, national sex symbol and icon, just wanted her mommy.

Rose couldn't believe her luck. She packed her things, left instructions for her adoring tenants at Witchwood Manor, and headed off to Hollywood. She had not been there in twenty years, since she'd fastened all her dreams to Baby June, told her ugly lies that coaxed pretty tears. She had made Gypsy a star in New York, and she would do the same out west, so long as her older daughter appreciated her effort and sacrifice.

As usual, she did not. Oh, Gypsy was fine at night, being her natural homebody self, knitting socks or sewing costumes or reading her current favorite author, Somerset Maugham. But as soon as the sun broke through the windows the girl headed out to the studio for rehearsals, forgetting all about the mother who was waiting, patiently, faithfully, back home. This was not New York, where the Minsky brothers punished her with what amounted to an informal restraining order, and Rose could go wherever she pleased, as she pleased. One day, when she could no longer stand being ignored, she pulled on a tattered old polo coat and dusted her face with white powder, looking, Gypsy said later, "like an old skyscraper nightlark without her bucket and mop." Drawing on every trick she'd perfected over the years—the raspy whispers, the downcast gaze, the threat of falling tears—Rose practiced her story, repeating it again and again until she herself believed it. It had worked on Grandpa Thompson's lodge brothers, on her various husbands and beaus of both genders, on hotel managers all along the Orpheum Circuit, and now it worked on the assistants to Darryl Zanuck, Hollywood honcho and Gypsy's boss. Once in his office, she shut the door behind her and gave it everything she had.

Would Mr. Zanuck be so kind as to pass a message on to her daughter, Gypsy Rose Lee? Tell Gypsy her mother is looking for her and needs her desperately. And was there any way she could get a bowl of hot soup? Thank you, Mr. Zanuck. Gypsy's selfish indifference had her living in poverty, begging on the streets. How did such a gentleman put up with the likes of her daughter?

Soon afterward, the daughter sent her back to Witchwood Manor.

———

𝒮he wanted it so badly she let them take Gypsy Rose Lee away from her. Despite promises that Gypsy would not appear in roles "influenced by her former experiences," the Hays Office, charged with monitoring morality in films, remained unconvinced. Darryl Zanuck capitulated, demanding she use her given name instead of the one she gave herself. She became Louise Hovick again, a striptease in reverse, dressing in a costume she had never found flattering. The layers hid everything worthwhile, even her fury, even her pride.

"To hell with them," she told June. "As long as they spell the name right and get me the money." Instead of protesting she told jokes, the only public reaction she trusted and the one that salvaged a bit of her dignity; they might not discount her or leer if she first made them laugh. As Louise Hovick, her old name turned new again, she sat for an interview with a syndicated "nudespaperman." But without her asking and to her perverse delight, he addressed her in the manner she preferred:

Q. You were a striptease artiste, or "stripeuse," in burlesque, were you not?

A. I was, but I'm not. I have discarded the habiliments of my earlier profession down to the last spangle and fragment of black lace. I now am a motion picture actress, and if you don't believe it you can ask the Hays office.

Q. I have asked the Hays office, Miss Lee, and it says you will not do any stripping for the screen.

A. Say, listen! These people are so cautious that I'm not even allowed to remove my coat for fear it will be misunderstood.

Q. What do you expect to accomplish in your cinema career, Miss Lee?

A. I could do straight drama because I believe in stark realism. I could do comedy because I have learned to grin and bare it. After all, a girl can't be both long-faced and broad-minded. Also, I should be a fairly good imitator because I know how to do take-offs.

In the end it didn't matter what they called her, or that she was being sold to the movie public as a "grande dame" or that, in accordance with this new image, she adopted a vaguely British accent, or that the studio executives (finally satisfied with her teeth) insisted she also raise her eyebrows, change the shape of her mouth, and remove the "slink" from her walk. By any name, by any measure, she was, in her own words, a "Hollywood floppo." The reviews of *You Can't Have Everything* were dismissive at best and scathing at worst. The movie, wrote *The New York Times,* "will go down in history—and we are careful not to say how far down—as the first time a strip tease artist has appeared before her public without revealing anything, not even her ability." The studio, quipped another reviewer, had given Gypsy Rose Lee the two things she needed least: clothing and a different name.

Even worse, her life back east kept intruding. Only her mother's hand could reach three thousand miles to clench her shoulder, only her mother's voice could burrow so deeply in her mind, an ear worm with an ominous bass line. Since Gypsy sent Rose back to New York she'd been waiting—for what, exactly, she wasn't sure—but when she received a peculiar letter from one of Mother's boarders, she knew that she should ready herself, that Rose wasn't content unless she laid claim to a piece of all her days.

The letter began oddly, addressing her as "My dear Miss Hovick" and alluding to reports Gypsy might have received concerning the girl's character—"detrimental" reports, replete with "false statements." The girl was anxious to clear her name, which was Genevieve Augustin, "Jean" or "Ginny" for short, and she insisted she had no "bad habits" and only two important interests at Witchwood Manor: assisting Rose Thompson Hovick in any way she might be of use to her (a task she rather enjoyed) and painting. The farm was everything an aspiring artist could want: she found the atmosphere ideal and Gypsy's family "very wholesome." Next week she planned to begin work on a life-size portrait of Rose—what did Gypsy think her mother should wear? Rose was leaning toward slacks and a simple colored smock, but Ginny was angling for something more conservative, more dignified. Next she'd paint Big Lady and Aunt Belle, who, as Gypsy surely knew, were at Witchwood Manor on an extended visit. She could see Big Lady "being done in the Monet style," while Belle lent herself to a Picasso version. "Miss Louise," the letter concluded, "I want you to know that I enjoy being here, and I love doing anything I can to make life more comfortable for your mother and your family, and I hope to continue doing so as long as I can be of assistance to any one of them."

And now Ginny Augustin was dead.

———

The reports were nebulous, but repeated certain details until they took on the sheen of truth. Ginny Augustin was a twenty-nine-year-old woman from Kenosha, Wisconsin, who had moved to Chicago and then to New York City. She was slim and pretty, with straight blond hair that swept her neck and pouty rosebud lips. She taught art classes at the Textile High School in Manhattan and displayed her work at the Municipal Art Gallery on West 53rd Street, watercolors that were deemed "a credible though not at all momentous showing." She had a history of depression and suicide attempts, most recently slashing her wrists with a razor blade. When she heard about the farm named Witchwood Manor up in Highland Mills, she knew she had to live there. She arrived and painted and tended to Rose and her family for months, without incident.

On the afternoon of Tuesday, June 1, 1937, Ginny Augustin went hiking in the woods around the property. Upon her return, she locked herself in her bedroom. She wore a white, short-sleeved blouse, black shorts, and thick cotton socks. Somehow she managed to point a rifle at her temple and pull the trigger. She landed on her back, her right leg folded under her in a limp, rag-doll pose. Blood soaked the carpet and spread as far as the door, but not one splatter marred the walls. She left no note. The body was discovered by Rose Thompson Hovick, and the coroner pronounced the death a suicide. Gypsy Rose Lee, former striptease artist, known as Louise Hovick in motion pictures, was not present at the cottage at the time of the shooting.

Maybe she was, and maybe she wasn't. Her old Minsky comrade Georgia Sothern would swear Gypsy had been there, as would a deputy sheriff named E. Sergio. Either way, she had to get involved. Mother and daughter, keepers of each other's secrets, hoarders of a devastating currency they couldn't afford to trade. Gypsy had never said a word about certain incidents from their vaudeville days—the unfortunate cow that wasn't really a cow at all, the hotel manager who "fell" from a window—and neither would she say anything about Ginny Augustin. The rumors would linger past Gypsy's lifetime, rumors she never confirmed or denied: there was a party attended by Rose's six boarders, numerous neighborhood men, assorted friends, and Gypsy. Ginny Augustin made a pass at Gypsy, which infuriated Rose; she did not want to compete for attention or affection with either one for either one.

Rose followed Ginny into her bedroom and shot her, once, in the head. She burned the girl's diary, full of what she called "crazy lies" that could hurt Gypsy's Hollywood career, and concocted her story.

"I didn't do a thing," Rose confided to June, and then contradicted the coroner's report of a shot through the temple. "She took the shotgun out of my hand, put the nozzle in her mouth, stepped on the trigger, and pow! I didn't actually offer the gun, don't you see? I just had it, that's all . . . she was deceitful and—and bad. With your sister trying so hard to be a Hollywood star, and that fool girl blowing the whole top of her head off. . . . I've never been able to stomach a poor loser. I never told her she was moving in with me. Why would I clutter up my life with a wild tramp like that? I'm tired of getting into other people's muckups, just because I know what loneliness is. . . . Abandoned, ig-nored. Sometimes I think I'd be better off dead, too. I told her that, I did. I said, 'Why not just check out if you're that unhappy?' And there was the gun, and—well, I think she knew what she was doing."

Rose sat back and trusted the incident would be covered up because of Gypsy, and it was. Sheriff Sergio took charge of quieting things down. Ginny Augustin's mother, unconvinced that her daughter com-mitted suicide, demanded an investigation. Members of a grand jury descended upon Witchwood Manor. They walked the grounds, toured the little theater room decorated with cutouts of Gypsy, saw the studio where Ginny painted portraits of Rose and Aunt Belle and Big Lady, sat on the bed where the girl got her final night's sleep. Four days later, they issued a report that the Orange County district attorney deemed "tan-tamount to refusal to indict."

The clamor subsided, Ginny Augustin was forgotten, but the after-shocks rumbled in Gypsy's ears. Mother was on the other side of the country, but Gypsy could sense the ominous jumble of her thoughts, anticipate her growing cache of trouble and threats.

———

She craved success so fiercely that she betrayed herself again: 20th Century–Fox suggested she marry a nice, ordinary man, a civilian, just to make her "more like everyone else." His name was Arnold "Bob" Mizzy. He was a dental supply manufacturer from New York and, at age twenty-five, just one year younger than she. He was also a friend of Eddy, who still darted in and out of her life; when the three of them were out together Bob pretended to be her date. Gypsy had dated Bob occasionally when Eddy was off with his wife and even developed a genuine affection for him, despite the fact that he was not at all her type.

Bob came from a wealthy family, had attended elite schools and sum-mer camps, spoke proper English, possessed a full head of hair and no rough edges. She liked his "intriguing frown" and regarded his normal childhood upbringing with a mixture of wonder and skepticism, as if it were some ancient artifact with dubious authenticity. "Think, June," she mused to her sister, "the same two parents all along the line. Mother, father." She reconnected with her own father, Daddy Jack Hovick, still living in Los Angeles and with his second family. He wrote her letters, calling Gypsy his "sweet lovely datter." Gypsy's stepbrother, Jack, and stepmother, Elizabeth, wrote, too, reminding her of the conventional civilian family she'd never known. "I remember when I was pregnant with Jack [your father] hoped it would be a girl," she wrote. "He did miss you and June so very much. . . . It is a sad thing when boys and girls have to be deprived of their dads."

The ceremony was scheduled for Friday the thirteenth of August, 1937, which Gypsy told the press was her lucky day. "I wanted to be married on the high seas," she said, and threw in a fib for the sake of publicity: "My father, grandfather, and great-grandfather were all married there . . . our name is a contraction of 'Ho, Viking!' But to keep all the records straight, we'll be married again—on land this time." On their first wedding night, after the water taxi pulled back to shore, Gypsy returned to her beachfront home in Santa Monica and Bob to his Hollywood hotel room, both of them alone.

Darryl Zanuck doubted the legality of the maritime marriage and ordered another wedding. On August 17, a Tuesday afternoon, Gypsy and Bob wed again, saying their vows before a justice of the peace on Santa Ana land.

Rose promised to meet the newlyweds at the Highland Mills cottage, along with a photographer from Life magazine. Two months had passed since the Ginny Augustin tragedy, and Gypsy and Rose maintained a cautious, deliberate peace, as if a sudden move by either might ruin both of them at once. Their letters were light and hazy, their endearments frequent but rote. Rose telegrammed when she couldn't make either of Gypsy's weddings to Bob—"Darling cant make trip call me at twelve heartsick love=Mommy"—and cracked jokes about the union, calling the newlyweds "Mr. and Mrs. Ha Ha High Tide."

But another shift began between Gypsy and Rose, deeper than any in the past, unfolding slowly and imperceptibly, a fever that cooled by fractions of degrees. Maybe it was prompted by a letter from June, who knew more than she cared to about her sister and mother's poisonous bond, about the suspicious deaths and questionable characters floating into and out of their world, about how vulnerable Gypsy became when a crack surfaced in her creation.

"Colossol [*sic*] Stupidity," June called her sister by way of greeting,

> Is this your idea of "The Glory Road"? And if I am not being too in-delicate—where is the end of the too, too thrilling road? You know Louise, I am younger than you are and poorer than you are, less lovely than you are and much less well, say—popular than you are— but By God I have three times the chance for happiness that you have—do you know it? . . . this illusion of yours isn't the only one you cherish—its one among many—your tinsel (stupid word but damn good) and fools you surround yourself with—drink with— live with—parasites—no—you aren't the big sister—I am. . . . I want to stay as far away from you and Momie as I possibly can.
>
> While I write to you and you write to me it generally stays right beside you where it belongs—but when I try to see and talk with ei-ther of you it bounces all over your faces and conversation and I come away sick and miserable—I hate every bit of it—it isn't even amusing—sad—tragic—anymore it stinks to high heaven—its rotten and unwholesome—its just plain garbage—and somehow while I am away from you it doesn't exist—and that is the only way we can manage . . . lets never mention your appetite or lack of it again.

Neither June nor Gypsy specified what that "appetite" was for.

Gypsy kept the letter, tucking it away along with her scrapbooks of press clippings, but she saw herself, perhaps for the first time, through June's eyes. There were disgust and outrage on those pages, yes, but also concern and, of all things, *disappointment*. It was that sentiment that bothered Gypsy most, this utter reversal of roles—the unbright, naïve Baby casting haughty judgment on the maddeningly self-assured Duchess—and the subtext, as obvious as it was undeniable: it was time once again to distance herself from Mother, or risk becoming her.

After a cross-country honeymoon drive, and after a brief stay at Witchwood Manor (during which Gypsy baked biscuits for Bob and treated her status as newlywed like a movie role, telling the press, "A gal has to know something besides wearing a jewel studded G-string if she's going to hold her husband"), she and Bob headed back to Holly-wood, leaving Mother behind.

From then on, when Gypsy turned her attention back to Rose her eyes were sharply focused, her ears attuned to nonsense passed off as fact. For the first time the three-thousand-mile distance began to do its job, and far away, on the east side of that divide, Rose could feel her grip slipping, her hold weakening, finger by clenched finger. She grasped and felt nothing, shouted and heard no response.

At last, in spring 1938, Gypsy ordered Rose and her lesbian harem to leave Witchwood Manor but continued an allowance that paid for a rental—for Mother only—two miles up the road. To Rose this meant war, and her mind began preparing for battle, tallying slights both re-cent and old. Her daughter had a habit of claiming and denying owner-ship at whim, whichever reaction was convenient in the moment, thinking always of how it would serve her image and never of the truth. How dare Gypsy complain when Rose went back to Witchwood Manor to collect certain items: antiques, books, dogs, even Waxey Gor-don's thirty-piece dining room set. Those were Rose's things, by God, and it was time Gypsy admitted it.

"Louise," Rose wrote,

> do you ever stop to think how much of the stuff in that house really belongs to me? Where did it all come from? How did most of it get there? I was your slave and colored maid for years and years, there I was a house keeper for you. I was never paid a salary I was given just enough to run your house on the few pennies I scraped together after expenses were taken care of I put back into your house never dreaming I would some day be turned out. . . . I am be-grudged $37.00 a week to live on, even called a thief and made out a leper.

And if Gypsy were being honest, she would take responsibility for the darker edges around their days, all of those strangers who stepped in and tinkered with their lives. Gypsy was fooling herself, feeling "so perfect" and turning everyone against Rose: Bob Mizzy, June, even Jack Hovick and his new family, who had the nerve to pretend they cared for

Gypsy more than did her own mother. Rose addressed all of it in the same handwritten letter, the force of her rage evident in every heavy word, the point of her pencil breaking several times: "What have I ever done that you haven't done <u>twenty</u> fold worse . . . you even advised the last fatal party that took place. . . . I mention all this because I want to know why am I so unwanted all of a sudden. It's a pretty tough time to let me down Louise."

No response, and Rose tried again, contrite and martyred. "I will regret as long as I live the unfortunate unhappiness I caused you through the Ginny affair that I was helpless to avoid," she wrote. "You can't hurt anything you love dear and I adore and love you. . . . Do you think you would feel better about me if I came to Cal. to live dear?"

Rose would not be ignored. She showed up in California, wielding a rifle no one knew was unloaded, and chased Bob around the house until she was tackled and restrained. For the first time Gypsy hired a lawyer to put some official space between them, but she knew she'd always feel the pull of her mother's hand, and hear the tune of her mad song.

———

She realized, too, that her Hollywood career as Louise Hovick was as insubstantial as her marriage. The studio never gave her a chance to do straight drama, and she couldn't rely on her striptease or its inherent humor. Her next four movies under contract—*Ali Baba Goes to Town, Battle of Broadway, My Lucky Star,* and *Sally, Irene and Mary*—were all critical and commercial failures. GYPSY FLOPPED IN HOLLYWOOD, one headline trumpeted, and she distracted herself by reconnecting with her activist friends. She became a fixture at Communist United Front meetings and charity events. The Dies Committee, so called after Representative Martin Dies, chairman of the House committee investigating un-American activities, began a dossier on Gypsy and issued her a subpoena to testify. "With my act and Dies' publicity," she joked to the press, "we could bring back vaudeville. . . . Sure, we gave parties in Hollywood to help poor Spanish kids. I thought it was American to help the downtrodden."

Some of her colleagues weren't quite sure what to make of her approach, especially when she reprised her role in the *Follies* for a roomful of sedate dowagers. She meant no offense; her act was the truest, easiest way she knew to raise money, and wasn't that the point? One of the offended ladies happened to be her mother-in-law, Ruth Mizzy, who afterward sent Gypsy a stern reprimand.

Dear Louise,

I realize now how very stupid I was not to have understood that when you were being advertised as Gypsy Rose Lee that you would appear in the role you played at the *Follies*. I have been trying to find a reason for your having given the Strip Tease performance at the Mecca Temple and to save my soul I really cannot find one. Perhaps you thought we would not mind seeing that it was a benefit for Spain . . . it was a serious Faux Pas. . . . I gather you are planning to continue in the show business doing the Strip Tease. . . . You have but a short time in which you can continue with this type of work— and as you definitely have a great deal of knowledge about the theatre and histrionic talent it would seem that with a very little bit of specialized training you could very easily find a most suitable and desirable place in the theatre which deals with drama. At this time you should make every effort to find the best material possible as a vehicle for your talent. Now, while you are still young, you can pass from one type of work to another.

Gypsy decided to cast aside Louise Hovick—for good this time. She didn't have it in her to argue; striptease *was* her talent, her theater, her drama, the one way she knew to get accolades and attention, and there was no room for it here. She left Bob and Hollywood and the memory of every failed take and awful review. Teaming up with Jimmy Durante, she launched a tour called the *Merry Whirl Review* and stripped her way back east, incorporating a parody of a character named "Mr. Censor." When reporters asked her what she thought about Sumner's battle against the Minskys, she deemed it "silly and rather provincial. If anyone's morals could possibly be jeopardized by burlesque, he's pretty far gone anyway."

She performed in every grand and musty old vaudeville theater across the country, spotting ghosts from that sad, sweet part of her life before she was anyone at all. New York was her final stop, the city that discovered her, and the only place she knew that offered redemption along with heartache.

Chapter Thirty-four

Wish I had a town I belonged to. All the towns we
drive through I see the lights on in the windows . . . it
looks as though it would be warm and friendly inside—
but I'm outside.

—GYPSY ROSE LEE, WRITING ABOUT HER
CHILDHOOD, 1956

New York City, 1958–1959

Despite June's resistance, David Merrick and his team move forward
with plans for the musical. One afternoon, Gypsy lounges in her drawing room, smoking a cigarette and sipping tar-thick tea, anticipating the
arrival of Arthur Laurents. His last work, *West Side Story,* was nomi-
nated for a Tony Award, and she is thrilled he's adapting her memoir for
the stage. He wants to ask a few questions, fill in some gaps about her
life, and she tells him to come over, darling, anytime, she'll be happy to
chat. Even his short walk through her front courtyard grants him insights not to be found in Walter Winchell's column or the *Police Gazette.*
In one section of her mansion on East 63rd Street, she rents out several
rooms to tenants on the condition that they leave their doors open.
"Closed doors," Laurents notes, "meant she was running a multiple

Gypsy (left) and June, 1959.

dwelling which meant permits and taxes, which meant money. Like mother, like daughter."

Gypsy knows it is Mother, in fact, who most intrigues Laurents, all those stories he's heard out in the Hamptons from some woman who claims Rose Hovick was her very first lover. Oh, she says, that Rose was curvaceous and charming and manipulative as Clytemnestra, somehow convincing a crew of women to work for nothing at her cottage up-state; she operated that place like a slave farm. Apparently, Mother confided to this lover all of her greatest hits. There was the time she took her ladies to a Chinese restaurant, crashed into another car, and black-mailed the other driver into paying for damages; the girls all vowed to be her witnesses. And the time, so long ago now, when she pushed a hotel manager out of the window. And of course the time she shot a girl who'd made a pass at Gypsy, and for this story Rose invented a twist ending: she buried the body in the backyard, and then asked, ever so sweetly, if some of the girls might like to hoe the dirt. She acted so surprised when she saw what turned up . . .

Erica, Gypsy's longtime and devoted secretary, leads Arthur Laurents into the drawing room. Gypsy can handle him, she knows. She learned her lesson with Mike Todd about telling men things that are better left unsaid.

"Was your son," Laurents asks, "named after your secretary?"

A clear reference, Gypsy thinks, to rumors that she is a lesbian, just like Mother, rumors she doesn't mind but sees no need to confirm or deny. She laughs and slips past the question, telling him that Erica is like a member of the family, darling, she doesn't know what she'd do without her.

Laurents tries again.

"Did the fifteen-year-old Hollywood Blondes your mother booked into a burlesque house ever appear partially nude?" he asks.

Gypsy crosses her legs. That was so long ago, a piece of that time she will never discuss. "I wouldn't know," she says.

She can see him replaying the answer in his head: she wouldn't know. *Really?*

She smiles at him, sweetly, showing the slightly bucked teeth he later describes as "endearing." She adds, "Wasn't Mother something?"

Laurents moves on. "What got you into stripping?" he asks.

Gypsy cocks her head, lets her gaze wander to the doorway. "Wasn't that the phone?" she says.

He stares at her and tries one more time.

"Where did you get your name?"

Gypsy laughs. "Oh, darling," she says, "I've given so many versions, why don't you make up your own?"

Laurents realizes that she is a much better actress offstage than on. He rises to leave and asks if he might come back to try again. "Anytime, darling," she says, and tells him she cares only about two things: that the show go on, and that it be called *Gypsy*.

By the end of 1958, Laurents delivers the first draft of the play. It is perfect, Gypsy thinks, tracking the course of her life precisely as she wishes she'd lived it. Of course, June feels differently. Who is this awful Baby June, this shrill, manic caricature of the child she remembers being? She headlined the most prestigious circuit in vaudeville at the age of seven—why does the first scene show her at an amateur contest? And why must she be the villain, eloping with the boy Gypsy loved, when in truth her sister never looked twice at Bobby?

Furthermore, does Gypsy think anyone will buy this little Louise? This frail, meek lamb who craves nothing more than her sister's talent and her mother's love? Where is the haughty Duchess who memorized Voltaire? Who doodled the word "Money" and dreamt of marrying kings? Who decided to perform that very first striptease out in Kansas City? Who has now stolen her little sister's past not once but twice?

"You want the world to believe that your credo says to hell with craft, with talent, with integrity, 'all you gotta have is a gimmick'?" June asks. "Is that your message? Do you really believe that?"

"Listen, June," Gypsy says, "you're the one who trusts all that craft stuff. I tried it, didn't I? Nothing worked but my gimmicks. That's what they bought, that's what they wanted. Wouldn't I be a stupid son of a bitch to disappoint them now?"

Gypsy pleads with her sister, makes promises that sidle away from the truth without being outright lies. June's concerns can be addressed through casting and direction. She will keep an eye on things, make sure June's interests are protected. Trust her, Gypsy says.

Eight days later, the production team convenes at her house.

"Grim," Gypsy scribbles in her journal. "I have to spend all my time and contractual points fighting for June's rights."

They are at an impasse. Laurents finds himself making a pilgrimage to the other Hovick sister, tracking June down in Stratford, Connecticut, where she is appearing as Titania in *A Midsummer Night's Dream*. He finds her in her dressing room, face shining with glitter dust.

"You didn't come to see me act," she says. "You came to get my name on a piece of paper."

Laurents has to admit it's true.

"What's a sensitive playwright like you doing writing this? It's vulgar! She's vulgar!"

"I found her funny," Laurents answers, "and rather touching."

"I'm touching! She's so cheap, she eats out of tin cans!"

Laurents leaves without June's signature and reports back to Gypsy, finding her at her home, hunched over a table, surrounded by doilies and bright construction paper hearts. She is preparing a Valentine's Day gift for her sister, a collage of June's recent clips, and she sighs as Laurents delivers the bad news. While he speaks, she arranges the glowing reviews around the perimeter and pastes the lone scathing notice on top, front and center, so the eye has no choice but to find it first.

On March 13, June calls and tells her she has hired a lawyer, that they are not to visit or talk. "I am ill and so confused by it all," Gypsy writes, but neither one of them can, nor wants to, shut the other out. One afternoon, as Laurents leaves Gypsy's home after another fruitless fact-finding mission, he notices a petite figure turn the corner on 63rd Street. Clad entirely in black, a heavy tulle veil shading her face, she tiptoes toward number 153, delicately, as if her footsteps might be heard above the clamor of the city. The string from a patisserie box coils like a bracelet around her wrist. The door swings open, slowly, before she has a chance to press the bell with her gloved finger, and Gypsy pulls her inside.

June never reveals what they discussed that day, but she sends a letter Gypsy doesn't have the capacity to answer:

You see, I love you but you don't let me very close. It's true . . . you are too pre-occupied. You don't know that I feel underfoot and damn boring to you unless I can grab and hold your attention, which makes a genuine exchange between us rare. We are "on"— the honest things aren't "BIG" enough to focus on. After I leave you I realize how superficial the hours were. And I never tell you that I love you. . . . I don't believe you fully realize what you are to me and I want so much to make you know.

The following month, June signs the release. She signs after begging to be written out entirely. She signs even though she is not guaranteed a royalty for the show past the first run. She signs even though, in the end, the play still opens with an amateur contest and has her run away with the boy Gypsy loves. She signs even though she's embarrassed that her own sister is "screwing me out in public." She signs even though the release is, she says, an "example of a nonlove that I don't understand." She signs because she knows what the play means to Gypsy. It is not only her monument but her surest chance for monumental revisionism. "It realizes," June says decades later, "who she wanted to be before the burlesque thing happened. She wanted to be this beautiful, idealistic, romantic person with dreams."

On May 21, a Thursday, Gypsy works on her rock garden and sends Erik to the home of producer Leonard Sillman, an old friend, to borrow a tuxedo. It is impossible to concentrate on anything but the rising of the curtain in a few short hours. When she has to, she sets down her tools, takes a long bath, and dresses in a full black taffeta skirt, white silk blouse, and sable jacket. She thinks, for a moment, of her mother. How sad that Rose isn't here to see Ethel Merman play her, to make her famous, an archetype, an icon in her own right. It would've been the greatest night of Mother's life.

She pins up her hair and hangs antique diamond pendants from her delicate seashell ears. She drives the Rolls-Royce to the theater and loops her arm through Erik's. They take their time walking down the aisle. Never have so many eyes stared so intently when she wasn't on stage, when she wasn't rolling down a stocking or peeling off a glove. And when little Louise strokes her lamb's soft head and wonders how old she is, Gypsy Rose Lee begins to cry.

Chapter Thirty-five

Broadway is New York intensified—the reflex of the
Republic—hustling, feverish, crowded, ever changing.
How the ranks and antagonisms of life jostle each
other on that crowded pave!

—JUNIUS HENRI BROWNE, *THE GREAT*
METROPOLIS, 1869

New York City, 1969

On the last weekend in June, Morton Minsky sat down at his desk to indulge in his favorite hobby, writing letters to *The New York Times*. He
was sixty-seven and would live for eighteen more years, long enough to
witness his beloved city thrive and decay and will itself back to life, long
enough to realize his favorite swath of it, Broadway, was always being
built but would never be finished, long enough to appreciate its fiercely
tender gift for retaining the spirit of those who shaped it along the way.

In 1942, he admired Gypsy Rose Lee and Michael Todd for doing the
impossible and bringing back old-time burlesque with *Star and Garter*,
right under Fiorello La Guardia's nose. He despaired as one theater
after another closed its doors in the 1950s, the worst serial shuttering
since the height of the Depression. In 1962, he scoffed at another license

Bud Abbott (standing) with Lou Costello (left) and Mayor Fiorello La Guardia.

commissioner's vow to eliminate "lurid and flamboyant" sidewalk displays. He followed the career of a revolutionary comedian named Lenny Bruce, who, in 1964, was barred from New York stages for being "obscene, indecent, immoral, and impure." He heard that 42nd Street between Seventh and Eighth Avenues was the worst block in the city, overrun by "deviant" males who wore teased hair and painted faces. He watched Minsky's Republic morph from a second-run movie house to a "grind house," showing pornography for twenty straight hours a day. He marveled when the State Supreme Court allowed the word "burlesque" to return to Times Square marquees and naked girls to its stages. "Given the nature of modern American life and letters," the *Times* asked, "do we need, *really* need, all those breasts and bellies and buttocks to feed our fantasies?"

Morton would have happily answered that question, but on this occasion he wished to address the recent debut of *Oh! Calcutta!* The play featured comedic sketches and full-frontal nudity and, more than anything in recent memory, brought to mind his three beloved, long-gone brothers and those glorious, maddening last days when Broadway still shined their name.

He rolled a piece of paper into his typewriter and began:

To the editor:

Was burlesque bad in the days of Minsky?

I doubt very much whether the status of the contributors to *Oh! Calcutta!* is above that of the comedy skit writers for Minsky Burlesque in the 20's and 30's, so admired by Nathan, Mencken, Edmund Wilson, and other respected critics of that era.

In the days before La Guardia's extinguishment of Minsky entertainment (for political expediency), the earthy comedy, delivered by such greats as Abbott and Costello, Rags Ragland, and Joey Faye, brought the wrath of the gods down on our heads. Nudity, bare bosoms à la Ziegfeld, popularized by Minsky's, was deemed shocking.

Yes, I saw *Oh! Calcutta!*. If permitted to run, it will be a sad commentary on the injustice rendered to the art form of burlesque so courageously developed by the Minskys, only to be banished by the great liberal, Fiorello La Guardia.

There was an honesty in early burlesque nowhere apparent in the current rash of "nudies."

Morton Minsky

He paused a moment, read over what he'd written, and added a tagline:

Of the Minsky Brothers. Remember?

Morton remembered; for the remainder of his years he'd do little else. He thought his city should remember, too, even after he was no longer there to remind it.

———————

*H*e remembered feeling a shift as the country tumbled into the thirties, a fin-de-siècle louche decadence yielding to grim sincerity. Beyond New York, far from Mayor La Guardia's frothing rants against Tammany and organized crime and imbecilic employees, tent preachers flourished in small towns of the South and Midwest, delivering the message that the ills of the Depression were God's protests against the wicked and unrighteous. Evangelists Gypsy Smith and Billy Sunday traveled from city to city, exhorting God's word and warning of His wrath to overflow crowds in ballparks and auditoriums. Every night, in every city, the Salvation Army invaded street corners and wooed passersby with tambourine music and curbside gospel.

The Catholic Church, along with a lay organization called the Legion of Decency, turned its considerable might toward Hollywood, demanding stricter adherence to the Hays Code, which, to Morton, read like an exceptionally uptight version of the Ten Commandments: No picture shall be produced that will lower the moral standards of those who see it. No picture shall ridicule religion, and ministers of religion shall not be represented as comic characters or villains. No picture shall contain nakedness or suggestive dances. No picture shall portray "excessive and lustful kissing" or any other activity that might "stimulate the lower and baser element." All this, he scoffed, from the same geniuses who believed that by changing Gypsy Rose Lee's name they could obscure who and what she really was.

———————

(M)orton remembered that John Sumner began invading his thoughts each night as soon as the curtain rose. He drove Morton crazy with his pious rhetoric and self-serving hyperbole, declaring that 1935 was the year "burlesque commenced to run wild." Was he out there in the audience, scribbling away on his little pad, paraffin whistle pursed by his lips? Did he have men stationed in all the Minsky theaters, monitoring each inch of bared skin?

Indeed he did, as Morton soon found out. On the night of June 22, 1935, one of Sumner's watchdogs attended the late show at the Repub-

Minsky "Rosebuds" and comic, shielding their faces after a raid.

lic, noting that during stripteaser Wanda Dell's encore she "dropped her dress to the floor, exposing her whole body, except her private parts, which were covered by a thin string of beads, leaving the cheeks of her rectum exposed," and that one of the Minsky comics defined a baby as "nine months' interest on a small deposit." This, Morton asked himself, was supposed to send audiences out in the streets "slavering to relieve themselves" at a nearby taxi-dance hall? "You'd think," he wrote, "we were holding a Roman orgy there."

He remembered Fiorello La Guardia joining the fray, giving a radio press conference that began with the melodramatic line, delivered in his trademark shriek, "This is the beginning of the end of incorporated filth." ("I wish," Morton wrote in 1986, the year before he died, "he could have lived to see [Times Square] as it is today, with open hard-core sex acts and no pretense at theater, comedy, or humor.") Of course, La Guardia then turned to John Sumner for counsel and assistance, imploring the reformer to link burlesque to the city's myriad problems and introducing him to the new license commissioner, Paul Moss. To Morton, the commissioner was something even worse than a reformer—an erstwhile "legitimate" Broadway producer.

Immediately upon taking office, Moss issued a sort of Hays Code for burlesque—some old restrictions, some new, all unreasonable. Stripteasers couldn't mingle with the audience or take off their bras but offer only the briefest flash of breast at the end. No more encores in which the girls slipped the curtain between their legs and whisked the velvet back and forth. No vulgar language or overtly suggestive double entendres. And, as the coup de grâce, a thorough dismantling of all lighted runways. Like their burlesque colleagues, Morton and Herbert obeyed only the final edict, feeling melancholy as the wood was stripped and the footlights darkened, thinking about Abe and his brilliant Parisian importation, and the distance that still festered between them.

Yet burlesque seemed to thrive in direct proportion to threats of its demise. Editorials pondered what would become of the "Minsky masterpieces" without the benefit of nudity. The painter Reginald Marsh created a series of sketches that captured what Morton loved most about his business, its phalanx of contradictions: the exquisite crudity;

the mechanical spontaneity; the wicked innocence; the hodgepodge audience and its palpably vacant gaze. During an extended visit to New York, sex researcher Alfred Kinsey took in several shows. "Burlesque at Broadway," he wrote, "has the most gorgeously thrilling girls I ever expect to see—and they stop at nothing. The g-strings to which they finally strip are half as wide as your little finger and not a button wider at the strategic spot. When the audience insists strenuously enough, she will remove even the string—slipping a finger in place (to live up to the law) with more damaging effect than the complete exposure of a nudist camp." A cadre of anonymous New York men calling themselves "The Mysterious Messieurs X" threw a "burlesque ball" for society hostess Elsa Maxwell. Hundreds of prominent New Yorkers, including Condé Nast and Theodore Roosevelt, Jr., packed the ballroom of the Waldorf-Astoria to watch a production titled *Gone with the Winski,* after the upcoming film with a similar name.

⸺

*M*orton remembered when he and Herbert opened their last burlesque house at 1662 Broadway, near 51st Street. They instructed the press to call them the "real, living Minskys" so as to distinguish themselves from Abe, who was "a renegade from the true Billy Minsky tradition." Minsky's Oriental Theatre would be different from anything else in burlesque's past or future, with spacious lounges, air-conditioning, and a "Park Avenue Row"—two hundred seats raised above the orchestra level and earphones for the dowagers, so they wouldn't miss the punch lines. Wait, there was more: an art gallery with "original oils" of nudes; a roof solarium complete with free lending library, so the girls could both sun and educate themselves in between shows; someone named Adrienne the Psychic offering free fortune-telling in the lobby; kimono-clad ladies serving fine champagne; and, in respectful homage to Billy, a cooch dancer, limber as a noodle, gyrating within the tight confines of a clear glass cage.

Everyone should come to the grand opening, scheduled for Christmas night 1936, to see for themselves. Formal attire, please.

A reporter asked about the schism from Abe.

Morton dropped his smile, rearranged his features into an expression of calm, and held up a hand. "We are on the most friendly terms with Abe," he insisted, and promptly changed the subject. "This house is going to be very different. Now it will be from the *Follies* to Minsky's." He thought about the ex-*Follies* girl he'd love to steal most of all. "Maybe," he added, "Gypsy Rose Lee will come back to us. You know she always said she could make more money in burlesque."

She did come back but for one night only, long enough to crack a bottle of champagne over the box office and launch her smile at the cameras.

There was a run of good luck, weekly box-office receipts of $19,000 at Minsky's Oriental and the chance for an unprecedented publicity coup. Representative Samuel Dickstein, Democrat from New York and one of the founders of the House Committee on Un-American Activities, introduced a bill to restrict foreign theatrical performers from entering the United States and stealing jobs from citizens. On February 18, 1937, Morton and Herbert dispatched a telegram to the congressman's office:

> FEEL WE COULD GREATLY INFLUENCE PUBLIC OPINION AS WELL
> AS COMMITTEE ON YOUR BILL STOP WOULD BE PLEASED COME TO
> WASHINGTON TO AID YOU

One week later, the brothers arrived in the nation's capital to discuss stripteasing with the country's most powerful men.

"Strange as it may seem to you gentlemen," Herbert began, "the striptease is a highly developed form of art. . . . It's not altogether what you take off, but how you take it off."

"And," Morton added, "*who* takes it off."

Herbert pulled an envelope from his pocket, offering it up as evidence. Hundreds of young American girls, he said, were "knocking at the doors of burlesque." And by concentrating on exotic dances, the

European performers often ruined the striptease, missing its nuances, vanquishing its humor.

"The American stripper," Morton said, "doesn't do that. She goes to school. Sometimes it takes twelve months just to learn how to peel off three garments."

"Maybe there aren't enough American strippers to go around," one congressman suggested.

"There are plenty of Americans," Herbert replied. "You've all heard of Gypsy Rose Lee. She started with us six years ago and now she is the greatest publicized star of today. I made every effort to get her to testify before this committee, but she was tied up with a contract and unable to come down."

A general sigh of disappointment looped around the committee table.

"About this bill," Herbert concluded, "we want to say that foreign governments have been stripping Uncle Sam for a long while. Now it's time to strip them, and we American Minskys should take care of the stripping."

From then on, Morton announced, the Minsky motto would be "The Stars and Strips Forever!"

Laughter and applause rushed through the hall, loud and gratifying as an opening-night ovation, so sweet and far removed from the trouble looming, inevitably, back in New York.

———

Morton remembered a wave of sex crimes across the city, and the way the newspapers divulged every detail with lurid, voracious glee. A four-year-old girl was strangled in the cellar of a deserted house in Staten Island. An eleven-year-old Brooklyn girl was raped and assaulted. An eight-year-old was raped and left to die in her old baby carriage, stored in the basement of her family home. A ten-year-old girl was attacked in a movie theater. A nine-year-old Catholic schoolgirl was raped and murdered in the back room of a Brooklyn barbershop. A thirty-four-year-old writer named Nancy Evans Titterton, wife of an

NBC radio executive, was raped and murdered in their Beekman Place apartment. Her battered body was found facedown in the bathtub, nude save for a slip, rolled-down stockings, and the pajama top used to strangle her.

Pundits and politicians suggested all manner of punishments for "criminal sexual perverts"—the electric chair, sterilization, segregation—and cast blame without discretion or direction. It was parents' fault for not teaching proper "sex hygiene." It was the state's fault for its lenient parole policies. It was the fault of every burlesque producer who allowed "salacious" performances, especially the Minsky brothers and, on one particular occasion, especially Abe.

How well Morton remembered that day in April 1937 when he and Herbert decided, five long years after Billy's death, to stand in the same room with their brother, especially since that room was in the Criminal Courts Building downtown. It had been so easy to push Abe to the periphery of their lives, to jab him with sly, subtle insults passed along through the press, to forget that the eldest Minsky, for all of his foibles and failures, was the one who first put the family name in lights. Morton knew it was a risk to show up on Abe's behalf—his brother could just as easily punch him as shake his hand—and also that, precisely because of the unknown outcome, the wild, hovering possibility of disaster, Billy would want him to do it.

So they showed up, he and Herbert, and took their seats in the courtroom where Abe would be accused of violating the penal code during a certain performance the prior August—a brilliant performance, Morton had to admit, with a girl swinging high from a trapeze, dropping a piece of clothing with every tantalizing to and fro. Abe, the brothers well knew, had violated the penal code numerous times—who hadn't?—but John Sumner and Commissioner Moss were determined to win this round.

Morton remembered his favorite part of the trial, when the district attorney examined a regular New Gotham patron, asking, in a powder-dry voice, "At any time during the performance were you excited?" and the guy's incredulous, no-shit look that served as his wordless reply. He remembered the unsettled, quicksand feeling in his gut when the judge found Abe guilty, and how it churned lower, faster, when the judge announced the revocation of Abe's license not just for a week but for months, until the fall.

At that news his brother stood. Abe's mouth curled and retracted into itself, like an earthworm poked with a stick, and he hurled his words with a vigorous, muttering fury.

"You think you are running the whole country," he said, stopping Commissioner Moss in midstride. "This has been going on for twenty-five years and you have been in office for three years and you haven't done anything." He stepped closer, situating his body inside the frame of the door. The courtroom fell into a prickled hush behind him. He lifted his chin.

"If you want to close them," Abe said, "close them."

The commissioner looked down at him and said, "Good-bye, Mr. Minsky."

———

Morton and Herbert formally reconciled with Abe, now using the press as a salve instead of a weapon. Morton kept his comments politic, impersonal. "In our case brother was pitted against brother," he said, "and that meant divided profits." Billy had been the fulcrum that kept them all in balance, and they had to learn how to work without him. They conferred, shared secrets and theories. It was obvious, now, why John Sumner and Commissioner Moss had postponed the trial against Abe for eight months; they wanted it to occur as closely as possible to May 1, 1937, when all burlesque licenses came up for renewal. Moss might not have the authority to padlock a theater without a conviction, but he could achieve the same end by refusing to issue a simple piece of paper.

On the afternoon of April 28, a Wednesday, the brothers convened in Moss's office at 105 Walker Street, aware that all forces were converging against them. Mayor La Guardia declared that "even the word striptease sounds dirty." A Brooklyn district attorney called burlesque dangerous to schoolchildren, lamenting how they "go into these places with their books under their arm." A man calling himself "a good Jewish subject" penned an adamant missive to the mayor: "For gods sakes," he wrote, "eliminate the most dangerous evil in the stage field. Do away with that name that has always spelled filth to the theatre-going public, and that is the name Minsky." Burlesque houses, said another city official, were the "habitats of sex crazed perverts." There was, the brothers noticed, a marked difference in tone between 1932 and now. Apparently burlesque no longer attracted degenerates and perverts but created them from scratch.

"All of us were fidgeting in the back row," Morton said, "irritated and embarrassed by all this ridiculous testimony. . . . Moss asked us over and over again if we had any defense, but none of us had anything to say."

———

𝒩othing he and his brothers tried worked: not the stays, writs, mandamuses, or superseding writs; not the pleas to La Guardia that thousands of actors, comics, chorus girls, stagehands, musicians, and stripteasers needed their jobs. Every Minsky theater now operated sporadically, in fits and starts. Mayor La Guardia vowed to "fight to the finish," a fait accompli with his landslide reelection in the fall.

"We tried to elevate burlesque," Morton told the press, "and look where it got us."

He remembered the eulogies from those who truly understood the loss, not only the brothers' but all of New York's. "As a patron of burlesque for more than forty years," wrote George Jean Nathan, "it is difficult for me to understand how the peculiar Mosses arrived at their concupiscent philosophy. If ever there was a male over sixteen years of age who, after giving ear to two hours of uninterrupted smut, felt otherwise than going right back straight home and getting a little relief by reading *Alice in Wonderland,* I haven't heard of him. Nothing so purges the mind of indecency as too much indecency. The most moral force in this world is a really dirty burlesque show."

At one of the Minsky Republic's final shows, a redheaded slinger named Ann Corio sheathed herself in gauzy organdy and performed a funeral dirge for her profession:

The old days forever are through
When we showed everything we had to you
'Cause now they've got us with our clothes on
No more will you see us strip
We can't even shake a hip
You'll see a little but that's your loss
That's by order of Commissioner Moss
Mr. Striptease is dead
And I'm his widow
He's gone but not forgotten
I'll just try to be brave
You should see the celebrities
Gathered at his grave
La Guardia, Moss were in the crowd
They had come by thousands to see the shroud
Herk was crying and so was Minsky
While music on a g-string was played by violinsky
Mr. Striptease is dead.

For her encore, she emerged from the curtain wearing a black negligee and a padlock encasing her hips.

---

*H*erbert fell into a deep depression, the days unraveling empty and endless before him. In 1942, he filed for bankruptcy, describing himself as a "theatrical manager, presently unemployed." He died in December 1959, of heart failure.

Morton remembered when Abe was on his deathbed ten years earlier, in late summer 1949. "Kid," he told Morton, "you're going to be the one to see the Minsky name in lights, I know it, and I want you to make every effort." In the end Abe was right. How Morton wished his brothers lived to see *The Night They Raided Minsky's*, based on Mademoiselle Fifi and that fabulous, fictitious raid of 1925, back when court hearings made for good publicity and even better jokes. In the film, a proper, pious Louis Minsky had neither ties to Tammany Hall nor a criminal record, and Billy was flamboyantly, magnificently alive.

Most of all he remembered what the city did to their name, banning the word "Minsky" from appearing anywhere on a marquee, anywhere in public, as if the brothers never defined or owned it at all. Yet for a long time those six letters remained visible across the Republic's facade, stubborn and deeply etched, brilliant even in the dark.

Chapter Thirty-six

Some people say that my collection is really quite

rare

and I can see the envy in their eyes

But if they only knew what I've been through, all that

wear and tear

I'm sure they wouldn't think it such a prize.

This key is to the cabinet where I keep my liquor

And here's one to a Hope chest I had in my youth

Feels like yesterday . . .

Though this ring holds every key, there is still no ring

for me

But I've had a lot of fun. And that's the truth.

—GYPSY ROSE LEE, "THAT'S ME ALL OVER"

Los Angeles, California, 1969–1970

June always says Gypsy is built like those cars of her heyday, a 1931 Chevy coupe or a Stutz, with a sleek, vibrant exterior unable to withstand the force of the engine within. Her body began turning on her long ago and she accepts her role in its demise: all those years of chain-

June and Gypsy, 1964.

smoking and chugging brandy, of sleeping either twelve hours a day or not at all, of telling herself that nothing matters as long as her accounts are full and her legend secure, of living in an exquisite trap she herself has set.

In the year leading up to the end she catalogues the minutiae of her days. She appears on *Hollywood Squares,* bleaches her hair, lunches with Merv Griffin, prepares for USO tours, interviews for *The Dating Game,* works in her aviary, itemizes even the smallest expenditures (a $2 tip for the grocery man, $2.25 on ashtrays), declines to appear with Frank Sinatra, Jr., because "I can't quite see myself with him," and marks the onset of the headaches. They are unlike any she's had before, the pain both sluggish and fierce, like a cement truck churning inside her skull. She makes this diary entry retroactively, perhaps realizing later that it represents a shift —the date her illness becomes a tool by which she measures her life. "Headaches begin about now," she writes on August 3, 1969. Her hand still has the strength to form bold letters across the page.

Never once does she write "cancer" in her very last journal, nor does she speak it aloud. Instead she veers around the word, as if acknowledging it directly will grant it power enough to win. "They've found a spot on my lung," she tells Erik, now a parent himself. "They took one look and sewed me back up. It has spread too much for them to operate. They've told me not to worry . . . yet. There's a good chance they'll be able to knock it out with radiation." In the meantime, would he mind calling Arm & Hammer for her? She did a commercial for them last month, soaking in a tub of baking soda and marveling at how smooth it made her skin. If word of her condition gets out, they'll never use the spot and she won't be paid her $10,000. God knows when she'll be able to work again. She wishes she had the time for one last face-lift.

Erik comes for a visit. He knows his Aunt June will be there, too, and he vows to keep the peace for his mother's sake. June was always trying to rip Gypsy off, once selling her a Rolliflex camera for more money than what it had cost in the store. He also never forgot what June told him, pointedly, when he was just eight years old: "All the men in this family never amounted to anything." Together, he thinks, Gypsy and June inherited all of Rose's characteristics—his mother got the good ones and Aunt June the rest. His mother's life was not an easy one, he realizes. She was "a wounded soul"—wounded by her mother, by Michael Todd, by June, and by Erik himself. He recalls their many disputes about money, about his thieving and disrespect, about the unconventional, exacting way she'd raised him. "We've never had a family," he told her once. "Families are supposed to love each other, and there's no love here. I can't even remember the last time we hugged or kissed good night."

Gypsy was taken aback but had her answer ready: "Well, you can hardly blame me for that. You never were a demonstrative little boy."

He knew his mother expected everyone to behave in ways that were bigger than human—herself included—and was always disappointed in the end. Now, as he leans in to kiss Gypsy, she shares one last confidence with her son. "After I go," she whispers, "don't let June in the house. She'll rob you blind."

June is working as the artistic director of the New Orleans Repertory Theatre, and as soon as a play opens she boards the next plane to Los Angeles. Nearly thirty years have passed since they lived together in Gypsy's double mansion on the Upper East Side, and the fragile thing between them is stashed, at least for the moment, in a place where it can't be harmed. "She was wonderful," June remembers, "she was gallant." June brings gifts, African violets and purple towels. Neither of them has ever seen purple towels—aren't they so lush, so cheerful?—and June cooks every meal. During the first few visits she actually convinces her big, fat sister to eat something, and they chatter about the kind of everything that means nothing real at all.

When the conversation changes, when it takes on weight and shape, it is Gypsy's doing and Gypsy's choice, and it lasts only as long as she allows. They are together in the bathroom, of all places, because Gypsy is too weak to stand on her own. June carries the enema bag and clasps Gypsy's waist, handling her as if she might tear. "Isn't this terrible, June?" she asks in a voice that has lost its exaggerated timbre and haughty trill, a voice that no longer speaks like Gypsy Rose Lee.

"Just ridiculously terrible," June answers. It is all she can think to say.

"This is a present," Gypsy adds, "from Mother."

And so the past moves in with them, uninvited but not unfamiliar. In the past few years Gypsy changed the way she spoke of Rose Hovick, reshaping her mother's motives, giving her credit for a love she might never have felt. The revisionist version began a few years earlier, during a television interview with Ethel Merman. "You remind me so much of Mother," Gypsy said. "You have her warmth and humor." Now the memories are all preserved inside delicate, gilded frames. June notices but says nothing. She is certain Gypsy has her reasons and also that she won't be inclined to share them. Maybe redeeming Mother is the fastest route to her own redemption. Maybe she decides the truth can be found somewhere in the shifting spaces between them.

Surely Gypsy knows that she is maddening and impossible, that she maintains her creation at the expense of those who have seen her naked, without it on. The creation rules her as much as she rules it; it is, along with Mother and Michael Todd, the great love of her life. It finally drives her last husband, Julio, away: the scenes, the yelling and stomping about, the inability to connect. He writes a poem for his wife that concludes with the lines

> *Strangled her*
> *To shut off*
> *Her torrent*
> *of*
> *verbal*
> *abuse*

He develops an ulcer because he just can't "stand the noise," as he puts it, the constant on-ness of being married to Gypsy Rose Lee, a woman who, for all of her bluster and might, can't take an aspirin without getting sick. The body reacts, June thinks, because the soul protests.

If she and Gypsy talked about things that could make them fight, June might begin with one night in particular at the 63rd Street house. Gypsy was throwing one of her fancy dinner parties and June was in bed with the flu, too sick to perform in her current show. Gypsy's cook, Eva, entered her darkened room.

"Here," she said, lowering a tray holding a cup of broth and a croissant. "You have to eat something."

No sooner had June taken a bite than Gypsy appeared in the doorway. June could track the course of her sister's gaze, from the tray to the croissant in June's hand, settling on her full mouth.

"June, Eva," she said coolly, distantly, as if meeting both of them for the first time. "You know I've only got twelve croissants for the dinner party tonight." Then, with raised volume: "You know I had so many guests, and it should come out even!" She stomped to the bed and leaned over June, as if to inspect the damage, and nearly scooped the crumbs from her sister's mouth. The ensuing scene—screaming, pacing, accusing, everything Gypsy had—carried on until the bell rang and the first guest arrived.

And there was the time June was in the hospital with a thyroid condition, nearly comatose, and Gypsy came to visit her. "Darling," she whispered, "I cannot stay. I have an engagement in Indianapolis that I cannot miss. Now, darling"—and here Gypsy leaned in so her mouth brushed June's ear—"can you hear me? Can you hear me?" June didn't stir. "In the side of your bed," Gypsy continued, "in the drawer, there's a check for four thousand dollars. You can pay me back at two percent interest, and you couldn't do better at a bank."

The worst of it, the memory that June pulled out time and again as evidence, was the night Gypsy gave her that card. After that nothing was as it had been before. She couldn't unsee those people, couldn't unhear that noise, and couldn't separate her sister from the moment Gypsy pressed the paper into her hand and told her to be bright. Seventy years later, bedridden, unable to walk let alone spin on her toes, ninety-five-year-old June Havoc made a confession: "Some things are just—" she said, and stopped short of filling in the space. "I'm still ashamed for her. I wish they hadn't happened . . . I was no sister. I was a knot in her life. I was nothing. Or else she wouldn't have given me that card."

Beneath all that, what June also left unsaid, was the unforgivable implication that she, too, lived to feed her own ravenous creation. That she had it in her to be just like Gypsy Rose Lee and, by extension, Rose.

And that's where Gypsy might join the forbidden conversation, if she cared to. She might recall every complimentary word June said about her: Gypsy knew how to "pick up an advantage" and use it. Gypsy was a marvelous storyteller. She was ruthless, she was brilliant, she was strong and sophisticated and elegant. She was the only one in her profession who "climbed out of the slime." She could do anything onstage that didn't involve actual talent. And beneath it all lay yet another tacit implication: Gypsy was too good for her own creation, and what a shame the creation was necessary at all.

"There came a day when she looked back on it all," June said, "and she herself was not pleased with what she'd created."

Time and again Gypsy endured the looks of disdain and pity, the rejections both silent and bold, the pressure to laugh at her own expense. She remembers trying to help June during those desperate early days in the best way she knew how: the audition at Minsky's, the blunt advice, the backroom party where the right people might notice her. One Christmas, when June was still struggling, she gave her sister a gorgeous fur coat. June hurled it straight into the fire. "I wouldn't take anything," she said, "that was made from stripping."

She remembers another time, when June was starring in a Broadway play and fielding offers from Hollywood. Gypsy was on the road, doing the same old act. June wanted Gypsy's opinion on a script, but there was a phone strike and very few calls could go through.

"What's the emergency?" the operator asked.

Gypsy identified herself and said, "This is my sister in New York, and she called me because she got an offer for a film and she wants my advice."

"Your advice?" the operator asked. "Well, you didn't do so well out there yourself." And she wouldn't permit the call.

They laughed about that for years, even though June—and June alone—knew Gypsy found it more painful than funny.

A few years later, in 1949, June was directing a production of Clare Boothe Luce's *The Women,* and Gypsy planned to play Sylvia. She was nervous and called June at all hours of the night with every concern, even those having nothing to do with the play. "June," she complained during one 3 A.M. chat, "you pay attention to everyone but me." Another time: "June, what earrings do you think I ought to wear?"

June declared that Gypsy's first performance was "fine." She followed the direction, she got her laughs. But when June left town for a few days, Gypsy had to compensate for her sister's absence. She put on her old monkey fur coat and the short dress that wouldn't let her sit down. She let Gypsy Rose Lee overtake Sylvia, and the company people called June and insisted she come back. June didn't have to say what she was thinking: Gypsy brought her gimmicks because they were all she had.

She tried, though, and June knew it. In 1960, she made a record, an actual record, called *That's Me All Over,* a dozen or so tracks of her singing about her strip days. She rushed to June's theater, grabbed her hand, and pulled her away from rehearsal. "Listen to me sing, June, I sing, I really sing!" she said. "Wait till you hear me." Gypsy put on the record, and they sat together on the floor. They listened to Gypsy rhyme "Tchaikovsky" with "take it offsky," boast that her "oven's the hottest you'll find," and lament everything she's been through, all that wear and tear. And June said only, "Boy, you're going to make a lot of money on that" in that voice of hers—that trained, professional voice, so skilled at slipping sly, private meanings beneath each word.

The cancer is the strongest part of her now. Each day it surges further beneath her skin, claiming new territory, staking fresh ground. One afternoon she and June lounge on chairs, side by side. Gypsy sits up suddenly, as if a bug is scuttling across her.

"June," she says, "look at this."

She pulls up her blouse to reveal the tumor under her breast. It has pushed clear through, a purple mass that pulses like a deadly second heart. June rises and starts toward her, arms outstretched. Gypsy asks her, kindly, not to hug her, and to please not say a word. And if she cries, Gypsy will beat the hell out of her.

In the beginning of February she calls her friends, one by one. Calmly, she finally says the word aloud: "I have cancer." The announcement makes the gossip columns. Everyone begins remembering Gypsy Rose Lee, the woman and the creation; they have never known the two as anything but connected, synonymous.

She had enjoyed the happiest time of her life just a few years earlier, during her syndicated talk show. For the first eight weeks, until the show found its rhythm, she did something she'd never done before:

work for free. Ironic, wasn't it, that the best audience she ever had was made up of conservative, conventional middle-aged women? The same group who once protested her Hollywood career en masse? Her "ladies," as she called them, tuned in faithfully at 4 P.M., Monday through Friday, from 1965 to 1968, for a peek into Gypsy's life, and she was more herself with them than she ever was onstage. Nothing was too private or trivial to share: letters from Erik when he was stationed overseas; the results of her latest face-lift; updates on her birds, fish, dogs, and flowers; tips on making jewelry out of bread dough; and recipes for French-fried chrysanthemum leaves. Everyone from Judy Garland to Liberace to Andy Warhol to Tom Wolfe sat down with her for interviews. Once she performed a dramatic reading from an article titled "How to Create a Compost Pile," beginning with "First you take a dead horse." She stashed potential fodder in a large, wheeled shopping basket and insisted on taking it to the studio in San Francisco. "I won't check it," she told airport security, "because my television show is in here and it's my entire life. I want the bulkhead seat, and I want this bag with me." And she always got her way.

The perfect description of her: Auntie Mame. She was eccentric, delightful, totally in another world. "Darling," she told Erik when he was just a boy, "I cannot sing. I cannot dance. But just remember your mother's a star." She took solace in that. She flopped in Hollywood and struggled on Broadway, but she could make the street a stage just by strolling across it. She traveled to Istanbul for impromptu weekends, taking only a change of clothes and a shopping bag. She nearly slugged Billy Rose at a dinner party for ordering her to stop talking. She was described, by the screenwriter Leonard Spigelgass, as having the "magic gifts of enthusiasm and incandescence, and the tenacity of a bulldog." She called Erik's fifteen-year-old girlfriend a "scheming little bitch" who just wanted money, and suggested her son lose his virginity to a prostitute. "Love," she told him. "You haven't the faintest idea of what that word involves." And when Erik, at age eighteen, demanded to know the name of his father, Gypsy responded by lighting a cigarette.

"I've decided not to tell you," she said.

"What do you mean?" Erik asked. "How come?"

"Because it's none of your business."

When she finally relented and said, "Otto Preminger," Erik was disappointed. He'd always suspected it was Michael Todd.

She never bought gifts. It wasn't just that she was tight—no one who knew her would suggest otherwise—but she preferred to make her own. They were personal and funny and said as much about the recipient as they did about Gypsy. She could make gorgeous, intricate lampshades by poking holes in tin cans. She knitted argyle socks while watching movies in the dark. For one friend's birthday she dressed a stuffed animal mouse in a hand-sewn prisoner's uniform and adorned its floppy ears with enormous hoops. She brought homemade ratatouille to dinner parties, a tiny jar meant to feed eight people, and exclaimed, "Darling, this is a delicacy, you're only supposed to have a taste." Her thriftiness pervaded her business dealings, as well. After a taping of *Hollywood Squares* she packed up all the leftover food. "This is for my animals," she said, but none of her costars believed it. When Edward R. Murrow came to interview her in her Upper East Side mansion, she accidentally dropped a hammer on her new marble floor—and then billed CBS for the damage. Her back-and-forth sparring with the notoriously difficult fashion designer Charles James was legendary. Gypsy recorded the disputes in her diary: "He said would count what he owes me (about $500, so he says) for making dress shape which I'm to pose in for him . . . he can't understand why he shouldn't be paid for his time. When I said what about my time, he called me a whore. Really!"

She notices, during one of her last radiation treatments, the queue of patients waiting behind her. "When I look at all these people," she says, "I can't bring myself to berate God for giving me this horrible disease. I've had three wonderful lives, and these poor sons-a-bitches haven't even lived once."

Still, Gypsy can't believe she is finally shutting down. "I'm going to beat this thing," she insists. "I'm going to beat it." She repeats this intention when she can no longer walk and spends her days in a wheelchair in her room. She repeats it when she exchanges her old bed for an electric one, when the oxygen tank is delivered, when she begins spending more time with a nurse than with her own sister. She repeats it when she weighs herself to measure how much she gained; she never notices—or pretends not to—when June leans on the back of the scale to make the needle jump. She repeats it when she douses herself with perfume, so as not to smell like death already lives inside her.

The gossip columns keep tabs on every setback, every trip to the UCLA Medical Center, every triumphant reprieve. On Sunday, April 26, 1970, the ambulance comes once again. Paramedics bind her to the stretcher and hoist her up, and the doors shut heavily at her feet. She is alive, Gypsy tells herself. Still in the ring, standing and taunting, still refusing to retreat to her corner. June will drop everything and meet her halfway, as always, bringing violets and forcing her to eat and knowing better than to cry. She wills her ears to hear the wail of the sirens, her face to feel the soft pressure of the mask that gives her air. It grows darker behind the lids of her closed eyes and her own breath teases her, letting her catch the tail end of each inhalation before slipping out of reach. Her body begins working in reverse, exhaling, exhaling, exhaling, giving everything it has, taking nothing in return. With her knowledge but never her permission, it relents at last.

Michael Todd and Gypsy at the World's Fair.

Chapter Thirty-seven

So we beat on, boats against the current, borne back
ceaselessly into the past.

—F. SCOTT FITZGERALD

New York World's Fair, 1940

Only she can transform a subdued return into a grand entrance. No one
will look at her and think she is less than what she'd been, or that she re-
gards tomorrow as warily as she does her recent yesterdays. She steps
into the city and wraps it tight around her, comfortable and sleek as one
of her old ermine coats, Gypsy Rose Lee wholly intact underneath.

She is everywhere at once, remaking her life as it was before she left
it: the East Side apartment with a calculated jumble of antique furniture, the chorus line of nosy cherubs, the lascivious portraits of naked
women, the thousands of erudite books teetering on shelves—some for
reading, some for show. She settles back into her good-natured jousting
with H. L. Mencken and her boldface status with Walter Winchell. She
continues her political activism, performing a strip to benefit the United
Committee for French Relief at the Ritz-Carlton, strolling out onto the
stage clad in a skirt, a few strings of beads, and a bolero. German bank-
ing heir Paul Felix Warburg scores her red garter for $50, and Mary
Pickford offers $400 if she'll keep her costume on. She references her re-
cent time in Hollywood under her old name as if it were passé, a tired

sketch she'd quickly outgrown; she'd much rather seduce a live audience than a phalanx of cameras, and it was all for a lark, anyway. "I guess my Fourteenth Street burlesque technique wasn't so good," she explains, shrugging. "There was never any Stanislavski in my methods. I just got up and said my lines. . . . I came back with a swell collection of autographs." She announces, with the subtlest touch of irony, her plan to strip to the song "I Want a Girl Just Like the Girl That Married Dear Old Dad."

She speaks of who she might become—Gypsy Rose Lee, author of mysteries—but says nothing about her plan to chronicle her life, a narrative every bit as mysterious as any she could invent. A page of notes is already tucked away in her scrapbook. "When I was a little girl," she's written in her boisterous, looping scrawl, "I was the #1 custodian of the family scrapbook. News photographers covered the first important event in my life—that was in Seattle, Wash when I won a healthy baby contest—then my sister June came along and could dance on her toes when she was 2½ years old. I was four and couldn't do anything."

On rare occasions she even speaks with candor, interviews that carry the burden of ulterior motives. "I want to do something serious and important in the theater some day," she admits, wistfully, to one columnist. "My sister is an actress. She's a real actress. She's been doing serious, important things for some time now."

"She has?" the columnist asks. "What's her name?"

June Havoc, Gypsy thinks but her mouth disobeys: "Jane Hovick."

Of course the columnist has never heard of her.

She and June are closing in on each other again, reshuffling their dynamic, wondering how best to fit into each other's lives. They are still the Duchess and the wunderkind—those original roles can never be stripped away—but they are nuanced and layered now, unafraid to step out of character. When June sent her that rabid, vicious letter after the murder at Highland Mills, Gypsy finally understood. June loves her in the same way she herself loved Mother: fiercely and irrevocably, and often against her better judgment.

June comes one day to visit while Gypsy is getting her usual "ass pounding," the masseuse chopping at her midsection while she lies spread-eagle across her mattress, her hands strangling the bedposts. "All that garbage, censor this, censor that," Gypsy mutters. "Well, I am Gypsy Rose Lee from now on, and the Ladies Mutual Admiration Society can stuff it up their noses." Her tone softens. "I don't know when I'm going to work again. . . . God alone knows what's next. Look over there—that's all I've been offered since I came back covered with glory." She pushes the masseuse away and sifts through a pile of paper, coming up with a sheet of music. "Wait a minute," she says. "There's a great song there. The writers are wonderful, June." She thrusts the page into her sister's hands. "They don't know I can't sing this, and I'll be damned if I'll prove I can't in public. Why don't you do it?" She has been taking from June for so many years, filching chapters from her life and diverting its path, and in a small, tentative way she seeks to atone.

June does do it. Through this project she meets Michael Todd and repays Gypsy the favor, suggesting that her sister be his star attraction at the New York World's Fair. Just like that Gypsy's grand reentrance is valid; she is no longer an impostor in her own skin.

The first time they meet, Gypsy knows Michael Todd instantly and makes an uncharacteristic decision, deciding to let him know her. Years later, after he damages her in places that were already broken, she realizes he also gave her a gift. When he marries Elizabeth Taylor in 1957, Gypsy says simply, "I hope he's finally found the person who is right for him" and means it, at long last happy for someone for the sake of it instead of for the show of it. He dies a year later when his private plane, *Lucky Liz*, crashes in New Mexico. Gypsy locks herself in her room at the 63rd Street mansion and cries for three days. (Joan Blondell, the actress he married instead of Gypsy, says, "I hope the son of a bitch screamed the whole way down.") Now, at the World's Fair, she tries not to mind that he calls her one of the two "greatest no-talent queens in show business"—the other being her Chihuahua, Popsy—or that in every photograph they take together, she gazes directly at him while he focuses on the lens.

At showtime, though, his eyes are heavy on Gypsy and she can't see him at all; he is one of thousands collected in the Hall of Music waiting to learn her private thoughts. She has just given an interview that asks her precisely that: what *is* she thinking when she performs her famous

routine "A Stripteaser's Education"? Reclining on a chaise longue in her
dressing room, done floor to ceiling in ivory and gold, Gypsy sips a
brandy and considers her answer. "So, basically, you want to know what
I think about?" she says. "Well, I don't think about love, and I don't
think of marriage, and I truly don't think too far ahead. . . . I can't help
but fervently hope that my lines are getting across, and that the audience doesn't really think I mean what I'm saying."

And here she is, dressed in an outfit that evokes gaslights and horse
cars—a welcome glimpse of nostalgia, on the eve of World War II—the
ruffles under her voluminous gown swishing with each step, hands
folded primly at her waist, eyes batting beneath the shadow of her hat.
Her inside-out strip, as she calls it, is inverted in both deed and word:
she first sheds the layers closest to her skin, all the while explaining the
aristocratic origins one must possess to become a stripteaser. Like
Gypsy herself it is a double-sided creation, the nuances intriguing to
many but understood by few, a tragic fable wrapped inside a brilliant
joke.

Peeling off white, elbow-length gloves, she cranes her languorous
neck and speaks as if the words were a poem:

> Have you the faintest idea of the private life of a stripteaser?
> My dear, it's New York's second largest industry.
> Now a stripteaser's education requires years of concentration
> And for the sake of illustration, take a look at me.
> I began at the age of three . . .

The crowd roars; she knows to wait for it. Just a hint of a smile, and
then she continues:

> . . . learning ballet at the Royal Imperial School in Moscow.
>   And how I suffered and suffered for my Art.
> Then, of course, Sweet Briar, oh those dear college days.
> And after four years of Sociology
> Zoology, Biology, and Anthropology—

She ticks each subject off on her fingers.

My education was complete
And I was ready to make my professional debut for the Minskys on
    14th Street.

The laughter rises and falls but never quite dies.

Now the things that go on in a stripteaser's mind
Would give you no end of surprise,
But if you are psychologically inclined,
There is more to see than meets the eye.

She swans across the stage and offers her hat to the bandleader. Strolling back to the center, she pulls at the shoulder of her gown to reveal a strip of collarbone.

For example—when I lower my gown a fraction
And expose a patch of shoulder
I am not interested in your reaction
Or in the bareness of that shoulder.
I am thinking of some paintings
By Van Gogh or by Cézanne
Or the charm I had in reading Lady Windermere's Fan
And when I lower the other side, and expose my other shoulder
Do you think I take the slightest pride in the whiteness of that shoulder?

She shakes her head, marveling at such a silly thought.

I am thinking of my country house
And the jolly fun in shooting grouse.

On to the pins now, dropping one at a time into the orchestra pit, the drummer tapping a cowbell as each one falls. Her blouse sways open just enough to expose her breasts, each covered by a black lace bow. She glances down and notices that one of the bows is askew. "Oh dear!" she exclaims, and adjusts it back into place. More laughter, and the music picks up tempo.

> *And the frantic music changes, then off to my cue*
> *But I only think of all the things I really ought to do.*
> *Wire Leslie Howard, cable Noël Coward*
> *Go to Bergdorf's for my fitting, buy the yarn for my mother's knitting*
> *Put preserves up by the jar, and make arrangements for my church bazaar.*
> *But there is the music, and that's my cue*
> *There is only one thing left for me to do, so I do it.*

She lifts her skirts and holds the pose, a blooming flower of ruffles and lace, her long, lovely legs the stem.

> *And when I raise my skirts with slyness and dexterity*
> *I am mentally computing just how much I'll give to charity.*

She leans and rolls down her stockings to the sweet, sliding notes of a violin, her hand imitating the dramatic flourishes of a conductor.

> *Though my thighs I have revealed, and just a bit of me remains concealed*
> *I am thinking of the life of Duse*
> *Or the third chapter of "The Last Puritan."*
> *None of these men are obscene*
> *They leave me apathetic, I prefer the more Aesthetic,*
> *Things like dramas by Racine . . . "Gone with the Wind."*

She removes her garter belt and drapes it around the neck of a man in the front row. "Oh, darling, you look so sweet," she coos, and turns him around for all to admire. The future fashion critic Richard Blackwell, just eighteen years old, watches, rapt. "Every slight smile, curved hip, raised arm and seductive thrust created a frenzy among the wide-eyed, open-mouthed men," he later writes. "She loved her audiences, as animalistic as they were."

Next she unhooks her petticoats, whirls them in a circle, and sends them soaring into the crowd. Suddenly she's shy again, realizing just how far she's gone.

And when I display my charms in all their dazzling splendor
And prove to you, conclusively, I am of the female gender
I am really thinking of Elsie de Wolfe, and the bric-a-brac I saw
And that lovely letter I received from George Bernard Shaw
I have a town house on the East River because it's so fashionable
To look at Welfare Island, coal barges, and garbage scows.
I have a Chinchilla, a Newport Villa . . .

She unfastens her skirt next and dangles it in front of her, a matador teasing with her cape.

And then . . . I take the last thing off!

The crowd screams a chorus of "No!" and laughs with her. The skirt drops and she tucks herself into the velvet curtain, holding it far enough to one side to show her G-string, lacy and black and adorned with a tiny pink bow, one last illusion for those who know to look. Her voice is a lullaby now, lolling and low, until the final punchline.

And stand here, shyly, with nothing on at all
Clutching an old velvet drop, and looking demurely at every man
Do you believe for a moment that I am thinking of sex?
Well, I certainly am!

She heeds their whistles and calls and reappears just once, giving what she has to, keeping all she can.

Acknowledgments

First and foremost, thank you to the late June Havoc—a fierce and lovely lady and a true national treasure—who so generously shared her time and her memories. Talking with her was like being magically escorted back to the 1920s and '30s, and I relish every moment I spent there. And my deepest gratitude to and affection for Tana Sibilio, who invited me into June's world, answered a million questions, supported me in a multitude of ways that have nothing to do with this book, and introduced me to the sublime grilled-cheese sandwich at the Lakeside Diner. The world is lucky to have you.

To Erik Preminger, for kindly inviting me into his home and sharing anecdotes and insights that made this a much richer book.

To the immensely talented Laura Jacobs, who provided me with every article, note, and interview transcription she used to write her groundbreaking piece on Gypsy, which ran in the March 2003 issue of *Vanity Fair*. I don't know another journalist who would have been so helpful and generous.

To my amazing editor, Susanna Porter, for her guidance, support, and superior editorial eye, and for finding Gypsy's story as fascinating as I do. And to her assistant, the efficient and ever-patient Sophie Epstein, for cracking the whip gently.

To Simon Lipskar, agent extraordinaire, for his general brilliance, unerring logic (his slavish devotion to the Yankees notwithstanding), tireless advocacy, and willingness to tell it like it is, even when I don't want to hear it. You gave me the single best piece of career advice I've ever received, a printout of which hangs on my office wall: "Just shut the fuck up and write the book." Indeed.

To the people who found files, checked facts, or lent a helping hand: the entire staff at the New York Public Library for the Performing Arts (a special shout-out to the unfailingly cheerful Tanisha Jones), Su Kim Chung of the University of Nevada at Las Vegas, Charlene Peoples at the Washington State Department of Health, Dotty King, Dianne Durante, Martha Davidson, Trish Nicola, Peter Dizozza, David Williams, Noralee Frankel, and, especially, the intrepid and delightful Carolyn Quinn.

To everyone who shared personal memories of Gypsy, the Minsky brothers, burlesque, and vaudeville, or who helped facilitate interviews: Arthur Laurents, Liz Smith, Dr. Edward Orzac, Bette Solomon, Dardy Minsky, George Bettinger, Satan's Angel, Kaye Ballard, D. A. Pennebaker, Gus Weill, Liz Goldwyn and Dominique Porter, Frank Cullen, Ava Minsky Foxman, and Mike Weiss. Thanks, also, to the vast and extraordinary neo-burlesque community, especially Laura Herbert, Franky Vivid and Michelle L'Amour, and the incomparable Jo Boobs.

To Sara Gruen and Joshilyn Jackson, my critique partners and dearest darlings (as Gypsy would say), who sustain me on a daily—even hourly—basis. Thank you for our decadent yet productive retreats, for reading this book more times than I care to count, for encouraging my inner Julia Child, for enduring my insufferable sore-winner poker-victory dance (okay, okay, I *occasionally* lose), for hating me hard, and for perfectly matching my own level of batshit crazy. Without you two I'd have quit this business long ago. My love and thanks, also, to the members of my writing group at large: the outrageously gifted Anna Schachner, the magnificent Lydia Netzer, the wicked and sharp Gilbert King, the whip-smart Emma Garman, the savvy Elisa Ludwig, and the fabulous and forgiving Renee Rosen.

To Julia "Edipist" Cheiffetz, Benjamin Dreyer, Tom Perry, Tom Nevins, Barbara Fillon, Sally Marvin, Debbie Aroff, Lynn Buckley, Susan Kamil, Gina Centrello, Steve Messina, Caroline Cunningham, Sandra Sjursen, Tom Schmidt, Rick Kogan, Erik Larson, Stephen J.

Dubner, Steven D. Levitt, Nick Barose, Jack Perry, Kathy Abbott, Melisa Monastero, Laura Dittmar, Beth France, Nora Skinner, Chip and Susan Fisher, Rachel Shteir, Jonathan Santlofer, Andrew "P. Pokey" Corsello, Mary Agnew, Sue Taddei, Jennifer Fales, and everyone who has supported me during my career, including the three-year process of writing this book. To quote old-time stripteaser Mae Dix, I'd do anything for all of you, within reason.

To Chuck Kahler, with whom, incredibly, I've spent half of my life: thanks for seeing through me, and for seeing me through.

And finally, a gutsy, ballsy, Ethel Merman–style *squawk!* to Poe and Dexter.

Notes and Sources

ix   "Genius is not a gift": Quoted in Joyce Carol Oates, *Blonde*, x.

ix   "May your bare ass": Telegram, Eleanor Roosevelt to Gypsy Rose Lee, May 8, 1959, Series I, Box 6, Folder 8, Gypsy Rose Lee Papers, Billy Rose Theatre Division (hereafter BRTD), New York Public Library.

CHAPTER 1: NEW YORK WORLD'S FAIR, 1940

3   "Everybody thinks": Havoc, *More Havoc*, 160.

3   the fair's 1,216 acres: Gelernter, 18.

3   seven hundred feet high: *The New York Times*, October 29, 1939. (Other sources say 610 feet; see Gelernter, 16.)

4   Joe DiMaggio: *The New York Times*, May 28, 1940.

4   "aquabelles": Gelernter, 308.

4   "We will be dedicating": Ibid., 344; *The New York Times*, December 29, 1938.

4   Westinghouse Time Capsule: *The New York Times*, September 24, 1938; Goldfield, 545.

4   General Motors' Futurama exhibit: Gelernter, 19–25.

4   "undesirable slum areas": Wood, 60.

4   They witness a robot: *The New York Times*, April 30, 1940.

4   "Sooner than you realize it": Trager, 515.

4   "Peace and Freedom": *The New York Times*, May 12, 1940.

4   hourly war bulletins: *The New York Times*, May 18, 1940; Philip Hamburger, "Comment," *The New Yorker*, June 1, 1940.

4   foreign section: *The New York Times*, May 18, 1940.

5   "American Common": *The New York Times*, May 19, 1940.

5   Fairgoers line up: *The New York Times*, June 4, 1940.

5   larger than the turnout: Gypsy received a louder ovation—based on an applause meter—than Roosevelt and Wilkie combined: J. P. McEvoy, "More Tease Than Strip," *Reader's Digest*, July 1941.

5   outpolling even Eleanor Roosevelt: John Richmond, "Gypsy Rose Lee, Striptease
     Intellectual," *American Mercury,* January 1941.
5   "larger than Stalin's": Preminger, 56.
6   "What's the matter in there?": Preminger, 57.
6   babies cry: Interview with Bette Solomon, granddaughter of Jack Hovick
     (through his second marriage), September 18, 2009.
6   dogs urinate: story by June Havoc as told to Tana Sibilio.
7   "I don't like poison darts": Geoffrey T. Hellman, "Author," *The New Yorker,* De-
     cember 7, 1940.
7   "I hope you are well": Rose Thompson Hovick to Gypsy Rose Lee, undated, Se-
     ries I, Box 1, Folder 14, Gypsy Rose Lee Papers, BRTD.
7   "Have you the faintest": The version of "A Stripteaser's Education" presented
     here (and later) is a composite; Gypsy performed this, her signature number, for
     many years and updated the lyrics every so often. In later years, she called it
     "The Psychology of a Stripteaser," likely in homage to Freud.

CHAPTER 2: SEATTLE, WASHINGTON, 1910S

9   "Do unto others": Cohn, 121.
9   hurling herself: Havoc, *Early Havoc,* 14, 92.
9   scalding water: Havoc, *More Havoc,* 39.
9   tearing her mother: Laura Jacobs, "Taking It *All* Off," *Vanity Fair,* March 2003;
     Havoc, *Early Havoc,* 122.
9   A caul: Lee, *Gypsy,* 44.
9   dark circles: Ibid., 10.
9   fit into a teacup: Havoc, *Early Havoc,* 14.
10   including her older daughter's name: Washington State certificate of birth,
     record number 193, file number 1388. This is the original birth certificate on file
     and specifies that there is "one child living of this mother"—clearly marking it
     as Louise's/Gypsy's. Though Rose Hovick certainly could have doctored a copy
     of a birth certificate, it would have been impossible for her to doctor the origi-
     nal. Charlene Peoples, a representative of the Washington State Department of
     Health, as well as officials at the King County Health Department, confirmed
     that this certificate is indeed the one that was filed at the time of birth. Though
     the birth certificate gives "Ellen June's" date of birth as January 8, 1911, I cite
     January 9 as Gypsy's birthday in the book since that is the date she used through-
     out her life (she also cited 1914 as the year of her birth). It's also possible, of
     course, that Rose never registered the name "Rose Louise" at all, and that, after
     the girls began their vaudeville careers, she requested that Gypsy's certificate be
     amended to read "Ellen June." The King County Health Department was un-
     able to verify when "Ellen June" was added to the certificate, or who, specifi-
     cally, updated the document. Erik Preminger also believes that his mother was
     born in January 1911.
        There are several theories and guesses about the Hovick sisters' true ages and
     names; I base my own conclusions on this birth certificate and several other
     pieces of documentation:
        a. June's letter to Gypsy, Series I, Box 2, Folder 9, Gypsy Rose Lee Papers,
           BRTD, dated April 25, 1949: "I wired to Vancouver and received a birth cer-
           tificate which makes me 35—born November 8, 1913. Here is the end of the

world. I am also called Ellen June. Mother requested they put down the same name as only she would do."

I tried to obtain a copy of June Havoc's birth certificate and was told that such records are not public information until 120 years after an individual's birth. A representative of the British Columbia Vital Statistics Agency said it would have been impossible for Rose Hovick to steal an original birth certificate, as June describes in *Early Havoc*.

b. The divorce records of Rose Hovick and John Hovick. Rose began divorce proceedings by filing a restraining order against John O. Hovick on July 3, 1914, which states "that there are two children the issue of the said marriage, to wit, Rose Louise Hovick and Ellen June Hovick, age respectively three years and one year."

If Louise had been born in January 1911, and June in November 1913, they would have been three and a half and nearly one, respectively, in 1914. Since the children were not yet in show business, Rose Hovick had no true motive to manipulate their ages. Judgment Decree for Rose E. Hovick vs. John O. Hovick, Filed August 20, 1915, #102195, Superior Court, State of Washington, King County, King Co. Court House, Docket Vol. 46, Folio 104, Journal 537, Folio 160.

c. Finally, in 1916, Rose Hovick enrolled Gypsy in the Seattle public school system using the name Rose Louise and a birth date of January 9, 1911: Frankel, 4; Seattle School District No. 1 enumeration record for J. O. Hovick, May 15, 1916, Seattle Public Schools.

11 Description of 4314 W. Frontenac Street: Office of the Secretary of State, Division of Archives and Records Management, Puget Sound Regional Archives, Bellevue, Washington.

11 square of Puget Sound: Residence, King County Assessor, Seattle, Washington, file number 3334.

11 "Her low tones": Havoc, *Early Havoc*, 22.

11 Rose had married: Marriage certificate, license no. 27327, filed on May 28, 1910, Seattle, King County, Washington. Both Rose's mother, Anna Thompson (aka Big Lady), and her grandmother Mary Stein (Dottie) signed the certificate as witnesses, which refutes the notion—invented by Rose and repeated by her daughters—that she fled a convent and eloped when she was fifteen. She lists her age as "18" on the marriage certificate, a number confirmed by the 1900 and 1910 U.S. censuses, both of which give her birth year as 1892: Year 1900; Census Place: Seattle Ward 8, King, Washington, Roll T623_1745; Page 7A, Enumeration District 114; Year 1910; Census Place: Seattle Ward 3, King, Washington; Roll T624_1659; Page 11A, Enumeration District 148.

11 Rose got her chance: July 8, 1914: Rose E. Hovick vs. John O. Hovick, Filed August 20, 1915, no. 102195, Superior Court, State of Washington, King County, King Co. Court House, Docket Vol. 46, Folio 104, Journal 537, Folio 160.

11 "damp and full of knot holes": Ibid.

11 "bad reputation": Ibid.

11 "struck and choked"; beat Louise "almost insensible": Ibid.

12 "any underwear to speak of": Ibid.

12 Professor Douglas's Dancing School: Series II, Box 14, Folder 7, Gypsy Rose Lee Papers, BRTD.

12 "I cannot recall": Havoc, *Early Havoc*, 15.

12   favorite bit of family lore: Preminger, 186–187.

13   "In a few years": Havoc, *Early Havoc*, 15.

13   "Mrs. Hovick, here you have": *New York Sunday News*, June 22, 1941. (In this article, the dance instructor is called "Professor Belcher.")

13   any child who: Lee, *Gypsy*, 10.

13   "We simply haven't the money": Havoc, *Early Havoc*, 15.

13   Jack Hovick told: Author's interview with Bette Solomon, September 18, 2009.

13   Would-be millionaires: Eugene Clinton Elliott, 35.

14   "jungle mother": Series VI, Box 42, Folder 4, Gypsy Rose Lee Papers, BRTD.

14   Judson Brennerman: Marriage Certificate No. 8289, State of Washington, King County.

14   newspapers reported: *The Fort Wayne Sentinel*, May 16, 1916.

14   "Daddy Bub": Havoc, *Early Havoc*, 123.

14   The following September: *Judson Brennerman v. Rose E. Brennerman*, Filed September 14, 1917, no. 124577, Superior Court, State of Washington, King County.

14   "cruel in many ways": Ibid.

14   "Men," she told her daughters: Havoc, *Early Havoc*, 122.

14   "God cursed them by adding an ornament": Ibid.

14   red rose . . . cabbage leaf: Lee, *Gypsy*, 61.

15   323 Fourth Avenue: U.S. Census, 1910.

15   drowning when he was nine: Author's interview with Erik Preminger, November 3, 2009; *Seattle Post-Intelligencer*, August 25, 1897.

15   died of a drug overdose: Havoc, *Early Havoc*, 24.

15   "Of course, he was only a man": Ibid.

15   Big Lady often fled: Havoc, *Early Havoc*, 23; Lee, *Gypsy*, 11.

15   embroidering an altar cloth: Series VI, Box 42, Folder 5, Gypsy Rose Lee Papers, BRTD.

16   "Dozens of tiny squares": Havoc, *Early Havoc*, 23.

16   Great Northern Railway: Ibid., 24.

16   "Indian necklaces": Carney et al., n.p.

16   "Vaudeville was America": Gilbert, 3.

17   the more popular term: Ibid., 4.

17   George Washington: *The New York Times*, April 24, 1927.

17   "coon shouters": Tucker, 4.

17   two dozen eggs: Gilbert, 53.

17   "The Haymakers": Ibid., 11.

17   Bertha Mills: Ibid., 20–22.

18   "This is a very": Gerald Marks interview, "Vaudeville," a PBS *American Masters* special, 1997.

18   Tony Pastor: *The New York Times*, August 16, 1908.

18   new commandments of vaudeville: Author's interview with June Havoc, March 2008.

18   Catholic boarding school: There is a record for an "R. Thompson" in an 1898 attendance book for Holy Names Academy in Seattle, Washington. This individual was enrolled for one semester, from August 1898 through December 1898. If "R. Thompson" is Rose Thompson, she would have been six years old during her tenure at Holy Names and certainly wouldn't have escaped to elope, or to run away with any vaudeville troupe (research contributed by Carolyn Quinn).

18   "learn manners and obedience": Havoc, *More Havoc*, 23.

18   "God wouldn't like": Ibid., 24.
18   paper doll family: Ibid.
19   she joined any roving vaudeville troupe: *New York Sunday News,* June 22, 1941.
19   "We always," June said: Ibid.
19   "Plug": Lee, *Gypsy,* 11.
19   "I'm a hard-boiled rose": Series VIII, Box 56, Folder 1, Gypsy Rose Lee Papers; BRTD.
20   "The rose step": Lee, *Gypsy,* 10.
20   "Fank you": Ibid.

CHAPTER 3: NEW YORK CITY, LATE SPRING 1912

21   "A Minsky never says die": *The New York Times,* September 7, 1930.
21   "Billy Minsky!": Minsky and Machlin, 19.
21   14th Street and Second Avenue: The Minsky family's home address was 228 Second Avenue, at Fourteenth Street. New York City telephone directory, May, October 1912–February 1913, Reel 23.
21   Wasn't it just a few weeks ago: Trager, 334–335.
21   "This is a get-things-done-quick age": Quoted in Barber, 27.
23   the most crowded neighborhood in the world: Trager, 697.
23   "As I enter": Barber, 58.
24   "gutter education": Minsky and Machlin, 18.
24   adult height: Michael William Minsky passport application; U.S. Passport Applications, 1795–1925 (database online), Provo, Utah, USA, www.ancestry.com.
24   "In God We Trust": *The New York Times,* November 14, 1907; undated clipping, Burlesque Clippings Files, Museum of the City of New York.
24   Billy counted it as a win: Barber, 77.
24   Gladys Vanderbilt's wedding: *The New York Times,* October 27, 1907.
24   behind the event's barred doors: Louis Sobol, "The Voice of Broadway," Burlesque Clippings Files, Museum of the City of New York.
25   laundry lines: Jackson, 1129.
25   Hit men abided by: *The New York Times,* November 8, 1908.
25   Billy's father had faced: Author's interview with Edward Orzac, nephew of Abraham Minsky, November 2009.
25   Louis Salzberg became: Ibid.
26   "How can you stand it?": Minsky and Machlin, 15.
26   "The politicians used to": Kisseloff, 37.
26   "Mayor of Grand Street": *The New York Times,* April 30, 1904.
27   "I would spend $10,000": *The New York Times,* September 16, 1898.
27   "Do you know who I am?": *The New York Times,* April 29, 1904.
27   Louis was arrested: Ibid.
27   "I will have stories": Ibid.
28   a cyclical pawning system: Barber, 23.
28   his scheme to defraud: *The New York Times,* May 14, 1909.
28   more than 45 million Americans: *The New York Times,* January 3, 1909.
28   "It amounts practically": *Billboard,* September 15, 1906.
28   Houston Street Hippodrome: Minsky and Machlin, 17.
29   S. Erschowsky & Sons Deli: National Winter Garden program, 1921, Burlesque programs after 1900, Museum of the City of New York.

29   "You know those slides": Barber, 24.
29   "Yiddish Broadway": Irving Lewis Allen, 61.
30   "Listen, Pop": Minsky and Machlin, 20.

CHAPTER 4: NEW YORK CITY, FALL 1940

31   "He was just a taker": June Havoc, interview with Laura Jacobs, 2002.
31   They pose for pictures: Series IX, Box 75, Folder 1, Gypsy Rose Lee Papers, BRTD.
31   "I am not a stripper" exchange: Cohn, 95–96.
33   "I like my men": Gypsy Rose Lee to Charlotte Seitlin, July 7, 1941, Series VI, Box 45, Folder 18, Gypsy Rose Lee Papers, BRTD.
33   When he was nine: Todd, Jr., 17.
34   "Dear Louise": Rose Thompson Hovick to Gypsy Rose Lee, January 27, 1940, Series I, Box 1, Folder 10, Gypsy Rose Lee Papers, BRTD.
34   "I thought you would like": Michael Todd to Gypsy Rose Lee, November 29, 1940, Series I, Box 3, Folder 8, Gypsy Rose Lee Papers, BRTD.
34   one girlfriend on the side: Cohn, 47–48.

CHAPTER 5: HOLLYWOOD, CALIFORNIA, 1916

35   "However paradoxical": Alice Miller, 10.
35   she played a frog: Series VI, Box 42, Folder 4, Gypsy Rose Lee Papers, BRTD.
37   "Come quickly, darling": Havoc, *Early Havoc*, 17.
37   "Baby June Hovick," etc.: Ibid., 62; *Los Angeles Times*, December 6, 1917.
38   the "little tot" led: *Los Angeles Times*, February 12, 1917.
38   "Hush, children": Havoc, *Early Havoc*, 26.
38   "the most beautiful child alive": Ibid., 15.
38   "Norwegian beak": Havoc, *More Havoc*, 18.
39   "She was haughty": June Havoc, interview with George Bettinger, 1997.
39   "Only actresses": Lee, *Gypsy*, 63.
39   "I wanted desperately": Ibid.
39   "Never lie, never steal": Havoc, *Early Havoc*, 58.
39   "If you don't succeed": Ibid., 25.
39   "Mother was," June thought: June Havoc, interview with Laura Jacobs, 2002.
40   "I know that Louise": From a vignette written by June Havoc about her family and career, courtesy of June Havoc and Tana Sibilio (June Havoc's papers are now housed in the June Havoc Collection, Howard Gotlieb Archival Research Center, Boston University).
40   "excess baggage": Ibid.
40   "What *is* the matter": Lee, *Gypsy*, 64.
40   "When she's away": From a vignette in the June Havoc Collection.
40   Aunt Hilma: Lee, *Gypsy*, 64 (Gypsy calls her "Aunt Helma" in her memoir).
40   a freak menstrual hemorrhage: Author's interview with Bette Solomon, September 18, 2009.
40   Rose enrolled Louise: Frankel, 4.
41   "Mother says you're the luckiest": Lee, *Gypsy*, 65–66.
41   "The Hollywood Baby": Havoc, *Early Havoc*, 121; *Wisconsin Rapids Daily Tribune*, June 6, 1922.

42   "beribboned, beflowered": Havoc, *Early Havoc*, 18.

42   "She'll do": Ibid., 19.

42   "Darling," she said: Ibid., 20.

42   "You're my trouper": Ibid., 62.

43   She unfurls her arms: See a clip of June's performance in *On the Jump* at www.KarenAbbott.net.

CHAPTER 6: PARIS, FRANCE, SUMMER 1916

45   "America is the only country": Quoted in Roger and Bowman, 181.

45   SS *Lafayette: The New York Times,* June 13, 1916.

45   "The second coming of Christ": *The New York Times*, May 22, 1916.

45   explosion on Black Tom Island: Trager, 359.

47   Charlie Chaplin: Castle, 77–79.

47   Anna Pavlova: Ibid.

47   "The Kangaroo Boxer": Ibid., 30.

47   These ladies were tradition: Ibid., 37.

47   Abe had been to the Moulin Rouge: Minsky and Machlin, 32.

47   before a fire closed: Pessis and Crepineau, 9.

48   "To deprive Paris": Castle, 28.

49   Access to the seats: Barber, 30.

49   the roof of Madison Square Garden: *The New York Times*, May 31, 1914.

49   *The Black Crook:* Zeidman, 21.

50   *Did You Ever Send Your Wife to Jersey?:* Brown, 524.

50   "Variety became vaudeville": Zeidman, 43.

50   "wheels": For an excellent discussion of the burlesque wheel system, see Zeidman, 76–100.

50   in late spring of 1916: Minsky and Machlin, 27.

50   belonging to shiksas: Roskolenko, 144–145.

51   a woman dressed: *The New York Times*, April 28, 1911.

CHAPTER 7: BROOKLYN, NEW YORK, FALL 1940

53   "You have made your stake": George Davis to Gypsy Rose Lee, undated (but likely December 1940), Series I, Box 3, Folder 2, Gypsy Rose Lee Papers, BRTD.

53   "If I have night lunch": Gypsy Rose Lee to Lee Wright, July 21, 1941, Series VI, Box 45, Folder 18, Gypsy Rose Lee Papers, BRTD.

53   the house at 7 Middagh Street: Tippins, photograph following page 146.

54   "like a whirlwind": Carr, *Paul Bowles,* 151.

54   "Leave them hungry": Carr, *The Lonely Hunter,* 118.

54   Annemarie Clarac-Schwarzenbach: Ibid., 119.

54   Nearly every night: Tippins, 107.

55   "We ran for several blocks": Carr, *The Lonely Hunter,* 121.

55   "H. I. Moss didn't care much": Lee, *The G-String Murders,* 7.

56   "get my ass pounded": Gypsy Rose Lee to Lee Wright, February 2, 1941, Series VI, Box 45, Folder 18, Gypsy Rose Lee Papers, BRTD.

56   "I read you are too smart": Michael Todd to Gypsy Rose Lee, undated, Series I, Box 3, Folder 8, Gypsy Rose Lee Papers, BRTD.

56   catering not to the elite: Todd, Jr., 69.

CHAPTER 8: SEATTLE, WASHINGTON, AND ON THE VAUDEVILLE CIRCUIT, 1917–1920

57   at least one more marriage proposal: A Seattle-based researcher and I checked the state of Washington for more marriage certificates under Rose Thompson Hovick, to no avail. Researcher Carolyn Quinn also checked records in California and found no evidence of another marriage. June says four husbands (*Early Havoc*, 25); Gypsy, three (*Gypsy*, 12–13).

57   "removed": Havoc, *More Havoc*, 75.

57   "They are little show kiddies": Lee, *Gypsy*, 14.

59   "nest egg": Ibid., 16.

59   "harum-scarum": Ibid., 18.

59   Four women played: *The Vancouver Sun*, April 29, 2009.

59   "I had a little bird": Ellis, 510.

59   Theaters across the country: *The New York Times*, October 6, 1918.

59   "June would be in pictures today": Series VI, Box 42, Folder 4, Gypsy Rose Lee Papers, BRTD.

60   a waiter, a bartender, and a pimp: Connors, 50.

60   He owned fifteen theaters: Tarrach, 22.

60   Each man shanghaied performers: Gilbert, 219.

60   "Take it or leave it": Tarrach, 22.

60   vowed to burn: Connors, 50.

60   occasionally disturbing: Tarrach, 51.

60   Guglielmo Marconi: Ibid., 88.

61   "You'll hear from us": Lee, *Gypsy*, 18.

61   "She was so ruffley": Laura Drake Seattle Historic Theaters Project Oral History Collection, Box 1 Folder 3, Mora Lucille Cody recollections, University of Washington Libraries.

61   always mistook Louise for a boy: Ibid.

61   "It's here, papa": Lee, *Gypsy*, 17.

61   "Master Laddie Kenneth": *Orlean Evening Herald*, December 29, 1922.

61   "King of the Ballad Songsters": *Eau Claire* (Wisc.) *Leader*, June 29, 1922.

61   "Baby June and Her Pals": Havoc, *Early Havoc*, 66.

61   "Honey Louise": *Wisconsin State Journal*, October 21, 1922.

61   "The Doll Girl": Havoc, *Early Havoc*, 66.

62   "clever Juvenile character actress": *Eau Claire* (Wisc.) *Leader*, June 29, 1922.

62   Pantages offered: Lee, *Gypsy*, 18. I couldn't find any such agreement with Pantages in Gypsy's papers at the New York Public Library, but it's likely those contract files aren't comprehensive.

62   On to Tacoma: Tarrach, 22.

63   Louise and Master Laddie Kenneth: Havoc, *Early Havoc*, 66–68.

64   "I got hurt a lot": June Havoc, commentary, "Vaudeville," a PBS *American Masters* special, 1997.

64   "It was safe": Author's interview with June Havoc, March 2008.

64   "Ten percent": Lee, *Gypsy*, 20.

64   "What are you getting?": Gilbert, 230.

65   William Morris: Ibid., 226.

65   "It's a wonder": Author's interview with June Havoc, 2008.

65   "A horse on you!": Ibid.

65   "You keep the change": Ibid.
65   fleeting and temporary "uncles": Havoc, *More Havoc*, 174.
65   "What are you doing here?": Author's interview with June Havoc, June 2008.
65   first pangs of shame: Ibid.
65   "I'll never forget": Ibid.
65   Murray Gordon Edelston: World War I Draft Registration Card, 1917–1918, Franklin County, Ohio; Roll 1832026; Draft Board: 2.
67   a child nearly the same age: Ibid.
67   "I lost their father": Lee, *Gypsy*, 23.
67   "I'm Baby June": Ibid.
67   "I hate him": Author's interview with June Havoc, March 2008; Series VI, Box 42, Folder 4, Gypsy Rose Lee Papers, BRTD.

CHAPTER 9: PHILADELPHIA, PENNSYLVANIA, DECEMBER 1940

69   "If you cry": Havoc, *More Havoc*, 269.
69   "talked about the things": Author's interview with June Havoc, 2008.
69   "original juke box voice": June Havoc to Gypsy Rose Lee (undated), Series I, Box 2, Folder 12, Gypsy Rose Lee papers, BRTD.
70   "I interviewed Leslie Howard": Rodgers, O'Hara, and Hart, 86–88 (I abbreviated the lyrics here).
71   She begins sobbing: Author's interview with June Havoc, March 2008.
71   "You always stopped the show": June Havoc, interview with Laura Jacobs, 2002.
71   "It wasn't hilarious": Ibid.
71   "I . . . I didn't think": Havoc, *More Havoc*, 226.
71   "Well, you see, June": Ibid., 227.
72   "Men yelling, 'Take it off' ": June Havoc, interview with Laura Jacobs, 2002.
72   Gypsy breaks the news: Tippins, 138.

CHAPTER 10: NEW YORK CITY, 1917–1920

73   "Puritanism: the haunting fear": Fessenden, Radel, and Zaborowska, 267.
73   "Ya know": Minsky and Machlin, 32–33.
75   They planned to advertise: Robert C. Allen, 231–232.
75   more motor vehicles than horses: Ellis, 509.
75   J. Montgomery Flagg's: *The New York Times*, May 20, 1917.
75   "The First Fifty": *The New York Times*, May 18, 1917.
75   "Booze or coal?": Lerner, 29.
75   City Hall bowed: *The New York Times*, November 2, 1917.
75   "a fascinating cross": Series I, Box 4, Folder 2, Gypsy Rose Lee Papers, BRTD.
76   he worked to cultivate: Hirsch, *The Boys from Syracuse*, 13, 17, 69.
76   Billy Minsky considered him: Undated clipping, Burlesque Clippings Files, Museum of the City of New York.
76   "The people must be amused": *The New York Times*, November 4, 1917.
76   a sad parade: Minsky and Machlin, 33.
77   Herbert took over "culture": Ibid., 49.
77   credit to "Will" Shakespeare: *Orlean* (N.Y.) *Evening Times*, December 19, 1925.
77   "plenty of short girls": *The New York Times*, September 4, 1927.
78   "No name in the history": Cantor, Freedman, and Johnson, 53.

78   *Nude Descending a Staircase*: Charyn, 46.

78   "One type is missing": Florenz Ziegfeld, "How I Pick Beauties," *Theatre Magazine,* September 1919; Florenz Ziegfeld, "Picking Out Pretty Girls for the Stage," *American Magazine,* December 1919.

78   "energetic Amazon": *Variety,* April 12, 1928.

78   "censorless ginger": Ziedman, 122.

79   "The Minsky brothers": Minsky and Machlin, 34.

79   "If people want it": Ibid.

79   He hadn't invented: Alexander, 17.

80   having lost his virginity: John S. Sumner, *Half and Half: Somewhat Autobiographical,* 42–44, John Saxton Sumner Papers, Wisconsin Historical Society.

80   Haymarket "resort": Ibid.; *The New York Times,* July 30, 1902.

80   "died of joy": Alva Johnston, "Contented Crusader," *The New Yorker,* February 20, 1937.

80   Two years prior: Shteir, *Striptease,* 93.

80   "I have never before": Minsky and Machlin, 35.

80   "Have your men drop in": Ibid.

80   a "Boston": Robert C. Allen, 247.

CHAPTER 11: CHICAGO, ILLINOIS, 1941

81   "Michael Todd was the toughest": Author's interview with June Havoc, June 2008.

81   "cruelly": *Hagerstown* (Md.) *Daily Mail* (AP report), January 28, 1941; *The New York Times,* January 28, 1941.

81   "obscene and abusive language": Ibid.

82   "I never try": J. P. McEvoy, "More Tease Than Strip," *Reader's Digest,* July 1941.

82   "Did you ever hold": Ibid.

82   "I'll do my specialty": Gypsy Rose Lee to Lee Wright, January 20, 1941, Gypsy Rose Lee scrapbooks, Reel 1, Gypsy Rose Lee Papers, BRTD.

82   "I'm delighted to hear": George Davis to Gypsy Rose Lee, January 15, 1941, Series I, Box 3, Folder 2, Gypsy Rose Lee Papers, BRTD.

82   "I think it very funny": George Davis to Gypsy Rose Lee, undated but circa December 1940, Series I, Box 3, Folder 2, Gypsy Rose Lee Papers, BRTD.

82   "Darling, I reread": Michael Todd to Gypsy Rose Lee, undated, Series I, Box 3, Folder 8, Gypsy Rose Lee Papers, BRTD.

83   "My father was unavoidably detained": Cohn, 107.

83   making $55,000 per week: Todd, Jr., 70.

83   Bertha Todd bursts into: Preminger, 58.

83   She has her superstitions: Ibid., 14–15.

CHAPTER 12: ON THE VAUDEVILLE CIRCUIT, 1920–1924

85   "Forty-five weeks of two shows": Tucker, 54.

85   Birth certificates were forged: "Gypsy Rose Lee: Naked Ambition," A&E *Biography,* directed by Jeff Swimmer, 1999.

85   "We never saw or heard": Author's interview with June Havoc, June 2008.

85   no salary for the boys: Lee, *Gypsy,* 25.

86 One singer, from Shamokin, Pennsylvania: Lee, *Gypsy,* 24; Havoc, *Early Havoc,* 126 (Gypsy's memoir says Sonny was from Shenandoah, Pennsylvania; June's, Shamokin, Pennsylvania).

86 Sonny Sinclair: 1924 Vaudeville Programs, Series V, Box 41, Folder 4, Gypsy Rose Lee Papers, BRTD.

86 "The disease is incurable": Havoc, *Early Havoc,* 127.

86 "He fondled her": June Havoc, interview with Laura Jacobs, 2002.

87 chewing the animals' food: Lee, *Gypsy,* 127.

87 "It's a wonder": Ibid., 24.

87 "The toothbrush," June said: Havoc, *Early Havoc,* 121.

87 "Why, they are only": Ibid., 223.

87 trench mouth: Ibid.

87 a gold pendant: Author's interview with June Havoc, March 2008.

87 "special" bars and restaurants and hotels: Ibid.

89 "Tough on Black Asses": "Vaudeville," a PBS *American Masters* special, 1997.

89 They met a performer: Story from June Havoc, as told to Tana Sibilio.

89 booking for $750 per week: Lee, *Gypsy,* 26.

89 no profane language: Series V, Box 41, Folder 2, Gypsy Rose Lee Papers, BRTD.

89 "licorice buttons": Havoc, *Early Havoc,* 132.

90 Mumshay was one: Lee, *Gypsy,* 127.

90 Sambo, perished after: Havoc, *Early Havoc,* 133–134.

90 "imitation children": Ibid., 131.

90 "She needs a lesson": Havoc, *More Havoc,* 208.

91 Chaz Chase: "Vaudeville," a PBS *American Masters* special, 1997.

91 Hadji Ali: Ibid.

91 "The Human Fish": Gilbert, 53–54.

91 a "cat piano": Ibid., 58. Though Gilbert claims that the vaudevillian who performed the "cat piano" actually pulled live cats' tails, this is unlikely; such a cruel act would not have gone over in family-friendly vaudeville houses. There was also a black-and-white Terrytoon cartoon called "Farmer Alfalfa's Barnyard Amateurs" that featured a "cat piano" and was popular screen fare in vaudeville houses. (November 2008 e-mail exchange with Frank Cullen, Director of the American Vaudeville Museum.)

91 Lady Alice: Author's interview with June Havoc, March 2008.

91 "insurance": "Vaudeville," a PBS *American Masters* special, 1997.

92 "kids," June said: Author's interview with June Havoc, March 2008.

92 It meant something when Martin Beck: Wertheim, 65.

92 Sarah Bernhardt at the New York Palace: Gilbert, 6.

92 "sophisticated little miss": *Wisconsin State Journal,* October 27, 1922.

92 "Pavlova's Own": Ibid.

92 "the greatest juvenile": *Orlean* (N.Y.) *Evening Herald,* December 28, 1922.

92 "I have seen and talked": Undated clipping from one of June Havoc's scrapbooks, June Havoc Collection, Boston University.

92 Dainty June dabbled: *Minnesota Daily Star,* March 12, 1924, Gypsy Rose Lee scrapbooks, Reel 1, Gypsy Rose Lee Papers, BRTD.

92 Dainty June and Company would soon: Passport application: Department of Washington State passport, no. 513399, issued February 1925.

92 "She is the most tender-hearted": *Wisconsin State Journal,* October 27, 1922.

92 "I love everybody": Ibid.

93   a patent: Researcher Carolyn Quinn checked the Library of Congress for the "Dainty June" patent and found none on record.

93   she once taught acting: Undated clipping from one of June Havoc's scrapbooks, June Havoc Collection, Boston University.

93   She had designed it herself: Series VI, Box 42, Folder 4, Gypsy Rose Lee Papers, BRTD.

94   "You know I wouldn't pay": Lee, *Gypsy,* 27.

94   grouch bag: Havoc, *Early Havoc,* 136.

94   "The Developer of Children": *Wisconsin State Journal,* October 27, 1922.

94   "We started fixing our room": Elizabeth B. Peterson, "Education for a Home Girl—Surprising Slant on Gypsy Rose Lee," undated, Gypsy Rose Lee scrapbooks, Reel 3, Gypsy Rose Lee Papers, BRTD.

95   "I just can't stand it": Lee, *Gypsy,* 42. June Havoc insists that Gypsy never slept with boys on the train (June Havoc, interview with Laura Jacobs, 2002).

95   "These child slaves": Stein, 143.

96   "They won't make me talk": Lee, *Gypsy,* 45.

96   "GO IMMEDIATELY TO MASTER": Series V, Box 41, Folder 3, Gypsy Rose Lee Papers, BRTD.

96   "SEATTLE WASH": Ibid.

97   "character, skill, and experience": *Wisconsin State Journal,* October 27, 1922.

97   They listened as she read: June Havoc, interview with Laura Jacobs, 2002.

97   "See for Yourself" field trips: Havoc, *Early Havoc,* 180.

97   "hideously" thin arms: Ibid., 181.

97   "gauche": Ibid.

97   at least $25,000: Havoc, *Early Havoc,* 136.

97   "It's a trillion dollars, I bet": Series VI, Box 42, Folder 4, Gypsy Rose Lee Papers, BRTD.

99   "Where did you children get those?": Lee, *Gypsy,* 49.

100   "How dare you?": Ibid., 51.

100   posing as Miss Thompson: *Gypsy Rose Lee: Naked Ambition,* documentary, 1999.

100   "The Duchess": Laura Jacobs, "Taking It *All* Off," *Vanity Fair,* March 2003.

100   "I'm going to marry": June Havoc, interview with Laura Jacobs, 2002.

100   "Money": Havoc, *More Havoc,* 253

102   "playing to the haircuts": "Vaudeville," a PBS *American Masters* special, 1997.

102   One of their programs: Series V, Box 41, Folder 2, Gypsy Rose Lee Papers, BRTD.

102   he performed before: *The Daily Freeman* (Kingston, N.Y.), August 28, 1923.

102   skit done in blackface: *The Daily Freeman* (Kingston, N.Y.), August 24, 1923.

102   Another boy's solo: *Capital Times* (Madison, Wisc.), February 25, 1924.

102   Louise displayed a flair: Gypsy Rose Lee scrapbooks, 1924, Reel 1, Gypsy Rose Lee Papers, BRTD.

102   "Won't You Be My Husband?": *Stevens Point* (Wisc.) *Daily Journal,* June 16, 1922.

102   "Dainty June and Company": *Wisconsin State Journal,* November 26, 1922.

102   first nervous breakdown: Author's interview with June Havoc, June 2008; Havoc, *More Havoc,* 27.

103   Franklin Delano Roosevelt: Murphy, 245–249.

103   There was, she said: Nathan Miller, 100–101.

103   The property damage: *The New York Times,* December 19, 1921.

103   It was the deadliest attack: Trager, 384.

104   Mme. Luisa Tetrazzini: *The New York Times,* December 4, 1920.

104   The Park Avenue Baptist Church: *The New York Times,* January 4, 1925.

104   "wireless vaudeville": *The New York Times,* March 14, 1921.

104   "Those earphones will never": Lee, *Gypsy,* 92.

104   "she couldn't dance that well": June Havoc interview with Laura Jacobs, 2002.

104   "I've got a cow": Lee, *Gypsy,* 34.

104   "Bring the kiddies": *The Daily Freeman* (Kingston, N.Y.), October 30, 1925.

104   "Every successful artist": Stein, 275–276.

105   "I can't wear this": Fanny Brice, "I Knew Gypsy Rose Lee When," *Cosmopolitan,* July 1948.

106   "You can't be too modest": Ibid.

106   "Does Mother know": Lee, *Gypsy,* 72.

106   "pink wax birds": Ibid., 73.

CHAPTER 13: NEW YORK CITY, 1942

107   "If only you knew": Quoted in Frankel, 135.

109   "You have to open": Cohn, 120.

109   "It was wartime": Quoted in Todd, Jr., 79.

110   his "princess": Preminger, 61.

CHAPTER 14: NEW YORK CITY, 1920–1924

111   "We'll get drunker": Quoted in Lerner, 260.

111   "Last rites and ceremonies": Trager, 388.

111   "mourning parties": *Daily News* (New York), January 16, 1920.

113   Uptown at Healy's: *New York Post,* January 17, 1920.

113   "I've had more friends in private": *Daily News* (New York), January 17, 1920.

113   Alphonse Capone: Walker, 11.

113   "I never was a crumb": *The New York Times,* January 27, 1962.

113   Arnold Rothstein: Walker, 11.

114   speakeasies sprouted: Lerner, 138.

114   "vaguely familiar": Walker, 102.

114   Izzy Einstein and Moe Smith: *The New York Times,* February 18, 1938.

114   Dozens lined East First: *The New York Times,* March 8, 1931.

114   "an itch to try new things": Lerner, 133.

114   "Give me a ginger ale": Ibid.

114   WAITER: Would the lady: Minsky and Machlin, 41.

115   shook a bottle: Zeidman, 149.

115   "Burlesque, like Broadway": *Billboard,* September 19, 1925.

115   half-page ads: *New York Clipper,* February 9, 1921.

115   Anne Toebe: "The History of Burlesque," *Billboard,* December 29, 1934.

115   Carrie Finnell: Ibid.

116   "My face ain't much to look at": Shteir, *Striptease,* 80–81.

117   "the girl with the $100,000 legs": Ibid., 81.

117   "Varicose Alley": Gilbert, 381; Zeidman, 110.

117   "I'll do anything": Zeidman, 133.

117   Minsky "Rosebuds": Minsky and Machlin, 11.

117   "a lavish and bounteous extravaganza": *The New York Times,* June 25, 1920.

118   "Look out, Minsky": Burlesque Clippings Files, Folder 30, Museum of the City of New York.

118   "They are far seeing youths": *The New York Times*, September 4, 1921.

118   "Burlesques": *The New York Times*, September 16, 1922; *Billboard*, November 11, 1922.

118   The company consisted of: *New York Clipper*, March 8, 1922.

118   "hulking": *The New York Times*, September 16, 1922.

118   "The Victoria": Van Hoogstraten, 41.

119   "Sober Sue": Gilbert, 247.

119   two retired Pinkerton detectives: Minsky and Machlin, 56.

119   intense conversations with his penis: L. Sprague de Camp, 119.

120   "The long-awaited uncorking": *New York Clipper*, September 20, 1922.

120   "People," Morton said: Minsky, 58.

120   closed after just twenty-three weeks: *New York Clipper*, February 14, 1923.

CHAPTER 15: GYPSY'S COUNTRY HOME, HIGHLAND MILLS, NEW YORK, AUGUST 1942

121   "By the time you swear you're his": Quoted in Meade, 143.

121   Gypsy Rose Lee wears black: *Orlean* (N.Y.) *Times Herald*, August 31, 1942.

121   the gathering downstairs: Preminger, 61; *Mansfield* (Ohio) *News Journal*, August 31, 1942.

123   "night club bad company": Rose Thompson Hovick to Gypsy Rose Lee, May 10, 1938, Series I, Box 1, Folder 9, Gypsy Rose Lee Papers, BRTD.

123   "Dear Bride Gypsy Rose Lee": June Havoc to Gypsy Rose Lee, Series I, Box 2, Folder 9, Gypsy Rose Lee Papers, BRTD.

123   "young, good-looking": *Oakland Tribune*, June 11, 1933.

123   "I don't think a woman": Ibid.

124   never to consummate: Author's interview with Erik Preminger, November 2009.

124   "Dearest Gypola": Alexander Kirkland to Gypsy Rose Lee, September 8, 1943, Series I, Box 1 Folder 3, Gypsy Rose Lee Papers, BRTD.

125   "charm the birds": Author's interview with Erik Preminger, November 2009.

125   twig of grapes: *Wisconsin State Journal*, August 31, 1942.

CHAPTER 16: ON THE VAUDEVILLE CIRCUIT, 1925–1928

127   "Their sincerity was greater": *Billboard*, December 26, 1936.

127   "I wanted to die": Richard E. Lauterbach, "Gypsy Rose Lee: She Combines a Public Body with a Private Mind," *Life*, December 14, 1942.

127   "Mind your own business": Lee, *Gypsy*, 126.

128   "Go and do it": Author's interview with June Havoc, March 2008. In *More Havoc*, June writes that "with the exception of [the doctor's] visits, and the hotel maid, I saw absolutely no one for two weeks" (27).

128   fourteen now and 165 pounds: Havoc, *More Havoc*, photo and caption: "Louise at fourteen, weight, 165 pounds," following page 54.

128   "Don't feel bad about it": Lee, *Gypsy*, 75.

129   "nutrition": Havoc, *More Havoc*, 128.

130   No fewer than 540: *The New York Times*, January 27, 1925.

130   playing the scores of the same shows: *The New York Times,* January 4, 1925.

130   "There is no more important question": *The New York Times,* January 27, 1925.

130   E. F. Albee: Stewart, 251.

130   old-time vaudeville houses succumbed: Ibid., 249.

130   The "film peril": *The New York Times,* July 20, 1928.

130   introduction of Vitaphone: Stewart, 252.

130   only five hundred theaters nationwide: Nathan Miller, 339.

130    $1.5 million "defense fund": *The New York Times,* June 30, 1928.

131   "that big boisterous American wench": *The New York Times,* April 24, 1927.

131   "Unique Pepologist": Series V, Box 41, Folder 2, Gypsy Rose Lee Papers, BRTD.

131   "The Joy Girl": Ibid.

131   "festival of splendor": *The Daily Freeman* (Kingston, N.Y.), October 29, 1925.

131   "Malcontent!": Havoc, *More Havoc,* 36.

132   made her bite June's favorite stagehand: June Havoc, interview with Laura Jacobs, 2002.

132   "The kids aren't babies": Lee, *Gypsy,* 92.

133   "What fights?": Havoc, *More Havoc,* 37.

133   a vision appeared: Author's interview with Erik Preminger, November 2009.

134   "one bright spot": Lee, *Gypsy,* 88.

134   "Everything going out": Ibid., 96.

135   "His very lack of pretension": Ibid., 95.

135   "You've told me to get out": Ibid., 96.

136   "I'm going to start": Ibid., 98.

136   "We'll just have to tighten": Havoc, *Early Havoc,* 190.

136   They had repaid: Lee, *Gypsy,* 154.

136   "That's interesting": Author's interview with June Havoc, March 2008.

137   "Why, that's an insult": Lee, *Gypsy,* 107.

137   they took all of them: Series V, Box 41, Folder 2, Gypsy Rose Lee Papers, BRTD.

137   "It is understood": Ibid.

137   "The experience will be": Havoc, *Early Havoc,* 191.

137   "danced like a bubble": Ibid., 192.

138   "show-offy": Lee, *Gypsy,* 138.

138   "cheap-looking": Ibid.

138   "I like being with you": Ibid., 139–140.

140   one-night stands: Gypsy Rose Lee scrapbooks, 1928, Reel 1, Gypsy Rose Lee Papers, BRTD.

140   Three Ormonde Sisters: Ibid.

140   Evelyn Nesbit: Ibid.

140   "Dainty June and the Happy Gang Revue": Gypsy Rose Lee scrapbooks, 1928, Reel 1, Gypsy Rose Lee Papers, BRTD.

140   "knock vaudeville out": Havoc, *Early Havoc,* 190.

141   she looped her arm through Rose's: June Havoc, interview with Laura Jacobs, 2002.

141   "Mother will be so glad": Lee, *Gypsy,* 133.

141   pushed that manager out: Author's interview with Arthur Laurents, October 2008; *Gypsy Rose Lee: Naked Ambition.* June calls this story "ridiculous," an assessment perhaps born of her changing views about her mother in later years. "Poor mother," she said to me. "She didn't know half the time what to do." I asked if Rose had realized how difficult it was for June to be working such ex-

hausting hours at such a young age, shouldering the financial burden for the entire family. "No, she didn't," June replied. "She was just so proud of me. And then later, when I was on Broadway, she wasn't interested at all." (Author's interview with June Havoc, March 2008.)

141   Jayhawk Theatre: Gypsy Rose Lee scrapbooks, 1928, Reel 1, Gypsy Rose Lee Papers, BRTD. "June eloped" is scrawled across the clipping. Bobby Reed's real name was Weldon C. Hyde, and the marriage certificate is dated November 28, 1928.

142   "She's only a baby": Lee, Gypsy, 143.

142   "She can't have gone far": Havoc, Early Havoc, 201.

142   She reached inside her coat: Ibid., 204.

143   "You're all I have now": Lee, Gypsy, 143.

CHAPTER 17: HIGHLAND MILLS AND NEW YORK CITY, 1942–1943

145   "All I ever wanted": Gettysburg Times, December 26, 1979.

145   "an Aztec virgin": Richard E. Lauterbach, "Gypsy Rose Lee: She Combines a Public Body with a Private Mind," Life, September 14, 1942.

145   "My Gawd!": Ibid.

145   "stay a bachelor forever": New York Daily Mirror, June 7, 1943.

146   "Sorry you are having trouble": Rose Thompson Hovick to Gypsy Rose Lee, December 24, 1942, Series I, Box 1, Folder 10, Gypsy Rose Lee Papers, BRTD.

146   "I miss you": Michael Todd to Gypsy Rose Lee, January 24, 1943, Series I, Box 3, Folder 8, Gypsy Rose Lee Papers, BRTD.

146   her play, The Naked Genius: Series VI, Box 44, Folders 1–9, Gypsy Rose Lee Papers, BRTD. The play's original title was The Ghost in the Woodpile.

146   "Doctor of Strip Teasing": Herbert Minsky to Gypsy Rose Lee, March 12, 1937, Series II, Box 14, Folder 2, Gypsy Rose Lee Papers, BRTD.

147   "the fizz on the soda": Daily Herald (Tyrone, Pa.), December 16, 1979.

147   she once bashed a producer: Daily Register (Harrisburg, Ill.), July 18, 1949.

147   less of a collaboration: Preminger, 63.

CHAPTER 18: NEW YORK CITY, 1925–1928

149   "When a burlesque producer": Mitchell, 53.

149   "bold invasion of Broadway": The New York Times, February 25, 1923.

149   "les frères Minsky": Billboard, January 2, 1937.

149   not to be confused with the Apollo: The Apollo of Harlem Renaissance fame was originally called Hurtig & Seamon's Theater and was a burlesque venue and competitor of Minsky's Apollo. Billy Minsky bought Hurtig & Seamon's lease in 1928 for $101,000 (Louis Sobol, "The Voice of Broadway," Burlesque Clippings Files, Museum of the City of New York). Six years later, the theater manager Frank Schiffman stepped in and renamed the venue the Apollo, after the Greek god. (The New York Times, February 19, 2006.)

149   Hurtig & Seamon's: Zeidman, 95.

150   "grossly inadequate": The New York Times, February 20, 1917.

150   "You won't last four weeks": Louis Sobol, "The Voice of Broadway," Burlesque Clippings Files, Museum of the City of New York.

150   corner barbershops: The New York Times, August 12, 1923.

150   a monkey had escaped and killed: *The New York Times*, September 22, 1924.

150   a triborough bridge: *The New York Times*, December 7, 1924.

150   The area boasted: Jackson, 523–524.

151   "There's no such thing": Van Vechten, *Parties*, 84.

151   rent parties: Adler, 57.

151   A'Lelia Walker: Nathan Miller, 220.

151   character called "Money": Adler, 57.

151   Sewing Machine Bertha: Caldwell, 292.

151   Madden's No. 1: Ibid., 238.

151   no darker than "high yellow": Kisseloff, 309–310.

151   *Super Black and White Sensation:* Burlesque Clippings Files, Museum of the City of New York.

152   Lucky Sambo: *Billboard*, August 29, 1925.

152   "You got any more material?": Minsky and Machlin, 61.

152   she was no longer Mary Dawson: South Florida *Sun-Sentinel*, April 17, 1974, Mary E. Dawson Papers, the University of Maine at Orono.

152   "Mademoiselle Fifi": Minsky and Machlin, 74.

153   "Dear Sir": *Variety*, September 3, 1924.

153   a queue that reached: *Variety*, September 17, 1924.

153   "gorgeous golden cape": *Billboard*, September 13, 1924.

153   "with a few cooch movements": Shteir, *Striptease*, 92.

154   "burlesque red hot": *Billboard*, September 13, 1924.

154   "I address you, sir": Barber, 35–36.

155   "Shakespeare Shimmies in His Grave": Minsky and Machlin, 78.

156   "splendid cooperation": Ibid., 177.

156   "Presenting the fair, the fragrant": Ibid., 265.

157   "This is it, Feef" and scene between Billy Minsky and Mlle. Fifi: Barber, 303–311.

159   the true whereabouts: South Florida *Sun Sentinel*, April 17, 1974, Mary E. Dawson Papers, the University of Maine at Orono.

160   "pelvic contortions" and courtroom scene: Barber, 330–332.

CHAPTER 19: ON AND OFF THE SET OF *THE NAKED GENIUS*, 1943

161   "The only time": *Gettysburg Times*, December 26, 1979.

161   until his ears "smarted": *The Evening Huronite* (Huron, S.D.), September 30, 1943.

161   "It is not a critic's play": *The New York Times*, November 7, 1943.

162   threatens to file a suit: Gypsy Rose Lee to George S. Kaufman, Series VI, Box 44, Folder 8, Gypsy Rose Lee Papers, BRTD.

162   "A waterfall gets 'em": Cohn, 145.

162   "Mike," she writes: Gypsy Rose Lee to Michael Todd, Series VI, Box 43, Folder 11, Gypsy Rose Lee Papers, BRTD.

162   "Every time I see": *The New York Times*, November 7, 1943.

163   "The critics will slaughter us": Cohn, 145.

163   "I'm taking it to New York": Ibid.

163   his pending $350,000 deal: *The New York Times*, November 7, 1943.

163   "Written by Louise Hovick": Todd, Jr., 107.

163   "Mr. Todd," he requests: Ibid.

163   It's the first time: Ibid.

163   "I can sort of understand": Quoted in Preminger, 64.
163   A gleaming gold compact: Ibid.

CHAPTER 20: ON THE VAUDEVILLE AND BURLESQUE CIRCUITS, 1928–1930

165   "The first hundred stares": Frankel, 19.
165   When Grandpa was a little boy: Series VI, Box 42, Folder 4, Gypsy Rose Lee Papers, BRTD.
166   "Mother," she said: Ibid.
166   "He can't do this, Rose!": Havoc, *Early Havoc,* 182–183.
167   died five days later: *Seattle Post-Intelligencer,* January 9, 1934.
167   "We'll comb the city of Seattle": Lee, *Gypsy,* 154.
167   The act consisted: Gypsy Rose Lee scrapbooks, 1929, Reel 1, Gypsy Rose Lee Papers, BRTD.
168   Mother sketched out prospective routines and personas: Ibid.
168   "two tiny swellings": Lee, *Gypsy,* 156.
168   the Tuesday-night entertainment: *El Paso Herald,* April 2, 1929, Gypsy Rose Lee scrapbooks, Reel 1, Gypsy Rose Lee Papers, BRTD.
168   "a kaleidoscopic pageant": Gypsy Rose Lee scrapbooks, 1929, Reel 1, Gypsy Rose Lee Papers, BRTD.
168   "Mother Machree": *Tucson Daily Citizen,* Gypsy Rose Lee scrapbooks, 1929, Reel 1, Gypsy Rose Lee Papers, BRTD.
168   "in the shadow": Havoc, *Early Havoc,* 8.
168   "It's the same as putting": Martin, 18.
169   visions of Jesus; another disrobed: Calabria, 77.
169   gnawed off the tops: *The New York Times,* June 23, 1928.
169   talked to imaginary friends: Calabria, 77.
169   dropped dead of heart failure: Martin, 19.
169   "complete Orpheum Circuit": Gypsy Rose Lee scrapbooks, 1929, Reel 1, Gypsy Rose Lee Papers, BRTD.
169   Attraction Extraordinary: Ibid.
170   "Look at us, Mother": Lee, *Gypsy,* 163.
171   "Seven Sunkist Sirens": Gypsy Rose Lee scrapbooks, 1929, Reel 1, Gypsy Rose Lee Papers, BRTD.
171   "really and truly from Hollywood": *Marion Daily Republican,* December 13, 1929, Gypsy Rose Lee scrapbooks, Reel 1, Gypsy Rose Lee Papers, BRTD.
171   "a number of the larger cities": Ibid.
171   having merged: *The New York Times,* December 9, 1927.
171   "I am vaudeville": Stewart, 252
171   Joseph Kennedy: Ibid., 253.
171   "washed up": Gilbert, 394.
171   only five straight vaudeville theaters remained: *The New York Times,* March 17, 1929.
172   "deliciosos" and "sugestivos" numbers: *El Paso Times,* April 2, 1929, Gypsy Rose Lee scrapbooks, Reel 1, Gypsy Rose Lee Papers, BRTD.
172   "They'd never get": Lee, *Gypsy,* 165.
172   "I am a hooker": Ibid., 166.
173   "A dime here, a quarter there": Ibid., 172.

173   daily expenses: Series V, Box 41, Folder 8, Gypsy Rose Lee Papers, BRTD.
173   "nothing will ever take": Lee, *Gypsy*, 158.
173   "If it weren't for that terrible revolution": Ibid., 171.
173   WALL ST. LAYS AN EGG: *Variety*, October 30, 1929.
173   "Happy Vic Allen": *Kansas City Star*, January 5, 1930.
174   "Now here's the deal": Lee, *Gypsy*, 176. In her memoir, Gypsy writes that they
       went to the Missouri Theatre, but there are no clippings in her papers from that
       venue. There are, however, plenty of clippings from the Gayety Theater, in-
       cluding one about a raid—which she cites as the reason they left Kansas City and
       headed for Toledo, Ohio.
174   "Burlesque!" she whispered: Lee, *Gypsy*, 178.
175   "Don't touch me!": Ibid., 179.
175   "Yes, it does": Ibid., 180.

CHAPTER 21: NEW YORK CITY, 1943

176   "How can we explain": June Havoc, interview with Laura Jacobs, 2002.
176   "I am sorry": June Havoc to Gypsy Rose Lee, December 1942, Series I, Box 2,
       Folder 9, Gypsy Rose Lee Papers, BRTD.
177    $12,500: Preminger, 63.
177   she'll claim it was built: Ibid., 44.
177   "Of course it goes without saying": Series II, Box 15, Folder 1, Gypsy Rose Lee
       Papers, BRTD.
177   "We know how well": J. P. McEvoy, "More Tease Than Strip," *Reader's Digest*,
       July 1941.
178   "Dear Miss Hovick": Seattle Welfare Department to Gypsy Rose Lee, Novem-
       ber 14, 1939, Series I, Box 1, Folder 1, Gypsy Rose Lee Papers, BRTD.
178   She was an "insane person": Aunt Belle and Big Lady to Gypsy Rose Lee, August
       27, 1943, Series I, Box 1, Folder 2, Gypsy Rose Lee Papers, BRTD.
178   "I'd rather put a gun to my head": Ibid.
178   "I can't imagine why": Big Lady to Rose Thompon Hovick, October 4 (year un-
       dated), Series I, Box I, Folder 7, Gypsy Rose Lee Papers, BRTD.
178   "a total state of heartache": June Havoc, interview with Laura Jacobs, 2002.
178   "They loved each other": Ibid.
178   "Louise dear," she writes: Rose Thompson Hovick to Gypsy Rose Lee, Decem-
       ber 24, 1942, Series I, Box 1, Folder 10, Gypsy Rose Lee Papers, BRTD.
179   accuse Gypsy of stopping: *Nevada State Journal*, May 13, 1943.
179   "he loves *his* mother": Rose Thompson Hovick to Gypsy Rose Lee, December
       24, 1942, Series I, Box 1, Folder 10, Gypsy Rose Lee Papers, BRTD.
179   "My life with you": Rose Thompson Hovick to Gypsy Rose Lee (echoing threats
       she'd made for years), April 30, 1951, Series I, Box 1, Folder 13, Gypsy Rose Lee
       Papers, BRTD.
179   "every tooth in my head": Gypsy Rose Lee to Rose Thompson Hovick, 1943, Se-
       ries I, Box 1, Folder 11, Gypsy Rose Lee Papers, BRTD.
179   "be brave and try to rise": Ibid.
179   "This isn't a pleasure trip": Gypsy Rose Lee to Rose Thompson Hovick, January
       11, 1944, Series I, Box 1, Folder 11, Gypsy Rose Lee Papers, BRTD.

CHAPTER 22: NEW YORK CITY, 1928–1930

181   "Viewed in retrospect": Adler, 57.
181   a floral horseshoe: *Billboard,* September 4, 1926.
181   the luminaries: Shteir, *Striptease,* 102.
183   "What fresh hell is this?": Meade, xvi.
183   "Outspoken buttocks in pink beads": Crane, 53–54.
183   "Beau Jimmy," the "Night Mayor," the "Jazz Mayor": Jeffers, 132.
183   his entire wardrobe was custom-made: *The New York Times,* February 19, 1928.
184   slip an illuminated wristwatch: Charyn, 108.
184   activate the siren: Mitgang, *Once Upon a Time,* 82.
184   "Jimmy Walker's Versailles": Charyn, 108.
184   "Why, that's cheap!": Mitgang, *Once Upon a Time,* 53.
185   He forbade: Author's interview with Ed Orzac, November 2009.
186   "presents": Minsky and Machlin, 70.
186   "Remember what Mama says": Ibid., 93.
186   a national sport: Phillips, 26.
186   "Hoover market": *The New York Times,* December 2, 1928.
187   "Any day now": Minsky and Machlin, 93.
187   dropped by dozens of points: Phillips, 30–31.
187   more than $32 billion worth: Ibid., 30–32.

CHAPTER 23: HOLLYWOOD AND NEW YORK CITY, 1944

188   "I only fucked": Author's interview with Gus Weill, former employee of Otto Preminger, July 2008.
188   "You always louse": Hirsch, *Otto Preminger,* 4.
188   "I'm going to have a baby": June Havoc, interview with Laura Jacobs, 2002.
189   has her stockings specially made: Havoc, *More Havoc,* 219.
189   "Hungarian Baroness": Hirsch, *Otto Preminger,* 36.
189   "delectable Viennese manner": Ibid., 30.
189   "sexual pleasure belonged to him": Ibid.
189   "good lover": Ibid.
189   "Louise dear," she writes: Big Lady to Gypsy Rose Lee, November 24, 1944, Series I, Box 1, Folder 4, Gypsy Rose Lee Papers, BRTD.
190   Gypsy sequesters herself in Reno: *Oakland Tribune,* September 5, 1944.
190   "People here ask": Bill Kirkland to Gypsy Rose Lee, November 6, 1944, Series I, Box 1, Folder 4, Gypsy Rose Lee Papers, BRTD.
190   "The cake and tea were good": Frankel, 149.
190   prematurely: *Moberly* (Mo.) *Monitor-Index and Democrat,* December 13, 1944.
190   "I can support my son": Hirsch, *Otto Preminger,* 116.
190   A radio newscast: From the diary of Rose Thompson Hovick (entries begin September 15, 1944), Series I, Box 1, Folder 11, Gypsy Rose Lee Papers, BRTD.
190   "O please God help her": Ibid.; Series I, Box 1, Folder 10, Gypsy Rose Lee Papers, BRTD.

CHAPTER 24: ON THE BURLESQUE CIRCUIT, 1930–1931

193 "I'm really a little prudish": "Gypsy Rose Lee: Dowager Stripper," *Look*, February 22, 1966.

193 "got a certain class": Lee, *Gypsy*, 195.

194 "The quicker you forget": Ibid., 195.

194 "a troupe a silly virgins": Ibid., 184.

194 "all of five minutes": Author's interview with June Havoc, March 2008.

194 "For a kid": Ibid., 194.

195 "I'm real": Ibid., 196.

195 a bottom-billing girl could earn: George Davis, "Gypsy Rose Lee: The Dark Young Pet of Burlesque," *Vanity Fair*, February 1936.

195 "Meet me round": Lee, *Gypsy*, 205.

196 The Depression affected female workers: *The New York Times*, March 13, 1932.

196 mothers with children: Dressler, 134.

196 75 percent of performers: Zeidman, 143.

196 Each applicant endured: Dressler, 137.

196 as easy as memorizing: John Richmond, "Gypsy Rose Lee: Striptease Intellectual," *American Mercury*, January 1941.

196 She learned that a "skull": Lee, *Gypsy*, 196.

196 G-strings might have been named: Briggeman, 34.

196 "catching the bumps": Ibid.

197 "If you were caught": Goldwyn, *Pretty Things*, 161.

197 "Oh, I like that": Ibid.

197 "G-String buyer": Goldwyn, *Pretty Things* (DVD).

197 prostitution thrived: Ibid., 129.

197 multiple scars from surgeries: Britton, 5.

197 If a girl couldn't afford: Brandt, 131.

198 "early-bird acts": June Havoc, interview with Laura Jacobs, 2002.

198 "Am I keeping the right rhythm": Goldwyn, 243.

198 "shocking" displays: Gypsy Rose Lee scrapbooks, 1930, Reel 1, Gypsy Rose Lee Papers, BRTD.

198 immoral "parties": Ibid.

198 "as big as a horse": Lee, *Gypsy*, 202.

199 "Close the flap": Ibid., 219.

199 she had murdered a cow: Author's interview with Erik Preminger, November 2009. Specifically, Preminger said, "This is more my guess" as to what really happened.

200 The cops threw Gladys in jail: Lee, *Gypsy*, 225. A May 12, 1930, article in *Zit's Weekly* claimed that Gladys was sick.

200 "When Miss Clark is showing": Shteir, *Striptease*, 113.

200 "There isn't any show": Lee, *Gypsy*, 225.

200 "I was a star": Ibid., 226.

200 "I have," Gypsy claimed: "Gypsy Rose Lee: Dowager Stripper," *Look*, February 22, 1966.

200 a pseudonym to trick Grandpa: Lee, *Gypsy*, 227.

200 when she wore a bandanna: Gypsy Rose Lee scrapbooks, Reel 2, Gypsy Rose Lee Papers, BRTD.

200   "lush, exotic beauty": John Richmond, "Gypsy Rose Lee, Striptease Intellectual."
201   her ability to read tea leaves: Richard E. Lauterbach, "Gypsy Rose Lee: She Combines a Public Body with a Private Mind," *Life*, December 14, 1942.
202   "Now stand up and show them": Lee, *Gypsy*, 230.
202   "They would always be so embarrassed": Frankel, 19.
202   "Well," she said: *Daily News* (New York), September 15, 1936.
202   "She was never an ingenue": June Havoc, interview with Laura Jacobs, 2002.
202   "There is a year my mother": Author's interview with Erik Preminger, November 2009.
203   "Well, don't stay": June Havoc, interview with Laura Jacobs, 2002.
203   "Would you like a cup": Ibid.
203   My god, she thought: Ibid.
203   "I couldn't stand it": Ibid.
204   Mother dropped a coat: Havoc, *More Havoc*, 157.
204   a vegetable "essence": Lauterbach, "Gypsy Rose Lee: She Combines."
205   "You should have told me": Lee, *Gypsy*, 240.
205   "gave him a lesson": Gypsy Rose Lee scrapbooks, 1930, Reel 1, Gypsy Rose Lee Papers, BRTD.
205   "You'd ought to read": Ibid.
205   helped themselves to June's history: Author's interview with Tana Sibilio, January 2010.
206   "No filth": *Zit's Weekly*, March 23, 1931.
206   "brunette of unusual face and form": Ibid.
206   "daytime person living in": "Gypsy Rose Lee: Dowager Stripper," *Look*, February 22, 1966.
206   "Darling! Sweetheart!": Davis, "The Dark Young Pet of Burlesque."

CHAPTER 25: NEW YORK CITY, 1930–1931

207   "You can become a winner": Quoted in Petras and Petras, 287.
207   The founder of a coal firm: *The New York Times*, October 30, 1929.
207   The president of the Rochester Gas: *The New York Times*, November 14, 1929.
207   The head of a major brokerage firm: *The New York Times*, November 24, 1929.
207   A man slit the throats: *The New York Times*, December 17, 1929.
207   The owner of a wholesale produce firm: *The New York Times*, November 17, 1929.
207   A Scranton man doused himself: *The New York Times*, November 18, 1929.
207   In the Bronx: *The New York Times*, December 12, 1929.
207   "improper schemes": *The New York Times*, October 26, 1929.
209   "that will reinstate courage": *The New York Times*, October 30, 1929.
209   More than four hundred leaders: *The New York Times*, December 6, 1929.
209   "work": Ibid.
209   "where all that money": *The New York Times*, October 28, 1929
209   A sixteen-year-old messenger boy: *The New York Times*, Nov. 17, 1929.
209    $5.50 for legitimate theater: Minsky and Machlin, 94.
210   The number of productions declined: Atkinson, 286.
210   "By 1930": Shteir, *Striptease*, 134.
210   Built in 1900: *The New York Times*, January 29, 1931.
210   By the time the show closed: *The New York Times*, October 22, 1927.

210   shot in the groin: Mitgang, *Once Upon a Time*, 10.
210   "Who shot you?": Ibid., 12.
211   "Arnold Rothstein has just been shot": Ibid., 2.
212   for twenty long years: *The New York Times*, January 29, 1931.
212   "Three years it took me": Lee, *Gypsy*, 257.
212   "Remote Control Girl": Corio, 74.
213   "She has trained": Ibid.
213   horizontal coochers: Shteir, *Striptease*, 137.
213 · "The only trouble": de Camp, 119.
213   "In the unnatural blaze of lights": Kazin, 87–88.
214   "dazzling and superabundant"; "Minsky-ized": *The New York Times*, September 13, 1933.
214   The producer came at him: Minsky and Machlin, 101.
215   "bump so vigorously": Zeidman, 156.
215   "strips like she just had dynamite": Mitchell, 57.
215   If she took too long: Sothern, 19.

CHAPTER 26: ENGLAND, 1952

217   "Once I chided her": Murray, n.p.
217   a "big lesbo": June Havoc to Gypsy Rose Lee, undated, Series I, Box 2, Folder 12, Gypsy Rose Lee Papers, BRTD.
218   "I hate like hell": Ibid.
218   "I'd like you even if": June Havoc, interview with Laura Jacobs, 2002.
218   Christopher Walken: Author's interview with Erik Preminger, November 2009.
219   Erik swallowed: Author's interview with Rosemary "Dardy" Minsky, a former wife of Harold Minsky (the son of Abe Minsky) and sister of the famous burlesque star Lili St. Cyr.
219   "I'm a woman alone": Preminger, 45.
219   "liberating": Ibid., 138.
219   "Honey, I wasn't even *born*": Ibid., 50.
219   someone hurls a rock: Series II, Box 10, Folder 3, diary entry for August 13, 1952, Gypsy Rose Lee Papers, BRTD.
219   "Rehearsal in three languages": Ibid., entry for April 30, 1952.
219   "Have decided": Ibid., entry for May 17, 1952.
220   "A stripteaser," she says: *Corpus Christi Times*, August 1, 1952.
220   "Dear June": Gypsy Rose Lee to June Havoc, undated, Series I, Box 2, Folder 12, Gypsy Rose Lee Papers, BRTD. I got the 1952 date from the prologue to *More Havoc*.

CHAPTER 27: NEW YORK CITY, 1931–1932

223   "It was all too discouraging": Frankel, ix.
223   "singing beggar" of Broadway: *The New York Times*, August 15, 1931.
223   coated in citronella: *The New York Times*, February 15, 2004.
223   "Hooverville": *The New York Times*, August 29, 1993.
224   "He wants us!": Lee, *Gypsy*, 249.
224   inventor of modern burlesque: Minsky and Machlin, 126.
224   "How old are you?": Lee, *Gypsy*, 251.

225   "Wear your hair like that": Ibid., 252.

225   Every day she rehearsed: Video footage of Gypsy practicing on the roof of the Republic, 1931, courtesy of Erik Preminger. The clip is silent, but you can see Gypsy mouthing the words. View it online at www.KarenAbbott.net.

226   "Come in and see her": Havoc, *More Havoc,* 17.

226   process of her own invention: Erik Preminger, interview with Laura Jacobs, 2002.

226   "Breasts more like molehills": Minsky and Machlin, 111.

227   "This is the only place left": Havoc, *Early Havoc,* 253.

227   "Louise wasn't a woman yet": Ibid., 255.

227   "cowboy production number": Lee, *Gypsy,* 252.

227   the *Poet and Peasant Overture*: Havoc, *Early Havoc,* 258.

228   "And now, ladies and gentlemen": Havoc, *More Havoc,* 257.

228   "And suddenly": Laura Jacobs, "Taking It *All* Off," *Vanity Fair,* March 2003.

228   "Seven minutes of sheer art": Minsky and Machlin, 98; John Richmond, "Gypsy Rose Lee, Striptease Intellectual," *American Mercury,* 1941.

228   "Gypsy Lee was a riot": *Zit's Weekly,* April 25, 1931.

228   "fan trouble": *New York Evening Graphic,* May 6, 1937, Gypsy Rose Lee scrapbooks, Reel 1, Gypsy Rose Lee Papers, BRTD.

229   "indecent performance": *The New York Times,* April 11, 1931.

229   "I wasn't naked": Minsky and Machlin, 144.

229   "Help!" she cried: Maeder (ed.), 78.

229   "My baby," Rose insisted: Minsky and Machlin, 144.

229   postraid fan mail: Series I, Box 7, Folder 1, Gypsy Rose Lee Papers, BRTD.

230    $900 salary: George Davis, "The Dark Young Pet of Burlesque," *Vanity Fair,* February 1936.

230   she stuffed the squares of paper: Shteir, *Gypsy,* 160.

230   Cameo Apartments: Lee, *Gypsy,* 254.

230   "I wish she was in": Havoc, *Early Havoc,* 257.

230   "You know," she told Gypsy: Lee, *Gypsy,* 257.

231   "Gypsy could really": Minsky and Machlin, 142

231   "I'm not giving anything away": Havoc, *More Havoc,* 160.

231   she accidentally spilled her lines: Richmond, "Gypsy Rose Lee, Striptease Intellectual."

231   No one could afford: Frederick Lewis Allen, 107.

231   seven out of ten: Ibid.

231   "feminine hygiene" and "marriage hygiene": Tone, 160.

232   a 14-karat gold button: Story from June Havoc, as told to Tana Sibilio.

232   Gypsy made one enemy: Briggeman, 41.

232   "*Fourteen?*": Minsky and Machlin, 123.

232   "I'll put this in the file": Ibid.

232   "like an animal": Sothern, 133.

233   "Gypsy had a style": Ibid., 131.

234   "Lew Costello": Minsky and Machlin, from an image of a Minsky program.

234   he yelled "Minsky!": Lee, *Gypsy,* 256.

234   "No actor should join": Shteir, *Gypsy,* 159.

234   "It takes time to be bad": Lee, *Gypsy,* 256.

234   "Seven days a week": Shteir, *Gypsy,* 159–160.

235   "all those down-and-outers": Minsky and Machlin, 99.

235   the largest investigation: Mitgang, *Once Upon a Time,* 98.
236   "When you're in politics": Edward Jean Smith, 225.
236   "by virtue of the Constitution": Mitgang, *The Man Who Rode the Tiger,* 170.
236   first few notes of "Ave Maria": Havoc, *More Havoc,* 64.
236   It cost $8,888: Lee, *Gypsy,* 266.
236   at the "funny parts": Havoc, *More Havoc,* 268.
236   Gypsy lost her virginity: Author's interview with June Havoc, June 2008.
236   "I'm going to have to rape": Havoc, *More Havoc,* 62.
236   "She *had* to get rid": Author's interview with June Havoc, June 2008.
236   "I would like to kiss you": Telegram from Rags Ragland to Gypsy Rose Lee, un-
       dated, Series I, Box 7, Folder 2, Gypsy Rose Lee Papers, BRTD.
237   Waxey Gordon was forty-three: Downey, 99.
237   an estimated 32,000 speakeasies: *The New York Times,* November 5, 1933.
237   At the height of Rothstein's operation: Lerner, 261.
237   the Bahamas' export of whiskey: Ibid.
237   New York City had its share: Lerner, 259–260.
238   a 6,000-foot beer pipeline: *The New York Times,* October 17, 1930.
238   "in the know": Lerner, 134.
238   "freedom of the seas": Frederick Lewis Allen, 25.
238   a five-year-old boy was killed: *The New York Times,* July 30, 1931.
238   just $10.76 in taxes: *The New York Times,* April 28, 1933.
238   "Compliments of Mr. W.": Lee, *Gypsy,* 262.
239   "Thank you for the champagne": Ibid., 263.
239   "No names": Ibid.
239   "Gyps," she whispered: Preminger, 74.
239   "I don't understand this": Lee, *Gypsy,* 263.
240   "brushed good": Ibid., 269.
240   "You can fuck or suck": Author's interview with Arthur Laurents, October 2008.
240   "She was very involved": Author's interview with June Havoc, June 2008.
240   3,600 hours on her feet: June Havoc, interview with George Bettinger, 1997.
241   "Plenty of popcorn, dear": Havoc, *More Havoc,* 68.
241   "Let go of me, June": Ibid., 61.
242   "And this is my baby": Ibid., 66.
243   "Gypsy assured us": Minsky and Machlin, 142.
244   Gypsy held out: Author's interview with June Havoc, June 2008.
244   "There are a lot of influential people": Ibid.
244   "It was a society": Ibid.
245   she didn't really love her: Ibid.

CHAPTER 28: NEW YORK CITY, 1931–1932

246   "There are three things": Mitgang, *Once Upon a Time,* 2.
246   "Where is the green room?": Lee, *Gypsy,* 251.
247   "Remember now": Ibid., 252.
247   "She had mastered the art": Minsky and Machlin, 97.
247   For the first time in burlesque history: Barber, 340.
247   Miss Seattle: *New York Evening Journal,* March 28, 1931, Gypsy Rose Lee scrap-
       books, Reel 1, Gypsy Rose Lee Papers, BRTD.
248   "I stuck a pin into you": James Thurber, "Robot," *The New Yorker,* August 29, 1931.

248   "No religious act": Lee, *Gypsy,* 254.

249   "had her idiosyncrasies": Minsky and Machlin, 140.

249   "She used foul words": Author's interview with Dardy Minsky, October 2009.

249   A day riding the Ferris wheel: Author's interview with Erik Preminger, November 2009.

249   "He could keep a hard-on": Havoc, *More Havoc,* 220–221.

250   "She had a monkey": Minsky and Machlin, 140.

250   More than eleven thousand: Ibid., 147.

250   the final night: *The New York Times,* September 19, 1931.

250   "Minsky American Wheel": *The New York Times,* May 16, 1931.

251   To Whom It May Concern: Minsky and Machlin, 130.

251   "Minskyville": Alva Johnston, "Tour of Minskyville," *The New Yorker,* May 28, 1932.

251   "Lose a few hundred": Ibid.

252   "I have never yet heard": Walsh, 35.

252   "a reformer is a guy": Walker, 224.

253   "Do you think anything's broken?": Minsky and Machlin, 131.

253   "Tweed Courthouse": *The New York Times,* December 2, 2001.

254   Q: Where did you keep these moneys: Mitgang, *Once Upon a Time,* 107–109.

254   "Atta boy, Jimmy!": Ibid., 147.

255   "Presumably by a *goy*": Minsky and Machlin, 106–107.

256   Paget's disease: Minsky, 131. I spoke with Charlene Waidman, executive director of the Paget and Bone and Cancer Foundations, who said that Billy Minsky's diagnosis was "undoubtedly due to a wrong assumption" by his doctor. At the time of Billy's death in 1932, little was known about Paget's disease; it is not a fatal condition.

256   "Never work north of Fourteenth Street": Minsky and Machlin, 132.

CHAPTER 29: NEW YORK CITY AND NYACK, NEW YORK, WINTER 1953–1954

257   "I am going to give": Rose Thompson Hovick to Gypsy Rose Lee, August 23, 1945, Series I, Box 1, Folder 12, Gypsy Rose Lee Papers, BRTD.

257   "Who is paying": Havoc, *More Havoc,* 3–4.

259   "Closer, please": Ibid., 4.

259   He's been stealing money: Preminger, 187–190; Series II, Box 10, Folder 4, diary entry for June 25, 1953, Gypsy Rose Lee Papers, BRTD.

259   "Is your mother home?": Erik Preminger, interview with Laura Jacobs, 2002.

260   She opened her purse: Ibid.

260   "So very elegant": Series II, Box 10, Folder 4, diary entry for November 8, 1953, Gypsy Rose Lee Papers, BRTD.

260   "I hope this is": Ibid., entry for November 23, 1953.

261   answering "Miss Lee's Residence": Author's interview with Erik Preminger, November 2009.

261   "Mother died at 6:30": Series II, Box 10, Folder 4, entry for January 28, 1954, Gypsy Rose Lee Papers, BRTD.

261   "I know about you": Havoc, *More Havoc,* 275.

262   "You'll fall": Ibid.

262   "You'll never forget": Ibid., 276.

263   "This isn't the end": Ibid.

263 Gypsy and one of Rose's neighbors: Details courtesy of researcher/writer Carolyn Quinn.

263 without any marker: Ibid.

CHAPTER 30: NEW YORK CITY, 1932–1936

264 "H. L. Mencken called me an ecdysiast": Lee, *Gypsy*, 2.

264 *"We take great pride"*: Ibid., 296.

264 "childishly leering": Shteir, *Striptease*, 88; Carl Van Vechten, "A Note on Tights," *American Mercury*, July 1924.

265 "kimonophobe": Kenneth Tynan, "Cornucopia," *The New Yorker*, May 30, 1959.

265 "went for Miss Lee": Russell Maloney, "Burlesk," *The New Yorker*, June 8, 1935.

265 "How vital!": Lee, *Gypsy*, 290.

265 "three stains bluer": Kyle Crichton, "Strip for Fame: Miss Gypsy Rose Lee, in Person," *Collier's*, December 19, 1936.

265 *La Traviata* at the Met: *The New York Times*, December 17, 1935.

265 a humming effect: Author's interview with D. A. Pennebaker, December 2008.

266 "Don't ask questions": Lee, *Gypsy*, 272.

266 "The moment I said it": Ibid., 273.

266 "depressing times": *The New York Times*, May 25, 1932.

266 "I don't know myself": Minsky and Machlin, 150.

266 "You were getting $60": Crichton, "Strip for Fame."

267 "It made me uncomfortable": Preminger, 75.

267 "I guess I wasn't used to": Crichton, "Strip for Fame."

267 when the show closed: *The New York Times*, April 18, 1933.

268 "burlesque moderne": *Boston Post*, November 24, 1933, Gypsy Rose Lee scrapbooks, Reel 1, Gypsy Rose Lee Papers, BRTD.

268 "limousine trade": *Boston Evening Transcript*, December 1, 1933, Gypsy Rose Lee scrapbooks, Reel 1, Gypsy Rose Lee Papers, BRTD.

268 Gypsy would even wear: J. P. McEvoy, "More Tease than Strip," *Reader's Digest*, July 1941.

268 "Burlesque pays well": *New York World Telegram*, June 11, 1934.

269 "Drive out the racketeers": Brodsky, 342.

269 "stands in need of": Mitgang, *Once Upon a Time*, 119.

269 "You let them shit": Brodsky, 399.

269 "Half Wop": Lawrence Elliott, 195.

269 "will be to Newark": *The New York Times*, September 10, 1937.

269 "you know I'd never end": Frankel, 234–235.

269 "Gypsy Rose Lee Guardia": *The New York Times*, March 7, 1937.

269 "incorporated filth": Zeidman, 230.

270 "the usual 50 showgirls": *The New York Times*, October 2, 1994.

270 "And now in Jimmy Savo's opinion": Walter Winchell column, syndicated in *Port Arthur* (Tex.) *News*, May 7, 1934.

270 "Get your money": Lee, *Gypsy*, 282.

270 "connected": Crichton, "Strip for Fame."

270 snubbed by the "café girls": *New York Daily Mirror* clipping, no headline, 1933, Gypsy Rose Lee scrapbooks, Reel 1, Gypsy Rose Lee Papers, BRTD.

271   "Darlings, please don't ask": John Richmond, "Gypsy Rose Lee, Striptease Intellectual," *American Mercury,* January 1941.

271   Edwin Bruns: *The New York Times,* May 16, 1925.

271   "mythical admirer": *New York Woman,* October 7, 1936.

272   "He's so darned handsome": Ibid.

272   he promised to take care of Gypsy: Author's interview with Erik Preminger, November 2009.

272   Billy Rose's gaudy circus: *The New York Times* November 18, 1935.

272   "ignoring the others": Havoc, *More Havoc,* 106.

272   "Among the death watch": *New York Journal American,* August 24, 1936, Gypsy Rose Lee scrapbooks, Reel 1, Gypsy Rose Lee Papers, BRTD.

272   "the hillbilly's Juliet": *Daily News* (New York), August 24, 1936.

273   "Keep them waiting": Fiske, 108.

273   81 Irving Place: Series I, Box 7, Folder 2, Gypsy Rose Lee Papers, BRTD.

274   Eva Morcur: Series VI, Box 24, Folder 1, Gypsy Rose Lee Papers, BRTD.

274   Every star had one: Havoc, *More Havoc,* 143.

274   Otis Chatfield-Taylors: George Davis, "The Dark Young Pet of Burlesque," *Vanity Fair,* February 1936.

274   courses of comfort food: Tippins, 90.

274   "We're broke or we wouldn't": *New York World Telegram,* November 28, 1936.

274   loosened a few: Havoc, *More Havoc,* 160.

274   *Strip Girl,* the show: "No Hits, Several Errors," *The New Yorker,* October 26, 1935.

274   "I consider that show": *New York Evening Journal,* October 21, 1935.

274   "Mae West," she said: McEvoy, "More Tease Than Strip."

274   "Leg art requires no protection": Ibid.

274   "I think he was a swell general": Ibid.

275   "Right End": *The Princeton Tiger,* November 5, 1935, Gypsy Rose Lee scrapbooks, Reel 1, Gypsy Rose Lee Papers, BRTD.

275   seasoning her conversation: "It was so contrived," June told Laura Jacobs in 2002. "She didn't know French . . . but she had all these bits and pieces and she knew when to lay them in and that they would be funny."

275   "Whither the New Negro?": Davis, "The Dark Young Pet of Burlesque."

275   "Dear, beloved, dazzling Gypsy": Bernard Sobel to Gypsy Rose Lee, Series I, Box 7, Folder 2, Gypsy Rose Lee Papers, BRTD.

276   "every ladies' luncheon": Havoc, *More Havoc,* 89.

276   "There was someone": Ibid., 91.

276   June, ironically: Author's interview with Erik Preminger, November 2009. Erik Preminger and June Havoc were estranged for many years.

276   "What in hell has happened": Havoc, *More Havoc,* 99.

277   "I'd like to be sure": Ibid., 106.

277   "Getting on my nerves": Ibid., 159.

277   "Look at that": Ibid., 160.

277   After Florenz Ziegfeld's death: *The New York Times,* July 23, 1932.

277   previously played by Josephine Baker: Lee, *Gypsy,* 289.

278   "saws, hatchets, chisels": *Orlean* (N.Y.) *Evening Herald,* August 17, 1923.

278   "Think I've got": Havoc, *More Havoc,* 161.

279   "I gave up marriage": Ibid., 109.

279   "Give Me a Lay!": Henry Miller, 3.

279   "The strippers talk": Ibid.

280   her rooster, Solly: Author's interview with June Havoc, March 2008.

280   "I guess he's not good enough": Lee, *Gypsy*, 279.

280   "Get the hell out of here": Havoc, *More Havoc*, 146.

281   "unnatural child": Ibid., 101.

281   "The world knows of Gypsy": Lee, *Gypsy*, 317.

281   filched from June's career: Author's interview with Tana Sibilio, January 2010.

282   "We know you are on dinner break": Havoc, *More Havoc*, 183.

282   "You mean," June said: Ibid.

CHAPTER 31: NEW YORK CITY, 1932–1936

283   "Whenever La Guardia talks": McIntyre, 130.

283   "Billy was dead": Minsky and Machlin, 132.

283   "I don't know how to tell you": Ibid.

284   "You're acceptable": Ibid., 231.

285   "Not one new burlesque": Ibid., 252.

285   He planned his own theater: *The New York Times*, July 29, 1932.

285   "I go my own way": Minsky and Machlin, 136.

285   "He thinks he can fill": Ibid., 137.

285   "battle of burlesque": *The New York Times*, July 19, 1932.

286   "His puritanical streak": Lawrence Elliott, 221–222.

286   at the Trocadero: Shteir, *Striptease*, 157.

286   "If I shake": Ibid., 115.

286   "that promised land": Minsky and Machlin, 154.

286   "Margie Hart Scholarship": Ibid., 247.

287   "Gypsy Rose Lee's act": Ibid.

288   developed an activist conscience: John Richmond, "Gypsy Rose Lee, Striptease Intellectual," *American Mercury*, January 1941.

288   "Gypsy called our theater": Shteir, *Gypsy*, 53.

288   "Morton," she began: Minsky and Machlin, 237.

289   "If you eliminated Waxey Gordon": Ibid., 238.

289   "She's *really* intelligent": Ibid.

289   "If the striptease is": Alexander, ix–x.

CHAPTER 32: NEW YORK CITY, 1956–1959

291   "the most publicized": Frankel, 220.

291   "There is," she concedes: Ibid., 218.

291   Her entire act: Author's interview with Erik Preminger, November 2009.

292   "Is a performer justified": Series II, Box 11, Folder 1, Gypsy Rose Lee Papers, BRTD.

292   Speak well of all: Ibid.

292   "I've had it": Preminger, 15.

292   "Good God, Erik!": Ibid., 24.

293   "I couldn't sing or dance": Lee, *Gypsy*, 5.

293   "an honest, unsparing document": *The New York Times*, April 28, 1957.

294   "From Hard-boiled Rose to Gypsy Rose": Lee, *Gypsy*, 319.

294   "I want to pay it": Ibid.
294   "The use of my character": Letter dated July 1957, courtesy of June Havoc and Tana Sibilio.

CHAPTER 33: HOLLYWOOD AND NEW YORK CITY, 1937–1940

295   "Nobody ever looked": June Havoc, interview with Laura Jacobs, 2002.
295   one of her new teeth: Richard E. Lauterbach, "Gypsy Rose Lee: She Combines a Public Body with a Private Mind," *Life,* December 14, 1942.
297   sinking the needle into her gums: June Havoc, interview with Laura Jacobs, 2002.
297   one of whom replenished: *New York Daily Mirror,* October 2, 1936.
297   Minsky's Oriental: *The New York Times,* December 25, 1936.
297   break a bottle of champagne: Minsky and Machlin, 263.
297   "Congress Learns of Gypsy's Art": Lee, *Gypsy,* 308.
297   "Serves them right!": Ibid., 330.
298   "Dear Louise": Rose Thompson Hovick to Gypsy Rose Lee, December 7, 1936, Series I, Box 1, Folder 8, Gypsy Rose Lee Papers, BRTD.
298   bought out the *Follies* contract: Author's interview with Erik Preminger, November 2009.
298   Rose underlined the words: Lee, *Gypsy,* 330.
298   "frowned" on her contract: *Boston Sunday Advertiser,* July 4, 1937.
298   a "headache": *The New York Times,* May 17, 1937.
298    $2,000 per week: Contract between Twentieth Century Fox Film Corporation and Rose Louise Hovick (professionally known as Gypsy Rose Lee), dated February 16, 1937, Series I, Box 4, Folder 2, Gypsy Rose Lee Papers, BRTD; author's interview with Erik Preminger, November 2009.
298   Gypsy visited the dressing room: Author's interview with Erik Preminger, November 2009. Preminger wasn't entirely sure the actress in question was Alice Faye; Phyllis Brooks was her other female costar.
299   "like an old skyscraper nightlark": Lauterbach, "Gypsy Rose Lee: She Combines," *Life,* December 14, 1942.
300   "influenced by her former experiences": *The New York Times,* May 17, 1937.
300   "To hell with them": June Havoc, interview with Laura Jacobs, 2002.
300   "Q. You were a striptease artiste": *Salt Lake Telegram* clipping, no headline, 1937, Gypsy Rose Lee scrapbooks, Reel 1, Gypsy Rose Lee Papers, BRTD.
301   "grande dame": *Los Angeles Times,* June 14, 1937.
301   vaguely British accent: *Los Angeles Times,* April 19, 1937.
301   remove the "slink": John Richmond, "Gypsy Rose Lee, Striptease Intellectual," *American Mercury,* January 1941.
301   "will go down in history": *The New York Times,* August 4, 1937.
301   "My dear Miss Hovick": Jean Augustin to Gypsy Rose Lee, February 21, 1937, Series I, Box 1, Folder 1, Gypsy Rose Lee Papers, BRTD.
302   a twenty-nine-year-old woman from Kenosha: *Portsmouth* (Ohio) *Times,* June 2, 1937.
302   "a credible though not at all": *The New York Times,* January 12, 1936.
303   She wore a white, short-sleeved: Description from crime scene photo, courtesy of Carolyn Quinn.
303   the coroner pronounced the death: *Wisconsin Rapids Daily Tribune,* June 2, 1937.

303   Gypsy Rose Lee: *Oakland Tribune,* November 30, 1937.

303   Georgia Sothern: Erik Preminger, interview with Laura Jacobs, 2002.

303   E. Sergio: Ibid.

303   Ginny Augustin made a pass: Author's interview with Erik Preminger, November 2009.

303   "I didn't do a thing": Havoc, *More Havoc,* 175.

304   "tantamount to refusal to indict": *Oakland Tribune,* November 39, 1937.

304   "more like everyone else": Havoc, *More Havoc,* 189.

304   when the three of them: Erik Preminger, interview with Laura Jacobs, 2002.

304   "Think, June," she mused: Havoc, *More Havoc,* 198.

305   "sweet lovely datter": John "Jack" Hovick to Gypsy Rose Lee, Series I, Box 1, Folder 6, Gypsy Rose Lee Papers, BRTD.

305   "I remember when I was pregnant": Elizabeth Hovick to Gypsy Rose Lee, May 31, 1966, Series I, Box 1, Folder 6, Gypsy Rose Lee Papers, BRTD.

305   "I wanted to be married": *Los Angeles Times,* August 1, 1937; Lauterbach, "Gypsy Rose Lee: She Combines," *Life,* December 14, 1942.

305   both of them alone: *Oakland Tribune,* August 15, 1937.

305   "Darling cant make trip": Rose Thompson Hovick to Gypsy Rose Lee, Series I, Box 1, Folder 8, Gypsy Rose Lee Papers, BRTD.

306   "Colossol [*sic*] Stupidity": June Havoc to Gypsy Rose Lee, undated, Series I, Box 2, Folder 12, Gypsy Rose Lee Papers, BRTD.

306   "A gal has to know": Frankel, 54.

307   continued an allowance: Rose Thompson Hovick to Gypsy Rose Lee, May 26, 1938, Series I, Box 1, Folder 9, Gypsy Rose Lee Papers, BRTD.

307   "Louise," Rose wrote: Rose Thompson Hovick to Gypsy Rose Lee, May 10, 1938, Series I, Box 1, Folder 9, Gypsy Rose Lee Papers, BRTD.

308   "What have I ever done": Ibid.

308   "I will regret": Rose Thompson Hovick to Gypsy Rose Lee, May 26, 1938, Series I, Box 1, Folder 9, Gypsy Rose Lee Papers, BRTD.

308   chased Bob around the house: Author's interview with June Havoc, March 2008.

308   "With my act": John Richmond, "Gypsy Rose Lee, Striptease Intellectual," *American Mercury,* January 1941.

309   "Dear Louise": Ruth Mizzy to Gypsy Rose Lee, December 20, 1938, Series I, Box 2, Folder 8, Gypsy Rose Lee Papers, BRTD.

309   "silly and rather provincial": Frankel, 35.

CHAPTER 34: NEW YORK CITY, 1958–1959

311   "Wish I had a town": Laura Jacobs, "Taking It *All* Off," *Vanity Fair,* March 2003.

311   "Closed doors": Laurents, 379.

313   the girls all vowed: Ibid., 377.

313   "Was your son": Ibid., 379.

313   "Did the fifteen-year-old": Ibid.

314   "Wasn't that the phone?": Ibid.

314   "Oh, darling": Ibid.

314   June feels differently: Author's interviews with June Havoc, March and June 2008; June Havoc, interview with Laura Jacobs, 2002.

314   "You want the world to believe": Havoc, *More Havoc,* 185.

314   "Listen, June": Ibid.

315   "Grim," Gypsy scribbles: Series II, Box 12, Folder 1, diary entry for January 22, 1959, Gypsy Rose Lee Papers, BRTD.
315   "You didn't come to see me": Laurents, 388.
315   "I found her funny": Ibid.
315   "I'm touching!": Ibid.
315   "I am ill": Series II, Box 12, Folder 1, diary entry for March 13, 1959, Gypsy Rose Lee Papers, BRTD.
315   he notices a petite figure: Laurents, 388–389.
315   "You see, I love you": June Havoc to Gypsy Rose Lee, Series I, Box 2, Folder 9, Gypsy Rose Lee Papers, BRTD.
316   she is not guaranteed a royalty: June Havoc, interview with Laura Jacobs, 2002.
316   "screwing me out in public": Author's interview with June Havoc, June 2008.
316   "example of a nonlove": Ibid.
316   "It realizes," June says: June Havoc, interview with Laura Jacobs, 2002.
316   sends Erik to the home: Preminger, 92.
316   She thinks, for a moment: Ibid., 101.

CHAPTER 35: NEW YORK CITY, 1969

317   "Broadway is New York intensified": Browne, 339.
317   the worst serial shuttering: *The New York Times,* June 27, 1955.
319   "lurid and flamboyant": *The New York Times,* November 29, 1962.
319   "obscene, indecent": *The New York Times,* June 27, 1971.
319   "deviant" males: *The New York Times,* December 9, 1955.
319   "Given the nature": *The New York Times,* June 26, 1966.
319   "To the editor": *The New York Times,* June 29, 1969.
320   the ills of the Depression: Phillips, 83.
320   "excessive and lustful kissing": Eyles, 14.
320   "stimulate the lower and baser": Ibid.
321   "burlesque commenced to run wild": John S. Sumner, *Half and Half: Somewhat Autobiographical,* 13, John Saxton Sumner Papers, Wisconsin Historical Society.
322   "nine months' interest": Minsky and Machlin, 253–254.
322   "You'd think," he wrote: Ibid., 254.
322   "This is the beginning": Zeidman, 230.
322   "I wish," Morton wrote: Minsky and Machlin, 277.
322   Moss issued a sort of Hays Code: *Billboard,* April 6, 1935.
322   "Minsky masterpieces": *Zit's Weekly,* February 16, 1935.
323   "Burlesque at Broadway": Shteir, *Striptease,* 382.
323   "The Mysterious Messieurs X": *The New York Times,* April 17, 1937.
323   *Gone with the Winski*: Ibid.
323   "real, living Minskys": *The New York Times,* December 26, 1936.
323   "a renegade from the true": Minsky and Machlin, 158.
324   "We are on the most": Ibid., 258.
324   "Maybe," he added: Ibid., 259.
324   FEEL WE COULD GREATLY: Morton Minsky and Herbert Minsky to Congressman Samuel Dickstein, February 18, 1937, National Archives and Records Administration, Record Group 233, Records of the 75th Congress, Box 114, Folder HR26-HR246.

324   "Strange as it may seem": Herbert K. Minsky, from U.S. Congress, Hearing of
        the House Committee on Immigration and Naturalization, "(75) H.R. 30: A Bill
        to Protect the Artistic and Earning Opportunities in the United States for Amer-
        ican Actors, Vocal Musicians, Operatic Singers, Solo Dancers, Solo Instrumen-
        talists, and Orchestral Conductors, and for Other Purposes" (2/24/1937),
        Microfilm, Library of Congress.
325   "The American stripper": *Cumberland* (Md.) *Evening Times,* February 25, 1937.
325   "About this bill": Herbert K. Minsky, from U.S. Congress, Hearing of the House
        Committee on Immigration and Naturalization for (75) H.R. 30, Microfilm, Li-
        brary of Congress.
325   A four-year-old girl: *The New York Times,* August 14, 1937.
325   An eleven-year-old Brooklyn girl: *The New York Times,* August 18, 1937.
325   An eight-year-old was raped: *The New York Times,* August 9, 1937.
325   A ten-year-old girl was attacked: *The New York Times,* August 12, 1937
325   A nine-year-old Catholic schoolgirl: *The New York Times,* March 23, 1937.
325   A thirty-four-year-old writer: *The New York Times,* April 11, 1936.
326   "criminal sexual perverts": *The New York Times,* October 1, 1937.
326   "sex hygiene": *The New York Times,* May 2, 1937.
326   It was the state's fault: *The New York Times,* August 26, 1937.
326   "salacious" performances: *The New York Times,* April 16, 1937.
326   "At any time during": Ibid., 271.
327   "You think you are running": *The New York Times,* April 16, 1937.
327   "If you want to close them": Ibid.
327   "In our case brother": *The New York Times,* September 4, 1937.
327   "even the word striptease": Shteir, *Striptease,* 171.
327   "go into these places": Friedman, 86.
327   "For gods sakes": Letter to Fiorello La Guardia, June 17, 1937, Papers of
        Fiorello H. La Guardia, Municipal Archives, City of New York.
328   "habitats of sex crazed perverts": *The New York Times,* May 4, 1937.
328   "All of us were fidgeting": Minsky and Machlin, 276.
328   "fight to the finish": *The New York Times,* May 3, 1937.
328   "We tried to elevate burlesque": *The New York Times,* May 6, 1937.
328   "As a patron of burlesque": Nathan, *The Theatre Book of the Year,* 23.
329   *"The old days forever are through":* Shteir, *Striptease,* 384.
329   "theatrical manager": *The New York Times,* May 13, 1942.
329   "Kid," he told Morton: Minsky and Machlin, 286.
330   banning the word "Minsky": Roland Barber, "The Sudden Raid That Ruined
        Real Burlesque," *Life,* May 2, 1960.

CHAPTER 36: LOS ANGELES, CALIFORNIA, 1969–1970

331   June always says: June Havoc, interview with Laura Jacobs, 2002.
333   "I can't quite see myself": Diary entry for July 17, 1969, Series II, Box 13,
        Folder 6, Gypsy Rose Lee Papers, BRTD.
333   "Headaches begin about now": Diary entry for August 3, 1969, Series II, Box 13,
        Folder 6, Gypsy Rose Lee Papers, BRTD.
333   "They've found a spot": Preminger, 260.
333   would he mind calling: Ibid., 263.

333   She wishes she had: Author's interview with Kaye Ballard, September 2008.

333   "All the men": Author's interview with Erik Preminger, November 2009.

334   "a wounded soul": Ibid.

334   "We've never had a family": Preminger, 193.

334   "After I go": Author's interview with Erik Preminger, November 2009.

334   "She was wonderful": June Havoc, interview with Laura Jacobs, 2002.

334   "Isn't this terrible, June?": Ibid.

334   "This is a present": Ibid.

335   "You remind me so much": Author's interview with Erik Preminger, November 2009.

335   Strangled her: Quoted in Shteir, Striptease, 161.

335   "stand the noise": June Havoc, interview with Laura Jacobs, 2002.

336   "June, Eva": Author's interview with June Havoc, June 2008.

336   "Darling," she whispered: Author's interview with Kaye Ballard, September 2008.

336   "Some things are just": Author's interview with June Havoc, June 2008.

336   "pick up an advantage": June Havoc, interview with Laura Jacobs, 2002.

337   "climbed out of the slime": Ibid.

337   "There came a day": Daily Herald (suburban Chicago), March 16, 1995.

337   "I wouldn't take anything": Author's interview with Erik Preminger, November 2009.

337   "What's the emergency?": June Havoc, interview with Laura Jacobs, 2002.

337   "June," she complained: Ibid.

338   "Listen to me sing": Ibid.

338   "Boy, you're going to make": Ibid.

338   "June," she says: Ibid.

338   "I have cancer": Lebanon (Pa.) Daily News, February 3, 1970.

339   recipes for French-fried: The New York Times, January 23, 1966.

339   "How to Create a Compost Pile": Erik Preminger, interview with Laura Jacobs, 2002.

339   "I won't check it": Ibid.

339   "Darling," she told Erik: Author's interview with Kaye Ballard, September 2008.

339   "magic gifts of enthusiasm": The New York Times, May 10, 1970.

339   "scheming little bitch": Preminger, 215.

339   "Love," she told him: Ibid.

339   "I've decided not to tell you": Ibid., 238.

340   "Darling, this is a delicacy": Author's interview with Kaye Ballard, September 2008.

340   "This is for my animals": Ibid.

340   billed CBS for the damage: Frankel, 221.

340   "He said would count": Entry for January 29, 1959, Series II, Box 12, Folder 1, Gypsy Rose Lee Papers, BRTD.

340   "When I look": Preminger, 266.

340   "I'm going to beat this": Ibid.

341   June leans on the back of the scale: June Havoc, interview with Laura Jacobs, 2002.

341   she douses herself with perfume: Preminger, 264.

CHAPTER 37: NEW YORK WORLD'S FAIR, 1940

343   performing a strip to benefit: *The New York Times,* May 10, 1940.

344   "I guess my Fourteenth Street": John Richmond, "Gypsy Rose Lee, Striptease Intellectual," *American Mercury,* January 1941.

344   "When I was a little girl": Gypsy Rose Lee scrapbooks, 1938, Reel 2, Gypsy Rose Lee Papers, BRTD.

344   "I want to do something serious": *Newark Ledger,* August 17, 1939.

344   "Jane Hovick": Ibid.

345   "I hope he's finally found": Erik Preminger, interview with Laura Jacobs, 2002.

345   "I hope the son of a bitch": Ibid.

345   "greatest no-talent queens": Richard E. Lauterbach, "Gypsy Rose Lee: She Combines a Public Body with a Private Mind," *Life,* December 14, 1942.

345   in every photograph they take together: Series IX, Box 75, Folder 1, Gypsy Rose Lee Papers, BRTD.

346   "So, basically, you want to know": *National Police Gazette,* August–September 1940.

348   "Oh, darling, you look so sweet": Erik Preminger, interview with Laura Jacobs, 2002.

348   "Every slight smile": Blackwell, 47.

$\mathcal{B}ibliography$

ARCHIVAL, GOVERNMENT, AND UNIVERSITY COLLECTIONS

Burlesque Clippings Files, Museum of the City of New York.

Gypsy Rose Lee Papers, Billy Rose Theatre Division, New York Public Library for the Performing Arts.

Harold Minsky Collection, Special Collections, University of Nevada, Las Vegas.

John Saxton Sumner Papers, Wisconsin Historical Society Archives.

June Havoc Collection, Howard Gotlieb Archival Research Center at Boston University.

La Guardia News Scrapbooks, Municipal Archives, City of New York.

Mary E. Dawson Papers, the University of Maine at Orono.

National Archives and Records Administration, Records of the 75th Congress, Washington, D.C.

Papers of Fiorello H. La Guardia, Municipal Archives, City of New York.

Papers of James J. Walker, Municipal Archives, City of New York.

Records of the Hearing of the House Committee on Immigration and Naturalization, the Library of Congress, Washington, D.C., February 1937.

The University of Washington Libraries.

Washington State Department of Health, Center for Health Statistics, Olympia, Washington.

BOOKS, ARTICLES, DISSERTATIONS, DOCUMENTARIES

Adler, Polly. *A House Is Not a Home.* New York: Rinehart, 1953.

Alexander, H. M. *Strip Tease: The Vanished Art of Burlesque.* New York: Knight, 1938.

Allen, Frederick Lewis. *Since Yesterday: 1929–1939.* New York: Bantam, 1961 (1940).

Allen, Irving Lewis. *The City in Slang: New York Life and Popular Speech.* New York: Oxford University Press, 1995.

Allen, Robert C. *Horrible Prettiness: Burlesque and American Culture.* Chapel Hill: University of North Carolina Press, 1991.

Alverson, Charles E. "The Story of Gypsy Rose Lee, from 'Take It Off' to 'Keep Them Talking.' " *TV Guide,* December 11, 1965.

Asbury, Herbert. *All Around the Town.* New York: Alfred A. Knopf, 1934.

Atkinson, Brooks. *Broadway.* New York: Macmillan, 1970.

Barber, Rowland. *The Night They Raided Minsky's.* New York: Simon and Schuster, 1960.

Batterberry, Michael, and Ariane Ruskin Batterberry. *On the Town in New York.* New York: Scribner, 1973.

Beaver, Frank E. *On Film: A History of the Motion Picture.* New York: McGraw-Hill, 1983.

Bianco, Anthony. *Ghosts of 42nd Street: A History of America's Most Infamous Block.* New York: William Morrow, 2004.

Blackwell, Richard, with Vernon Patterson. *From Rags to Bitches: An Autobiography.* Los Angeles: General Publishing Group, 1995.

Blair, Thomas. "What Gypsy Rose Didn't Tell in 'Gypsy.' " *Uncensored,* January 1960.

Blessing, Jennifer. "The Art(ifice) of Striptease: Gypsy Rose Lee and the Masquerade of Nudity." In *Modernism, Gender, and Culture: A Cultural Studies Approach.* New York: Garland, 1997.

Block, Alan A. *East Side–West Side: Organizing Crime in New York, 1930–1950.* Cardiff, Wales: University College Cardiff Press, 1980.

Brandt, Allan M. *No Magic Bullet: A Social History of Venereal Disease in the United States Since 1880.* New York: Oxford University Press, 1987.

Brice, Fanny. "I Knew Gypsy Rose Lee When." *Cosmopolitan,* July 1948.

Briggeman, Jane. *Burlesque: Legendary Stars of the Stage.* Portland, Ore.: Collectors Press, 2004.

Britton, Sherry. *The Stripper, by the Hon. Brigadier General Sherry Britton.* Unpublished memoir, courtesy of her attorney, Peter Dizozza.

Brodsky, Alyn. *The Great Mayor: Fiorello La Guardia and the Making of the City of New York.* New York: St. Martin's, 2003.

Brown, Thomas Allston. *A History of the New York Stage from the First Performance in 1732 to 1901.* New York: B. Blom, 1964.

Browne, Junius Henri. *The Great Metropolis: A Mirror of New York.* Whitefish, Mont.: Kessinger Publishing, 2007 (1869).

"Burlesque." *Fortune,* February 1935.

Burrows, Edwin G., and Mike Wallace. *Gotham: A History of New York City to 1898.* New York: Oxford University Press, 1999.

Butterfield, Isabel. *Manhattan Tales: 1920–1945.* Oxford: Isis, 2004.

Calabria, Frank M. *Dance of the Sleepwalkers: The Dance Marathon Fad.* Bowling Green, Oh.: Bowling Green State University Popular Press, 1993.

Caldwell, Mark. *New York Night: The Mystique and Its History.* New York: Scribner, 2008.

Cantor, Eddie, David Freedman, and Alfred Cheney Johnson. *Ziegfeld: The Great Glorifier.* New York: Alfred H. King, 1934.

Carney, Robert, Pat Filler, Cathy Fulton, Roger Fulton, and Marge Saffer. *West Seattle Memories.* Seattle: The Southwest Seattle Historical Society, 1999.

Carr, Virginia Spencer. *The Lonely Hunter: A Biography of Carson McCullers.* New York: Anchor, 1976.

———. *Paul Bowles: A Life.* New York: Scribner, 2004.

Castle, Charles. *The Folies Bergère.* New York: Franklin Watts, 1985.

Charyn, Jerome. *Gangsters & Gold Diggers: Old New York, the Jazz Age, and the Birth of Broadway.* New York: Thunder's Mouth, 2003.

Chauncey, George. *Gay New York: Urban Culture and the Making of the Gay Male World, 1890–1940*. New York: Basic, 1994.

Cohen, Rich. *Tough Jews: Fathers, Sons, and Gangster Dreams*. New York: Vintage, 1999.

Cohn, Art. *The Nine Lives of Michael Todd*. New York: Random House, 1958.

Connors, Timothy David. *American Vaudeville Managers: Their Organization and Influence*. Doctoral thesis, the University of Kansas, 1981.

Cooper, Morton. "Profile of a Character: Gypsy Rose Lee." *Modern Man*, September 1959.

Corio, Ann, with Joseph DiMona. *This Was Burlesque*. New York: Madison Square, 1968.

Costello, Chris, and Raymond Strait. *Lou's On First*. New York: St. Martin's, 1981.

Crane, Hart. *The Bridge*. New York: Liveright, 1933.

Crichton, Kyle. "Strip for Fame: Miss Gypsy Rose Lee, in Person." *Collier's*, December 19, 1936.

Davis, George. "The Dark Young Pet of Burlesque." *Vanity Fair*, February 1936.

de Camp, L. Sprague. *Time and Chance: An Autobiography*. Hampton Falls, N.H.: Donald M. Grant, 1996.

Dewey, John. *New York and the Seabury Investigation*. New York: City Affairs Committee of New York, 1933.

Douglas, Ann. *Terrible Honesty: Mongrel Manhattan in the 1920s*. New York: Farrar, Strauss and Giroux, 1995.

Downey, Patrick. *Gangster City: The History of the New York Underworld, 1900–1935*. Fort Lee, N.J.: Barricade, 2004.

Dressler, David. *Burlesque as a Cultural Phenomenon*. Doctoral thesis, New York University, 1937.

Drutman, Irving. *Good Company: A Memoir, Mostly Theatrical*. Boston: Little, Brown, 1976.

Elliott, Eugene Clinton. *A History of Variety-Vaudeville in Seattle: From the Beginning to 1914*. Seattle: University of Washington Press, 1944.

Elliott, Lawrence. *Little Flower: The Life and Times of Fiorello La Guardia*. New York: William Morrow, 1983.

Ellis, Edward Robb. *The Epic of New York City*. New York: Basic, 2004.

Eyles, Allen. *That Was Hollywood: The 1930s*. London: Batsford, 1987.

Farnsworth, Marjorie. *The Ziegfeld Follies*. New York: G.P. Putnam's Sons, 1956.

Farrell, Edythe. "An Unusual Strip-Tease: Gypsy Rose Lee Is First to Do a 'Talking' Strip." *National Police Gazette*, August–September 1940.

Fessenden, Tracy, Nicholas F. Radel, and Magdalena J. Zaborowska (eds.). *The Puritan Origins of American Sex: Religion, Sexuality, and National Identity in American Literature*. New York: Routledge, 2000.

Fiske, Dwight. *Without Music*. New York: Chatham, 1933.

Frankel, Noralee. *Stripping Gypsy*. New York: Oxford University Press, 2009.

Friedman, Andrea. "The Habitats of Sex-Crazed Perverts: Campaigns Against Burlesque in Depression-Era New York City." *Journal of the History of Sexuality*, vol. 7, October 1996.

Gavin, James. *Intimate Nights: The Golden Age of New York Cabaret*. New York: Back Stage, 2006.

Gelernter, David. *1939: The Lost World of the Fair*. New York: Avon, 1995.

Gilbert, Douglas. *American Vaudeville: Its Life and Times*. New York: Dover, 1963.

Goldfield, David R. *The Encyclopedia of American Urban History, Volume I*. Newbury Park, Calif.: Sage, 2006.

Goldman, Herbert G. *Fanny Brice: The Original Funny Girl.* New York: Oxford University Press, 1992.

Goldwyn, Liz. *Pretty Things: The Last Generation of American Burlesque Queens.* New York: Regan, 2006.

———. *Pretty Things* (DVD). Liz Goldwyn Film Productions, 2005.

Gottlieb, Polly Rose. *The Nine Lives of Billy Rose: An Intimate Biography.* New York: Crown, 1968.

Granlund, Nils Thor. *Blondes, Brunettes, and Bullets.* New York: D. McKay, 1957.

"Gypsy Rose Lee: A General Collector." *Hobbies,* October 1942.

"Gypsy Rose Lee and Her Golden G-String." *Uncensored,* August 1954.

"Gypsy Rose Lee: At Home at Witchwood Manor." *Pic,* August 6, 1940.

"Gypsy Rose Lee: Dowager Stripper." *Look,* February 22, 1966.

"Gypsy Rose Lee: She Takes It Off for Charity." *Sir!,* August 1942.

Havoc, June. *Early Havoc.* New York: Simon and Schuster, 1959.

———. *More Havoc.* New York: Harper & Row, 1980.

Hellman, Geoffrey T. "Author." *The New Yorker,* December 7, 1940.

Hirsch, Foster. *The Boys from Syracuse: The Shuberts' Theatrical Empire.* New York: Cooper Square, 2000.

———. *Otto Preminger: The Man Who Would Be King.* New York: Knopf, 2007.

Hochman, Louis. "The Mechanix of Gypsy Rose Lee." *Mechanix Illustrated,* June 1943.

"Hovick-Kirkland: Miss Gypsy Rose Lee, Author, Weds Broadway Actor." *Life,* September 14, 1942.

"How to Undress Gracefully in Front of Millions." *TV Guide,* September 12, 1964.

"Intimate Secrets of a Strip Dancer: Gypsy Rose Lee Tells of Her Love and Life." *Romantic Stories,* April 1937.

Jacobs, Laura. "Taking It *All* Off." *Vanity Fair,* March 2003.

Jackson, Kenneth T. *The Encyclopedia of New York City.* New Haven: Yale University Press, 1995.

Jeffers, Harry Paul. *The Napoleon of New York: Mayor Fiorello La Guardia.* Hoboken, N.J.: Wiley, 2002.

Jennel, Joseph. "Interview with: Gypsy Rose Lee." *Jem,* February 1960.

Johnston, Alva. "Tour of Minskyville." *The New Yorker,* May 28, 1932.

Kahn, Roger. "Strip Teaser: The Ups and Downs of Gypsy Rose Lee." *Real: The Exciting Magazine for Men,* November 1956.

Kazin, Alfred. *Starting Out in the Thirties.* Boston: Atlantic Monthly Press / Little, Brown, 1962.

Kessner, Thomas. *Fiorello H. La Guardia and the Making of Modern New York.* New York: McGraw-Hill, 1989.

Kibler, M. Alison. *Female Varieties: Gender and Cultural Hierarchy on the Keith Vaudeville Circuit, 1890–1925.* Doctoral thesis, the University of Iowa, 1994.

Kisseloff, John. *You Must Remember This: An Oral History of Manhattan from the 1890s to World War II.* Baltimore: Johns Hopkins University Press, 1989.

Lait, Jack, and Lee Mortimer. *New York: Confidential!* New York: Crown, 1951.

Laurents, Arthur. *Original Story by: A Memoir of Broadway and Hollywood.* New York: Alfred A. Knopf, 2000.

Laurents, Arthur, Stephen Sondheim, and Jule Styne. *Gypsy.* New York: Theatre Communications Group, 1998.

Lauterbach, Richard E. "Gypsy Rose Lee: She Combines a Public Body with a Private Mind." *Life,* December 14, 1942.

Lee, Gypsy Rose. *The G-String Murders.* New York: Simon and Schuster, 1941.

———. *Mother Finds a Body.* New York: Simon and Schuster, 1942.

———. "I Was with It." *Cowles,* June 1950.

———. "Fanny Brice and I." *Town & Country,* April 1957.

———. "Stranded in Kansas City." *Harper's,* April 1957.

———. *Gypsy: A Memoir.* New York: Harper & Row, 1957.

Lerner, Michael A. *Dry Manhattan: Prohibition in New York City.* Cambridge, Mass.: Harvard University Press, 2007.

Linn, Edward. "Mike Todd: The Man Who Can't Go Broke." *Saga,* August 1955.

Maeder, James (ed.). *Big Town, Big Time: A New York Epic: 1898–1998.* New York: Daily News Books, 1999.

Maloney, Russell. "Burlesk." *The New Yorker,* June 8, 1935.

Marks, Robert. "Trill on the G-String." *Esquire,* June 1942.

Martin, Carol J. *Dance Marathons: Performing American Culture of the 1920s and 1930s.* Jackson: University Press of Mississippi, 1994.

McEvoy, J. P. "More Tease Than Strip." *Reader's Digest,* July 1941.

McGovern, Dennis, and Deborah Grace Winer. *Sing Out, Louise!: 150 Stars of the Musical Theatre Remember 50 Years on Broadway.* New York: Schirmer, 1993.

McIntyre, O. O. *The Big Town.* New York: Dodd, Mead & Company, 1935.

Meade, Marion. *Dorothy Parker: What Fresh Hell Is This?* New York: Penguin, 1989.

Mencken, H. L. *The American Language* (fourth edition). New York: Alfred A. Knopf, 1936.

Meredith, Scott. *George S. Kaufman and His Friends.* New York: Doubleday, 1974.

Miller, Alice. *The Drama of the Gifted Child: The Search for the True Self.* New York: Basic, 1997.

Miller, Henry. *Aller Retour New York.* New York: New Directions, 1991.

Miller, Nathan. *New World Coming: The 1920s and the Making of Modern America.* Cambridge, Mass.: Da Capo, 2003.

Minsky, Morton, and Milt Machlin. *Minsky's Burlesque.* New York: Arbor House, 1986.

Mitchell, Joseph. *My Ears Are Bent.* New York: Pantheon, 1938.

Mitgang, Herbert. *The Man Who Rode the Tiger.* Philadelphia: Lippincott, 1963.

———. *Once Upon a Time in New York.* New York: Free Press, 2000.

Montague, Art. *Meyer Lansky: The Shadowy Exploits of New York's Master Manipulator.* Alberta: Altitude, 2005.

Morgan, Lane, Murray Morgan, and Paul Dorpat. *Seattle: A Pictorial History.* Norfolk, Va.: Donning, 1982.

Murphy, Lawrence R. *Perverts by Official Order: The Campaign Against Homosexuals by the United States Navy.* New York: Haworth, 1988.

Murray, Kathryn. *Family Laugh Lines.* Englewood Cliffs, N.J.: Prentice-Hall, 1966.

Nasaw, David. *Going Out: The Rise and Fall of Public Amusements.* Cambridge, Mass.: Harvard University Press, 1999.

Nathan, George Jean. *Art of the Night.* New York: Alfred A. Knopf, 1928.

———. *The Theatre Book of the Year, 1942–1943.* Madison, N.J.: Fairleigh Dickinson University Press, 1972.

New York Times Company. *The New York Times Page One, 1851–2001.* New York: Galahad, 2001.

Oates, Joyce Carol. *Blonde.* New York: Ecco, 2000.

Palmer, Greta. "She Undressed Her Way to Fame." *New York Woman,* October 7, 1936.

Pessis, Jacques, and Jacques Crepineau. *The Moulin Rouge.* New York: St. Martin's, 1990.

Petras, Kathryn, and Ross Petras. *Don't Forget to Sing in the Lifeboats: Uncommon Wisdom for Uncommon Times.* New York: Workman, 2009.

Phillips, Cabell. *From the Crash to the Blitz: 1929–1939.* New York: Macmillan, 1969.

Preminger, Erik Lee. *My G-String Mother: At Home and Backstage with Gypsy Rose Lee.* New York: Little, Brown, 1984.

Richmond, John. "Gypsy Rose Lee, Striptease Intellectual." *American Mercury,* January 1941.

Robert, Shirley. "When Gypsy Rose Lee Ratted on Her Mother." *On the QT,* February 1960.

Rodgers, Richard, John O'Hara, and Lorenz Hart. *Pal Joey: The Libretto and Lyrics.* New York: Random House, 1952.

Roger, Philippe, and Sharon Bowman. *The American Enemy: The History of French Anti-Americanism.* Chicago: University of Chicago Press, 2006.

Roskolenko, Harry. *The Time That Was Then.* New York: Dial, 1971.

Runyon, Damon. *The Bloodhounds of Broadway and Other Stories.* New York: Morrow, 1981.

Schwartz, Daniel R. *Broadway Boogie Woogie: Damon Runyon and the Making of New York Culture.* New York: Palgrave Macmillan, 2003.

Shteir, Rachel. *Striptease: The Untold History of the Girlie Show.* New York: Oxford University Press, 2004.

———. *Gypsy: The Art of the Tease.* New Haven and London: Yale University Press, 2009.

Silvers, Phil, and Robert Saffron. *This Laugh Is on Me.* Englewood Cliffs, N.J.: Prentice-Hall, 1973.

Singer, Stanford Paul, Ph.D. *Vaudeville West: To Los Angeles and the Final Stages of Vaudeville.* Doctoral thesis, University of California, Los Angeles, 1987.

Slide, Anthony. *The Encyclopedia of Vaudeville.* Westport, Conn., and London: Greenwood, 1994.

Smith, Bill. *The Vaudevillians.* New York: Macmillan, 1976.

———. *Prurient Interests: Gender, Democracy, and Obscenity in New York City, 1909–1945.* New York: Columbia University Press, 2000.

Smith, Edward Jean. *FDR.* New York: Random House, 2007.

Snyder, Robert W. *The Voice of the City: Vaudeville and Popular Culture in New York.* New York: Oxford University Press, 1989.

Sobel, Bernard. *Broadway Heartbeat: Memoirs of a Press Agent.* New York: Hermitage House, 1953.

———. *A Pictorial History of Burlesque.* New York: Bonanza, 1956.

———. *A Pictorial History of Vaudeville.* New York: Citadel, 1961.

Sothern, Georgia. *Georgia: My Life in Burlesque.* New York: New American Library, 1972.

Stagg, Jerry. *The Brothers Shubert.* New York: Random House, 1968.

Stein, Charles W. (ed.). *American Vaudeville as Seen by Its Contemporaries.* New York: Alfred A. Knopf, 1984.

Stewart, Travis D. *No Applause—Just Throw Money: The Book That Made Vaudeville Famous.* New York: Faber & Faber, 2005.

Stravitz, David. *New York, Empire City, 1920–1945.* New York: Harry N. Abrams, 2004.

Swimmer, Jeff. "Gypsy Rose Lee: Naked Ambition." *Biography,* A&E, 1999.

Tarrach, Dean Arthur. *Alexander Pantages: The Seattle Pantages and His Vaudeville Circuit.* Master's thesis, University of Washington, 1973.

Teachout, Terry. *The Skeptic: A Life of H. L. Mencken.* New York: HarperCollins, 2002.

Thompson, Craig, and Allen Raymond. *Gang Rule in New York.* New York: Dial, 1940.

Thurber, James. "Robot." *The New Yorker,* August 29, 1931.

Tippins, Sherill. *February House.* New York: Houghton Mifflin, 2005.

Todd, Michael, Jr., and Susan McCarthy Todd. *A Valuable Property: The Life Story of Michael Todd.* New York: Arbor House, 1983.

Tone, Andrea. "Contraceptive Consumers: Gender and the Political Economy of Birth Control in the 1930s," *Journal of Social History,* Spring 1966.

Trager, James. *The New York Chronology: The Ultimate Compendium of Events, People, and Anecdotes from the Dutch to the Present.* New York: HarperCollins, 2003.

Traub, James. *The Devil's Playground: A Century of Pleasure and Profit in Times Square.* New York: Random House, 2004.

Tucker, Sophie. *Some of These Days.* Garden City, N.Y.: Doubleday, Doran, 1945.

Tynan, Kenneth. "Cornucopia." *The New Yorker,* May 30, 1959.

Van Hoogstraten, Nicholas. *Lost Broadway Theatres.* Princeton, N.J.: Princeton Architectural Press, 1991.

Van Vechten, Carl. *Parties: Scenes from Contemporary New York Life.* New York: Alfred A. Knopf, 1930.

———. "A Note on Tights." *American Mercury,* July 1934.

"Vaudeville." *American Masters,* PBS, 1997.

Walker, Stanley. *The Night Club Era.* New York: Frederick A. Stokes, 1933.

Walsh, George. *Gentleman Jimmy Walker: Mayor of the Jazz Age.* New York: Henry Holt, 1976.

Wertheim, Arthur Frank. *Vaudeville Wars: How the Keith-Albee and Orpheum Circuits Controlled the Big Time and Its Performers.* New York: Palgrave Macmillan, 2009.

Wilson, Edmund. *The Twenties: An Intimate Portrait of the Jazz Age.* New York: Farrar, Straus and Giroux, 1975.

Winchell, Walter. *Winchell Exclusive.* Englewood Cliffs, N.J.: Prentice Hall, 1975.

Witchel, Alex. *Girls Only.* New York: Random House, 1996.

Wood, Andrew. *New York's 1939–1940 World's Fair.* Mount Pleasant, S.C.: Arcadia, 2004.

Zeidman, Irving. *The American Burlesque Show.* New York: Hawthorn, 1967.

Zullo, Allan. *Wise Guys: Brilliant Thoughts and Big Talk from Real Men.* Naperville, Ill.: Sourcebooks, 2005.

Index

Illustration Credits

ABOUT THE AUTHOR

KAREN ABBOTT is the *New York Times* bestselling author of *Sin in the Second City*. A native of Philadelphia, she now lives in New York City with her husband and two African Grey parrots who do a mean Ethel Merman. Visit her online at www.KarenAbbott.net.

ABOUT THE TYPE

This book was set in Monotype Dante, a typeface designed by Giovanni Mardersteig (1892–1977). Conceived as a private type for the Officina Bodoni in Verona, Italy, Dante was originally cut only for hand composition by Charles Malin, the famous Parisian punch cutter, between 1946 and 1952. Its first use was in an edition of Boccaccio's *Trattatello in laude di Dante* that appeared in 1954. The Monotype Corporation's version of Dante followed in 1957. Though modeled on the Aldine type used for Pietro Cardinal Bembo's treatise *De Aetna* in 1495, Dante is a thoroughly modern interpretation of that venerable face.